Susanne Epple, Getachew Assefa (eds.)
Legal Pluralism in Ethiopia

Culture and Social Practice

Susanne Epple (PhD), born in 1968, is a social anthropologist and research affiliate at the Frobenius Institute in Frankfurt/Main. She has undertaken extensive fieldwork in Southern Ethiopia for 25 years, and has taught and published extensively on issues related to gender and age in agropastoral societies, cultural contact and change, hereditary status groups, and legal pluralism.
Getachew Assefa (PhD), born in 1973, is associate professor of law at Addis Ababa University. He has published widely on issues related to minority rights, federalism and constitutional litigation, and legal pluralism. His areas of interest include comparative constitutional law and federalism, human rights, traditional governance and justice systems, as well as law and religion.

Susanne Epple, Getachew Assefa (eds.)

Legal Pluralism in Ethiopia

Actors, Challenges and Solutions

[transcript]

Bibliographic information published by the Deutsche Nationalbibliothek
The Deutsche Nationalbibliothek lists this publication in the Deutsche Nationalbibliografie; detailed bibliographic data are available in the Internet at http://dnb.d-nb.de

First published in 2020 by transcript Verlag, Bielefeld

transcript Verlag | Hermannstraße 26 | D-33602 Bielefeld | live@transcript-verlag.de

Cover layout: Maria Arndt, Bielefeld
Cover illustration: Bashada elders and government officials during a meeting (photo: Susanne Epple 2016)
Proofread by Kay Celtel
Printed by Majuskel Medienproduktion GmbH, Wetzlar
Print-ISBN 978-3-8376-5021-1
PDF-ISBN 978-3-8394-5021-5
https://doi.org/10.14361/9783839450215

Printed on permanent acid-free text paper.

Contents

IV.
Incompatibilities and conflict

Acknowledgements

This volume is part of the results of a research project on 'The negotiation of law in the peripheries of southern Ethiopia'. It was funded by the German Research Foundation (DFG) and hosted at the Frobenius Institute at the Goethe University in Frankfurt/Main. Susanne Epple – a social anthropologist – was the principal investigator of the project and did her own research in the very south of Ethiopia. In order to widen the scope of the research and get an interdisciplinary perspective, she invited Getachew Assefa – a lawyer and expert on constitutional law and legal pluralism in Ethiopia – to cooperate. Together they organized two interdisciplinary events: an international conference organized at Jinka University (JKU) in Jinka, southern Ethiopia in January 2018, and a panel at the 20th International Conference of Ethiopian Studies (ICES) at Mekelle University, northern Ethiopia in October 2018. Both were titled 'Legal pluralism in Ethiopia: The interplay of international, national and customary law'. Most of the papers in this volume are results of these events; some joined the group at a later stage.

We are grateful to the German Research Foundation (DFG) for the generous funding of the project, the conference and panel, and most of the publication costs. We would also like to take the opportunity to thank the staff at Jinka University for their great support in making the conference in Jinka possible, and express our gratitude to the organizers of the ICES 20 in Mekelle.

We are also indebted to the Frobenius Institute, which hosted the project from 2016–2019. The institute has a long history of research and has shown continued interest in the ethnic diversity and cultural complexity of Ethiopia. Since its expeditions into Ethiopia in the early twentieth century, numerous well-known publications have come out of the institute, by authors such as Adolf E. Jensen, Eike Haberland, Helmut Straube, Werner Lange, Elisabeth Pauli and Ulrich Braukämper, to mention only a few.[1] Professor Karl-Heinz Kohl, the then director of the Frobenius Institute, offered to host the project in 2016. We would like to thank him,

1 For an overview of the engagement of the Frobenius Institute in Ethiopia see Dinslage, Sabine and Sophia Thubauville (eds.), 2017 *Seeking out wise old men: Six decades of Ethiopian studies at the Frobenius Institute*. Berlin: Reimer

and the current director, Professor Roland Hardenberg, as well as the staff of the Frobenius Institute for their welcoming and indefatigable cooperation, and also for co-financing the publication of the book. Special thanks go to Sophia Thubauville, a colleague at the Frobenius Institute and a co-researcher in Ethiopia, who has been very helpful throughout in many different ways.

To address the complexity of customary law and legal pluralism in contemporary Ethiopia from an interdisciplinary perspective, the editors invited experienced scholars from both of their disciplines – social anthropology and law – to contribute. We wish to thank all the authors for their great efforts and the patience they have shown in the course of publishing this volume.

Finally, we are grateful to the many informants in the field, both private people and government officials. Through their trust and openness to discuss partly very sensitive topics they have given us an insight into the problematic and conflicting aspects of their lives.

Last but not least we would like to thank Kay Celtel for her fast and professional copy-editing.

1. Introduction

Susanne Epple

Ethiopia is currently facing a delicate challenge, as it attempts to balance different priorities in the country: respecting religious and cultural diversity, ensuring the implementation of state law throughout its territorial domain, and committing itself to international standards of human rights through the ratification of global conventions and agreements.

With more than eighty officially listed ethnic groups (Central Statistical Agency/CSA 2008) and languages (Lewis 2009), there exists a great plurality of livelihoods, social organisations, belief systems, and political and legal systems in the country. For the first time in Ethiopian history, this cultural diversity has been officially acknowledged and respected in the new Constitution of 1995. Through the Constitution, each ethnic group has been given the space to promote its own culture and language, and legal pluralism is officially recognized. Today, conflicts in the areas of family and civil law can legally be resolved using local laws, procedures and mechanisms, as long as the Constitution is not contradicted, international humans rights standards are not violated and all the parties in conflict have agreed. The same rights and respect have been given to religious laws, so that Sharia law and courts have received a special place in contemporary Ethiopia.[1]

The existing legal arrangement seems to offer many advantages, as it seeks to combine the diverse interests of its inhabitants and the government. It is, therefore, generally welcomed and appreciated by many people, especially as previous

1 See the Ethiopian Constitution (FDRE 1995), especially Art. 34(5) which says that 'the adjudication of disputes relating to personal and family laws in accordance with [religious or] customary laws, with the consent of the parties to the dispute' shall not be precluded by the Constitution, and Art. 78(5), which grants the right to 'establish or give official recognition to religious and customary courts' to the House of Peoples' Representatives and State Councils. See also the Cultural Policy (endorsed in 1997), in which the government clearly distances itself from previous governments, who are said to have followed a discriminatory policy by seeding enmity among peoples and promoting the domination of the culture of one nation or nationality at the expense of others (http://www.ethioembassy.org.uk/fact%20file/a-z/culture.htm), and the recent publication by Getachew, Yonas and Muradu (2016) on *Economic, social and cultural rights in Ethiopia*.

Ethiopian governments ignored and forbade the application of customary law, though it nonetheless continued to operate unofficially and partly in hiding. However, in practice, the multiplicity of the often opposing and competing norms of the different legal forums poses a challenge to both legal practitioners and justice seekers. As will be shown in this volume, certain gaps in the law have left the system open to abuse and exploitation for personal advantage. There are also examples of power being accumulated by individuals who hold prominent positions in more than one legal system, and in some places offenders are being sanctioned more than once for the same wrongdoing. The criminalization of certain cultural practices that contradict the state law and international human rights - labelled as 'harmful traditional practices' – has caused disappointment among local communities and occasionally led to avoidance of and resistance to the state law. At the same time, state institutions have remained difficult to access especially in rural areas, not only because police stations and courts do not exist everywhere and often lack staff and equipment where they do, but also because local acceptance is still low. In addition, in some places pressure is put on individuals to not take their cases outside the community.

A lot of the existing literature on legal pluralism places an emphasis on contradictions between the legal systems, and on the problems arising from the implementation of state law and international law in local communities. However, as one can see from the case studies in this volume, in places where the communication between the different legal forums is open and respectful, the various stakeholders do cooperate and the legal institutions and procedures complement rather than contradict each other – at least to some extent. Where mutual distrust and insufficient communication prevail, problems among the customary, religious and state legal forums are abundant, and many complaints arise.

The intention of this volume is therefore not only to shed light on the diverse connections between various legal actors and their day-to-day experiences, but also – and particularly – to highlight the conditions that contribute to the cooperative co-existence of different legal systems. It includes the views, perspectives and opinions of government representatives (e.g. legal practitioners, administrative personnel, other officials), various representatives of local communities (both customers seeking legal services and practitioners of customary law and administration), and religious actors (Muslim and Christian legal practitioners and communities). The case studies examine how state law is implemented locally, partly accepted, combined with local and/or religious law, or rejected. They also look at how state officials make use of local institutions, norms and actors in order to 'make things work' and apply state law in their daily practice. While friction, contradictions and clashes are not denied, a closer look is taken at the potential of legal pluralism, in the hope of identifying how the existing and inevitably plural legal setting can become a win–win situation for all.

The interplay of plural legal orders

Legal pluralism

Early studies in legal anthropology looked at 'traditional law', that is, at the question of how people maintained social order without Western law (Malinowski 1926, Nader 1969). Later, the focus shifted to the co-existence and intersections of customary and European law in the colonial context, nowadays referred to as 'classical legal pluralism'. Studies in the 'new legal pluralism', in which scholars looked at the existence of plural normative orders in non-colonized states, emerged in the late 1970s, mainly in the USA and Europe (Merry 1988:873).

Since then it has been widely agreed that legal pluralism is a 'situation in which two or more legal systems coexist in the same social field' (Pospisil 1971, Griffiths 1986, Moore 1986). Concepts of legal pluralism and law have been debated and redefined in the last decades by anthropologists, sociologists, lawyers and others. In the social sciences, most scholars now generally agree that every society is legally plural 'whether or not it has a colonial past' (Merry 1988:869), as official and unofficial social orderings operate side by side everywhere (Macaulay 1986 in Merry 1988:868–869). While there has been intense debate on whether the term 'law' should be reserved for state law only (Woodman 1996, Griffith 1986, Tamanaha 2007), the concept of 'semi-autonomous social fields' introduced by Moore in 1973 focuses instead on the arenas (economic, social, political etc.) that operate with their own specific sets of formal and informal norms. These norms are partly newly created within the given social field itself. They originate partly from the specific environment (formal laws, rules determined by the economic system, cultural norms etc.), and partly from other social fields with which they are interconnected and interdependent (Moore 1973:720). As Moore emphasizes (1973:723), there is no presupposed hierarchy between different normative orders interacting in the same social field. This means that state law is not necessarily or automatically dominant over other normative orders, and other social arrangements can be stronger in determining individuals' actions. It also implies that new legal systems brought into or imposed on a specific social field can have unpredictable results.

Human rights and local contexts

Legal systems have always been dynamic and have always influenced each other. Since the mid-1990s, the transnational flows of legal models in the context of globalization have become a focus of scholarly interest (F. and K. von Benda-Beckmann 2006, Tamanaha 2007, Nader 1969). In particular, the promotion and implementation of human rights standards have been widely discussed. Since human rights standards have become a kind of benchmark for the quality of governments in the developing world, national and international NGOs have begun exerting direct and indirect pressure to ensure that such rights are enforced (F. von Benda-Beckmann 2009). Issues pertaining to gender equality and the protection of women and children (number 5 in the Sustainable Development Goals) have been given high priority. Indeed, they were already strongly addressed in the 'Convention on the Elimination of all Forms of Discrimination against Women' (CEDAW) adopted by the UN General Assembly in 1975, which gave a clear priority to women's rights over the protection of cultural diversity.[2]

Running parallel to discussions on the implementation of human rights standards has been concern about the universality of human rights (Goodale 2009).[3] The widespread incompatibilities of human rights and customary laws and values have been discussed in various theoretical publications (Eriksen 2001, Kinley 2012, Preis 1996), and some authors have accused human rights of Western bias (An-Na'im 1992, 2002). Merry (2003a) has even identified certain parallels between the transnational transfer of law in times of globalization and during colonialism. She argues that, in both instances, the transfer of legal ideas, institutions and technologies was justified with the argument that it would contribute to an improved society. Moreover, the 'reformers' involved – both colonial and contemporary – were convinced they were doing a morally right thing: contributing to a better life and more civilized society by overcoming primitivism in the colonial context, and promoting the rule of law, democracy and human rights today. Merry also points out that the diffusion of new legal ideas has been taking place among countries and peoples of extremely unequal power and resources, e.g. in relations where economic, political and cultural considerations also play a role (Merry 2003a:570).

Scholars who have studied how law and human rights are discussed in international forums have complained that, especially in reference to rural communities or developing countries, 'culture' is still presented as something static and a hindrance to change and development.[4] As such, 'culture' appears to be an obstacle to

2 The Convention is very clear about its aims to eradicate all practices discriminating against women, even if that means changing cultural values, and even if women belonging to a specific culture do not perceive them as harmful (see www.un.org/womenwatch/daw/cedaw).

3 Anthropologists were long aware of but only marginally involved in the debate on how 'global law can be translated into the vernacular' (Merry 2006:2). It was only after the end of the Cold War in the late 1980s that anthropology engaged actively in research and debates around International Human Rights (Goodale 2009:2). The 'Declaration on Anthropology and Human Rights', voted on and approved by the general membership of the American Anthropologists Association (AAA) in 1999, clearly expressed the 'commitment to human rights consistent with international principles' and declared it mandatory for anthropologists 'to be involved in the debate on enlarging our understanding of human rights on the basis of anthropological knowledge and research' (Goodale 2009:7).

4 Conversely, in anthropology it has long been agreed that culture is something fluid, contested, dynamic, and fundamentally hybrid.

the realization of human rights (Merry 2003b). In viewing culture as the source of all problems, attention is drawn away from other sources of subordinate groups' suffering, such as economic or political problems, which might actually be caused by Western countries' domination (Merry 2003b:63). Only in the context of heritage management are 'culture' or 'cultural diversity' internationally declared as worth protecting. The 2003 UNESCO 'Convention for the safeguarding of intangible heritage' promoted the idea of 'cultural rights' and declared the right to live according to one's own traditions as a form of human right, albeit only provided that those traditions do not contradict existing human rights instruments and meet the requirement for mutual respect among communities, groups and individuals (Langfield *et al.* 2010). Once the rights of less powerful individuals like women and children, stateless persons, the weak or destitute are violated, cultural rights are no longer protected (Logan *et al.* 2010:14).

Many case studies have looked at the problems of implementing human rights in local contexts (Cowan *et al.* 2001, Foblets and Yassari 2013, Langfield *et al.* 2010), and have uncovered how women's rights and gender equality in particular are often contradictory to local values and customs (Merry 2006, Hodgson 2011). One of the main reasons why human rights and local culture do not easily converge is that there is a contradiction between individual rights and group rights. As Foblets *et al.* (2018:6) have elaborated, a general principle in human rights is that an individual cannot renounce his or her fundamental human rights. This rule is especially applied in cases involving the interests of children, gender equality and fair trials. In the name of human rights, any practices considered as deviant or contentious can be prohibited under state law. This 'imposed protection' can lead to individuals being prevented from following their traditions. This, in turn, can mean that they are denied the capacity to renew and adapt their cultural practices in their own way and at their own pace. In practice, Foblets *et al.* (2018:6–7) conclude, this is itself a denial of personal autonomy[5] that can – as a side effect – give rise to the unintended marginalization of those who decide to avoid courts in order to be able to follow their own traditions.

As certain cultures do not support personal autonomy, Foblets *et al.* (2018:8) question whether individual autonomy should realistically be a universal goal. Individuals feel strongly attached to their groups and often find it impossible to make a decision independent of, or against, the interests of their family, clan or community. This explains why people refrain from abandoning certain aspects of their culture (*ibid.*:2). When an individual in a case voluntarily renounces the freedom granted to them by international law, the legal practitioners involved face an ethical

5 Foblets *et al.* (2018:2, fn9) define 'autonomy' as a 'person's capacity to make independent decisions and exercise choice', and differentiate it from 'agency', which refers to a person's 'acting on decisions made'.

dilemma in deciding how to deal with someone who has personally chosen a path prohibited by law (*ibid.*:5).

The dilemma of government officials

Within any given legally plural social field, diverse actors operate and pursue their individual interests. Many studies on legal pluralism have investigated the decision-making processes of justice-seeking members of local communities, and have explored how the specific background, gender, age, or profession of individuals influences their decisions about which legal forum to choose or 'shop from' (K. von Benda-Beckmann 1981).[6] However, the perspective of state actors, the 'paradox' (Zenker and Hoehne 2018) of their having to deal with custom in order to get their work for the state done, their background and personal interests, their actions and choices, and the contexts in which they work have only become of interest in the decade (Lentz 2010, Bierschenk 2014, Olivier de Sardan 2008, 2015; de Herdt and Olivier de Sardan 2015, Beek *et al.* 2017).

In their day-to-day work, government officials act in 'complex normative universes', and they undergo an informal professional socialization in order to be able to navigate in a rather unpredictable environment (Bierschenk 2014). They have to comply with contradictory messages stemming from official norms – including rules of law, conventions, local regulations, professional or administrative procedures, all of which are *formalized* or *codified* in public action or professional practice – (Olivier de Sardan 2008:4, fn 15) and from practical norms that are 'absent from the public discourse, absent from the official moral rhetorics and absent from the teaching' but that are nevertheless important to know (ibid.:15). State officials therefore flexibly orient themselves towards these 'rules of the game' to get their daily work done. At the same time, they also change them strategically. They play the 'game of the rules' in a way that can be seen as 'skilful and flexible manoeuvring within and between norms and modes of engagement' (De Herdt and Olivier de Sardan 2015:25). Aside from the external framework and constraints, the personal backgrounds of the individual officials influences their behaviour and decisions as they put state law into practice locally, determining their way of interpreting, implementing and also innovating norms 'in the interest of accomplishing the organizational goals' (Lentz 2010:5).

6 Studies have shown, for example, that females prefer to turn to new forums, as state law and its 'non-traditional' values can be an important resources in the struggle for emancipation, while the local law is often the law of local elites and/or the senior male population (K. von Benda-Beckmann 2001:50). At the same time, gender can also limit access to legal forums (Griffith 1997, Hirsch 1998).

Demise or rise of customary law in Africa?

Customary law continues to play an important role in Africa, and is now officially recognized in many African constitutions, although – due to differing histories and colonial experience – the degree of recognition and the legal areas recognized vary greatly (Merry 1991:891). In a comparative analysis of 190 constitutions worldwide, Cuskelly (2011) found that African constitutions offer the highest level of recognition of customary law: of 52 African constitutions, 33 referred to customary law in some form, with good recognition of traditional and customary institutions and customary law in the courts and relating to land issues. An even larger number of African constitutions generally protect culture or tradition (Cuskelly 2011:6–11, see also Gebre, this volume).

What is customary law?

Although regularly used in the literature, the term 'customary law' has been criticized for being misleading. What is actually meant by the term depends on the contexts it refers to. In the literature, three types of customary law referred to by authors can be discerned.

First, there is the precolonial non-written law of the past: the 'customary law' described by many anthropologists in the first half of the twentieth century. It is seen as a continuation or remnant of precolonial cultures and traditions, and some authors perceived it to be 'timeless and static' (Zenker and Hoehne 2018:5). Since the 1970s and 1980s this view has been questioned. Researchers have emphasised that law (like culture in general) is dynamic, and that a second kind of customary law found in post-colonial Africa (and elsewhere) was actually created out of the struggles between and among colonizers and colonized during the colonial period.[7] Emerging African elites – mostly those who were educated, lived in towns

---

7 A dual legal system existed in most African colonies: one (imported European) law for the colonizers, and one (indigenous African) for the colonized (Merry 1991:890). Despite the room given to the local law to regulate the lives of the colonized, local law was nevertheless strongly influenced by the imported European legal system: indigenous structures and institutions were integrated into the colonial administration and regional authorities were identified and made responsible for regional administration (Kohlhagen 2008:79). European law was used to handle major criminal cases, control the local labour force, exploit local resources and establish an administrative structure that facilitated national and international trade. Local practices that contradicted key values of the colonizers were forbidden. In British colonies this was enforced through the repugnancy doctrine, which prohibited courts from enforcing any customary law considered 'uncivilized' or inhuman' by British standards and values or 'repugnant to natural justice, equity and good conscience' (Ibhawoh 2007:60–63). The central works highlighting the creation of 'customary law' are by Snyder (1981), Gordon and Meggitt (1985), Chanock (1985) and Moore (1986). Merry (1991) provides a detailed overview and re-

and tried to adapt to the lives and values of the colonizers – supported this process. The adaptation of the local law to imported law not only changed the local law's content, but also its general character, as the originally very flexible and adaptable local law was substantively transformed by codification (Merry 1991:891–893).[8] Thus, many authors consider the codified customary law used to handle the cases of the colonized in former colonies to be distinct from the pre-colonial law, and they speak of the 'creation of a customary law' (Zenker and Hoehne 2018:5–7) or 'invention of tradition' (F. von Benda-Beckmann 1989).[9]

A third version of the local law continued to exist next to the codified customary law (F. von Benda-Beckmann 1984). To distinguish between the second kind, e.g. the transformed versions of codified African law that developed under colonial rule and the third, that is the normative orders that actually guide daily lives in contemporary Africa, some scholars use the term 'customary law' or 'official customary law' (also 'lawyers' customary law' or 'judicial customary law') for the former, and 'living customary law' (also: 'sociologists' customary law', 'practiced customary law') for the latter (Woodman 2011:224–225). The 'living customary law', Himonga (2011:48) emphasizes, is also dynamic, though the changes it undergoes come from within the community instead of being enforced by any external authority.

Other terms used in the literature for unwritten or non-state legal systems include 'people's law', 'traditional law', 'folk law' and 'indigenous law'. All of these terms have been discussed and partly discarded for different reasons.[10] The expressions 'traditional law' and 'customary law' have been criticized for suggesting non-state law is unchanged and static, while law is – like other aspects of culture – dynamic and subject to continuous change (K. von Benda-Beckmann 2001). The terms 'people's law' and 'folk law' have been rejected for romanticizing and minimizing the forms of non-state law (Roberts 1986, in Merry 1988:877). The expression 'indigenous law' has been seen as giving the wrong impression, as indigenous societies

---

view of important literature on the emergence of customary law under colonialism in Africa, pointing out that the indigenous law changed from a 'subtle and adaptable system often unwritten, to one of fixed, formal and written rules enforced by native courts' through adaption to the imported European law (Merry 1991:897).

8 This pattern of adaptation of the subordinate law to the dominant one, Merry (1991:893) argues, is also found in other contexts of domination, for example, when states incorporate ethnic minorities.

9 Franz von Benda-Beckmann (1989) describes how the Minankabau developed a legalistic version of their customary *adat* system, which they present and refer to when they communicate with state bureaucrats. By claiming that certain practices (such as land ownership or transfer) were violating one of their customary laws they could defend their interests against the dominant state in a convincing way. If they simply claimed that land ownership did not exist or was disliked among them, they would appear as backward and uncivilized.

10 See Merry (1988) for an overview of the discussion.

that seemed untouched by European influence at the time of early ethnographic research had, in fact, already been vulnerable to outside influences (Fitzpatrick 1985 in Merry 1988:876–877). The rather neutral term 'local law' has been suggested as 'a generic term for law that is being used and maintained at a local level, from whatever source it is derived' (K. von Benda-Beckmann 2001).

Alongside the diverse forms of customary law, the imported European law has also been reinterpreted and transformed into local versions (F. von Benda-Beckmann 1984) – a process that Merry and Levitt (2017) have called the 'vernacularization of law'. Thus, in reality, there exists a much greater variety of normative orders in Africa than just 'state law and 'customary law'.

Discussions on the correct terminology referring to the various forms of local and imported law channelled into the notion that the boundaries between different systems of ordering are fluid and that the systems are not separate but constitute a continuum (Galanter 1981 in Merry 1988:877). Moore's concept of the 'semi-autonomous social field' (1973), which can generate rules and norms internally but is also influenced by external forces, has been widely accepted and has endured.

Despite all the criticism, the term 'customary law' is still widely in use, not only in academia but also in national and international laws and policy documents. It is also commonly used in the Ethiopian context, both by scholars and legal practitioners and policy makers, though the context is slightly different to that of other African countries. Ethiopia was never colonized and there exist no codified versions of local normative orders (though some indigenous notions are reflected in areas of family law, successions and property law (Vanderlinden 1966/67:59 in Getachew, this volume). Most of Ethiopia's numerous non-state normative orders continue to be functional today, and run in parallel with the state system. When used in the Ethiopian context, the expression 'customary law' is therefore only used to refer to those local laws that are a dynamic continuation of past forms of legal ordering. While these local laws have certainly changed over time, in most cases, the extent to which a given customary legal system has been shaped or influenced by the law of previous and/or the current regimes remains to be explored. With all this in mind, the term 'customary law' is also used in this volume.

The presence and future of customary law in Africa

Many scholars acknowledge that customary justice systems, despite their oft-claimed fundamental differences and incompatibility with state law (Woodman 2011:20), are resilient and continue to be relevant in the lives of many people worldwide, especially among the poor (Ubink 2011a:7).

As Gebre (this volume) has pointed out for Ethiopia, customary laws are deeply rooted in cultural and religious values. Customary conflict resolution mechanisms have been praised not only by the local communities using them, but also by state legal practitioners. The proximity of customary courts or elders' councils and their speedy handling of cases at low or no cost make customary conflict resolution attractive and easily acceptable to the public. Local legal practitioners are personally known and respected, and procedures are embedded and legitimated in local values and beliefs. Customary law is seen as highly credible and transparent because cases are usually handled in public and with the involvement of community members as observers, witnesses and commentators, and final decisions are usually publicly accepted and respected. This limits the chance for corruption and unfair judgment. In addition, individuals who do not conform to the verdicts of elders or customary courts risk being considered as rebellious against community values and interests. Customary institutions are also often more successful in finding out the truth in criminal cases than the formal justice system, as the social pressure to tell the truth within communities is very high. Besides, customary institutions can employ religious or spiritual pressure, for example, by asking a suspect to speak under oath. As lying under oath is believed to bring misfortune or disease, this tactic is usually succesful. Furthermore, while the state courts aim to punish wrongdoers, customary insitutions primarily intend to restore broken relationships. This again means that their decisions are usually well accepted and supported by the community, which hopes to avoid coercive measures and enhance social cohesion (Pankhurst and Getachew 2008a:260). As the restoration of social order often includes the relatives or clans and communities from both the perpetrator's and the victim's sides, possible relapses and spill over effects are avoided and community peace is ensured (Gebre, this volume). Alongside its role in dispute settlement and conflict resolution, Ubink (2011c) emphasizes that customary law has particular value in the way it regulates daily life, the management of and access to land and natural resources, as well as social life and family issues. As customary legal institutions reduce the workload of formal courts and are known for their effectiveness, they are often coopted by government officials.

However, for all their positive attributes, customary laws and norms have also been criticized, especially for their frequent incompatibility with the modern state and international law. As mentioned earlier, some aspects of customary law do not comply with human rights standards because they contradict ideas of gender equality, the rights of women, children and minorities, and the rights of the individual. Yet, many voices claim that despite the shortcomings of customary laws, their strengths can be used to shape Africa's future (Mgbako and Baehr 2011) and contribute to its legal development in the twenty-first century. Himonga (2011) sees potential not in the 'official codified customary law', as used by magistrates and courts in postcolonial Africa, but rather in the 'living customary law', i.e. the nonencoded normative orders people live by. The ability of the 'living customary law' to adapt to changing circumstances, he argues, will enable it to live on despite the fact that it often contradicts national laws and international human rights standards

(Himonga 2011:34). While efforts should be made to reconcile 'living customary law' with human rights, its local values and fundamental features should be retained as much as possible (Himonga 2011:48).

Adding to the voices in support of customary systems, Ubink and van Rooij (2011:8) have pointed to the contribution made by customary laws and administration, natural resource management and local knowledge on food security to the enhancement of sustainable development in Africa. The authors' hope is that the involvement of local people and their normative systems should not be seen as a hindrance, but as assets in the creation of a fruitful link between state and customary law and institutions.

The potential of legal hybridity

Legal hybridity is not a new phenomenon. Indeed, it is rather the norm, as legal institutions – whether state or customary – have always been dynamic and borrowed from and been influenced by other legal institutions. However, the focus in academia on legal hybridity is somewhat recent, probably because the number of legal forums coming into contact with each other has been increasing with globalization.

Santos (2006:46) uses the words 'porosity and interpenetration' to describe 'legal hybridity', and sees it as the result of the bringing together of distinctive and often contradictory legal orders or cultures that leads to the emergence of 'new forms of legal meaning and action'. In a wide sense, 'hybridity of law' refers to a legally plural situation, in which 'two or more legal systems coexist in the same social field'. More specifically, it means that 'two legal traditions blend in the same social field' – something sometimes referred to as 'mixed jurisdictions' or 'hybrid systems of law'. This is the case, for example, in countries or jurisdictions where both civil law and common law traditions coexist (De Cruz 1999:202). 'Legal hybridity' can refer to the whole justice sector, but also to individual (state or customary) legal institutions. When they borrow from each other or function in a hybrid manner, this is often referred to as 'internal hybridity' (Clark and Stephens 2011).

In contemporary Africa, the complexity of legal forums is greater than in the past (Santos 2006). Due to the transformative processes at play in Africa's states in the context of globalization, the focus of research has shifted from the intra-state legal orders that coexist with official, national law, to the influence of the emerging supranational legal orders. Today, we find today subnational legal plurality in combination with supranational legal plurality in many African countries (Santos 2006:7). While the interaction between the local, national and global (each of which has its own rationale and norms) often creates tensions, it always also leads to mutual influence. Thus, each legal order can only be defined in relation to the legal constellation of which it is part (Santos 2006:45–46).

As Clark and Stephens (2011:70) have shown for Indonesia and the South Pacific, this borrowing of elements occurs in both directions. Their work elaborates how on one hand customary authorities tend to codify their rules and structures in order to 'be seen like the state' and thus to be respected and not regarded as 'backward'. On the other hand, the state also borrows from non-state normative traditions to apply state law more effectively. The creation of hybrid institutions, the authors argue, can be a chance to blend the strengths and mitigate the weaknesses of formal and customary systems. Also, in contexts where neither state nor non-state justice system can fully deliver justice, hybrid institutions can help overcome the weaknesses and injustices of both systems (Clark and Stephens 2011:68). Berman (2007) also sees the normative conflicts among multiple, overlapping legal systems as a potential source of new ideas that can lead to the creation of a wide variety of procedural mechanisms and institutions. The *gacaca* courts in Rwanda, for example, are an oft-mentioned recent example of a creative and resourceful hybrid of 'retributive, deterrent and restorative justice with the ultimate aim of being restorative and reconciliatory' (Clark 2007:61–62). This hybrid form of court was launched to handle the less serious cases related to the 1994 genocide, and combined 'prosecution with national unity and reconciliation' (Hermann 2012:90). Mgbako and Baehr (2011) mention the constructive role played by paralegal organizations, which are usually comprised of non-lawyers – for example, paralegal experts who receive some training in formal law and at the same time have intimate knowledge of customary law – who assist communities and individuals in the resolution of justice disputes. These non-lawyers' knowledge of both areas of law enables them to assist communities in navigating between the formal and customary systems. Harper (2011) has highlighted some examples of productive engagement with customary law in Africa, and has shown that impediments to accessing equitable justice through customary forums can be addressed by the creation of alternative institutions. These include i) NGO-created forums for dispute resolution based on customary values and procedures that can be expanded and built on; ii) paralegals (laypersons with some legal knowledge and skills to negotiate with court system) who can provide a bridge between the formal legal system and society; and iii) legal aid services and mobile courts designed to extend the reach of the state's justice services to remote communities (Harper 2011:35–38). Ubink (2011b) has explored the positive effects of participatory codification of customary law in Namibia, and uncovered a successful attempt to bring customary and state law together. In the 1990s, traditional Ovambo authorities of northern Namibia selected a number of the most essential and procedural customary norms for codification. Even though some of these codified norms (for example, on the status of widows) were adapted to conform to the constitution, local acceptance of their legitimacy still seems to have been rather high. The fact that the norms chosen for codification were selected by local elders and not enforced by the government had an overall strengthening effect on the Uukwambi (traditional kingdom of Ovambo) customary justice system (Ubink 2011b:145–147). The formalization of customary law has not, however, contributed to the legal empowerment of women in either customary or state court contexts (Peters and Ubink 2015). In South Africa, the philosophical and legal concept of *ubuntu*, 'the right to be treated with respect and dignity',[11] is frequently used in state court cases (Himonga 2011:45–46).

Preconditions for productive cooperation

Transferring laws from one cultural context to another often means interfering with communities' key values, and carries the risk of knowingly or unknowingly creating disturbance and irritation. Such transfers mostly also occur in unequal relationships: they are usually initiated by a dominant state imposing new laws on local communities, even if both sides influence each other in the long run. However, even though the state seems to be in the more powerful position, if the targeted recipients cannot be convinced that the legal innovations are to their benefit, the imposition of new laws can lead to disappointment, withdrawal, resistance and conflict. Mutual recognition is one of the bases for peaceful relations and trust (Taylor 1997).[12] Thus, respectful and polite forms of interaction must be found in order to avoid distrust, disrespect and perceived insult. As trust, respect and deference are rather complex social and culture-specific phenomena (Broch-Due and Ystanes 2016, Finkelstein 2008), mutual knowledge about cultural values and practices are important for success. In addition, the character of social relationships, whether interpersonal or between groups, radiates from the past as much as the present, so successful intercultural encounters need careful and open-minded approaches, especially when negative experiences have shaped perceptions and stereotypes.

---

11 *Ubuntu* has been translated as 'humaneness', 'human dignity'. Being a traditional concept, it has to some extent influenced the way people are treated in the state legal system.

12 In his discussion on the contemporary politics of 'multiculturalism', Charles Taylor (1997:99) acknowledged the importance of 'recognition' as a 'vital human need' and not just a 'courtesy we owe people'. The absence of recognition (i.e. misrecognition) can actually be considered as a form of oppression, and can inflict harm (*ibid*.:98–99). In the politics of equal recognition, this has led to two forms of conceptions. The first, based on the perception that all humans are the same, equal recognition is commonly understood as an offering of equal rights for all. The second acknowledges the need to recognize difference and the need for special rights and entitlements for groups who have been disadvantaged or whose culture is at stake if they are to preserve their personal and cultural integrity (*ibid*.:105–107).

Customary law and legal pluralism in Ethiopia

The normative systems in Ethiopia are highly diverse. They include the formal state system, the customary normative orders of more than eighty ethnic groups, the *Sharia* courts, the certified commercial arbitration forums, and spirit mediums operating as mediators between humans and supernatural forces (Gebre 2014). International law now also has a place in Ehtiopia's legal landscape, as Ethiopia has adopted the Universal Declaration of Human Rights (UDHR) and related conventions and treaties, and has included laws protecting human rights of the individual in its 1995 Constitution and in numerous government and NGO programmes. Concepts

As mentioned earlier, customary laws and conflict resolution mechanisms continue to be applied both in the absence and presence of state institutions in both rural and urban contexts. Efforts by earlier regimes to ignore or forbid local normative orders, institutions and authorities have been rather unsuccessful in Ethiopia (Pankhurst and Getachew 2008, Getachew, this volume). Unlike in former colonies, Ethiopia's customary legal systems have continued to function unimpeded by outside influence in many places (especially in the peripheries). However, as elsewhere, changing conditions and external influences have led to changes in customary conflict resolution that have, especially in the twentieth century, led to new forms, hybrid institutions and some cooperative interaction between state and customary institutions (Pankhurst and Getachew 2008:73).[13]

The first Ethiopian Constitution was enacted in 1931 and revised in 1955 (Aberra 2012:166, 170). The country's first modern codified law was developed in the late 1950s and early 1960s. It was inspired mainly by various European civil law models, with efforts made to blend Ethiopian concepts of justice into the civic law (Aberra 2012:183ff). However, despite these efforts, it is clear that the incorporated elements were very limited and did not represent the diversity of customary laws in the country; customary legal institutions were also not given any recognition (Pankhurst and Getachew 2008:5). Similarly, the socialist Derg regime's (1987–1991) consitution emphasized the formation of a unitary state under one national law (*ibid.*:5–6).

The current Ethiopian Constitution, created in 1995, emphasizes cultural and ethnic diversity in a federal state. Article 34(5) makes direct reference to settlement

13 In some areas state law was extended, especially in areas of serious crime (such as homicide, breaches of law and order, and after 1975 in relation to land issues). The introduction of the *balabat* institution (local leaders selected for local administration) constituted a form of indirect rule. The formalization and monetization of economy led to changes in compensation payments –no longer given in kind but in cash – and the influence of writing led to the codification of law. Besides, the monotheistic religions (Islam and Orthodox and Protestant Christianity) replaced customary law in some places or removed some of its key elements (Pankhurst and Getachew 2008:73ff).

of disputes relating to personal and family laws in accordance with customary laws, and Article 78(5) states that the House of People's Representatives and State Councils can give official recognition to customary courts.[14] Local institutions and courts are thus officially recognized and, in some contexts, even considered as more cost and time effective than the state system (Gebre *et al.* 2012a). While there exist many studies on customary conflict resolution in Ethiopia (see the collected essays in Fekade *et al.* 2011, Pankhurst and Getachew 2008, Gebre *et al.* 2011, 2012b, Tarekegn and Hanna 2001, and the monograph by Nicolas 2011) – both appreciative and cricital – there are very few on legal pluralism. Most of the case studies on customary dispute resolution in Pankhurst and Getachew (2008) have a short section on the interaction between state and customary legal institutions of half a page or so. Only Dereje (2008, in the same volume) gives a more detailed example, in his discussion of the *sefer shum*, a kind of hybrid legal institution (court) among the Nuer. Some very recent publications look specifically at the cooperative coexistance of state and customary laws and the emergence of hybrid institutions and procedures. Among the very few offerings from anthropology are the works of three authors: Seidel (2013), who examines the coexistence of Sharia law and state law; Kairedin (2018), who looks at the very complex situation in Siltie, where Sharia, state and customary legal institutions function and interact; and Prigge (2012), who describes the realities of legal pluralism among the Amhara. Legal experts, meanwhile, have made efforts to develop models of how the various legal systems could cooperate productively and contradictions be eliminated. Among them are Donovan and Getachew (2003), who discuss the handling of homicide in the context of legal pluralism in Ethiopia from a legal perspective, Mohammed (2011), who discusses the position of Sharia courts in the constitutional framework of Ethiopia, and several authors in the volume edited by Stebek and Muradu (2013), who examine the role of legal pluralism in the process of development and modernization of the Ethiopian state.

Somewhat paradoxically, it was with the introduction of ethnic federalism in 1995, and the official recognition of cultural diversity and customary laws in the constitution, that major changes in local normative orders began to occur. Since 1991, the current government has been putting increased effort into integrating all areas and people into the state apparatus. The penetration of the state into the local communities has taken different forms. First, the decentralization process has empowered local people to administer their own affairs using the national and subnational law. Second, the government has practically come to the 'doorsteps' of many rather isolated communities through major development and investment projects, the improvement of local infrastructure (construction of roads, establishment of telecommunication networks), and the expansion of social services (educa-

14 Constitution of the Federal Democratic Republic of Ethiopia (accessible online at http://www.ethiopia.gov.et/constitution, last accessed 22 October 2018).

tional and healthcare institutions, awareness-raising programmes). This has been accompanied by government efforts to increase enforcement of the state law, which meant that state law has come to be seen as offering a viable alternative legal forum for local communities.

Given that the federal decentralization of power was inspired by the right to self-determination of the ethno-cultural communities, one might expect that customary justice systems would have been given robust recognition. However, the formal state's approach to customary justice systems has not in fact shown much change from the pre-1995 scenario. While the state seems to be continuing with its policy of creating a pervasively applicable formal legal system (to the exclusion of customary institutions), many researchers have the impression that customary institutions not only continue to exist but are, in fact, flourishing. Although their position has been altered, customary leaders continue to play important roles in managing community affairs in many parts of the country, especially in the Southern Nations Nationalities and Peoples Region (SNNPR), parts of Oromia region and the border regions of Afar, Somali, Gambella and Benishangul-Gumuz, where most pastoral groups live (Tronvoll and Hagmann 2012a:7–8). Local legal institutions and courts are appreciated by both, the communities and state officials, who value them for their cost and time effectiveness and their sustainable resolution of conflicts (Gebre *et al.* 2012).[15]

The co-existence of different legal systems has led to constant negotiations across normative divides between state, religious and customary legal practitioners, government officials, justice-seeking members of local communities, local leaders and political functionaries. The provision that parties to a dispute have to agree to have their case handled in a particular legal forum makes communication between justice seekers and government officials necessary. The fact that a growing number of government officials are native to the area in which they work has led to a merging of knowledge about different value and legal systems; although, the normative dilemma for native government officials of having to serve different sides necessitates great sensitivity, flexibility and tolerance. The high caseload in state courts and an awareness of the effectiveness of customary conflict-resolution mechanisms motivates many legal practitioners to send cases back to the customary or religious legal forums for resolution, and this demands at least a certain degree of knowledge of, and respect for, customary laws. As the case studies in this volume will show, the better the communication, mutual respect and knowledge about the differences between the values and laws of the existing legal systems, the more sustainable and satisfying the outcome of

15 There are many appreciative and also critical studies on customary conflict resolution in Ethiopia (see the collected essays in Fekade *et al.* 2011, Pankhurst and Getachew 2008, Gebre *et al.* 2011, 2012, Tarekegn and Hanna 2001, and the monograph by Nicolas 2011).

resolved conflicts. Misunderstandings, resistance and conflict are common – and previously abandoned harmful traditional practices might even be taken up again (see Epple, this volume, on infanticide in Bashada and Gabbert 2014, on female genital cutting in Arbore) – where distrust continues to prevail, cultural differences are great, and the flexibility of legal practitioners is low (see for example Aberra, Yohannes, this volume).

Finally, the study of legal pluralism in contemporary Ethiopia needs to be understood in the context of its history, which has long been marked by the domination of the centralist state over the country's diverse cultural groups. Some studies looking at the continuities and changes of the mutual perceptions of local populations and the government under subsequent regimes have shown that past experiences still influence the way present day Ethiopian citizens relate to their government.[16] As Strecker and Lydall (2006a:1) put it, in situations of cultural contact, 'notions of pride, honour, name and self-esteem come into play, which – once people are hurt – have great explosive power leading to destruction and self destruction'. However, people have the chance to 'act imaginatively and creatively' if given enough space and time to understand and adapt, even if the changes they experience are unwanted and painful (Strecker and Lydall 2006a:3).

Organization of the book

The contributions were made by lawyers and social anthropologists working on legal pluralism in Ethiopia. The book is divided into four thematic sections. Fol-

16 See the collection of articles in Strecker and Lydall (2006b), which examine how the different peoples in the Ethiopian south remember their past, especially their forced inclusion into the Ethiopian Empire at the end of the nineteenth century under Emperor Menelik II, and their lives under a dominant central state until the end of the socialist Derg regime in 1991. The one hundred years of unequal cultural contact between government and local populations led to various mutual conceptions and stereotypes, which still influence the way people think of each other, interact, communicate, adapt, avoid or reject each other. For example, Miyawaki (2006) has shown how the memories of the Ethiopian conquest still shape the way the Arbore people interpret present-day disturbances in their country. Taddesse (2006) recounts the Guji experience of past humiliation and strongly suggests that minority groups must be given opportunities for voluntary rather than enforced assimilation. Strecker (2013) published the memories of a Hamar elder about the Ethiopian conquest and the Italian occupation. Lydall (2010) depicted the relationship between the Hamar and the government and described it as paternalistic in that Hamar traditions are challenged by the dominant 'highlanders' with the assumption that they know better what is good for them than the Hamar themselves. Epple (2012) showed that, in the context of modern education, the Bashada cooperate with the government as long as the people feel they are being taken seriously and treated respectfully, and do not fear that the key values of their culture are under threat.

lowing the introduction, which constitutes chapter one, the first section gives an overview of the history and constitutional context of legal pluralism in Ethiopia, a critical view on the international status of indigenous rights, and a conceptual discussion of customary law in the context of legal pluralism. The second, third and fourth thematic section provide insights into the experiences and daily practice of justice-seeking individuals and legal practitioners. Based on original and recent fieldwork, they show that the relationships between the existing legal forums in Ethiopia are very dynamic and prone to constant negotiation by the actors concerned, who strive to achieve their rights, keep their personal and cultural integrity and defend their interests. Many of the authors have also made efforts to indicate the historical context for their case studies. Descriptions of customary legal systems and the normative differences and tensions with state and international law are provided as these create the framework in which actual interactions take place. However, the greatest emphasis has been given to the real-life experiences of justice seekers and legal practitioners.

The first section on *The interplay of international, national and local law* contains three contributions. First, Getachew Assefa discusses the past and continuing relationship between the formal and customary justice systems in his chapter entitled 'Towards widening the constitutional space for customary justice systems in Ethiopia'. He begins by providing an historical overview of the relationship between the two justice systems up until the early 1990s, and explains the formal linkages created among them by the 1995 Ethiopian Constitution. He argues that the constitutional position, which requires that only customary (and religious) family and personal laws are recognized and only customary and religious courts only have power to preside over such matters, and not – for example – criminal matters does not reflect the reality in the country. He suggests that the vibrancy of customary justice systems in all areas of dispute settlement in all corners of the country must be reflected in the formal legal institutions. The author cautions, however, that the de jure recognition of customary justice systems must be done in a way that ensures customary justice is not subordinated to the formal system, and that only mechanisms – such as a constitutional review system – be put in place to ensure that customary justice systems function consistently with constitutional and international human rights standards.

The next chapter, written by Gebre Yntiso, aims at 'Understanding customary laws in the context of legal pluralism'. While the plural legal orders in Africa are the object of growing attention from researchers, the author argues that better and more comprehensive knowledge is needed for comparative analysis, scientific generalization and policy application. The deficiency lies mainly in the inconsistent use of terminology, especially around conceptual issues in the study of customary law. In his contribution, the author clarifies the meaning of concepts borrowed from the literature on alternative dispute resolution (ADR), and examines the extent to which these concepts could be used to refer to customary legal practices. Next, he identifies and organizes the core values, structures and procedures of customary laws, and examines their relevance in the analysis of legally plural situations.

Karl-Heinz Kohl looks at the UN 'Declaration on the Rights of Indigenous Peoples', and examines why many African governments remain reluctant to accept it as a basis of policy. Unlike in many former colonial settings around the world, where 'indigenous' peoples usually form a minority, the vast majority of people in Africa are indigenous to the continent: they were born there and regained freedom to live according to pre-colonial tradition after independence. Consequently, labelling all African peoples as indigenous would mean that there is no need to protect and privilege some of them. However, Kohl argues, the situation of smaller groups in Africa is comparable to, if not worse than, that of indigenous groups on other continents, as they are often considered as an obstacle to development and modernization, their cultures discriminated against and their access to natural resources and traditional lands threatened.

In the first of three thematic sections, the case studies explore *Cooperation and competition between legal forums,* and look at the productive aspects of the interplay between various legal forums in urban and rural contexts, which have led to the sustainable resolution of conflicts to the satisfaction of all parties involved, though not without elements of competition and abuse of gaps in the law. More specifically, the case studies presented look at i) the continued strength and widespread popularity of customary law; ii) the efforts made by legal practitioners and the justice-seeking clientele of parallel legal systems to communicate and cooperate, learn and be inspired from each other; iii) the daily handling of legal plurality, the negotiations between the actors, and the strategic application and manipulation of law.

The first case study in this section looks at 'The handling of homicide cases in the context of legal pluralism: Cooperation between government and customary institutions in the Gamo highlands'. The author, Temechegn Gutu, looks at how state and customary institutions cooperate in the area of criminal law. Although officially the exclusive domain of the government, in practice, homicide cases are also handled locally. This is not only because the Gamo people believe that rituals of purification are needed to restore social order and prevent misfortune, disease and natural calamities caused by the offender's pollution, but also because state institutions need the local population to cooperate in the collection of evidence and to help identify and detain suspects. As he shows in several case studies, the police and courts not only give local communities room to restore and maintain peace through their own conflict resolution mechanisms, but also make creative use of customary mechanisms to get hold of perpetrators and thus to serve the state's interests in prosecuting criminals.

The next contribution, by Melaku Abera, is on 'The interplay of customary and formal legal systems among the Tulama Oromo: Cooperation and competition'. Using several cases as examples, he highlights cooperative as well as problematic aspects of the relationship between the two legal systems. The author shows how the transfer of cases and notification of decisions made between jurisdictions contribute to mutual recognition and respect between state and local courts. Their activities even overlap at times: disputes may be settled jointly, or legal practitioners may be part of both systems, as elders in the local elders' court and judges in state courts, for example. At the same time, he points out, this emerging cooperation is vulnerable, especially when customary and state courts fail to respect each other's decisions, which leads to a lack of mutual trust and, in some cases, to wrongdoers being punished by both legal forums. The absence of clear regulations over the responsibilities of state and customary courts in some areas of law has led to the rejection of both systems in the handling of certain disputes.

In his chapter on 'Sharia Courts in Addis Ababa', Mohammed Abdo looks at the nature of the cases, the kinds of litigants and the procedures used in Sharia courts in Ethiopia's capital. After giving a detailed account of the history of Islamic courts in Ethiopia, he examines their current condition and how well accepted they are in light of recent developments, such as the growing consciousness of human rights and women's rights and the increasing Muslim demand for self-autonomy over religious matters. His findings show that most cases submitted to the Federal Sharia Courts – whose jurisdiction is confined to personal and family matters – concern divorce, with the great majority being submitted by well-educated Muslim women. Despite their modern outlook and economic independence, many Muslim women prefer to have their marriages dissolved in Sharia courts out of religious conviction. Mohammed also shows that Sharia courts have developed ways to interpret and employ the state procedural rules, by which they are bound, so that they appear to be in line with Sharia procedures.

Desalegn Amsalu has done research on the 'Use and abuse of "the right to consent": Forum shopping between *shimgilinna* and state courts among the Amhara of Ankober, north-central Ethiopia'. The transfer of a case from state court to customary legal forum demands the consent of all parties in dispute, and cases can be transferred back to the formal court if one of the parties withdraws consent. However, the author demonstrates, the lack of further elaboration of this rule in law has left room for manipulation and abuse. Plaintiffs or defendants may give and rescind their consent several times during the course of litigation, switching between courts in the hunt for a favourable decision. In Ankober, where many cases have been moved back and forth several times between the state court and the elders' council, this abuse of the right to shop between different legal forums has led to a general weakening of both the customary dispute resolution culture and the formal justice system.

The third thematic section looks more specifically at the *Emerging hybridity of legal institutions and practices*, examining how the boundaries between legal forums can become less rigid, and how new forms of legal concepts, values and practices can emerge through the effects of close cooperation, mutual understanding and influence. Case studies focus on i) the creativity of legal actors and recipients/users in making national and international law applicable to the local context; ii) the emergence of hybrid forms of law and legal procedures in some places, and iii) cross-cutting legal procedures.

Susanne Epple looks at 'Local strategies to maintain cultural integrity: The vernacularization of state law among the Bashada and Hamar of southern Ethiopia'. She argues that local communities have developed different kinds of mechanisms to handle unavoidable change brought from outside with the aim to protect their key values and cultural practises. As could be demonstrated, these strategies of avoidance range for very soft ones, such as hiding crimes or criminals and pretending cooperation to open confrontation when the pressure gets very high. Wherever possible, people try to avoid government interference in areas where they feel their cultural integrity is threatened. Innovations that cannot be turned away are adapted to, reinterpreted or customized in ways that allow the people to be, or at least to feel in control of their own affairs.

Julian Sommerschuh writes about the role of religion. In his chapter on 'Legal pluralism and Protestant Christianity: From fine to forgiveness in an Aari community', he demonstrates that, alongside customary conflict resolution mechanisms and state courts, Protestant churches offer an additional forum for dispute resolution. In an area where about 60 per cent of the population has converted, Protestantism has become an important player in the legal arena. By privileging forgiveness over retribution, prohibiting litigants from going to court without asking permission, and introducing Protestant logic into the formal courts through the judges' personal religious convictions, the author argues, the Church is gaining influence over the functioning of local formal institutions.

Muradu Abdo's chapter on '*Kontract*: A hybrid form of law among the Sidama' discusses three legal forums that are used to govern land transfer among the Sidama: Sidama customary norms and institutions (*utuwa*), state land laws, and a hybrid form of land rental agreement (*kontract*). Examining the genesis and nature of *kontract*, he shows that it holds elements of both customary practice and legal contracts used for land transfer. He then elaborates on the related processes employed during land transference, and on their implications for the livelihoods of smallholder farmers who are suffering from agricultural land alienation and loss. He presents two contrasting theoretical perspectives to interpret the practice of *kontract:* i) efficiency-oriented thinking, which characterizes *kontract* as a practice that gives free juridical expression to a peasant's demand for the lifting of state-law-imposed restrictions on the transferability of farmland; and ii) the legal positivist view that *kontract* emerged as an effective legal regime with detailed, clear and specific rules sanctioning those who enter into land sales is lacking. He then develops a third approach that sees *kontract* as constituting a third layer of the land tenure regime, lying between *utuwa* and state land law.

Kairedin Tezera looks at 'Legal pluralism and emerging legal hybridity: Interactions between the customary, state and religious law among the Siltie of southern Ethiopia'. He first provides a detailed description of the intra-plurality of the religious, state and customary legal forums among the Siltie and then explores how actors from the different courts communicate and complement, support and compete with each other for local power positions. His findings show that dispute settlers from the three courts borrow norms and legal concepts from each other in order to pass verdicts in their respective courts. This points to the porousness of the boundaries between the various legal systems, and to the emergence of a hybridized legal practice in the area.

Andrea Nicolas looks at how the normative and legal systems of Amhara and Oromo people influence each other. In chapter thirteen, 'A matter of perspective: Of transfer, switching and cross-cutting procedures. Legal processes among Oromo and Amhara of East Shewa Central Ethiopia', she introduces different forms of legal institutions co-existing in the study area. These include traditional Oromo law and legal forums, the Orthodox Church, the courts of spirit followers, the federal state law, courts and village tribunals, as well as some 'intermediate' forms, such as newly founded 'clan assemblies' and modern NGOs. By providing several case studies, she shows how justice seekers cross the institutional boundaries and consecutively appeal to different legal institutions – in her view possibly a legitimate choice for those involved. Alongside the option to forum shop, she suggests that a kind of 'meta-procedure' has emerged, such as when, for example, Amhara priests and Oromo legal experts jointly participate in common settlement procedures. Here, the cross-cutting of different legal institutions is no longer the exception but has become the standard, in that different legal institutions have become 'elements' of one and the same legal procedure.

Despite the many efforts to cooperate and develop mechanisms to cope with the diversity of legal forums in Ethiopia, disparities often end in miscommunication and mutual disappointment. The fourth thematic section therefore focuses on *Incompatibilities and conflict between legal forums in Ethiopia*, and shows that the way things are handled often depends on the goodwill and flexibility of individuals on the ground. Thus, the contributions in this part focus on areas where legal forums have been unable to come to satisfying solutions, either because the contradictions are too great, or because the parties involved are exploiting, denouncing or working against each other. More specifically, the authors explore i) the difficulties stakeholders face in attempting to harmonize international, national and local law; ii) the conflicts that arise when communication fails or the involved parties treat each other with disrespect or ignore each others' needs and constraints; and iii) the negative effects on the local population when legal systems fail to cooperate.

Aberra Degefa's chapter titled 'When parallel justice systems lack mutual recognition: Negative impacts on the resolution of criminal cases among the Borana Oromo' looks at the competition between the two justice systems in the area of criminal law, and the negative effects this has on the community. The Borana have fully functional laws and procedures based on their Gada age-system, where clan elders make sure that all clan members respect the customary laws. Criminal cases, though handled by the state courts, continue to be treated locally as well. As is shown in several case studies, the denial of mutual recognition has meant that many offenders have been subjected to the jurisdictions of both systems and have, consequently, been sanctioned twice: through imprisonment by the state and through compensation payments in the community.

In 'Combatting infanticide in Bashada and Hamar: The complexities behind a "harmful traditional practice" in southern Ethiopia', Susanne Epple explores the problems that arise from contradictions between international law/human rights and customary laws and values in local contexts. Specifically, she examines the negotiation on harmful traditional practices (HTPs) in Hamar Woreda, looking at the perspectives and priorities of both local communities and external agents. After elaborating the cultural meaning and explanations of infanticide among the Bashada and Hamar people, she explores the views and priorities of state representatives: administrative personnel at the zonal and district level, and legal practitioners (prosecutors and judges). Examining the different strategies that have been employed to eliminate infanticide in South Omo, as well as the population's reactions and various local strategies, she shows that certain changes could be achieved through the creativity, flexibility and patience of actors on both sides, even though frequent set backs are part of daily reality.

Yohannes Yitbarek's research on 'Clashing values: The 2015 conflict in Hamar district of South Omo Zone, southern Ethiopia' constitutes chapter sixteen. The author explores the causes of certain major conflicts between the Hamar people and the local government, the reasons for their escalation in 2014/15, as well as the efforts made by both sides to resolve the crisis. As he demonstrates, differing perspectives on what it means to live a good life, how local resources should be used, and how conflicts should be resolved led to many deaths during violent encounters in 2015. Such deaths, he suggests, could be avoided in the future if differences in values are respected and solutions sought through equitable communication.

References

ABERRA Jembere, 2012 *An introduction to the legal history of Ethiopia 1434–1974*. Addis Ababa: Shama Books

AN-NA'IM, Abdullahi (ed.), 1992 *Human rights in cross-cultural perspectives: A quest for consensus*. Philadelphia: University of Philadelphia Press.

2002 *Cultural transformation and human rights in Africa. Human rights under African constitutions: Realizing the promise for ourselves.* Philadelphia: University of Philadelphia Press

BEEK, Jan, Mirco GÖPFERT, Olly OWEN, Jonny STEINBERG (eds.), 2017 *Police in Africa: The street-level view*. London: Hurst

BENDA-BECKMANN, Keebet von, 1981 "Forum shopping and shopping forums: Dispute processing in Minangkabau Village", *Journal of Legal Pluralism* 19:117–159

2001 "Folk, indigenous, and customary law", in: Neil J. Smelser and Paul B. Baltes (eds.), *International Encyclopedia* of the *Social* and *Behavioural Sciences* 8, 5705–5708. Amsterdam: Elsevier

BENDA-BECKMANN, Franz von, 1984 "Law out of context: A comment on the creation of traditional law discussion", *Journal of African Law* 28 (1/2):28–33

1989 "Scape-goat and magic charm: Law in development theory and practice", *Journal of Legal Pluralism* 28:129–148

2009 "Human rights, cultural relativism and legal pluralism: Towards a two-dimensional debate", in: Franz von Benda-Beckmann, Keebet von Benda-Beckmann and Anne Griffiths (eds.) *The power of law in a transnational world: Anthropological enquiries*, 115–134. Oxford and New York: Berghahn

BENDA-BECKMANN, Franz von and Keebet von BENDA-BECKMANN, 2006 "Change and continuity in plural legal orders", *Journal of Legal Pluralism* 53–54:1–44

BIERSCHENK, Thomas, 2014 "States at work in West Africa: Sedimentation, fragmentation and normative double-binds", in: Thomas Bierschenk and Jean-Pierre Olivier de Sardan (eds.) *States at work: Dynamics of African bureaucracies*, 221–245. Leiden: Brill

BIERSCHENK, Thomas and Jean-Pierre OLIVIER DE SARDAN (eds.), 2014 *States at work: Dynamics of African bureaucracies*. Leiden: Brill

BROCH-DUE, Vigdis and Margit YSTANES (eds.), 2016 *Trusting and its tribulations: Interdisciplinary engagements with intimacy, sociality and trust*. New York: Berghahn

CENTRAL STATISTICAL AGENCY (CSA), 2008 *Summary and statistical report of the 2007 population and housing census*. FDRE: Population Census Commission

CHANOCK, Martin, 1985 *Law, custom and social order: The colonial experience in Malawi and Zambia*. Cambridge: Cambridge University Press

CLARK, Phil, 2007 "Hybridity, holism, and 'traditional' justice: The case of the gacaca courts in post-genocide Rwanda", *George Washington International Law Review* 39 (4):765–837

CLARK, Samuel and Matthew STEPHENS, 2011 "Reducing injustice? A grounded approach to strengthening hybrid justice systems: Lessons from Indonesia", in: Janine Ubink (ed.) *Customary justice: Perspectives on legal empowerment*, 67–90. Rome: International Development Law Organization

COWAN, Jane K., Marie-Bénédicte DEMBOUR, Richard A. WILSON (eds.), 2001 *Culture and rights: Anthropological perspectives*. Cambridge: Cambridge University Press

CUSKELLY, Katrina, 2011 *Customs and constitutions: State recognition of customary law around the world*. Bangkok: IUCN

DE CRUZ, Peter, 1999 *Comparative law in a changing world*. London, Sydney: Cavendish Publishing

DE HERDT, Tom and Jean-Pierre OLIVIER de SARDAN (eds.), 2015 *Real governance and practical norms in sub-Saharan Africa: The game of the rules*. London: Routledge

DEREJE Feyissa, 2008 "Customary dispute resolution institutions in Gambella Region: The case of the Nuer", in: Alula Pankhurst and Getachew Assefa (eds.) *Grassroots justice: The contribution of customary dispute resolution*, 133–154. Addis Ababa: CFEE

DONOVAN, Dolores A. and GETACHEW Assefa, 2003 "Homicide in Ethiopia: Human rights, federalism, and legal pluralism", *American Journal of Comparative Law* 51 (3):505–552

EPPLE, Susanne, 2012 "Local responses to externally induced cultural change in Southern Ethiopia: The introduction of formal education in Bashada (southern Ethiopia)", *Paideuma: Mitteilungen zur Kulturkunde (Special focus issue)* 58:197–212

ERIKSEN, Thomas Hylland, 2001 "Between universalism and relativism: A critique of the UNESCO concept of culture", in: Jane K. Cowan, Marie-Bénédicte Dembour, Richard A. Wilson (eds.) *Culture and rights: Anthropological perspectives*, 127–148. Cambridge: Cambridge University Press.

FEDERAL DEMOCRATIC REPUBLIC OF ETHIOPIA(FDRE), 1995 *The Constitution of the Federal Democratic Republic of Ethiopia*. Addis Ababa (accessible online at https://www.wipo.int/edocs/lexdocs/laws/en/et/et007en.pdf, last accessed, 25 February 2019).

FEKADE Azeze, ASSEFA Fiseha, GEBRE Yntiso (eds.), 2011 *Annotated bibliography of studies on customary dispute resolution mechanisms in Ethiopia*. Addis Ababa: The Ethiopian Arbitration and Conciliation Center

FINKELSTEIN, Ellis, 2008 "Toward an anthropology of respect", *Social Analysis*: 99–117.

FOBLETS, Marie-Claire and Nadjma YASSARI (eds.), 2013 *Legal approaches to cultural diversity*. Leiden/Boston: Martinus Nijhoff

FOBLETS, Marie-Claire, Michele GRAZIADEI and Alison D. RENTELN (eds.), 2018 *Personal autonomy in plural societies: A principle and its paradoxes*. New York: Routledge

GABBERT, Echi Christina,2014 "Powerful mothers, radical daughters: Tales about and cases of women's agency among the Arbore of southern Ethiopia", *Paideuma: Mitteilungen zur Kulturkunde*(Special focus issue) 60:187–204

GEBRE Yntiso, FEKADE Azeze, ASSEFA Fiseha (eds.), 2012a "Introduction: Customary/alternative dispute resolutions: Values, operations and legal status", in: Gebre Yntiso, Fekade Azeze, and Assefa Fiseha (eds.) *Customary dispute resolution mechanisms in Ethiopia*, 23–48. Addis Ababa: The Ethiopian Arbitration and Conciliation Center

2012b *Customary dispute resolution mechanisms in Ethiopia*. Addis Ababa: The Ethiopian Arbitration and Conciliation Center

GEBRE Yntiso, 2014 "Systematizing knowledge about customary laws in Ethiopia", *Journal of Ethiopian Law* 26 (2):28–54

GETACHEW Assefa, YONAS Birmeta, MURADU Abdo (eds.), 2016 *Economic, social and cultural rights in Ethiopia*. Addis Ababa: Eclipse Printers

GOODALE, Mark, 2009 "Introduction: Human rights and anthropology", in: Mark Goodale (ed.) *Human rights: An anthropological reader*, 1–19. Oxford: Miley–Blackwell

GRIFFITH, Anne, 1997 *In the shadow of marriage: Gender and justice in an African community*. Chicago: University of Chicago Press.

GRIFFITH, John, 1986 "What is legal pluralism?", *Journal of Legal Pluralism* 24:1–55

GORDON, Robert J. and Mervyn J. MEGGITT, 1985 *Law and order in the New Guinea highlands: Encounters with Enga*. Hanover, N.H.: University Press of New England

HARPER, Erica, 2011 "Engaging with customary justice systems", in: Janine Ubink (ed.) *Customary justice: Perspectives on legal empowerment*, 29–42. Rome: International Development Law Organization

HELFAND, Michael A. (ed.), 2015 *Negotiating state and on-state law: The challenge of global and local legal pluralism*. New York: Cambridge University Press

HERRMANN, Judith, 2012 "A critical analysis of the transitional justice measures incorporated by Rwandan gacaca and their effectiveness", *James Cook University Law Review* 5 (19):90–112

HIMONGA, Chuma, 2011 "The future of living customary law in African legal systems in the twenty-first century and beyond, with special reference to South Africa", in: Jeanmarie Fenrich, Paolo Galizzi, Tracy E. Higgins (eds.) *The future of African customary law*, 31–57. Cambridge: Cambridge University Press

HIRSCH, Susan, E., 1998 *Pronouncing and persevering: Gender and the discourses of disputing in an African Islamic court.* Chicago: University of Chicago Press

HODGSON, Dorothy L. (ed.), 2011 *Gender and culture at the limits of rights*. Philadelphia: University of Pennsylvania Press

IBHAWOH, Bonny, 2007 *Imperialism and human rights: Colonial discourses of rights and liberties in African history*. Albany: State University of New York Press

KAIREDIN Tezera, 2018 *Dynamics of identity formation and legal pluralism: The case of customary, religious and state dispute resolutions among the Siltie people, southern Ethiopia*. Bayreuth: Bayreuth University (PhD Thesis)

KINLEY, David, 2012 "Bendable rules: The development implications of human rights pluralism", in: Brian Z. Tamanaha, Caroline Sage, Michael Woolcock (eds.) *Legal pluralism and development: Scholars and practitioners in dialogue*, 50–65. Cambridge: CUP

KOHLHAGEN, Dominik, 2008 "State law and local law in sub-Saharan Africa", in: Alula Pankhurst and Getachew Assefa (eds.) *Grassroots justice in Ethiopia: The contribution of customary dispute resolution*, 77–90. Addis Ababa: CFEE

LANGFIELD, Michele, William LOGAN and Máiréad Nic CRAITH (eds.), 2010 *Cultural diversity, heritage and human rights: Intersections in theory and practice*. London, New York: Routledge

LENTZ, Carola, 2014 "'I take an oath to the state, not the government': Career trajectories and professional ethics of Ghanaian public servants", in: Thomas Bierschenk and Jean-Pierre Olivier de Sardan (eds.) *States at work: Dynamics of African bureaucracies*,175–204. Leiden: Brill.

LEWIS, M. Paul (ed.), 2009 *Ethnologue: Languages of the world* (16th edition). Dallas, Texas: SIL International (acc. online at http://www.ethnologue.com)

LOGAN, William, Michael LANGFIELD and Máiréad Nic CRAITH, 2010 "Intersecting concepts and practices", in: Michele Langfield, William Logan and Máiréad Nic Craith (eds.) *Cultural diversity, heritage and human rights: Intersections in theory and practice*, 3–20. London, New York: Routledge

LYDALL, Jean, 2010 "The paternalistic neighbor: A tale of the demise of cherished traditions", in: Echi Cristina Gabbert and Sophia Thubauville (eds.) *To live with others: Essays on cultural neighborhood in Southern Ethiopia*, 314–334. Köln: Köppe

MALINOWSKI, Bronislaw, 1926 *Crime and custom in savage society*. New York: Harcourt, Brace & Co

MERRY, Sally Engle, 1988 "Legal pluralism", *Law and Society Review*, 22 (5):869–896

1991 "Law and colonialism", *Law & Society Review* 25 (4):889–922

2003a "From law and colonialism to law and globalization", *Law and Social Inquiry* 28 (29): 569–590

2003b "Human rights law and the demonization of culture (and anthropology along the way)", *PoLAR* 26 (1): 55–76

2006 *Human rights and gender violence: Translating international law into local justice*. Chicago and London: The University of Chicago Press.

MERRY, Sally Engle and Peggy Levitt, 2017 "The vernacularization of women's human rights", in: Stephen Hopgood, Jack Snyder, Leslie Vinjamuri (eds.): *Human rights futures*, 213–236. Cambridge: Cambridge University Press.

MGBAKO, Chi and Kristina Scurry BAEHR, 2011 "Engaging legal dualism", in: Jeanmarie Fenrich, Paolo Galizzi and Tracey E. Higgins (eds.): *The future of African customary law*, 170–201. Cambridge: Cambridge University Press

MIYAWAKI, Yukio, 2006 "Hor memory of Sidaama conquest", in: Ivo Strecker and Jean Lydall (eds.) *The perils of face: Essays on cultural contact, respect and self-esteem in southern Ethiopia*, 185–205. Berlin: Lit

MOHAMMED Abdo, 2011 "Legal pluralism, Sharia courts, and constitutional issues in Ethiopia", *Mizan Law Review* 5 (1):72–104

MOORE, Sally Falk, 1973 "Law and social change: The semi-autonomous social field as an appropriate subject of study", *Law and Society Review* 7 (4):719–746

1986 *Social facts and fabrications: 'Customary' law on Kilimanjaro, 1880–1980*. Cambridge *et al.*: Cambridge University Press

NADER, Laura (ed.), 1969 *Law in Culture and Society*. Berkeley and Los Angeles: University of California Press

NICOLAS, Andrea, 2011 *From process to procedure: Elders' mediation and formality in central Ethiopia*. Wiesbaden: Harrassowitz.

OLIVIER DE SARDAN, Jean-Pierre, 2008 "Researching the practical norms of real governance in Africa", *APPP Discussion paper Nr 5*. London: Overseas Development Institute

2015 "Practical norms: Informal regulations within public bureaucracies (in Africa and beyond)", in: Tom de Herdt and Jean-Pierre Olivier de Sardan (eds.) *Real governance and practical norms in sub-Sahara Africa: The game of the rules*, 19–62. London: Routledge

PANKHURST, Alula and GETACHEW Assefa (eds.), 2008a *Grassroots justice in Ethiopia: The contribution of customary dispute resolution*. Addis Ababa: CFEE

2008b "Understanding customary dispute settlement in Ethiopia", in: Alula Pankhurst and Getachew Assefa (eds.) *Grassroots justice in Ethiopia: the contribution of customary dispute resolution*, 1–76. Addis Ababa: CFEE

PETERS, Eline and Janine UBINK 2015 "Restorative and flexible customary procedures and their gendered impact: A preliminary view on Namibia's formalization of traditional courts", *Journal of Legal Pluralism and Unofficial Law* 47 (2):291–311

POSPISIL, Leopold J., 1971 *Anthropology of law: A comparative theory*. New York: Harper and Row

PREIS, Ann-Belinda S., 1996 "Human rights as cultural practice: An anthropological critique", *Human Rights Quarterly* 18 (2):286–315

PRIGGE, Judit, 2012 "Friedenswächter: Institutionen der Streitbeilegung bei den Amhara in Äthiopien", FB-*Governance Working Paper Series* Nr. 28, DFG, SFB 700

SANTOS, Boaventura de Sousa 2006 "The heterogeneous state and legal pluralism in Mozambique", *Law and Society Review* 40 (1):39–75

SEIDEL, Katrin, 2013 *Rechtspluralismus in Äthiopien: Interdependenzen zwischen islamischem Recht und staatlichem Recht*. Köln: Köppe

SNYDER, Francis, 1981 "Colonialism and legal form: The creation of 'customary law' in Senegal", *Journal of Legal Pluralism* 19:49–90

STEBEK, Elias N. and MURADO Abdo (eds.), 2013 *Law and development and legal pluralism in Ethiopia*. Addis Ababa: JLSRI Publications

STRECKER, Ivo, 2013 *Berimba's resistance: The life and times of a great Hamar spokesman: As told by his son Aike Berinas*. Münster: Lit

STRECKER, Ivo and Jean LYDALL (eds.), 2006a *The perils of face: Essays on cultural contact, respect and self-esteem in southern Ethiopia*. Berlin: Lit

2006b "Introduction", in: Ivo Strecker and Jean Lydall (eds.) *The perils of face: Essays on cultural contact, respect and self-esteem in southern Ethiopia*, 1–15. Berlin: Lit

TADESSE Berisso, 2006 "The pride of the Guji-Oromo: An essay on cultural contact and self-esteem", in: Ivo Strecker and Jean Lydall (eds.): *The perils of face: Essays on cultural contact, respect and self-esteem in southern Ethiopia*, 207–226. Berlin: Lit

TAREKEGN Adebo and HANNA Tsadik (eds.), 2008 *Making peace in Ethiopia: Five cases of traditional mechanisms for conflict resolution*. Addis Ababa: Peace and Development Committee

TAMANAHA, Brian, 2007 "Understanding legal pluralism: Past to present, local to global", *Sydney Law Review* 30:374–411

TAYLOR, Charles, 1997 "The politics of recognition", in: Ajay Heble, Donna Palmateer Pennee, J.R. Tim Struthers (eds.) *New contexts of Canadian criticism*, 98–131. Peterborough: Broadview Press

TRONVOLL, Kjetil and Tobias HAGMANN (eds.), 2012 *Contested power in Ethiopia: Traditional authorities and multi-party elections*. Leiden, Boston: Brill

2012 "Introduction: Traditional authorities and multi-partyelections in Ethiopia", in: Kjetil Tronvoll and Tobias Hagmann (eds.) *Contested power in Ethiopia: Traditional authorities and multi-party elections*, 1–30. Leiden, Boston: Brill

UBINK, Janine and Benjamin VAN ROOIJ, 2011 "Towards customary legal empowerment: An introduction", in: Janine Ubink (ed.) *Customary justice: Perspectives on legal empowerment*, 7–27. Rome: International Development Law Organization

UBINK, Janine (ed.), 2011a *Customary justice: Perspectives on legal empowerment*. Rome: International Development Law Organization

2011b "Stating the customary: An innovative approach to the locally legitimate recording of customary law in Namibia", in: Janine Ubink (ed.) *Customary justice: Perspectives on legal empowerment*, 131–150. Rome: International Development Law Organization

2011c "The quest for customary law in African state courts, in: Jeanmarie Fenrich, Paolo Galizzi and Tracey E. Higgins (eds.) *The future of African customary law*, 83–102. Cambridge: Cambridge University Press

WOODMAN, Gordon, 1996 "Legal pluralism and the search for justice", *Journal of African Law* 40 (2):152–167
2011 "A survey of customary laws in Africa in search of lessons for the future", in: Jeanmarie Fenrich, Paolo Galizzi and Tracey E. Higgins (eds.) *The future of African customary law*, 9–30. Cambridge: Cambridge University Press
ZENKER, Olaf and Markus Virgil HOEHNE (eds.), 2018 *The state and the paradox of customary law in Africa*. London and New York: Routledge
2018 "Processing the paradox. When the state has to deal with customary law", in: Olaf Zenker and Markus Virgil Hoehne (eds.) *The state and the paradox of customary law in Africa*, 1–40. London and New York: Routledge

Webpages

www.ethioembassy.org.uk/fact%20file/a-z/culture.htm
www.un.org/womenwatch/daw/cedaw

I.

The interplay of international, national and local law

2. Towards widening the constitutional space for customary justice systems in Ethiopia

Getachew Assefa

Introduction

Ethiopia exhibits a typical feature of many non-Western societies, wherein the formal state sponsored legal system functions alongside a multitude of non-formal legal systems. The state judicial system, which began in a rudimentary way at the beginning of the twentieth century, took a definite shape in 1942 with the enactment of the first proclamation on judicial administration. Through this law, Emperor Haile Selassie's government intended to create a judicial system with jurisdiction throughout the country. With the enactment of six codified laws (Penal Code, Civil Code, Commercial Code, Maritime Code, Criminal Procedure Code and Civil Procedure Code) from the late 1950s to mid 1960s, the imperial government made it clear that legal relations in Ethiopia would no longer be governed by any customary legal system.

The drafters of the codes, especially those of the Civil Code of 1960 (with a total of 3367 articles), attempted to incorporate some customary norms in areas dealing with family, successions and property (Vanderlinden 1966–67:259). The Civil Code then declared that any rules – written or customary – dealing with matters covered in the Code that had not been saved by explicit reference or incorporated into the Code were repealed (Art. 3347). Although the other codes did not include such clear repeal provisions, they were enacted with the aim of bringing about the complete displacement of any non-formal sources of law that were hitherto in operation.

The Ethiopian government's policy of derecognizing customary justice systems continued until the fall of the military government (also known as Derg or Dergue) in 1991. But, contrary to the official policy of the government, the customary justice systems of the various ethno-cultural communities of Ethiopia have never stopped functioning. As studies by Gebre *et al.* (2012), Donovan and Getachew (2003), Pankhurst and Getachew (2008) and others show, most of the non-urban population of the country – about 85 per cent of its population – primarily uses the customary justice system to settle their disputes.

The government led by the Ethiopian Peoples' Revolutionary Democratic Front (EPRDF), which ousted the Derg and came to power in 1991, introduced – among other things – a policy of cultural self-determination for the ethno-linguistic communities of the country. As part of this policy shift, the 1995 Constitution recognized the right of customary and religious laws and courts to preside over cases in the areas of family and personal matters where the disputants have given consent to be heard by these forums. The Constitution is, however, silent regarding the place of customary justice systems in other areas of civil law and in criminal law. The central argument of this chapter is that Ethiopia needs to undertake a legislative reform at both federal and state levels to clearly recognize customary justice systems in criminal matters and additional areas of civil law. At the same time, legislative reform needs to put in place mechanisms for creating and sustaining harmonious cooperative relations between the formal and customary legal systems. Any law enacted should also make sure that the interpretation and application of customary law is undertaken in a manner consistent with the fundamental rights and freedoms guaranteed by the Ethiopian Constitution and international human rights standards applicable to Ethiopia. The chapter makes suggestions on how these legislative aims could be met.

The chapter proceeds as follows. The next section (section two) presents a succinct summary of the trajectory of customary justice systems to the coming into force of the 1995 Constitution. Section three explores the space given to customary justice system under the 1995 Constitution of Ethiopia. Section four presents arguments and options for the full recognition of customary justice system in Ethiopia. Finally, the chapter closes with a brief conclusion.

Customary justice system in Ethiopia before the 1995 constitution

Ethiopia has more than eighty different ethno-linguistic communities. These communities have memberships that range from millions to a few hundred. Each of them has its own indigenous governance and dispute settlement institutions, laws and mechanisms that have enabled them to live harmoniously and at peace internally as well as with others with whom they share land, water or other resources. Each cultural community may have more than one internal dispute settlement institution, each of which applies to certain sections of the group and has developed separately owing to geographical or other reasons.

Customary dispute settlement institutions and norms have been in existence for perhaps as long as the communities themselves and certainly long before the formal state laws and institutions were created and applied to these communities. Based on the existing evidence, the history of customary justice systems in Ethiopia can be categorized into four broad eras: the whole period preceding the mid-fourteenth century; the period between the mid-fourteenth century and early twentieth century; the period from the early twentieth century to the ratification of the Ethiopian Constitution in 1995; and the post 1995 constitutional order.

Before the fourteenth century justice was predominantly administered on the basis of the Biblical precepts of the Old Testament (Fetha Nagast:xvii). Although not much is known about the legal norms utilized by most of the non-Christian parts – including those professing Islam–of the population during that time, it is safe to assume that the cultural groups applied their own norms to govern their relations internally and with their neighbouring groups. This, however, is not to say that customary norms were not in use in the Christian or Judeo-Christian parts of the country. Rather, customary norms were used alongside the Old Testament precepts to fill gaps or otherwise supplement the royal sources of law (Bililign 1969:152). It is also known that, at least from the Aksumite period (around the tenth century BC), the monarchical regime exerted its control over the populace through royal edicts and proclamations to collect tax, declare war and make peace.

In the mid-fourteenth century, the Fetha Nagast ('Law of Kings') was imported from Alexandria Egypt at the request of Emperor Za'ra Ya'qob (r. 1434–68) for use in the Christian part of the country (which had large Judaic community before the advent of Christianity in the fourth century[1]). According to Abba Paulos Tzadua[2], the Fetha Nagast 'was originally written in Arabic by the Coptic Egyptian writer Abu-l Fada'il Ibn al-Assal' in the 1230s (Fetha Nagast:xv). It replaced the Old Testament of the Bible as the main source of law at the formal level for the Judeo-Christian part of the Ethiopian society and remained so until the early twentieth century. But, for various reasons, the application of the Fetha Nagast was not pervasive. In fact, its application is said to have been limited to the clergy, the imperial court and limited sections of the Christian community. The ecumenical code was not readily accessible to those who were in charge of the administration of the law, both physically as there were few copies of the code in the entire country and because most people did not understand Ge'ez, the language in which it was expressed (Singer 1970:74). Thus, again, most people continued to use their customary dispute settlement institutions and laws to maintain peace and order and to go about their daily lives (Fetha Nagast:xxvii).

The third era began with the coming to power of Emperor Menelik II (r. 1889–1913). In 1907, for the first time in the country's history, ministerial departments were established. Hitherto, at least theoretically, the Emperor made all the

1 Kaplan (1992:17) for example notes, that "according to some Ethiopian traditions, half the population of Aksum was Jewish prior to the advent of Christianity".

2 Paulos Tzadua is a Catholic bishop who translated the *Fetha Nagast* from Ge'ez to English, originally published in 1968 by the Law Faculty, Haile Selassie I (current Addis Ababa) University. 'Ge'ez' (also sometimes referred to as 'Ethiopic') is a classical language of the Christian and Jewish population of Northern Ethiopia. It is currently a liturgical language of the Ethiopian Orthodox Tewahido and also Catholic churches in Ethiopia and Eritrea.

decisions single-handedly with the help and advice of some very close personnel. The Emperor's decision to create various departments was motivated by his desire to 'modernize' the governance and justice system of the country for the benefit of all its inhabitants (Mahteme-Selassie 1970:53). Among the ministries established was the Ministry of Justice. It was declared that the Minister of Justice was to serve as the head (chief) of all the judges in the country and that he was responsible for ensuring that all judgments conformed to the Fetha Nagast. From that time on, the formal institutions for the administration of justice were more pervasively applied, at least in theory.

The establishment of the ministries was followed quickly by the creation of a division of courts under the Minister of Justice known as *Afe Negus*, (lit. 'mouth of the king', Amharic), that were to preside over every territory in the country. Before this, appeals within a particular province were passed to the provincial governor, who acted as both administrator and high court judge. In the new courts, appeals from the provinces were heard by the *Afe Negus* himself, while appeals regarding the death penalty were heard by the Emperor. Accordingly, six divisions of courts, with two judges each, were created to have local jurisdiction over the parts of the country that were placed under their remit. This court structure continued until the Italian invasion in 1935. It was formally replaced through a law promulgated in 1942 by four tiers (*mikitil woreda,*[3] *woreda, awraja*[4], high courts) below the *Afe Negus*, with the Imperial Supreme Court presiding over the latter. A decree issued after the 1942 judicial administration law allowed governors and lower officials to sit as presiding judges in the lower (*mikitil woreda, woreda* and *awraja*) courts (Geraghty 1970:443).

Attempts were also made to enact procedural and substantive laws especially in the areas of criminal justice. The Penal Code enacted in 1930, and the judicial administration decree of 1943, are the two important laws worth mentioning in this regard. The 1930 Penal Code drew heavily on the criminal law part of the Fetha Nagast (Singer 1970:131) and superseded it. It is also noteworthy that Haile Selassie's policy of legal unification set in motion with the enactment of the 1942 judicial administration law left room for Sharia law and customary law, the latter of which was to deal with small claims and petty offences. A law passed in 1942 (replaced by another law enacted in 1944), allowed *khadis* and *naibas* councils[5] to adjudicate cases based on Islamic law (Singer 1971:136). This law was replaced by a subsequent law on the same subject passed in 1944 (*ibid.*).

---

3 The *mikitil woreda* court level was later abolished by Judicial Administration Proclamation No. 195/1962. *Mikitil woreda* was an administrative unit below *woreda* (district) level.

4 *Awraja* was an administrative unit encompassing some *woredas* under it. It is not in use currently.

5 *Khadi* (also *qadi*) was a mid-level Sharia court judge, and *naiba* was the lowest Sharia court judge.

In 1947, a proclamation (No. 90) was passed establishing local judges called *atbia dagnias*. Proclamation No. 90/1947 allowed the *atbia dagnias* to adjudicate civil claims up to the value of 26 Ethiopia Birr (about 9 USD at the time), and to impose a criminal fine of up to Birr 15 (Singer 1970:313). The men appointed as *atbia dagnias* were highly regarded local people, such as large landholders, who had already been unofficially exercising the power formally given to them by Proclamation No. 90/1947. The *atbia dagnia* was empowered to settle disputes by compromise (Amharic '*erq*') within his local jurisdiction without limit as to the amount or type of dispute. If unable to broker a compromise in a dispute within his material jurisdiction, he could then move to adjudicate the case, but if the case exceeded his material jurisdiction, he would pass it to the appropriate court (Singer 1970:313).

Between the late 1950s and mid-1960s, Emperor Haile Selassie I (r. 1930–1974) made a comprehensive move, on a revolutionary scale, to replace all existing laws (customary or otherwise) with codified formal law. This was the pinnacle of the drive to 'modernize' Ethiopia's legal system begun by Emperor Menelik II. It seems ironic, however, that while maintaining that 'no modern legislation which does not have its roots in the customs of those whom it governs can have a strong foundation' (Fetha Nagast: Preface), Emperor Haile Selassie instructed foreign experts who had no or very little knowledge about Ethiopian society to draft the major codes of law.[6] The Emperor believed that 'law is a unifying force in a nation' and that 'one of the goals sought to be attained by the enactment of modern codes and other legislation is that the law be uniform throughout the Empire' (Haile Selassie I 1964:vi). He also averred that although the codes drew in part on foreign sources, they were drafted to accord with Ethiopia's needs and ancient legal traditions' (ibid.).

However, it is questionable whether Emperor Haile Selassie's convictions resonated with the drafters of the codes who, it seems, understood their task to be to create a new set of laws for Ethiopia. For example, Rene David, speaking about the civil law, stated that Ethiopia's approach was aimed at the total abolition of customary law (outside those customary rules that would be incorporated into the code) and the enactment in its place of a ready-made system of foreign law (David 1962/63:188–189). David made an assumption that 'Ethiopians do not expect the new Code to be a work of consolidation, the methodical and clear statement of actual customary rules. They wish it to be a program envisaging a total transformation of society and they demand that for the most part, it set out new rules appropriate for the society they wish to create' (David 1962/63:193). David also spoke about the fact that some customs might not be worth preserving as they were repugnant

6 The 1957 Penal Code was drafted by Professor Jean Graven (Swiss); 1960 Civil Code was drafted by the French comparative law jurist Rene David; the Commercial Code (also of 1960) was drafted by professors Escarra and Jauffret (also French jurists); 1961 Criminal Procedure Code by Sir Mathews of the UK (Sand 1974:12,14).

to justice and likely to be rejected by the people in the future (David 1962/63:194). David further justified the almost wholesale importation of foreign civil law into Ethiopia by the fact that there was no custom at all in certain areas of the civil law, such as contracts, and that the multiplicity of cultures with diverse customary laws in Ethiopia made it impossible to codify or follow custom in the country (David 1962/63:195). Thus, except in certain areas of the Civil Code dealing with family law, successions and property law, where the rules reflected indigenous notions (Vanderlinden 1966/67:59), most of its provisions were essentially based on European legal rules. It needs to be noted that the Civil Code made it poignantly clear in its repeal provision (Art. 3347) that it abrogated or replaced all laws, written or customary, previously in force.

The ideas reflected by Rene David with regard to the Civil Code were shared by all the foreign experts that drafted Ethiopia's legal codes at that time. Indeed, it seems they were acting on instructions from the Emperor's government to draft the laws based on the legal systems of developed nations (Sand 1971:5). The Penal Code (1957) and the Commercial Code (1960) hardly gave any regard to the customary laws and institutions of Ethiopian society. The only reference the Penal Code made to 'customary law' was in Art. 10 dealing with transitory issues, which states that applications for the cancellation and reinstatement of judgments made under penal legislation repealed by this Code or 'customary law fallen into disuse' shall be governed by the Penal Code. The expression 'customary law fallen into disuse' makes it clear that the intention of the Code was to supersede customary law. In a few other places (Art. 97, confiscation of property; Art. 550, duels; Art. 770, disturbance of work or rest of others; and Art. 806, petty theft) the Penal Code refers to 'custom' as fact, not law. The fact that the 2004 Criminal Code, which replaced the 1957 Penal Code, does not have provisions analogous to Art. 10 of the 1957 Penal Code makes it clear that customary law in criminal law areas had already been nullified by the 1957 Penal Code, and that the Criminal Code had no intention of reviving it.

The same was the case with the Criminal Procedure Code of 1961, which – aside from its incorporation of a section on the *atbia dagnias*, entitled 'Atbia Dagnias with summary jurisdiction'[7] – was almost totally based on European (mostly Anglo-American) rules of criminal procedure. The *atbia dagnias*, as earlier noted, were established in 1947 as local judges to hear very minor civil and criminal cases.

---

7 Arts. 223 and 224 of the Criminal Procedure Code, the *atbia dagnias* were empowered to whenever possible settle by compromise all cases arising within their local jurisdiction of minor offences of insult, assault, petty damage to property or petty theft where the value of the property stolen does not exceed 5 Birr. If he cannot bring about a compromise, the *atbia dagnias* can then move to adjudicate the case with the help of two assessors and, on conviction, can impose a fine not exceeding 15 Birr. His decisions are appealable to the *woreda* court with local jurisdiction.

While the Criminal Procedure Code maintained the *atbia dagnias* and gave them jurisdiction over minor criminal offences, the Civil Procedure Code enacted in 1965 did not mention them as having any civil jurisdiction. A Ministry of Justice circular sent out to the provincial governors immediately after the adoption of the Civil Procedure Code did, however, state that the *atbia dagnias* courts could continue to exercise their civil jurisdiction if the parties agreed to submit their disputes to them (Geraghty 1970:428).

The dominant paradigm of replacing customary law with foreign-influenced formal laws and institutions of justice continued under the Derg regime (1974–1991). The defining character of the Derg was its importation of a socialist-oriented legal system based on Marxist-Leninist teachings, and its rejection of the liberal notions of the West. But when it came to customary justice systems, the Derg's policy position had the same effect of relegating and disregarding customary justice systems as that of the previous regime.

The fall of the Derg and coming to power of the EPRDF in May 1991 ushered in the current era in the development of the relationship between the Ethiopian state and the customary justice system. The EPDRF government clearly distanced itself from earlier regimes by proclaiming, among other things, the cultural self-determination of the country's ethno-cultural communities as official state policy. The EPDRF's interim constitution, the 1991 Charter of the Transitional Government (the Charter), states that every nation, nationality or people in Ethiopia is, among other things, guaranteed the right to: preserve its identity and have it respected; promote its culture; and administer its own affairs within its own defined territory (Art. 2). However, while the Charter openly embraced the cultural and other rights of self-determination of nationalities, it did not make specific reference to customary laws or courts. In this regard, it followed suit with all the earlier Ethiopian constitutions. Moreover, one of the most important pieces of legislation enacted during the transitional period (1991–1995) under the ambit of the Charter was Proclamation No. 7/1992, which organized the national/regional self-governments of the country and divided up judicial power between central and regional formal courts without any mention of non-formal courts (see Art. 10(9) and Arts. 23–24). The 1995 Constitution, on the other hand, reflected a clear policy shift in its embracing of customary (and also religious) laws and courts, albeit only in the areas of family and personal matters. The next section of this paper will explore the relevant constitutional, legal and policy regimes regarding customary justice under the current constitutional dispensation.

Customary justice system and the 1995 constitution of Ethiopia

As earlier noted, the 1995 Constitution of Ethiopia signalled a move away from the abolitionist position with regard to non-state justice system pursued by Ethiopia's governments since Haile Selassie's time. The framers of the Constitution adopted an approach that opened up space for the application of some customary laws and courts on the basis of subject matter. Accordingly, Art. 34(5) of the 1995 Constitution states:

> This Constitution shall not preclude the adjudication of disputes relating to personal and family laws in accordance with [religious or] customary laws, with the consent of the parties to the dispute. Particulars shall be determined by law.

To go full circle on the matter, the Constitution makes provisions for religious and customary courts in Art. 78(5), thus:

> Pursuant to sub-Article 5 of Article 34 the House of Peoples' Representatives and State Councils can establish or give official recognition to religious and customary courts. Religious and customary courts that had state recognition and functioned prior to the adoption of the Constitution shall be organized on the basis of recognition accorded to them by this Constitution.

Art. 34 of the Constitution, which is part of the Bill of Rights of the Constitution, deals with 'marital, personal and family rights'. Other provisions of this article enshrine constitutional standards that need to be respected regardless of religious or cultural or communal considerations. Thus, it is declared that men and women without any distinction as to race, nation, nationality or religion, have equal rights while entering into, during marriage and at the time of divorce, and that marriage shall be entered into only with the free and full consent of the intending spouses. The Constitution also makes clear that the recognition of marriages concluded under systems of religious or customary law must be based on normative standards to be specified by law. Furthermore, the Constitution stipulates that laws shall be enacted to ensure the protection of the rights and interests of children at the time of divorce.

The Constitution's substantive standards in its other provisions are likewise noteworthy. Art. 35 enshrines the rights of women, underscoring their complete equality with men in the enjoyment of constitutional rights and their right to protection by the state against harmful customs. The Constitution explicitly states that 'laws, customs and practices that oppress or cause bodily or mental harm to women are prohibited' (Art. 35 [4]). In its declaration of the cultural objectives of the country (Art. 91), the Constitution also states:

> The Government shall have the duty to support, on the basis of equality, the growth and enrichment of cultures and traditions that are *compatible with fundamental rights, human dignity, democratic norms and ideals, and the provisions of the Constitution* (emphasis added).

Added to these is the Constitution's supremacy clause, which emphatically states that 'any law, customary practice … which contravenes [the] Constitution shall be of no effect'.

Therefore, the statement in Art. 34(5) of the Constitution, cited above, needs to be viewed within the context of the broad normative position taken in the Constitution. The Constitution gives primacy to individual rights even in the face of possible challenges to such rights from religious, cultural or communitarian positions. It has taken the position that the human rights standards enshrined in it shall apply uniformly to men and women that come under the Constitution's jurisdiction, regardless of their religious and cultural background. But at the same time, the Constitution has also chosen not to force its rights' standards on those who may want to settle disputes arising in the areas of family and personal matters in accordance with the rules ordained by religion or custom. By allowing an exception to the uniform standards it espouses with regard to fundamental rights and freedoms, the Constitution accommodates the wishes of those individuals who, while being aware of their right to have personal and family matters regulated by the country's civil law, consent to having their disputes in these areas adjudicated on the basis of religious or customary law. Therefore, the Constitution as such does not subject individuals to the operation of religious and customary laws but rather gives individuals themselves the right to choose.

The Constitution stated in Art.34(5) that particulars regarding the adjudication of disputes by customary and religious laws would be determined by a law to be enacted on the matter. In pursuance of that, Proclamation No. 188/1999 (*Federal Courts of Sharia Consolidation Proclamation*) was enacted by the House of Peoples' Representatives and deals comprehensively with the structures and hierarchies of the Federal Sharia Court, the jurisdiction of each hierarchy, the applicable substantive and procedural laws, the appointment of judges and the governance system of the Court. However, to date, no law has been enacted regarding customary laws and courts. Indeed, regulating the particulars of customary courts and laws in Ethiopia is not an easy task because of the sheer number of cultural communities in the country, each with their own customary norms. It is hoped that the suggestions made later in this chapter indicate some ways of surmounting this difficulty.

The constitutions of the Ethiopian regional states have the same dispensations as the Federal Constitution regarding the customary and religious laws, courts and other normative standards discussed in the preceding paragraphs. As is the case at the federal level, although most regional states have enacted legislation on the Sharia courts, none has enacted laws regarding customary laws and courts.

Now that we have seen the place of customary (and religious) family and personal laws and courts in the Ethiopian constitutional order, the next question is whether the customary justice system has any de jure place with regard to other civil matters and in criminal matters. The answer to this question is not readily available in the constitutional texts. And the issue has been further complicated by the discrepancy between what seems to be the position of the constitutions (both federal and regional) and the provisions of some sub-constitutional laws enacted by the regional states' legislative councils.

To begin with, the Federal Constitution – to which all regional constitutions conform – does not make any further reference to customary laws and courts beyond its reference to them in relation to family and personal matters in Arts. 34(5) and 78(5). The Federal Constitution empowers the federal legislature, the House of Peoples' Representatives (HoPR), to make major laws such as penal law – although the state may enact penal laws on matters that are not specifically covered by the federal penal legislation – commercial law and labour law. The HoPR is also empowered to make laws on the utilization of land and other natural resources, interstate commerce and foreign trade, patents and copyrights, and to enact civil laws that the House of the Federation deems necessary for establishing and sustaining the economic unity of the federation (if not decided as such by the House of the Federation, civil matters remain part of the states' competences).

The laws that fall under the law-making competence of the federal legislature are applied nationally: they apply throughout the territory and to all persons that happen to be within the territorial jurisdiction of Ethiopia. This by implication means that, except for the customary family and personal laws (which have been clearly given formal space by the Constitution), all other matters – civil and criminal – fall within the remit of formal laws and are governed by them. Thus, because of the silence of the Federal Constitution – and, as they currently stand, of all regional state constitutions – regarding the place of customary law in areas other than family and personal matters, it would be plausible to conclude that customary law is not given any formal (de jure) recognition to deal with matters falling outside family and personal laws.

While the above-presented reading of the federal and regional states' constitutions is correct, I hasten to add three important points. First, many studies have shown that, in reality, the customary justice systems of Ethiopia's ethno-linguistic groups have always exercised jurisdiction over all kinds of disputes involving family, personal, civil and criminal matters without any jurisdictional limitations based on the matters in dispute (see for example Gebre *et al.* 2012, Pankhurst and Getachew 2008, Melaku 2018). Thus, although the formal constitutional structure ignores the vitality of customary justice systems, the reality has always been that most disputes – from the simplest to the most complex, such as homicide cases (see Donovan and Getachew 2003, Pankhurst and Getachew 2008) – especially outside urban locations, get resolved through customary systems. This makes it plain that the formal constitutional position does not reflect reality.

The second point regards a development that emerged after the 1995 Federal Constitution came into force and that is a reason for optimism about the gradually widening space for customary justice systems. As earlier noted, the Federal Constitution seems to be in favour of a uniform application of the formal legal system with regard to all matters other than family and personal matters. This is also the position of regional state constitutions. However, of late, there seems to have been a policy shift on the part of the federal government in the direction of being more accommodative towards customary justice systems in the area of criminal matters. In 2011, the federal government of Ethiopia endorsed a 'Criminal Justice Policy'. The Policy declared the government's resolve to recognize the customary justice system as an integral part of the country's criminal justice system. The two relevant paragraphs of the Policy read as follows:

> Even if the crime committed is a serious crime, if the Attorney General (AG) is of the opinion that the settlement of the dispute by customary means brings about the restoration of lasting harmony and peace among the victim and the wrongdoer than it would be the case if the case was to be resolved by the formal justice avenue, then the AG may in consideration of public interest decide not to prosecute such a crime. In cases of crimes that are punishable with simple imprisonment or upon complaint, the investigation or prosecution can be interrupted if the disputing parties have settled their differences through reconciliation and upon the initiation or request of the parties (FDRE Criminal Justice Policy 2011:14–15).

The Policy underscores that any decision by the Attorney General not to prosecute crimes shall be based on public interest considerations. It further states that what constitutes public interest shall be stipulated in the criminal procedure law and directives to be issued by the Attorney General. The Policy does not specify how the formal and customary justice systems should communicate and interact in the event that the Attorney General decides to leave a case to the customary justice system. Thus, although the Policy suggests the government has shifted its policy towards embracing customary justice systems, more concrete steps need to be taken to work out the relationship between the two systems. The most effective way to do this would obviously be through legislative reform, which could be effected at the sub-constitutional level without necessarily involving an amendment to the Federal Constitution.

The third point is that, through their sub-constitutional legislation, the regional states have already entrusted customary justice institutions with certain jurisdictions in areas other than family and personal matters. This, again, arguably does not accord with what seems to be the shared position of the federal and regional states' constitutions. But, in my view, these legal developments show the policy shift towards opening up space for customary justice systems, which was not the case in the early 1990s when the constitutional norms were being negotiated.

The customary justice system in states' sub-constitutional laws

As earlier noted, laws passed by regional states, notably in relation to rural land administration and utilization and social courts, have bestowed different levels of jurisdiction on customary institutions. A few examples are presented here.

The lowest judicial structures found in the *kebeles*, the lowest administrative units, are the social courts. Some regional states have established and defined the jurisdiction of the social courts, empowering them to settle disputes based on customary law. For example, the Amhara Social Courts Proc. No. 246/2017 stipulates that one of its objectives is to enable the settlement of disputes amicably through the *shimgilinna*[8] process. The proclamation also states that social courts shall undertake their activities based on the local custom, tradition and practices, and that the judges of social courts shall be directed solely by formal (state enacted) law or local tradition and custom. Similarly, the Social Courts Proclamation No. 127/2007 of Oromia Region states that judges in social courts can settle disputes based on the regular law or through customary means.

Rural land use and administration laws provide another set of laws through which regional governments allow customary institutions to settle disputes. According to the Oromia Rural Land Use and Administration Proclamation No. 130/2007, anyone who has a land-related case should first apply to the *kebele* administration where the land is situated. Then, the disputing parties should select two arbitral elders each, after which they should agree on a chairperson for the elders' panel. The chairperson may also be co-opted by the four elders. If both the parties and the elders can not agree on the presiding elder, the *kebele* administration will appoint one. The law states that the elders' panel is to be given 15 days to submit a written decision on the dispute. Once submitted, the decision of the elders' panel should be registered, and officiated copies given to the disputing parties. Dissatisfied parties can lodge an appeal – attaching the copy of the elders' decision –with the *woreda* (district) court with local jurisdiction, and they also have the right to appeal to the high court with local jurisdiction. The Afar Regional State's Rural Land Use and Administration Proclamation No. 49/2009 takes a similar approach to that of Oromia, except that it does not require the decision of the arbitral elders to be submitted in writing. Likewise, the Amhara Rural Land Use and Administration Proclamation No. 252/2017 provides that if disputing parties fail to settle their disputes amicably, they can entrust their case to elders of their choosing. If that fails, the case can be taken to the *woreda* court, with a right to appeal to the high court. The Rural Land Use and Administration Proclamation No. 110/2007 of SNNPR sets forth an almost identical procedural approach to the settlement of land-related disputes. The above examples of regional land-use and

8 Reconciliation through local elders.

administration laws regarding the use of social courts give a clear indication that formal government institutions at the regional level have determined to extend the jurisdiction of customary justice institutions beyond what seems to be allowed by their constitutions. Of course, this still represents only a fraction of the variety of disputes that customary institutions settle in reality.

Challenges faced by customary justice systems

As noted earlier, although the formal legal system at the regional state level does carve out more space for customary justice systems beyond family and personal matters, there is still a huge gap between what these institutions do in reality and the recognition accorded to them. This situation has created many challenges for the customary justice institutions and for people who happen to be disputants before them, especially those who benefit from the decisions that are handed down by these institutions (see Desalegn and Melaku, this volume).

In addition, customary justice systems continue to face challenges even in the areas of family and personal matters. The main reason being that the legislation that was supposed to formally establish customary courts and delineate their jurisdiction, composition and the substantive and procedural laws they may apply, as well as their relationship with the formal laws and institutions, has yet to be enacted. This has made their legal standing very precarious. It has exposed them, for example, to abuse and exploitation by disputants who strategically engage in forum shopping, i.e. those who move back and forth between the customary and formal courts (see Desalegn, this volume).

Disputants in a case also live through a state of uncertainty, as one side may have addressed their complaint to the formal justice system while the other approached the customary justice institutions. This results in the matter ping ponging between the courts and the customary institutions. Since the formal courts do not consider customary legal systems as a legitimate avenue for dispute settlement, they do not take into account any processes that might have begun before the case was brought to them. So cases can start afresh with the formal courts after having been 'settled' through customary justice avenues. This raises the possibility that wrongdoers might be subjected to punishment twice for the same wrongdoing. In the case of homicide or grave bodily injury, a wrongdoer tried by the formal criminal justice system could still be subjected to the customary justice process of compensation payments, and vice versa (see Aberra, this volume). These are just some examples showing the challenges brought by the current imperfect recognition of customary justice system as part of the country's justice system. The need to workout the most acceptable and productive way of creating an interface between customary and formal justice systems is clear, and the next section explores ways in which the two systems could be productively integrated.

Options for an interlink between formal and customary justice systems

The problem of integrating formal and customary justice systems is shared by many countries in Africa, Latin America and Asia that were at the receiving end of legal transplantation, primarily from the legal systems of the colonial powers of the West. As noted at the beginning of this chapter, although Ethiopia does not share this colonial history, it has the same problem as a result of its voluntary borrowing of legal norms from the West.

Upon independence, many post-colonial states – and others like Australia and the USA – that inherited plural legal systems adopted various approaches to accommodating the non-formal legal system of their native communities. In the USA, for example, Indian Americans are generally subject to tribal law (not state or federal law) when the offender and victims are both Indians (18 USC § 1152). However, under the Indian Major Crimes Act, violent crimes are exempted from this exclusive grant of jurisdiction (18 USC §1153). In Papua New Guinea, under the Native Customs (Recognition) Act 1963, custom is recognized as a cultural fact (not law) in the formal court's determination of the guilt of a native offender (Dinnen 1988:25–26). Yet, at the same time, it should be noted that some people in the country, including judges, argue that customary compensation should be considered as a legitimate form of punishment and that courts should be seen 'as a consensual forum in which people actively participate in restoring harmony in communities disturbed by law breaking' (Dinnen 1988:9–10).

The state of various customary systems in Ethiopia is fundamentally different from those in Africa's postcolonial countries. There, customary systems were subject to various kinds of interference from the colonial administrators and their legal institutions (Pimentel 2010, Snyder 1981, Ige 2015). Various attempts were made to codify the local law, thereby creating a state version of customary law, different to the living or unofficial version of customary law. In Ethiopia, however, the customary justice system never lost its original character because the formal state remained aloof from the functioning of the customary systems and kept them at a distance from state institutions. For example, at no point in Ethiopia's history have customary court personnel been appointed by the government. As a result of this autonomy, the customary justice system has maintained its integrity and natural character.

The natural state of the customary law and institutions of Ethiopia's various communities needs to be maintained in any attempt to link customary and formal justice systems in the future. It is advisable for any government policy or legal intervention to allow customary institutions to be the sole interpreters and enforcers of customary law, but procedures need to be put in place to ensure that the workings of the customary justice system are consistent with constitutional human rights standards. This approach, as Pimentel (2010:4) observes, enables customary justice systems to maintain their vitality and adaptability. It also rejects the creation of customary divisions within formal courts, such as were in place in Eritrea when it was federated with Ethiopia (Geraghty 1970:450), in which it is the formal court/judge who interprets and applies the customary law, and not the customary court.

Following David Pimentel (2010:15), I suggest that the linkages between formal and customary justice systems need to be guided by the following considerations: (1) the need to recognise and respect traditional cultures and customs; (2) the need to ensure that customary law and institutions do not violate the fundamental rights and freedoms enshrined in the Ethiopian Constitution, and those protected by the international human rights standards applicable to Ethiopia; and (3) the need to uphold the rule of law. These considerations will no doubt require some trade-offs, particularly as some cultures do not treat women as equal to men or have practices that violate fundamental rights of children (see Epple, chapter 14, this volume). But, this needs careful handling and any trade-offs should not strike at the heart of the fundamental rights of women and children. One of the most effective ways through which the primacy of the fundamental rights of women and vulnerable groups such as children and minorities can be protected is – as noted below – by empowering the reviewers of constitutions to uphold the constitutional human rights standards against any contrary rules in the communities' customary justice systems.

The above suggestion calls for the maintenance of the separation between the customary and formal justice systems (what Pimentel 2010:23 calls 'the equal dignity approach'), but at the same time for the creation of a review mechanism to ensure that the former upholds constitutionally protected rights and freedoms. There is no rational reason why the formal justice system should crush the customary systems and become the sole justice dispenser, so long as the customary systems conform to the minimum standards of human rights protection (Donovan and Getachew 2003:539). What the formal state machinery must be concerned with is ensuring that those subject to its jurisdiction benefit from the minimum human and group rights protections guaranteed by the Constitution. With a mechanism to achieve this in place, customary justice systems should generally be left alone to evolve, adapt and change through their own internal dynamics, as they have always done.

As stated above, the creation of a productive interlink between formal and informal justice systems demands that customary justice systems should not be subordinated to the formal system through appeal or other such means. The question arises, thus, of how it is possible to check whether customary courts and institutions are observing the minimum human rights guarantees outlined in the Constitution if their decisions are not appealable to the formal courts. There are ways to do this. First and foremost, it is necessary to believe in the capacity of customary justice systems to change and adapt to keep abreast of the world in which they function and with which they interact (Pimentel 2010:25, Donovan and Getachew 2003:550). Then, the constitutional review system, whereby the decisions of customary courts are reviewed for violations of constitutionally guaranteed rights and international human rights standards, can be used. My suggestion is that the decisions of customary courts should not be subjected to the appellate review of federal or regional state courts but rather should be subjected directly to the constitutional review process. The constitutional reviewer – in Ethiopia's case, the House of the Federation with the technical recommendation from the Council of Constitutional Inquiry (Ethiopian Constitution: Arts. 62(1):83–84) – could then fashion its decision in a manner that respects the autonomy of the customary system involved and allows its adherents to engage in what Abdullahi An-Na'im (1992:27) calls 'internal cultural discourse' to readjust its position vis-à-vis the constitutional standards.

I believe that, as part of the above suggestion, it is also possible to design a cooperative system in which jurisdiction over serious crimes that endanger national security and social harmony and that jeopardize constitutionally protected rights, such as the right to life, may be either ceded to the formal justice system or handled by the two legal systems jointly, and in a manner that allows the traditional justice system to fully embrace any joint activity. This limited intrusion into the territory of customary institutions is justifiable given the state's constitutional responsibilities to maintain a minimum protection of rights (Donovan and Getachew 2003:538).

The realization of the above suggestions would inevitably call for new laws at both federal and state levels detailing the interlinkage, cooperation and autonomy of the two legal systems. The requirement to be consistent with the minimum human rights standards of the Constitution would, of course, also need to be clearly spelled out in the law.

The question of how to determine the jurisdiction of the formal and customary justice systems is another major issue that needs to be settled in law. The suggestion that the customary justice systems should be kept separate from the formal system normally creates a situation whereby both the formal and customary courts can have concurrent jurisdiction over a given case. For example, in a civil dispute involving a hire-purchase contract, both the formal court with local jurisdiction in the area and the customary court of the community there have jurisdiction over the case. How then should a disagreement between the plaintiff and the defendant on the legal forum to be used be resolved? Is it plausible to state in the law that the forum where the case was filed first has the jurisdiction? Or should the law provide that the court, whether formal or customary, where the case was filed should decide whether it should decide the case or transfer it to the other court? These are very difficult questions that the law needs to somehow settle. One way to deal with this – at least for most civil law disputes – is to extend the consent requirement in article 34(5) of the Constitution, whereby both parties are required to formally give their consent to their case being lodged with a customary court. The law could also make provision for the transfer of cases from the formal court to the customary courts when both parties demand it. It might also be possible to explore whether there are circumstances under which customary institutions would voluntarily relinquish jurisdiction over certain individuals that do not abide by the customs of the community (see Aberra, this volume).

Summary and conclusion

This chapter has shown the state and development of customary justice systems in Ethiopia, and explored the relationship between the formal (state) law and legal institutions and the informal (customary) ones. As explained, from the late 1940s the Ethiopian government directed its attention to putting in place legal institutions following the model of Western legal systems. This attempt was accompanied by a policy of uprooting customary justice systems and replacing them with codified law. With the coming into force of the 1995 Constitution, the policy of hostility to customary law and institutions was replaced by an accommodative policy that explicitly recognizes customary family and personal laws and courts. However, as we have seen, the space given by the Constitution to the various customary justice systems in Ethiopia does not match the practical vitality of these systems, which encompass all areas of law. Therefore, recognition of customary justice systems should be widened to acknowledge the fact that they work on cases from all areas of dispute, including criminal cases. In order to do so successfully and sustainably, the government should formalize this recognition through a well-crafted law to be made by the federal, and regional, legislatures. It is hoped, the suggestions made in this chapter will assist policy-makers in accomplishing that task.

References

AN-NA'IM, Abdullahi Ahmed, 1992 "Toward a cross-cultural approach to defining international standards of human rights: The meaning of cruel, inhuman, or degrading treatment or punishment", in: Abdullahi Ahmed An-Na'im (ed.) *Human rights in cross-cultural perspectives: A quest for consensus*. Philadelphia: University of Pennsylvania Press

BILILIGN, Mandefro, 1969 "Agricultural communities and the Civil Code", *Journal of Ethiopian Law* 6 (1):145–199

DAVID, René, 1962/63 "A civil code for Ethiopia: Considerations on the codification of the civil law in African countries", *Tulane Law Review* 37:187–204

DINNEN, Sinclair, 1988 "Sentencing, custom and the rule of law in Papua New Guinea", *Journal of Legal Pluralism and Unofficial Law* 27:19-54

DONOVAN, Dolores A. and GETACHEW Assefa, 2003 "Homicide in Ethiopia: Human rights, federalism, and legal pluralism", *American Journal of Comparative Law* 51 (3):505–552

FEDERAL DEMOCRATIC REPUBLIC OF ETHIOPIA (FDRE), 1996 *Proclamation No. 25/1996, Federal Courts Proclamation 2nd Year No.13*. FDRE: Federal Negarit Gazeta

1995 *Constitution of the Federal Democratic Republic of Ethiopia*. Addis Ababa: FDRE

GEBRE, Yntiso, FEKADE Azeze, and ASSEFA Fiseha (eds.), 2012 *Customary dispute resolution in Ethiopia*. Addis Ababa: The Ethiopian Arbitration and Conciliation Center

GERAGHTY, Thomas, 1970 "People, practice, attitudes and problems in the lower courts of Ethiopia", *Journal of Ethiopian Law* 6 (2):426–512

HAILE SELASSIE I, 1964 "Preface", *Journal of Ethiopian Law* 1 (1):v–vi

IGE, Rhoda Asikia, 2015 "Legal pluralism in Africa: Challenges, conflicts and adaptation in a global village", *Journal of Law, Policy and Globalization* 34:59–66

KAPLAN, Steven, 1992 *The Beta Israel (Falasha) in Ethiopia from earliest times to the twentieth Century*. New York and London: New York University Press

MAHTEME-SELASSIE, Woldemeskel, 1970 *Zikre Neger*, 2nd edition (in Amharic). Addis Ababa: n.p.

MELAKU Abera, 2018 *Legal pluralism among the Tulama Oromo of Ethiopia: Preference and interplays between customary and formal laws*. Addis Ababa: Addis Ababa University (PhD Thesis)

PANKHURST, Alula and GETACHEW Assefa (eds.), 2008 *Grass-roots justice in Ethiopia: The contribution of customary dispute resolution*. Addis Ababa: United Printers

PAULOS, Tzadua Abba (transl.), 2009 *The Fetha Negast: The law of the kings*. Durham, North Carolina: Carolina Academic Press

PIMENTEL, David, 2010 *Legal pluralism in post-colonial Africa: Linking statutory and customary adjudication in Mozambique* (accessible online http://works.bepress.com/david_pimentel/7/)

SAND, Peter, 1971 "Current trends in African legal geography: The interfusion of legal systems", *African Legal Studies* 5:1–24

SINGER, Norman, 1970 "Modernization of law in Ethiopia: A study in process and personal values", *Harvard International Law Journal* 11:73–125

1971 "Islamic Law and the development of the Ethiopian legal system", *Howard Law Review* 17:130–168

SNYDER, Francis, 1981 "Colonialism and legal form: The creation of 'customary law' in Senegal", *Journal of Legal Pluralism and Unofficial Law* 13 (19):49–90

VANDERLINDEN, Jacques, 1966/67 "Civil law and common law influences on the developing law of Ethiopia" *Buffalo Law Review* 16:250–266

Legislations and policies

Judicial Administration Proclamation, 1942
Judicial Administration Proclamation, 1962
Local Judges Proclamation, 1947
Charter of the Transitional Government of Ethiopia, 1991
Penal Code of Ethiopia, 1957
The Civil Code of Ethiopia, 1960
Criminal Procedure Code of Ethiopia, 1961
Federal Sharia Courts Proclamation, 1999
Criminal Code of Ethiopia, 2004
The Criminal Justice Policy of Ethiopia, 2011
Afar Regional State's Rural Land Use and Administration Proclamation, 2009
Amhara Social Courts Proclamation, 2017
Amhara Rural Land Use and Administration Proclamation, 2017
Oromia Social Courts Proclamation, 2007
Oromia Rural Land Use and Administration Proclamation, 2007
SNNPR Rural Land Use and Administration Proclamation, 2007
Crimes and Criminal Procedure, United States Code (18 USC § 1152)

3. The UN Declaration on the Rights of Indigenous Peoples and African Societies

Karl-Heinz Kohl

Introduction

Alongside the institutions of local, national and international law, the United Nations also plays an important role in currently on-going legal disputes in Ethiopia, as well as in other African nations, even though it does not want to interfere directly in the internal affairs of these states. Since its direct interventions are strictly limited to peace-building activities and involve long and complicated bureaucratic procedures, one of the UN's preferred means of contributing to such and other disputes are through the declarations adopted by its General Assembly. These declarations have the character of recommendations and do not contain any legally binding obligations. In the terminology of the UN, they are only 'documents of intent'.[1] Nevertheless, they try to formulate some principles according to which legal decisions should be taken. This is the case with the UN 'Declaration on the Rights of Indigenous Peoples'. As I will show, its primary intent was to grant more rights to the marginalized and long-disenfranchised indigenous peoples of the former European colonies in North and South America, Australia and New Zealand. But the extent to which its principles can also be applied to African societies remains a controversial point of discussion. On the one hand, the Declaration contains a moral appeal to Africa's political leaders to help their many small-scale local communities to preserve their language and cultural traditions and to protect them from land robbery at the hands of the big international agricultural corporations. On the other hand, there is also the wish of African governments to unify all societies within a given country under one national law.

1 http://www.unesco.org/new/en/social-and-human-sciences/themes/international-migration/glossary/declaration/ (last accessed 28 February 2019)

The UN Declaration on the Rights of Indigenous Peoples

After debating for more than 25 years, the General Assembly of the United Nations adopted the 'Declaration on the Rights of Indigenous Peoples' in autumn 2007. The Declaration grants a special status to indigenous peoples inside the state to which they belong, emphasizing their right to speak their own language, to maintain their social and cultural institutions, to preserve their cultural heritage and above all to control and use their traditionally owned land. Today, more than ten years later, the Declaration is regarded as one of the cornerstones of the international Human Rights Movement.

The Declaration's beginnings go back to the late 1960s and early 1970s, when Native Americans in the United States, First Nations in Canada, Australian Aborigines and New Zealand Maoris joined the worldwide civil rights movement and protested against their on-going oppression and discrimination. Other autochthonous groups, especially in Latin America, followed them. But it was still a long time before the United Nations decided to support their demands. In 1985, the UN set up a Working Group on the Rights of Indigenous Populations. In 1993 this Working Group prepared the first draft of the Declaration. But it had to be revisited more than ten times in the following years because a number of UN member states expressed concern about some of its key issues such as self-determination and exclusive land use. These reservations were also shared by a group of African states, which then prompted a formal decision by the African Union in December 2006 that almost blocked the final adoption of the Declaration.[2] After new negotiations, on 13 September 2007, 143 members of the UN General Assembly voted for the Declaration;[3] 14, including Nigeria and Kenya, abstained; and 4, namely Australia, Canada, New Zealand and the United States, voted against it. But a very high number of UN members, at total of 34, did not participate in the vote at all; of these, 15 were African states, including Ethiopia.

Since then, Australia, Canada and New Zealand have revised their decision and have transposed some of the Declaration's principles into national law. In the US, the situation seems to be more complicated. On December 2010, President Barack Obama declared that the United States would 'lend its support' to the Declaration. Yet, as the recent events in the Lakota Standing Rock Reservation have shown, President Trump is unwilling to fulfil his predecessor's promise. On the African conti-

2 According to Pelican and Maruyama (2015:51) the adoption of the Declaration 'has been particularly problematic for southern African states, such as Botswana and Namibia, which excluded the provision for any differential treatment of their citizens based on race or ethnicity to distance themselves from apartheid politics.'

3 See the United Nations Permanent Forum of Indigenous Issues 2006: *Declaration on the rights of indigenous peoples* (accessible online at http://www.un.org/esa/socdev/unpfii/documents/FAQsindigenousdeclaration.pdf).

nent too, many governments remain reluctant to accept the Declaration's principles as a basis of policy. What are the reasons for the African States' enduring scepticism?

We may find an answer to this question in the African Union's aforementioned decision from December 2006. Besides noting the many political problems that self-determination and the recognition of indigenous land-ownership may cause for national and territorial integrity, the decision named explicitly 'the lack of a clear definition of indigenous peoples', although it affirms at the same time, 'that the vast majority of the peoples of Africa are indigenous to the African Continent'. This is, without doubt, a contradictory statement. If there is 'no clear definition of indigenous peoples', one cannot contend that almost all African peoples are 'indigenous'. Where does this contradiction stem from?

Actually, how to define indigeneity and indigenous peoples had been one of the biggest problems in the period when the Declaration was being prepared. From an etymological point of view, 'indigenous' means nothing more than having been born in the land or territory where one lives, in contrast to all the people who came later, be they migrants or conquerors. Historically, however, the English word 'indigenous' and other derivations from the Latin word '*indigena*', such as 'indigène' in French or '*indigéna*' in Spanish were derogatory. European colonizers and settlers applied them to the subdued inhabitants of their colonies and associated them with backwardness and primitiveness. Yet, during its long struggle for recognition, which began half a century ago, the international indigenous movement has been very successful in purifying the word 'indigeneity' of these old racist stereotypes. What once was an insult has now become a title of honour. Today, more than 5,000 ethnic groups all over the world share the term 'indigenous' as a common denominator.

Yet, there is such a great diversity between these groups that one may ask oneself what main features the Kwakwaka'wakw of the American Northwest Coast, who live mainly from fishing, share with the Aranda hunters and gatherers of the Australian Desert, the crop-growing Yanomami of the Amazonian rain forest, the Pokot pastoralists of Kenya or the Sami reindeer herders of Finland? This was exactly the problem that the UN's suborganizations were confronted with when they looked for a clear and distinct definition of indigeneity. It proved to be very difficult, indeed, almost impossible. Instead of defining in legal terms what indigenous peoples are, they could only give a description of what most of them have in common. One of the most cited of these descriptions or working definitions was drafted by José Martinez Cobo, the former Special Rapporteur on the Problem of Discrimination against Indigenous Populations in 1986. It reads as follows:

> Indigenous communities, peoples and nations are those, which, having a historical continuity with pre-invasion and pre-colonial societies considers themselves distinct from other sectors of the societies now prevailing in those territories or part of them. They form at present non-dominant sectors of society and are determined to preserve, develop and transmit to future generations their ancestral territories, and their ethnic identity, as the basis of their continued existence as peoples, in accordance with their own cultural patterns, social institutions and legal systems.[4]

Since then, a number of other characteristic features, such as their strong maintenance of their cultural traditions, language and belief systems have complemented José Martinez Cobo's description and found their way into the final version of the Declaration adopted in 2007. The most important of these new features concerns the indigenous peoples' 'distinctive spiritual relationship with their traditionally owned or otherwise occupied and used lands, territories, waters and coastal seas', as expressed in Article 25 of the UN Declaration. This 'distinctive spiritual relationship' is so important because it also legitimizes those peoples' right 'to own, use, develop and control the lands, territories and resources that they possess by reason of traditional ownership'. Actually, this passage contains political dynamite, because it grants to indigenous peoples not only absolute usage rights of the territories they live in, but could also be used as a legal basis to claim back from the majority population the land once stolen from their ancestors. This was, without any doubt, one of the main concerns and reasons why four former British colonies voted against the UN Declaration in 2007.

Indigenousness (or indigenity) and African society

Against this background, we can understand better the reluctance of so many African states to adopt the UN Declaration, as well as the contradictions in the text of the African Union's decision of 2006 mentioned above. On the one side, the African Union states that 'the vast majority of the peoples of Africa are indigenous to the African Continent' because they were born there and became victims of European colonization. On the other side, however, all of them have also regained their freedom to live according to their pre-invasion and pre-colonial tradition

4 UNCHR (Sub-Commission), 'Report of the Special Rapporteur on the Problem of Discrimination against Indigenous Populations' (1986) UN Doc E/CN.4/Sub.2/1986/7/Add.1–4, quoted by Lidetu 2016:6. Cobo is also the author of 1986's important three-volume *Study on the problem of discrimination against indigenous peoples*, 'where he promotes the use of the word ethnicity and group rather than race' and 'initiated a shift in focus away from mainly biological definitions of indigenous peoples' (Lidetu 2016:25).

after the fight for independence and the end of the European rule. The corollary of this is: if all African peoples are indigenous, all of them also stand in a special spiritual relationship to their homeland and it is *not* necessary to protect and privilege some of them.

The inherent logic of this argumentation shows where that the problem lies in the difficulty of applying the UN Declaration's categories of 'indigenous', 'indigeneity' and 'indigenous peoples' to African societies. These difficulties stem from the fact that these categories grew out of the historical experiences of the aboriginal inhabitants of the former British colonies in North America, Australia and New Zealand, as well as the Spanish and Portuguese conquests in Latin America. Not only some small parts but all of the land of these vast continents and islands belonged to them before the arrival of European conquerors and settlers. It is largely forgotten that the biggest genocide in history of humankind happened after Columbus's so-called discovery of the New World. According to recent estimations, between 7 and 20 million native people lived in the territory of what is now the United States of America before the arrival of the Europeans. At the end of the nineteenth century their number had decreased to 500,000, while the total population of the US had grown to 62 million. Today less than 1 per cent of the US population identify themselves as Native Americans (United States Census Bureau 2011). In Australia, the aboriginal population rate is 2.7 per cent, and in Canada 4.3 per cent. This means that in those countries, in which the indigenous movement came into being in the early 1970s, indigenous peoples had been reduced to very small and unimportant minorities, living at the margins of a white majority society, strongly discriminated against and denied full citizenship. Indeed, in Australia, Aborigines remained under state guardianship until 1976. Their rights to the small territories and reservations in which they had lived for generations were recognized by the national governments only after decades of struggle.

Conclusion

At its core, talking of indigeneity and indigenous peoples is a Eurocentric construction. Both categories are meaningful in states that grew out of colonial settler societies in which the progeny of the foreign invaders represent the vast majority, while the descendants of the aboriginal landowners have become small and insignificant minorities. But it is hard to transfer this dichotomous model to most African states, because – with some exceptions – there was no such overwhelming dominant or racially different sector of society that succeeded in the course of history in subduing all other ethnic and linguistic units under its rule. And there is still another, even more important, difference. In the U.S., Australia, Canada and New Zealand, the aboriginal populations' traditional forms of life and even their languages were largely destroyed under the pressure of the white majority. Among most African peoples identifying themselves as indigenous, such a radical rupture never took place.

In the final analysis, however, it is not only a question of terminology whether you call these local communities indigenous peoples or not. Although indigenous political activists in the former colonies have appropriated the term, it has gained international political recognition and became an effective weapon in the worldwide fight against oppression and ruthless exploitation. The African local communities with their own languages and traditional ways of life share their fate with marginalized indigenous populations in Asia, South America and other parts of the world. In Africa, their situation seems to be even harder because national politicians and urban elites regard them as an obstacle to development and modernization. Instead of recognizing their traditional land rights, they ban them from their ancestors' lands and support the activities of international agricultural agencies exploiting it for commercial purposes. This happened to the pastoralist and semi-sedentary societies in Southern Ethiopia, where Government officials tried to force them to give up their traditional way of life in order to transform them into agriculturalists and wage labourers, as we can see in Human Right Watch's staggering report on 'Abuses against the Indigenous Peoples of Ethiopia's Lower Omo Valley' (2012). As already stated in 2006 by the African Commission on Human and Peoples' Rights already, the cultures of African indigenous peoples are also

> under threat, in some cases to the point of extinction. A key characteristic for most of them is that the survival of their particular way of life depends on access and rights to their traditional lands and the natural resources thereon. They suffer from discrimination as they are regarded as less developed and less advanced than other more dominant sectors of society. They often live in inaccessible regions, often geographically isolated, and suffer from various forms of marginalization, both politically and socially (African Commission on Human and Peoples' Rights (ACHPR 2006:11).

While indigenous peoples in Australia, Canada, New Zealand and the US remind the white majority society of their forefathers' sins, and measures taken to protect their customs and reinstall their rights can be regarded as making amends for the crimes done to them, Africa's indigenous peoples have another, more important, significance and deserve protection even more, because they stand in a continuous relation to the contemporary African societies whose great cultural and social heritage they represent. Leading African politicians of the independent movement in the 1960s and 1970s, such as Jomo Kenyatta or Léopold Sedar Senghor, and leading intellectuals, such as Chinua Achebe or Amadou Hampâté Bâ, were convinced that the true African values and norms, with their complete governance and restorative dispute settlement institutions, could still be found in the villages. But this was almost two generations ago. Since then, things really have fallen apart. The urbanization process is speeding up considerably, and modern techniques are infiltrating agriculture in some rural areas. Nevertheless, there are still many semi-autonomous, small-scale societies, subsistence farmers, pastoralists, hunters and gatherers who have shown an astonishing resilience to the seductive power of modernity and have succeeded in maintaining central parts of their traditions. And obviously, they did it by their free will, because they are so far out of our world that they do not know the possible alternatives to their way of life. I freely confess that my view may be a deeply romantic one. But who knows: if the endeavours to solve the continent's economic problems by a globally oriented neo-liberal policy should fail, a new African Renaissance may come, comparable to what happened fifty years ago. And then, everybody will be glad that not all of these small-scale societies have been sacrificed on the altar of modernity.

References

African Commission on Human and Peoples' Rights (ACHPR), 2006 *Indigenous peoples in Africa: The forgotten peoples? The African Commission's work on indigenous peoples in Africa*. Banjul, The Gambia: ACHOR and Copenhagen: International Work Group for Indigenous Peoples Affairs

COBO, José R. Martínez, 1985/86 *Study of the problem of discrimination against indigenous populations* (3 Volumes). New York: United Nations

Human Rights Watch, 2012 "What will happen if hunger comes?' Abuses against the indigenous peoples of Ethiopia's Lower Omo Valley", in: *Human Rights Watch* June 2012 (accessible online at https://reliefweb.int/report/ethiopia/'what-will-happen-if-hunger-comes'-abuses-against-indigenous-peoples-ethiopia's, last accessed 22 October 2018)

LIDETU Yimer Ayele, 2016 *Definition and rights of indigenous peoples: The case of Ethiopia*. Addis Ababa: Addis Ababa University (MA thesis)

PELICAN, Michaela and Junko MARUYAMA, 2015 "The indigenous rights movement in Africa: Perspectives from Botswana and Cameroon", in: *African Study Monographs*, 36 (1):49–74

UNITED NATIONS PERMANENT FORUM OF INDIGENOUS ISSUES, 2006 *Declaration on the rights of indigenous peoples* (accessible online at http://www.un.org/esa/socdev/unpfii/documents/FAQsindigenousdeclaration.pdf)

UNITED NATIONS CENSUS BUREAU, 2011 *Overview of race and Hispanic origin: 2010* (accessible online at https://www.census.gov/prod/cen2010/briefs/c2010br-02.pdf, last accessed 6 July 2012)

Websites

http://www.unesco.org/new/en/social-and-human-sciences/themes/international-migration/glossary/declaration/ (last accessed 28 February 2019)

4. Understanding customary laws in the context of legal pluralism

Gebre Yntiso

Introduction

Legal pluralism, which is defined as the co-existence of more than one legal system in a given social field (Pospisil 1971, Griffiths 1986, Moore 1986 in Merry 1988:870), is prevalent in contemporary Ethiopia, as in other parts of Africa. Five normative legal regimes (one state law and four non-state laws) can be identified in the country. The codified state law was introduced from Europe in the 1960s and subsequent laws were issued later. The non-state legal systems include: i) the numerous forms of customary law characterized by both commonalities and differences between and within ethnic groups operating independently; ii) the *Sharia* courts that have been in existence for a long time, have been recognized by three successive governments, and currently operate with jurisdiction over family and personal issues; iii) the certified commercial arbitration forums that provide arbitration and mediation services in commercial, labour, construction, family and other disputes; vi) the spirit mediums believed to operate as mediators between humans and supernatural forces.

The customary laws operate in parallel with the other forms and, despite pressure from the state law, have proved to be resilient and dominant in the entire continent. Hence, it is tempting to investigate the persistence, the characteristics, the effectiveness and the prospects of these popular legal systems. Despite identifiable gaps and drawbacks, customary laws have been recognized as the best option for handling group conflicts and ensuring peaceful coexistence among families and communities.

However, due to certain inadequacies studies on customary laws run short of informing theory and policy. First, concepts borrowed from Western alternative dispute resolution (ADR) literature have been used interchangeably and confusingly. Hence, a lack of conceptual clarity has hindered communication and prevented in-depth understanding of the functional differences between the various legal orders. Second, the absence of efforts to identify and analyse customary laws systematically has constrained our knowledge about which of the core values underlying customary laws are worth appreciating and which key challenges are worth addressing. In other words, the lack of comprehensive knowledge has prevented the development of theoretical frameworks and concrete policy ideas. This paper, therefore, intends to shed light on these two issues by drawing illustrations from a few countries, with a special focus on Ethiopia as a case study.

Prior to colonization in the nineteenth century, customary laws governed all the affairs of the people of Africa. Following the introduction of codified modern legal systems from the West, legal pluralism became the reality in African legal systems. Many customary laws survived colonialism and marginalization by formal justice systems(Kariuki 2015, Mutisi and Sansculotte-Greenidge 2012). These deep-rooted and widely accepted institutions are likely to remain relevant and crucial in addressing intra- and inter-group conflicts on the continent (Mutisi and Sansculotte-Greenidge 2012). The popularity of customary laws may be explained with reference to the qualities that make them preferable to the state law, as will be shown further below.

Many African states have given constitutional recognition to customary laws. For example, in South Africa, Section 166(e) of the Constitution and Section 16(1) of Schedule 6 recognize the judicial powers of traditional leaders. Likewise, Articles 34(5) and 78(5) of the Ethiopian Constitution make reference to customary laws. In Rwanda, where the famous *gacaca* courts handled genocide cases, the integration of *abunzi* mediation into the legal system (Organic Law No. 31/2006) is one of the recent developments that point to the relevance of customary courts in contemporary Africa. According to Cuskelly (2011:6)

> The highest level of recognition of customary law is found in African constitutions, both in terms of the number of countries with relevant provisions and the breadth of aspects of customary law covered. Of 52 African constitutions analysed, 33 referred to customary law in some form.... there is a high level of recognition of traditional and customary institutions, as well as a broad recognition of customary law in the courts and relating to land. At the weakest level of recognition of customary law, a large number of African constitutions have provisions relating to the protection of culture or tradition.

Besides the recognition, in many countries the actual relationship between the state law and the customary laws has been inadequately articulated. The Ethiopian Constitution (Articles 39:2 and 91:1) provides, in broad terms, for the promotion of the cultures of nations, nationalities and peoples of the country. Article 34:5 makes more specific and direct reference to adjudication of disputes relating to personal and family matters in accordance with customary laws, with the consent of the parties to the dispute. Article 78:5 also states that the House of People's Representatives and State Councils can give official recognition to customary courts. Thus far, the particulars of Article 34:5 have not been determined by law and the official recognition stipulated in Article 78:5 has not been given.

The inadequate constitutional provision in Ethiopia led to the existence of different views about the relevance of customary laws in the country: while the proponents of the state law want the customary legal forum to give way to the modern unitary legal forum, the advocates of customary laws argue that the state-centred unitary approach must give way to different alternative paradigms. Many legal experts justify the relevance of non-state law by the fact that it reduces the caseload of formal courts. Ordinary people welcome the existence of legal pluralism because it provides multiple options to justice seekers. And still others (scholars, practitioners, etc.) advocate for a reform of the legal system in order to create a hybridized brand that contains elements of the formal and the informal laws.

Customary dispute and conflict handling mechanisms have received increasing scholarly attention as evidenced by the growing number of studies and publications. The regional level comparative works of Zartman (2000), Ogbaharya (2010), Mutisi and Sansculotte-Greenidge (2012) and Kariuki (2015), among others, deserve mention. Country-specific studies and publications are also numerous. The depth and breadth of studies in Ethiopia have been revealed by the edited volumes on customary conflict handling mechanisms by Alula Pankhurst and Getachew Assefa (2008), Gebre Yintiso *et al.* (2011, 2012) and Elias Stebek and Muradu Abdu (2013). However, as Kane *et al.* (2005:3) rightly argue, research on African customary laws has not been systematic and comprehensive:

> [I]t is important to note that insufficient research has gone into understanding both the dynamics and the operation of customary law tribunals and into assessing the content and status of most customary laws to ensure that they in fact reflect the values and mores of the communities (...). We recommend comprehensive research into the universe of dispute resolution services (...). We recommend that a participatory assessment of the contemporary status and content of customary laws be carried out in order to open up knowledge of customary laws and ensure that the voices of all stakeholders are actually heard as these laws naturally evolve.

It is equally important to acknowledge the weaknesses of customary legal practices, which can be challenged on grounds of gender insensitivity, discrimination against minorities, breach of other human rights, weak procedural fairness in adjudication and punishment, lack of uniformity and lack of records. The practices are sometimes incompatible with national laws and international standards and norms. Some of the most serious weaknesses, such us gender insensitivity, discrimination against minorities and breach of human rights, have to do with established cultural values and practices that perpetuate social inequality. In societies where men are viewed as superior to women and the participation of the latter in customary legal practices remains limited or non-existent, customary laws tend to disregard or violate the rights of women. Similarly, in cultures where minority groups such as artisans or hunters experience social exclusion, customary laws tend to reinforce the existing inequality and discrimination. On the whole, breaches of human rights in the application of customary legal practices emanate from structural factors that warrant change through awareness creation and the legal enforcement of laws protecting the rights of disadvantaged groups. In today's world, where transnationalism, multiculturalism and rapid social transformation are bridging the global – local divide, the incompatibility of customary laws with the changing context in which they operate has become an issue that must be addressed.

This chapter has been written with the firm conviction that its approach will enable researchers to generate knowledge amenable to comparative analysis, scientific generalization and/or policy application.[1] I recognize that a comprehensive study of African customary laws would be extremely difficult and rather unrealistic given their vastness and their diversity. However, systematization of the existing knowledge we have will lead to a consolidation of perspectives on the communalities and differences of the customary laws, to an identification of the essential underlying values worth promoting, and an evaluation of the principles and practices viewed as unfavourable in today's world.

Towards conceptual clarity

As stated in the introduction, the undifferentiated and at times confusing use of certain concepts has hindered our understanding of and communication about the functional differences between the various legal orders. The key terms often used to describe customary laws – dispute, conflict, negotiation, mediation, arbitration, conciliation, dispute settlement, conflict resolution, conflict management, and conflict transformation – come from the 'alternative dispute resolution' (ADR) literature of the West. This section, therefore, attempts to reflect on the meaning of these terms and the appropriateness of their use in the context of customary laws. Before discussing each term, it is important to present briefly the context and the historical background of ADR.

ADR was conceived in the United States by legal practitioners and law professors with the intention of reforming the justice system through the introduction of

1 This paper is based on my own research on customary conflict resolution in various parts of Ethiopia (see Gebre 2012, 2016a, 2016b) and extensive literature review. Earlier versions were published in the Journal of Ethiopian Law (Gebre 2014) and in an edited volume I co-edited with Itaru Ohta and Motoji Matsuda (2017).

non-litigious methods (Nader 1993). The early advocates of ADR in the US turned for inspiration to customary laws, which were viewed as more humane, therapeutic and non-adversarial (Avruch 2003:352). Ugo Mattei and Laura Nader (2008:77) argued that ADR was used as a disempowering tool, 'to suppress people's resistance, by socializing them toward conformity by means of consensus-building mechanisms, by valorising consensus, cooperation, passivity, and docility, and by silencing people who speak out angrily.' In England, the history of voluntary conciliation and arbitration goes back to 1850, where these methods were used to address industrial disputes, with 'the highest hopes of abolishing strikes completely by the most ruthless application of arbitration' (Hicks 1930:26).

ADR as applied in the West is different from the customary laws practised in Africa. For example, the Western institutional settings focus on individuals, while African cultures consider the collective as the unit of social organization (Grande 1999). Accordingly, ADR procedures in the West are closed, while African conflict handling procedures are open to the public, and therefore transparent. Because of the differences in focus, context and procedures, the terminology used in ADR cannot be transferred to customary laws without customization. In the West, there are four common ADR methods: negotiation, mediation, conciliation, and arbitration. During mediation, mediators do not propose a solution, while conciliators can suggest non-binding agreement ideas during conciliation. During arbitration, arbitrators apply the law, start the process by receiving a written consensus from the parties, and have the power to administer a legally enforceable award, even internationally. ADR also differentiates between dispute settlement, conflict resolution, conflict management and conflict transformation. Simply transferring these concepts from ADR to customary laws without explanation leads to confusion and misunderstanding.

Half a century ago two prominent anthropologists – Paul Bohannan and Max Gluckman – espoused a debate on whether universal categories and terminologies should be used to depict the legal systems of different societies. Bohannan (1969:403) advocated for the use of native terms to be accompanied by ethnographic meaning, arguing that the use of universal categories acts as a barrier to understanding and representing the legal systems in different cultures. Gluckman (1969:535), on the other hand, argued in favour of translating native concepts into English, stating that the excessive use of local terms was serving as a barrier to cross-cultural comparison of legal practices. As Kevin Avruch (1998:60) rightly stated, the etic approaches that allow comparative analysis and the emic approaches that provide much deeper and contextualized insights are equally important in dealing with dispute/conflict. Since terminological usage has discrete implications for the outcome of a dispute/conflict situation, ensuring conceptual clarity is indispensable.

For analytical purposes, the terms that require differentiation are categorized into three: types of incompatibility (dispute and conflict); methods of handling incompatibility (negotiation, mediation, arbitration, and conciliation); and approaches to ending incompatibility (dispute settlement, conflict management, conflict resolution, and conflict transformation). This section attempts to clarify the meanings of these concepts to find out whether they have equivalent practices in Ethiopia and to reflect on the aptness of their use in the literature on Africa.

In this chapter, as part of the knowledge systematization effort, the concept of 'customary laws' has been used, intentionally avoiding the interchangeable use of such terms as 'indigenous law', 'traditional law', 'informal law' and 'customary dispute/conflict resolution mechanisms'. The term customary laws is preferred because of its common use in law schools, legal documents (e.g., constitutions), and major international publications.

Types of incompatibility

There exists a lack of uniformity in the literature in the use of the terms 'dispute' and 'conflict'. While some writers stress the differences between the two, others use them interchangeably. In the Ethiopian literature on customary laws, dispute and conflict have not been adequately differentiated. In *Grassroots justice in Ethiopia* (Pankhurst and Getachew 2008), the titles of ten out of eleven chapters carry the term dispute, but nowhere in the volume is it made clear whether the choice was meant to convey the message that the issues discussed are specifically about disputes and not conflicts. Likewise, the two volumes on *Customary dispute resolution mechanisms in Ethiopia* (Gebre *et al.* 2011) failed to differentiate between the two concepts. Many chapter contributors to these two books and others published in Ethiopia have used dispute and conflict without providing operational definitions, and at times interchangeably.

In order to ensure conceptual clarity in the field of dispute/conflict handling research, this chapter adopts John Burton's (1990:2) approach, which describes dispute as a short-term disagreement between two persons or groups over a specific set of facts and/or issues that are negotiable in nature, and conflict as a long-term and deeply rooted incompatibility associated with seemingly 'non-negotiable' issues between opposing groups or individuals. Non-negotiable issues include the denial of basic human rights and deprivation of essential economic resources such as land and water. If not settled, a specific dispute could turn into conflict, but a conflict cannot turn into a dispute.

Methods of handling incompatibility

The methods commonly employed to address individual or group disputes/conflicts outside of the formal court include negotiation, mediation, conciliation, and arbitration. The four methods of alternative dispute resolution, as practised in Western societies, vary in their respective meanings and approaches. For example, in the context of Western ADR mediators do not suggest solutions, conciliators suggest non-binding agreement ideas, and arbitration results are final and legally binding.

Scholars describing customary laws in Africa have used the terms listed above without questioning them. For example, Francis Kariuki (2015:13) wrote, 'conflict resolution amongst African communities has since time immemorial and continues to take the form of negotiation, mediation, reconciliation or arbitration by elders', without elaborating on the meanings of these terms in the African contexts. It is incumbent on researchers of African customary laws to make sure that the concepts they borrow from the ADR or other international literature adequately represent the local realities. In the literature on Ethiopia, these terms are also not sufficiently differentiated from each other and from their usage in the ADR literature. Tirsit Girshaw (2004:49), for example, states: 'Mechanisms like reconciliation and arbitration are common features of indigenous conflict resolution mechanisms.' Wodisha Habtie (2011:438–440) notes that negotiation, mediation and arbitration exist as distinct methods among the Boro-Shinasha. Among the Nuer, according to Koang Tutlam (2011:412), kinsmen and elders arrange mediation to determine the fine and ask the culprit to pay compensation to the victim. However, these and many other authors do not explain what they mean by concepts like mediation, reconciliation and arbitration.

This section therefore discusses the meanings of the four concepts (namely, negotiaion, mediationreconciliation and arbitration) and ADR proceedings (private in nature), so that researchers can establish whether there is a resemblance with the proceedings of the customary laws (public in nature) that they are studying.

In ADR, 'negotiation' is a mechanism whereby the parties that are directly involved in a dispute/conflict meet to resolve their differences, and reach an agreement without the involvement of a third party (Assefa 2012:245). If conducted without influence and intimidation, negotiation is known to be the most efficient and cost effective approach to handle a dispute/conflict. Since it is conducted on the principles of give-and-take and willingness to ease tension, private negotiators are expected to opt for compromise. Apart from this specific and narrow usage, the term negotiation is flexibly and broadly employed to refer to any discussion aimed at finding a middle ground, be it in the context of mediation, conciliation or an early phase of arbitration.

Mediation as a dispute/conflict handling method involves the appointment of a neutral and impartial third party, e.g. a mediator, often a trained person or a legal expert. He facilitates the dialogue between the parties in conflict and helps them reach a mutually acceptable agreement. It does not impose a binding solution (Le Baron-Duryea 2001:121). Mediation is often preferred to litigation because it is confidential, faster, fairer, cheaper, more efficient and addresses the unique needs of parties. The guiding principles of mediation are that it be voluntary, non-binding, confidential and interest-based. The parties are free to reach or withdraw from negotiated agreements. In order to facilitate the resolution of a conflict, a mediator performs a series of activities. He is expected to understand the perspectives of the parties, set ground rules for improved communication, encourage them to discuss in good faith and articulate their interests or concerns, remind them to make decisions on their own, and convince them to remain committed to a peaceful result. In mediation, parties may be represented by lawyers who argue their case, advocate for their clients and negotiate on their behalf. One might wonder whether mediation as practised in the West is consistent with African customary laws, where non-professionals handle disputes/conflicts in public.

The 1960 Civil Code of Ethiopia does not clearly recognize a mediation procedure. According to Assefa Fiseha (2012:247), it appears that the Ethiopian Civil Code combines mediation and conciliation. Researchers of African customary laws should bear in mind the fact that a mediator in the ADR context would not dictate the process, make a judgment, or suggest any solution.

Conciliation (or reconciliation) is another dispute/conflict handling method that involves the appointment of a neutral and impartial third party – a conciliator – to help parties reach a satisfactory agreement. Conciliators are appointed on the basis of their experience, expertise, availability, language and cultural knowledge. Louis Kriesberg and Bruce Dayton (2012:305) have stated that parties expect four important dimensions to be present in reconciliation for it to succeed: truth, justice, regard and security.

Conciliation and mediation have a lot in common, and sometimes the two terms are used interchangeably. In both methods, the parties retain the power to select their conciliators, the venue, the language, the structure, the content and the timing of the proceedings. Both techniques are flexible, time and cost-efficient, confidential and interest-based. The parties also retain autonomy to make the final decision without imposition by a third party. The difference between conciliation and mediation is that a conciliator can play a direct/active role in providing a non-binding settlement proposal. The Ethiopian Civil Code (Articles 3318–3324) duly recognizes conciliation and provides, among other things, details about the role of conciliators and conciliation proceedings.

Arbitration is the fourth major dispute/conflict-handling method. Here, parties voluntarily present their disagreement to an unbiased third-party arbitrator or arbitral tribunal. Arbitrators are expected to apply the law, and start the proceedings after receiving a written consensus (arbitration agreement) from the parties on the content of their disagreement and their willingness to accept the 'arbitral award' in advance – the verdict issued after the hearing. Arbitral proceedings are conducted under strict rules of confidentiality, e.g. they are not open to the public. Like mediation and conciliation, arbitration is supposed to be more efficient, easier, faster and cheaper than litigation, and to be relatively flexible. Parties are free to choose their arbitrators, the venue, the language and the timing of the arbitral proceedings. Arbitration is different from mediation and conciliation in that: i) arbitrators have the power to administer a legally enforceable award; and ii) parties lose control over their ability to make a decision on their own. Arbitral awards are enforced even internationally because of the 1958 New York Convention on the Recognition and Enforcement of Foreign Arbitral Awards. As practised in the West, the decisions of arbitrators are final and binding, and they cannot be reversed, even by the formal courts, unless the arbitration agreements were invalid. It would be interesting to know whether there exist customary courts in Africa that apply the formal law, require the submission of written arbitration agreements, and conduct private hearings away from the public.

Arbitration as an ADR method is legally recognized in Ethiopia and has been used to handle different disputes/conflicts (Tilahun 2007). Although the procedure seems to be similar to Western practices, Assefa (2012:25) notes that arbitration in the Ethiopian context is becoming more expensive than litigation and that arbitral awards are not necessarily final and binding, as courts tend to accept appeals from parties dissatisfied with the decisions of arbitrators. Such court interference is inconsistent with the principles of arbitration and unfairly diminishes the relevance and the credibility of the method.

Approaches to ending incompatibility

The ending of a conflict takes four major forms: dispute settlement, conflict management, conflict resolution and conflict transformation. In the Ethiopian literature, the terms dispute settlement, conflict resolution and conflict management are not sufficiently differentiated, while conflict transformation is a new concept, the local equivalent of which is yet to be found. Hopefully, the following discussions will clarify the common usage of the four terms, therby avoiding future confusion and interchangeable use.

Dispute settlement is an approach that removes dispute through negotiation, mediation, conciliation and arbitration. A dispute is settled – rather than resolved, managed or transformed – because it represents an easily addressable short-term problem that emanates from negotiable interests. Establishing the facts of the dispute and satisfying the interests of disputants are among the basic conditions that need to be met for successful dispute settlement. Depending on the methods employed, a third party may use persuasion, inducement, pressure or threats to ensure that the disputants arrive at a satisfactory settlement. Dispute settlement strategies aim to end the dispute through compromises and concessions, without addressing the fundamental causes of the dispute or satisfying the basic demands of the disputants (Burton and Dukes 1990:83–87). Since it does not change the existing structures and relationships that cause disputes, the efficacy and durability of the settlement approach, compared to the resolution and transformation approaches, are considered to be limited.

Conflict management refers to the process of mitigating, containing, limiting or temporarily controlling conflict through the intervention of a third party. Conflict management steps are taken with the recognition that conflicts cannot be quickly resolved, and with the conviction that the continuation or escalation of conflicts can be somehow controlled as an interim measure. The conflict management process can succeed only when the conflicting parties have respect for the integrity, impartiality and ability of the third party. However, the strategy neither removes a conflict nor addresses the underlying causes (Lederach 1995:16–17). As Morton Deutsch (1973:8) notes, the main intention is to make the situation more constructive to the conflicting parties through lose–lose, win–lose, or win–win results. The management of a conflict must therefore soon be followed by other strategies that resolve the problem permanently.

Conflict management as defined in ADR has equivalent cultural and religious practices in Ethiopia. For example, among the Orthodox Christians, a priest might place a religious injunction on adversaries in order to temporarily halt offensive actions. In some cultures, offenders take refuge with individuals and institutions believed to be culturally and religiously sanctified to protect them against revenge (Alemu 2011:41).

Conflict resolution is an approach that decisively removes the underlying causes of conflict. Peter Wallensteen (2012:8) defines conflict resolution as 'a situation where conflicting parties enter into an agreement that solves their central incompatibilities, accept each other's continued existence as parties and cease all violent action against each other.' From this definition it is apparent that conflict resolution follows a mutual understanding about the problem to be solved and a firm commitment to address the root causes of the conflict. This can be accomplished through changes in the behaviours, attitudes, structures and relationships that incite or perpetuate conflict. A third party facilitates communication and enables the conflicting parties to come to a comprehensive agreement. Generally, the resolution approach leads to a long-term solution, as resolving conflicts – as opposed to settling disputes – demands more than just establishing the facts or satisfying the interests of the parties. However, it is important to note that conflict resolution may not remove all differences and may not lead to major structural changes that would avoid a relapse into conflict.

Conflict transformation provides the deepest level of change, which results from an improved and accurate understanding of the conflict in question. Conflict transformation underlines the need for major structural and relational change to address similar causes that might prompt a relapse into conflict. The structures, relations, issues and interests that have led to a conflict are all expected to change and allow the establishment of a new system and a new environment. In this regard, the transformational approach seems to have an interest in the aftermath of conflict and or post-conflict peace-building processes. John Paul Lederach (1995:17), the leading advocate and proponent of conflict transformation, writes:

> Transformation provides a more holistic understanding, which can be fleshed out at several levels. Unlike resolution and management, the idea of transformation does not suggest we simply eliminate or control conflict, but rather points descriptively toward its inherent dialectic nature. Social conflict is a phenomenon of human creation, lodged naturally in relationships. It is a phenomenon that transforms events, the relationships in which conflict occurs, and indeed its very creators. It is a necessary element in transformative human construction and reconstruction of social organization and realities.

The gist of Lederach's argument is that conflict – created by people in some kind of relationship – transforms the creators and their relationship. If unchecked or left alone, it can have destructive consequences for the people involved in the conflict. However, the adverse effects of hostile relations and negative perceptions can be modified through long-term and sustained processes that involve education, advocacy and reconciliation, and that improve mutual understanding and transform the people, relationships and structures for the better. Hence, conflict transformation is explained in terms of healing and major structural change, and as having positive implications for social transformation and nation building.

Values and virtues of customary laws

The studies undertaken thus far in Ethiopia indisputably reveal that customary laws are deeply rooted in cultural and religious values and are widely practised throughout the country. Especially in the countryside of Amara and Oromia Regions, it seems that comparatively few cases are taken to the state court (Woubishet 2011:194) and that most plaintiffs (more than 76 per cent according to Dejene) withdraw cases filed with formal institutions before proper investigation (Dejene 2011:271). It appears that the degree of resistance to the formal law depends on the intensity of state influence, which gets weaker from the centre to the periphery.

In 2011, I had the opportunity to coordinate research on customary laws in Ethiopia and organize a series of validation workshops in different regions. Many of the professionals and practitioners in the justice sector who participated in the workshops acknowledged that customary courts have been helpful in reducing the workload of formal courts. As often seen on TV screens, in their efforts to address inter-ethnic conflicts, government officials have been openly co-opting influential customary authorities and judges. It is apparent that legal experts and authorities, who in the past were antagonistic towards customary laws, have now begun to recognize their virtues. This section therefore focuses on the underlying core values that may have contributed to the perpetuation, resilience and, in some cases, dominance of customary laws.

Restoration of social order

In places where people live in settings with strong networks of kinship, clanship, ethnicity, and other social groupings, disputes/conflicts between individuals are likely to engulf much larger groups. Unlike the formal courts, which define justice in terms of the penalization of perpetrators, customary laws focus on the larger groups (e.g., families, communities, clans, etc.) from both the perpetrators' and the victims' sides who may have been drawn into the trouble. This is because discord is viewed not only as a matter of individual differences that should be addressed, but also as something that disrupts the social order. The restoration of social order can therefore only be ensured when the larger groups drawn into a dispute/conflict come to grips with it and move forward, leaving the trouble behind them. Hence, the deliberations of customary laws often end with the repentance of the perpetrator's group and the forgiveness of the victim's group, which help bridge the social divide and heal the social scar.

From many case studies on customary laws in Ethiopia (Gebre *et al.* 2011, 2012), it is apparent that families and large groups in many parts of Ethiopia are involved during the handling of disputes and conflicts initiated by individuals or small groups. To give an example, in 1999 I witnessed the reconciliation process in an adultery case involving two Gumz families, in which a young married woman admitted to having been impregnated by a young man in the same village. The case was brought to the attention of elders and clan leaders, who immediately summoned the family and relatives of the impregnator and those of the young woman's husband (who was away from the village at the time, in education). The problem between the two families was resolved through repentance and forgiveness in the absence of the husband, who was expected to agree to the deal upon his return to the village.

The staging of a forum for group involvement in customary peace-making processes is meant not only to resolve the dispute/conflict itself but also to help avoid possible relapses and spill over effects, and to ensure social order and community peace. Hence, justice and peace are served at the same time. It could be argued that in communities with a strong sense of social bonding and group loyalty customary laws are well suited to transform hostility to solidarity at both the individual and group levels without creating a winner–loser situation. In this respect, customary laws exhibit irrefutable advantages over the formal law, which focuses only on the prosecution of the perpetrator, a measure that does not lead to community peace.

Quest for truth

The second important quality of customary laws is their unique and unparalleled strength in discovering the truth, which often poses a challenge for the formal justice system. The police often finds offences committed in secret and lacking evidence makes it difficult or even impossible to investigate. In the context of customary law, the victim's side is not expected to be open to discussion and forgiveness before the truth has been disclosed. Hence, the primary role of the actors who deliberate in cases under customary law is to discover the facts through a confession of the perpetrator or through investigation. In closely organized communities, people do not hesitate to expose culprits, and it is not uncommon for family members to testify against loved ones involved in unlawful acts. Thus, alleged perpetrators are rarely convicted on the basis of circumstantial evidence, and offenders rarely get away with wrongdoing for lack of witnesses or evidence.

Telling the truth is given high value for practical and religious reasons. On the practical side, the social life of people in communities is built around mutual trust. People make agreements and entrust things to each other without witnesses and without formal records. If the social contract of trust was allowed to crumble, the consequences for the individuals and the society at large would be grave. For example, untrustworthy individuals risk being dishonoured and disgraced among their own families and communities. A society would become dysfunctional without the basic principles that govern the behaviours and actions of its members. Hence, there exists a great deal of social pressure to tell the truth.

Regarding the religious aspect, telling lies while under oath is associated with a betrayal of faith that might have supernatural consequences. The case of the Nuer, for example, reveals the value attached to truth and its association with belief systems. There, '(t)he disputants swear an oath of innocence and the person who doesn't tell the truth is bound to suffer misfortune' (Koang 2011:425). Among the Woliso Oromo, 'customary courts attempt to prove the truthfulness of cases through the flow of information, directly from the disputants. Both parties are expected to be honest in providing information. (...) It is believed that the *waaqa* (higher spiritual being) easily identifies the truthfulness and falsity' (Dejene 2011:261–262). In short, while state legal institutions struggle to find the truth as people do not feel indebted to them, customary institutions can employ social and religious pressure to learn the truth from a community.

Public participation

As opposed to the closed and confidential ADR proceedings of the West, customary laws allow people to attend the publically held deliberations into disuputes/conflicts and to provide opinions on the validity or falsity of the evidence provided and/or the fairness of the verdict reached. Before Ethiopia was occupied by Italy in 1936, this was also the case for the customary justice system of the Ethiopian government: the Imperial Courts invited bystanders and passers-by to attend hearings and air their opinions.

Participation in the administration of justice characterizes the customary laws of many Ethiopian people (see for example Assefa Fiseha (2011:366–7) on Tigray and Abraham Tadesse (2011:123) on Sidama). Dejene (2011:261–276), who studied the Woliso Oromo, writes: 'Apart from direct participation, the community provides information and suggests ideas on the issue under litigation. Such informal discussions and public views are important to arrive at consensus at the end of the day. The final decisions are the outcome of these various views and suggestions from the community.' In addition, the openness of customary procedures and the participation of the community members in the administration of customary justice tend to limit opportunities for corruption and nepotism, as Koang (2011:429) noted about the Nuer.

Why is popular participation so important? First, the involvement of community members as observers, witnesses and commentators increases the credibility and transparency of customary laws. Second, non-confidential proceedings help to put public pressure on parties to honour and respect agreements. Non-compliance to decisions is rare, mainly because nonconformity is likely to be interpreted as a rebellion against community values and interests. Finally, since decisions are passed in the presence of community observers, the possibility for corruption and prejudiced judgment is limited.

Collective responsibility

Collective responsibility refers to a situation where social groups take the blame for offences perpetrated by their members and take responsibility for the consequences. This principle is widely common in cultures where group identification and group control mechanisms are strong, and where the idea of the individualization of crimes is uncommon. In such societies, members of a perpetrator's family may be subjected to retaliation as a form of collective punishment. Hence, to avoid such retribution, the families and relatives of wrongdoers often take the initiative to make peace. The perpetrator's family, lineage or clan may be required to take responsibility, express repentance as a group, and contribute towards compensation for the victim. In Dassanech and Nyangatom, South Omo Zone, even government authorities seem to employ the principle of collective responsibility to put pressure on communities to apprehend and bring criminals to justice.

From a Western perspective, collective responsibility for any wrongdoing does not seem fair or appropriate. One might well challenge the appropriateness of holding communities/groups responsible for offences committed by individuals. Yet, in an African context, blame-sharing seems to serve important purposes that are worth appreciating. First, blame-sharing represents a tacit recognition that the family or the group to which the perpetrator belongs failed to detect, discourage, stop or report an unjustified offence, and as such, they should take some responsibility. Second, when a verdict involves costly compensation being awarded to the victim's group, the principles of reciprocity, solidarity and sharing are often evoked to help members in trouble. Third, in a situation where the group (rather than the individual offender) is the target of retribution, the cost of not taking collective responsibility could be much higher than that of sharing the blame and jointly paying the fine.

One might also wonder whether sharing of the consequences of wrongdoing might encourage further crimes. However, it is unpleasant for a group to go through such trials and tribulations, which tarnish the group's reputation and image in society.Thus, repeated offences may strain the relationship between the perpetrator and his group, leading to harsher measures, such as humiliation, ostracism, expulsion from the community, capital punishment, etc. In other words, there are internal mechanisms that discourage and control offenders.

Accessibility, efficiency and affordability

In Ethiopia, the formal legal institutions are largely inaccessible to a significant proportion of rural communities. Most rural communities lack easy physical access to the formal courts because the district courts are located in the woreda (district) capitals, far away from most villages. Travelling to a *woreda* (district) capital to file a case would, undoubtedly, incur costs: money, time and energy. Moreover, dealing with the district courts can involve having to face unfamiliar and intimidating judges, return visits to the court, unexpected delays, and issues with language, for example, if local languages are not used in the courts. Although quasi-formal social courts exist in villages, their mandate is limited to civil cases and petty crimes, the punishments for which do not exceed one-month in jail and a 500 Birr (US $18) fine.

Conversely, customary laws provides alternatives that fairly adequately address these gaps and challenges. The people who apply customary law, often elders who speak the local languages and are appointed and entrusted by the parties, are readily available in every locality and provide speedy services free of charge (or for a nominal fee). Hence, customary law provides a more affordable and accessible way to settle disputes than the formal courts. Unlike the formal courts, which are complicated and known for their rigidity, customary forms are characterized by flexibility and simplicity, making them more efficient. The inconvenience and dissatisfaction associated with repeated court appearances, unbearable delays, intimidating court procedures and corruption are also limited in the customary context.

Systematic and comparative research

Studies on customary law may be undertaken in a variety of ways depending on their purpose and design. In this section, with the idea of knowledge systematization in mind, attempts are made to outline and explain the salient variables useful for understanding the structures and procedures of customary law and the state of legal pluralism in Ethiopia. It is assumed that systematic study of customary law requires a structured research approach that ensures the collection and analysis of comparable data.

The structure of customary courts

This sub-section attempts to identify the judicial levels and frameworks, and the identity, legitimacy and terms of office of the people who handle cases. It needs to be noted that despite the constitutional provisions (i.e., Articles 34:5 and 78:5, discussed later), the customary legal systems operate independently of the formal court. Hence, the structure discussed in this section relates only to the customary legal order.

Regarding court levels, some societies have customary courts that are hierarchically organized and have procedures for appeal, while others lack fixed courts, hierarchy and the possibility of appeal. The absence of hierarchical structure does not necessarily deter complainants from taking their cases to other parallel levels for rehearing (Debebe 2011:348, Mesfin 2012:181). Some customary courts, such as the *mad'a* of the Afar people, handle different types of cases (Kahsay 2011:326), while others, such as those among the Woleyta, specialize in handling only specific cases (Yilma 2011:106).

In customary legal systems, the customary court judges are influential clan leaders, ritual specialists, religious leaders, senior elders, village administrators and lineage heads. These well-versed individuals are known for their wisdom, impartiality, knowledge of their culture, rhetorical skills or power to convince, and rich experience in handingling disputes/conflicts.

The power of the customary judges and others handling conflicts emanates from at least one of four sources: i) the consent of the parties to have their case handled by them; ii) an administrative position (e.g., clan chief) in the society; iii) participation in certain rituals that entitle them to become judges, as is the case among the Sidama (Abraham 2011) and the Dassanech (Gebre 2012), or iv) leadership in religious institutions, as in some parts of Amhara (Birhan 2011). The legitimacy of legal authorities and their power are derived from secular and/or spiritual sources.

The terms of office of people who handle dispute/conflict vary depending on the sources of their authority. The role of those appointed by the parties in a dispute/conflict ends the moment the discord is dealt with. However, judges who acquire their authority by virtue of their religious or administrative posts, or by performing rituals, may continue to serve until they are formally replaced, unless they are required to step down for legitimate reasons, such as inability to function, poor performance or malpractice. While individuals with an excellent record of service are invited to handle cases repeatedly, those who fail to meet expectations are rarely given another chance. In all cases, those who handle disputes are under close public scrutiny and this helps to ensure their impartiality and competence.

The procedures of customary courts

This sub-section focuses on the events/activities that occur between when a dispute arises and when it is resolved. These include: reporting cases, evidence collection and verification, deliberation and verdict, closing rituals, and enforcement mechanisms. Reporting cases to customary courts is a collective responsibility rather than a matter to be left to those directly involved. Family members, relatives, neighbours or anyone who has knowledge about the dispute/conflict is expected to report it. In many cases, the culprit or his/her kin will admit their guilt and report incidents to ensure quick conciliation. It is also common for the party of the victim to file a case with the judicial body instead of resorting to vengeance.

The ultimate objective of customary courts is to achieve genuine conciliation after the disclosure of the truth. The truth is expected to surface through confession or public investigation, which may involve a review of the evidence and witness testimony. Thanks to the high value accorded to truth, serious offences committed in secret and in the absence of witnesses are often solved through customary procedures. The handlers remind disputants to restrain themselves from doing things that can derail the process, hurt feelings or exacerbate social disorder. Apart from those directly involved in a dispute/conflict and their witnesses, representatives of the parties (often family members) and ordinary spectators of the deliberation may be asked to air their views and comment in the interests of reconciliation and community peace.

When guilt is admitted or proven with evidence, the case comes to a close, and a verdict will be passed, often by consensus between the parties involved, although it does not preclude coercion by customary judges (when persuasion fails). The offender's group may have to pay compensation to the victim's side, and express sincere repentance, which is often reciprocated with forgiveness by the victim's group. Regarding compensation, there exist significant variations across cultures. In some societies, fixed payment regimes exist, while in others, fines are determined later based on the severity of the offence and sometimes the economic capacity of the offender. Compensation may be paid immediately, in piecemeal over a short period of time, or as a long-term debt inherited by generations.

Most customary court rulings end with closing ritual performances that involve sacrificial animals, the expression of a commitment to the agreements made, curses for wickedness and nonconformist behaviours, and blessings for righteousness and conformity. Such rituals of partly divine content are believed to deter rebellious tendencies and avoid a relapse into discord. Alongside the spiritual harm that such rituals are believed to inflict on the defiant, social pressure (e.g., defamation, ostracism, etc.) and physical measures (e.g., punishment, property confiscation, etc.) may be used to enforce customary court decisions. Handing an offender to the formal justice system provides another way of dealing with the disobedient.

Summary and conclusion

The plural legal orders of Africa came into being as a result of three processes: transplantation from Western countries, imposition from authoritarian states, and derivation from local values and traditions. Compared to the transplanted and imposed law, the local level customary laws seem to enjoy widespread acceptance throughout the continent and especially in rural areas, where the majority of African population resides. Moreover, they have received growing attention by researchers, as evidenced by an increaing number of research reports and publications.

However, this unprecedented study of customary legal practices has not led to comprehensive knowledge amenable to comparative analysis, scientific generalization, or policy application because of gaps in the use of terminologies, identification of the virtues of customary laws, and articulation of research strategies. This has warranted the need to systematize knowledge about customary laws. With this in mind, this chapter hopes to have accomplished the following. First, besides clarifying the meaning of concepts borrowed from the ADR literature, attempts have been made to shed light on the comparability of the various terms to customary legal practices. Second, the core values of customary laws worth recognizing have been identified and organized. These include the restoration of community peace, transparency, accessibility, efficiency, affordability, flexibility, simplicity, familiarity, and sense of belongingness. Third, the variables useful for understanding the structures and procedures of customary laws have also been discussed. In this way, the chapter has made a modest contribution to better understanding and informed appreciation of customary laws.

Customary law faces existential challenges that have put it at crossroads. It is criticized for gender insensitivity, weak procedural fairness in adjudication and punishment, breach of human rights, lack of uniformity, and incompatibility with changing contexts. The application of some customary laws obviously violates classic liberal rights, such as privacy, personal dignity and bodily integrity. The breach of the rights of women and minority groups in the application of customary legal practices are structural problems that largely emanate from the established cultural norms in every society and culture. In order to remain relevant and effective in the twenty-first century, the custodians of customary legal practices should demonstrate adaptation, flexibility and sensitivity.

In Ethiopia, the constitutional recognition of customary laws remains inadequate in that the particulars of Article 34:5 have not been determined by law and the official recognition stipulated in Article 78:5 has not yet been given. Consequently, the interactions between state law and customary law are arbitrary, inconsistent, unregulated, and quite unpredictable. In some cases, the two legal systems unofficially recognize each other and cooperate to the extent of transferring cases or exchanging information. There are instances where government authorities and custodians of customary laws work together in addressing inter-ethnic conflicts. There are also situations where the formal and customary courts operate side-by-side exhibiting indifference and tolerance. Sometimes, both get antagonistic, especially when one intervenes in the domains and activities of the other. The inadequate constitutional provision and the consequent anomalous practices have led to the existence of different views about the relevance of customary laws.

There is a need to regulate the relationship between the two legal systems within the context of legal pluralism and avoid anomalies within a country. Policy makers have to reckon with the relative indispensability and the manifest irreplaceability (in addressing group conflicts) of the customary laws discussed in this paper, and fulfil the constitutional promises without further delay. Given the historical factors, the cultural differences, and the limitations of the state law, the ideal strategy would be to maintain and strengthen legal pluralism to provide multiple legal service options to citizens.

References

ABRAHAM Tadesse, 2011 "Customary conflict resolution among the Sidama" (in Amharic), in: Gebre Yntiso, Fekade Azeze, and Assefa Fiseha (eds.) *Customary dispute resolution in Ethiopia*, 121–132. Addis Ababa: The Ethiopian Arbitration and Conciliation Center

ALEMU Kassaye, 2011 "Blood feud reconciliation in Lalomama Midir District, North Shoa" (in Amharic), in: Gebre Yntiso, Fekade Azeze, and Assefa Fiseha (eds.) *Customary dispute resolution in Ethiopia*, 157–180. Addis Ababa: The Ethiopian Arbitration and Conciliation Center

ASSEFA Fiseha, 2012 "Business-related alternative dispute resolution mechanisms in Addis Ababa", in: Gebre Yntiso, Fekade Azeze, and Assefa Fiseha (eds.) *Customary dispute resolution in Ethiopia*, Vol. 2. Addis Ababa: The Ethiopian Arbitration and Conciliation Center

AVRUCH, Kevin, 2003 "Type I and type II errors in culturally sensitive conflict resolution practice", *Conflict Resolution Quarterly* 20 (3):351–371

1998 *Culture and conflict resolution*. Washington DC: United States Institute of Peace

BIRHAN Assefa, 2011 "*Yamare fird* [customary court] in Wogidi and Borena District, South Wollo" (in Amharic), in: Gebre Yntiso, Fekade Azeze, and Assefa Fiseha (eds.) Customary dispute resolution in Ethiopia, 133–156. Addis Ababa: The Ethiopian Arbitration and Conciliation Center

BOHANNAN, Paul, 1969 "Ethnography and comparison in legal anthropology", in: Laura Nader (ed.): *Law in culture and society*, 401–418. Chicago: Aldine

BURTON, John, 1990 *Conflict: Resolution and prevention*. New York: St. Martin's Press

BURTON, John and Frank DUKES, 1990 *Conflict: Practices in management, settlement and resolution*. New York: St. Martin's Press Cuskelly, Katrina

2011 Customs and constitutions: State recognition of customary law around the world. Bangkok: IUCN

DEBEBE Zewde, 2011 "Conflict resolution among the Issa community" (in Amharic), in: Gebre Yntiso, Fekade Azeze, Assefa Fiseha (eds.) Customary dispute resolution in Ethiopia, 341–369. Addis Ababa: The Ethiopian Arbitration and Conciliation Center

DEJENE Gemechu, 2011 "The customary courts of the Waliso Oromo", in: Gebre Yntiso, Fekade Azeze, Assefa Fiseha (eds.) *Customary dispute resolution in Ethiopia*, 251–278. Addis Ababa: The Ethiopian Arbitration and Conciliation Center

DEUTSCH, Morton, 1973 *The resolution of conflict: Constrictive and destructive processes*. New Haven: Yale University Press

EMPIRE OF ETHIOPIA, 1960 *Civil Code of the Empire of Ethiopia*, Proclamation No. 165/1960, Negarit Gazeta Extraordinary Issue, 1960-05-05, Year 19, No. 2

GEBRE Yntiso, Itaru OHTA and Motoji MATSUDA (eds.), 2017 *African virtues and the pursuit of conviviality: Exploring local solutions in light of global prescriptions*. Mankon, Bamenda (Cameroon): Langaa Research & Publishing

GEBRE Yntiso, 2016a "Borderland conflicts in East Africa: The unnoticed wars in the Ethiopia-Kenya border", *Ethiopian Journal of Development Research* 38 (1):1–30

2016b "Ethnic boundary making in East Africa: Rigidity and flexibility among the Nyangatom people", *African Study Monographs*, 37 (4):143–160

2014 "Systematizing knowledge about customary laws in Ethiopia", *Journal of Ethiopian Law* 26 (2):28–54

2012 "Arra: Customary conflict resolution mechanisms of the Dassanech" (in Amharic), in: Gebre Yntiso, Fekade Azeze and Assefa Fiseha (eds.) *Customary dispute resolution in Ethiopia* Vol. 2, 51–79. Addis Ababa: The Ethiopian Arbitration and Conciliation Center

2012 with Fekade Azeze, and Assefa Fiseha (eds.): *Customary dispute resolution in Ethiopia,* Vol 2. Addis Ababa: The Ethiopian Arbitration and Conciliation Center

2011 with Fekade Azeze, and Assefa Fiseha (eds.): *Customary dispute resolution in Ethiopia* Vol. 1. Addis Ababa: The Ethiopian Arbitration and Conciliation Center

GLUCKMAN, Max, 1969 "Concepts in the comparative study of tribal law", in: Laura Nader (ed.): *Law in culture and society*, 349–373. Chicago: Aldine

GRANDE, Elisabetta, 1999"Alternative dispute resolution, Africa and the structure of law and power: The Horn in context", *Journal of African Law* 43 (1):63–70

GRIFFITH, John, 1986 "What is legal pluralism?", *Journal of Legal Pluralism* 24:1–55

HICKS, John R., 1930 "The early history of industrial conciliation in England", *Economica* 28:25–39

KAHSAY Gebre, 2011 "Mad'a: The justice system of the Afar people" (in Amharic), in: Gebre Yntiso, Fekade Azeze and Assefa Fiseha (eds.) *Customary dispute resolution in Ethiopia,* 323–340. Addis Ababa: EACC

KANE, Minneh, Joe OLOKA-ONYANGO and Abdul TEJAN-COLE, 2005 "Reassessing customary law systems as a vehicle for providing equitable access to justice for the poor", paper presented for the Arusha World Bank Conference titled *New Frontiers of Social Policy*, held on 12–15 December

KARIUKI, Francis, 2015 "Conflict resolution by elders in Africa: Successes, challenges and opportunities", *Alternative Dispute Resolution* 3 (2):30–53

KOANG Tutlam, 2011 "Dispute resolution mechanisms of the Nuer", in: Gebre Yntiso, Fekade Azeze and Assefa Fiseha (eds.) *Customary dispute resolution in Ethiopia,* 407–434. Addis Ababa: The Ethiopian Arbitration and Conciliation Center

KRIESBERG, Louis and Bruce W. DAYTON, 2012 *Constructive conflicts: From escalation to resolution*. Lanham, Maryland: Rowman & Littlefield Publisher

LE BARON-DURYEA, Michelle, 2001 *Conflict and culture: A literature review and bibliography*. Revised edition. Victoria, BC: Institute for Dispute Resolution

LEDERACH, John Paul, 1995 *Preparing for peace: Conflict transformation across cultures.* Syracuse, NY: Syracuse University Press

MAMO Hebo, 2006 *Land, local custom and state policies: Land tenure, land disputes and dispute settlement among the Arsii Oromo of Southern Ethiopia*. Kyoto: Shoukadoh

MATTEI, Ugo and Laura NADER, 2008 *Plunder: When the rule of law is illegal*. Oxford: Wiley-Blackwell

MERRY, Sally, 1988 "Legal pluralism", *Law & Society Review* 22 (5):869–896

MESFIN Melese, 2012 "Customary dispute resolution mechansims in Tach Armahiho Woreda, North Gondar" (in Amharic), in: Gebre Yntiso, Fekade Azeze, and Assefa Fiseha (eds.) *Customary dispute resolution in Ethiopia*, Vol 2. Addis Ababa: The Ethiopian Arbitration and Conciliation Center

MUTISI, Martha and Kwesi SANSCULOTTE-GREENIDGE (eds.), 2012 *Integrating traditional and modern conflict resolution experiences from selected cases in Eastern and the Horn of Africa*. Durban: ACCORD (accessible online at http://accord.org.za/publications/special-issues/994-integrating-traditional-and-modern-conflict-resolution, last accessed 20 November 2018)

NADER, Laura and Elisabetta GRANDE, 2002 "Current illusions and delusions about conflict management in Africa and elsewhere", *Law & Social Inquiry*, 27 (3):573–594

NADER, Laura, 1993 "Controlling process in the practice of law: Hierarchy and pacification in the movement to reform dispute ideology", *Ohio State Journal on Dispute Resolution* 9:1–8

OGBAHARYA, Daniel, 2010 "Alternative dispute resolution (ADR) in sub-Saharan Africa: The role of customary systems of conflict resolution (CSCR)", paper presented at the *23rd Annual International Association of Conflict Management Conference Boston*, Massachusetts, 24–27 June 2010

PANKHURST, Alula and GETACHEW Assefa (eds.), 2008 *Grass-roots justice in Ethiopia: The contribution of customary dispute resolution*. Addis Ababa: French Center of Ethiopian Studies

POSPISIL, Leopold J., 1971 *Anthropology of law: A comparative theory*. New York: Harper and Row

STEBEK, Elias and MURADU Abdo (eds.), 2013 *Law and development and legal pluralism in Ethiopia*. Addis Ababa: Justice and Legal Systems Research Institute

TILAHUN Teshome, 2007 "The legal regime government arbitration in Ethiopia: A synopsis", *Ethiopian Bar Review* 1 (2):117–140

TIRSIT Girshaw, 2004 "Indigenous conflict resolution mechanisms in Ethiopia", in: *First national conference on federalism, conflict and peace building* (organized by the Ministry of Federal Affairs and German Technical Cooperation), 49–65. Addis Ababa: Ministry of Federal Affairs

WALLENSTEEN, Peter, 2012 *Understanding conflict resolution* (3rd edition). London: SAGE

WODISHA Habitie, 2011 "The Nèèmá: Conflict resolution institution of the Boro-Šinaša", in: Gebre Yntiso, Fekade Azeze and Assefa Fiseha (eds.) *Customary dispute resolution in Ethiopia* Vol 1, 435–460. Addis Ababa: The Ethiopian Arbitration and Conciliation Center

WOUBISHET Shiferaw, 2011 "Spirit medium as an institution for dispute resolution in North Shoa: The case of Wofa Legesse, in: Gebre Yntiso, Fekade Azeze and Assefa Fiseha (eds.) *Customary dispute resolution in Ethiopia* Vol 1, 181–202. Addis Ababa: The Ethiopian Arbitration and Conciliation Center

YILMA Teferi, 2011 "Mediation and reconclitiation among the Woleyta ethnic group", in: Gebre Yntiso, Fekade Azeze and Assefa Fiseha (eds.) *Customary dispute resolution in Ethiopia* Vol 1, 103–121. Addis Ababa: The Ethiopian Arbitration and Conciliation Center

ZARTMAN, William (ed.), 2000 *Traditional cures for modern conflicts: African conflict 'medicine'*. Boulder: Lynne Rienner

II.

Cooperation and competition between legal forums

5. The handling of homicide in the context of legal pluralism

Cooperation between government and customary institutions in the Gamo highlands

Temechegn Gutu

Introduction

In the Gamo highlands, as in many parts of Ethiopia, customary law continues to be applied, even in areas where the constitution does not allow it. The current study attempts to understand how the Balta community in the Gamo highlands handles homicide and makes use of the availability of parallel legal systems: the customary and state law.

In the Gamo worldview, taking human life is believed to be *gome* – a transgression of a social norm or sin that leads to the pollution of the wrongdoer and can cause misfortune, disease and natural calamities. Therefore, when someone is killed, a ritual of purification is enforced to cleanse the wrongdoer and to restore the social order violated by the act. While customary law perceives homicide as an issue that affects the whole group and therefore emphasizes the restoration of normal social order between the families and clans of the slayer and the deceased, state law defines it as an individual wrongdoing and punishes the criminal.

While the Gamo people's philosophical position in relation to homicide sets its customary legal system apart from the formal state law, this chapter shows that the two legal systems work together in the process of handling homicide cases in a number of different ways. The cooperation between the police, the *ogade* (mediator between two or more communities), and the elders of the community in the collection of evidence is a case in point. Moreover, based on the findings, it seems that the attention given to reconciling the victim's and the slayer's sides in the customary dispute settlement process makes an indispensable contribution in restoring and maintaining peace and harmony in the community, an effect that is also valued and supported by government officials.

Legal anthropology in the colonial context often viewed state and customary law as co-existing but separate areas of authority and adjudication, which used different procedures rooted in distinct moralities. Recent studies have conceptualized the interplay between state and customary law in increasingly sophisticated ways: seeing each as pursuing its own interests and creating a complex hybrid of overlapping legal jurisdictions (Mann and Roberts 1991:264). However, the existing body of knowledge on this issue is still limited.

Many scholars from different backgrounds have studied the indigenous conflict resolution mechanisms that Ethiopian societies in different regions have developed (Donovan and Getachew 2003, Gebre *et al.* 2011, 2012; Pankhurst and Getachew 2008, Dejene 2002, Ayalew 2012). Gonfa (2014), for example, reported that among the Oromo people, the court, police and the prosecutors encourage conflicting parties to resolve all simple criminal cases through their traditional *jaarsummaa* (elder's council) system. With the consent of the conflicting parties, such cases are formally referred to the elders with an appeal to resolve the conflict and report the result. Some authors have demonstrated that formal and customary institutions are working closely on homicide cases, despite the fact that the law stipulates they should be handled exclusively by the state courts. Esayas (2015:104–108) has shown that, among the Gofa, the council of elders is closely cooperating with the police, the prosecutors and the court to provide evidence or witnesses in, for example, homicide cases.

However, only a few anthropologists are engaged in comparative studies of customary law and the coexistence of customary and state law (see Gebre *et al.* 2011, Alemayehu 2004). This chapter attempts to contribute to the scientific knowledge on legal pluralism in Ethiopia from an anthropological perspective by exploring the experiences of the Balta community of the Gamo highlands in south Ethiopia.

The Gamo people

The Gamo ethnic group lives in Gamo Gofa Zone in the Southern Nations, Nationalities and Peoples Regional State (SNNPRS). Predominantly, they live in nine districts of the zone and its capital, Arba Minch. The term Gamo refers to both the people and the land where they live (Gebreyohannes 1993 E.C).

Much of the Gamo territory is highland, where the people grow *ensete* (false banana), barley, wheat, peas, beans, potatoes and cabbages. In some lowland areas they herd cattle and grow sorghum and maize (Freeman 1999, 2001). *Ensete* is a staple food grown across the highland communities and every house in the highland is surrounded by an *ensete* grove. However, recently introduced cash crops, such as bananas, mangos and avocados, have become the main source of livelihood in the lowlands. Besides agriculture, weaving is also an important activity in many parts of Gamo (Getaneh 2014).

The Gamo people have more than 200 clans, and Gamo society is further subdivided into different social classes or strata, some of which are based on occupation and descent, including farmers (*malla*), craft workers (*mana, tsoma* or *digela*) and slave descendants (*ayle*) (Arthur 2013, Bosha 2013, Weedman 2013, Olmstead 1975, Freeman 2004).

Before the introduction of Orthodox Christianity to the highlands in the fifteenth century, the Gamo people followed only their own belief system (Getaneh 2014). Despite the influence of Christianity, the local people managed to maintain their own beliefs until the twentieth century, when Protestant Christianity was introduced to Gamo with the help of the Sudan Interior Missions (SIM), who visited the area in the 1920s and 1930s (Freeman 2004).

The Gamo highlands have some forty self-administered communities (*dereta*)[1] (Bureau 2012). According to Freeman (2004), every *dere* has its own *kawo*[2] (hereditary ruler), its own *halaqa* (initiate in small-sized *dere), huduga* (initiate in medium-sized *dere)* or *maga,* as well as its own *dubusha* (assembly place), where the public assembly (*dere dulata*) meets to discuss communal matters. Each *dere* also has its own *ogade* (spokesman),[3] responsible for inter-*dere* affairs and official communication with other *dere* on various socio-economic and political issues. As such, each *dere* is a self-administrating unit. Though there exist many parallels, there are also slight differences in the way conflicts are handled and resolved in each *dere*.

The Gamo highlands were incorporated into the Ethiopian state in the second half of the nineteenth century. As stated by Freeman (2004), knowing that their neighbours found it difficult to withstand Menelik II's forces, the Gamo people quickly submitted to the emperor's soldiers in 1897, though – as several Gamo elders recounted – there was some unorganized resistance in different places. Following the subjugation of the Gamo, the soldiers established their administrative centre at Chencha, a small town that served as the capital of Gamo Gofa Province before the centre was shifted to Arba Minch in the 1960s (Freeman 2004:37). Since their incorporation into the Ethiopian state, the Gamo have experienced many changes in their socio-political and economic life (Freeman 2004, Zenebe 2014, Mahe 2013). These can be summarized as changing power relations, an increase in religious alternatives, and improvements in transport and trade (Freeman 2004:31–38).

Under imperial rule (1897–1973) many local dignitaries received new titles (Freeman 2004:31–32). In Gamo, the *kawo* became *balabat* – a title given to the landlords

---

1 *Dereta* is the plural form of *dere*.

2 Zenebe (2014), citing the Gamo Gofa Zone Culture and Information Department, argued that the title of *kawo* or *kati* was introduced in Gamo indigenous governance in the sixteenth century. My own research in 2008 E.C showed that not all Gamo *dereta* were ruled by a *kawo*: ten *dereta* were ruled by a *halaqa* and Ganta was ruled by a *kati* (king).

3 In some *dere* this office is called *gaanna*.

responsible for managing a territory and collecting tax from tenants. As such, the local leaders retained their local power but, at the same time, had to be loyal to the centre. In turn, they were given certain different privileges and positions, becoming, for example, juridical officials or being put in charge of the local police. While, in principle, all criminal cases were to be brought to the newly established courts, at first they were heard by the *balabat* (Bureau 1978:282, Abeles 1981:62).

In this way, the people of the Gamo highlands were exposed to the state legal system from the early years of their incorporation into the Ethiopian state. However, the newly introduced courts and police were not positively accepted by the local people (Bureau 2012). Rather, as Bureau has described, there was little interaction between the newcomers and the local population: the Gamo people generally avoided visiting the new markets established by the newcomers and continued to use their own courts and Orthodox churches. In terms of settlement, the northerners were confined to garrison towns while the local people stayed in the rural areas (Bureau 2012). Besides Chencha, the main administrative centre of Gamo, several smaller towns – such as Ezzo, Gulta, Gerese, Baza and Kamba – were founded elsewhere in the highlands as local administrative outposts; each had its own state institutions (Freeman 2004).

The Balta community of the Gamo highlands was exposed to this new administration through the garrison town of Kamba, which is some 15 km away from the Balta area. While the regimes of emperors Menelik II and Haile Selassie were based on indirect rule, when the Derg regime took over in 1974, many local institutions central to the life of Gamo people – such as the public places (*dubusha*), ritual places, and the traditional palace (*gadho*) – were destroyed. Since the coming of the FDRE government to power in 1991, many Gamo institutions have been revitalized (Zenebe 2014:31).

The research for this chapter was undertaken in Balta *dere*, one of the eleven *dereta* in Kamba district of Gamo Gofa Zone. Balta was chosen because traditional institutions for conflict resolution, including those for cases of homicide, are still central to the life of the local people and now work side-by-side with state law. The aim is to understand how this community handles homicide cases in the context of plural legal system, with a focus on the cooperation between government and customary institutions.

The traditional political and legal system of Balta *dere*

In the Gamo political system, each *dere* has various offices with specific duties that are hierarchically structured. As mentioned above, although they are generally similar, there exist slight differences between the different *dere* (see Freeman

1999, 2000; Getaneh 2006, Wondimu 2010, Zelalem 2016).[4] In the following I will describe the political offices as found in Balta and most other *dere*.

At the top of the hierarchy is the *kawo*, a politico-religious leader who is often referred to as 'king' in the literature (Abeles 1981, Freeman 2004, Zelalem 2016). Succession to this position is hereditary and usually governed by the rule of primogeniture. The office holder has different administrative and religious duties. Accordingly, the *kawo* is a senior office holder politically and a senior sacrificer in Balta traditional religion. He makes the final decisions in the internal matters of the community of his jurisdiction, adjudicates over serious crimes and administers the territory (Freeman 2004, SNNPR Council of Nationalities 2008 E.C, Gamo Gofa Culture and Information Department 2004 E.C).

Below the *kawo* is the *huduga*, a politico-religious position. The title is acquired through an initiation ceremony. The *huduga* is responsible for governing the sub-administrative unit within the *dere* and making sacrifices on behalf of the community under his jurisdiction. The office holder is accountable to the *kawo* and his community. Below the *huduga* is the *ogade* (also: *gasaa maga*), a kind of spokesman or mediator between different *dere*. The position is hereditary and passes from father to eldest son on the father's death. The *ogade* is responsible for handling all matters concerning inter-*dere* affairs, more specifically inter-*dere* conflict and homicide mediations. The *ogade* is followed by the *maga*, a kind of mediator within one *dere* who has to handle conflicts and homicides within the *dere*. Working closely with these officials on multiple social issues is the *dere cima* (council of elders). It plays a central role during social gatherings and public assemblies and works closely with the *maga*, the *ogade* and the police on conflict resolution.

Conceptualizing conflict and homicide in Gamo

As explained by one of my informants,[5] the term 'conflict', *ooshsha* in the Gamo language, refers to a condition in which disagreement over a particular issue has occurred between two or more individuals or groups. Conflicts in Gamo may be inter-personal, inter- and intra-family, inter- and intra-clan, inter and intra-*dere*. Their causes lie in the economic, political and social life of the people. Whether interpersonal or at the inter-group level, conflict is perceived as a group issue; and a conflict between individuals from two families, clans or *dere* can easily become a

4 The reason for the differences in the traditional political structure (but also some other aspects of life) of the *dereta* is that the Gamo *dereta* used to be relatively autonomous.

5 Wondifraw is a native Gamo from Dorze village and an experienced researcher in the Gamo Gofa Zone Culture and Tourism Department. He was field assistant in the research project entitled 'Shared Values of the Gamo, Gofa, Gidiccho, Zayse and Oyda ethnic groups' in 2015–2016.

conflict between the respective groups. Less serious crimes can be settled through mediation and compensation payments, after which social peace is re-established between conflicting parties. Homicide cases within Gamo[6] are handled differently, as killing someone from the same ethnic group is believed to lead to a state of pollution for the perpetrator that has the potential to affect the well-being, health and fertility of both humans and animals belonging to his family and clan. Being *gome* (polluted) is also believed to affect the natural order. As such, it can cause drought, disease and, therefore, harm to the whole community. Thus, the homicide of a Gamo by another Gamo must be followed by ritual purification of the slayer. The procedure for handling intra-*dere* homicide is slightly different to that used for inter-*dere* homicide.

Intra-dere homicide

In the past, when homicide occurred within one *dere*, the slayer reported the case to his/her family and then took refuge in the *kawo gadho* (residence of the *kawo*), seeking protection from the deceased person's family, who might come for revenge. Not only the slayer but also his relatives would take refuge in another place and stay in exile until the families had been reconciled. Nowadays, once the slayer's family have reported a case to *maga*, the perpetrator is kept in the police station rather than in the *kawo gadho*. Then the reconciliation process between the two families is initiated through the *maga*.

In consultation with the *kawo*, the *maga* identifies the elders of the community (*dere cima*) with whom he will progress the reconciliation ritual. With the selected elders, he then travels to the residence of the deceased person's family, where they explain that the crime constitutes a violation of the customary law (*dere woga*) and, as such, is an unacceptable act. They also condemn the homicide as *gome*. Further, they outline the position of the slayer, his family and clan, who regret what has happened, feel guilty and wish to reconcile. It is common for the family of the deceased to initially reject the request to forgive the killer. However, the social norm obliges them to accept in the end. As Solomon, a retired teacher from Kamba town stated, failing to accept the *maga's* request to forgive the family of the slayer potentially brings *gome* to the family members of the deceased person, so they eventually accept.

Once the family of the deceased has agreed to reconcile, the ritual of purification and re-integration of the slayer's family and clan into the society is carried out on the *dubusha* ('public meeting place'). After this, they can return to their houses

6 This applies only when a Gamo kills a fellow Gamo; killing a member of a group considered an enemy turns the killer into a local hero and brings fertility to him.

and continue their lives as before. After finishing his time in prison, the slayer himself can never return to his *dere* and has to settle elsewhere.

Inter-*dere* homicide

Adala, the *ogade* of Balta *dere*, explained that when homicide occurs between two *dere*, the case is handled by the *ogade* through *ayidama*, a customary mechanism for resolving conflicts between the different Gamo communities. *Ayidama* is carried out in special places, also called *ayidama*, which are located at the boundary between two adjacent *dere*. These places exist at every corner of each *dere* so that local people do not have to travel far.[7]

The reconciliation process is initiated by the *ogade* of the slayer's *dere*. He rubs his body with mud and ashes before he travels to the *ayidama*, thereby expressing that a particular group in his community (i.e. the culprit and his entire family and clan) is impure. He walks on his knees to show that someone from his group has done wrong and therefore cannot stand upright and be equal with those who are free of wrongdoing. Standing on the *ayidama* he shouts, 'I made a mistake, I killed a person, I am dirty, please forgive me!' until his counterpart from the deceased person's side approaches him. The *ogade* from the deceased person's side cannot refuse to meet the other *ogade*, as it is believed that this would turn him *gome*. Upon his arrival, he is received by the *ogade* from the slayer's *dere*. While on the *ayidama*, they discuss the issue with each other and agree on a date for resolving the case. Once back home, the *ogade* from the *dere* of the deceased person informs his community about his counterpart's request and convinces them to accept. On the agreed date he takes them to the *ayidama*, where they meet the other *ogade* and the slayer's family. From the first contact between the two *ogade* until the re-integration of the slayer into the community, all the steps in the process of resolving inter-*dere* killing cases take place on the *ayidama*.

When the purifying ritual is performed, a member of the *maakka* clan – which has spiritual power to purify wrongdoers – spears the abdomen of a live sheep. When the chyme comes out, the clan head of the slayer is ordered to touch it with his foot. While approaching the chyme, he must hide himself from the public gathered to attend the peace-making ceremony.[8] Then the clan head of the deceased

---

7 There are five *ayidama* places at the borders of Balta *dere*: Mucalo (between Bonke and Balta), Eshata (between Kamba and Balta), Maazee (Sorba and Balta *dere*), Gongolo (Balta and Kole) and Qeqello (Haringa and Balta).

8 This man should not expose himself to the general public before the ritual is accomplished. If he is seen, he might be killed by the family of the deceased person out of revenge. If he or any relative of the slayer are killed before the clan head has touched the chyme of the speared sheep, the ritual ends immediately as it is believed that both families have thus equally harmed each other and blood has been compensated with blood.

person is told to touch the chyme, but he does not have to hide himself from the public.

After this, the *maakka* cleanses the family and the clan of the slayer by using *ercho*, a kind of grass, to purify the wrongdoers and their relatives from *gome*. Finally, compensation (*susaa qantso*) – currently about 150 ETB – is given to the relatives of the victim for the spilling of his blood. The family of the slayer do not hand the compensation payment directly to the relatives of the victim; both families are instead represented by their respective *ogade*. While handing over the compensation, the *ogade* of the slayer walks on his knees, kissing the ground until the money has been accepted by the *ogade* of the deceased person. This ritual cleansing is crucial for re-establishing peace and thereby allowing normal social interaction between the families of the slayer and the deceased. It symbolizes the accomplishment of the resolution and is still performed today; although, while traditionally the slayer had to hide somewhere until the process was over, today it is done while he is in police custody or prison.

Prevalence of government institutions in the study area

Administratively, Ethiopia is divided into nine regional states and two city administrations. The regional states are sub-divided into zones, districts (*woreda*), and *kebeles* (smallest administrative unit) in order to decentralize power to the grass roots level as specified in the 1995 FDRE constitution (FDRE 1995).

As noted earlier, Balta *dere* is located in Kamba district in Gamo Gofa Zone. In Kamba district, there are a number of government institutions, including offices for the police, women and children's affairs, education, health, social affairs, agriculture and rural development, culture and tourism, and the court. A number of schools, police stations and posts, a court, health centres and posts have been established under these different offices in order to ensure that their services are accessible to the communities. Over time, the traditional geo-political administration of the Gamo highlands has undergone some significant changes. Accordingly, the former Balta *dere* was restructured and now consists of nine *kebeles* in the current administrative structure of Kamba district. However, as the local people continue calling it Balta *dere*,[9] I have decided to use this name throughout this chapter to refer to all nine *kebeles*.

9 In most cases, but not necessarily all, the *dere* are bigger than the *kebele*. For instance, like Balta *dere*, which consists of nine *kebeles*, Dorze *dere* consists of thirteen *kebeles*.

Several different government agencies operate at the *kebele* level in Balta *dere*, including the *kebele* administration, the *kebele* social court,[10] the *kebele* militia, and schools, a health centre and police stations have been established to serve the local communities. These agencies are headed by various personnel, such as the *kebele* chief, the social court committee, local militia, development agent workers, teachers, nurses and policemen. The majority of them are from Balta and only a few are from other *dereta* in Kamba district or other parts of the Gamo highlands. Specifically, the chairman of the *kebele*, local militia, social court workers, teachers, nurses, development agent workers and the policemen are from the Gamo ethnic group. As one informant stated, the duties of these personnel and institutions are highly integrated. As an example he mentioned that the school principal participates in *kebele* administration affairs in the belief that he should participate in the affairs of the community in which the school is established.

Cooperation between government and customary institutions in handling homicide

In collaboration with traditional leaders and elders, state institutions at different levels engage directly or indirectly in conflict resolution for crimes ranging from the minor to the serious, including homicide. As mentioned above, customary institutions have continued to exist side by side with government institutions. As I was informed by several policemen in Kamba and during interviews with local authorities in Arba Minch, state institutions need to cooperate with customary institutions and vice versa to resolve certain conflicts. In the following, the factors that make their cooperation necessary as well as the areas in which they support each other will be described in more detail.

Factors contributing to cooperation

(i) Preference for customary mechanisms

As is the case in many other places in Ethiopia (Gebre *et al.* 2011, 2012; Pankhurst and Getachew 2008), customary conflict resolution mechanisms in Gamo continue to be preferred over state institutions by the local population. The accessibility, restorative power and participatory nature of the Gamo people's customary in-

10 The social courts can be categorized as what *Ayke and Mekonnen* (2011:201–215) *call* 'semi-formal institutions', that is, institutions that have both formal and informal features. They seem formal since they are established by proclamation, but look informal since the so-called 'judges' are untrained and receive no salary.

stitutions, as well as the transparency of their processes and impartiality of the decisions made, all work to make them preferable to state institutions.

The restorative effect and potential to bring sustainable peace is achieved through the ritual of purification and reconciliation. My informants emphasized that the families of the slayer and deceased family can engage in the same social arena after the ritual: members of the two families can intermarry and attend the same market without any fear, and the family of the slayer can also freely travel in the *dere* of the deceased person.

The participatory nature of customary conflict resolution lies in the fact that, for example in the context of homicide, all family members from both sides take part in the reconciliation process. As crime itself is perceived at the collective level, its resolution requires the participation of all family and clan members, who are represented by their respective clan heads.

The transparency and impartiality of the customary institutions stems from the fact that, throughout the whole process of reconciliation, the discussions are carried out in public places, where every witness presents their evidence in the presence of the public. Both victim and perpetrator are given an equal chance to talk about the case. Nothing is hidden from the public on this stage, and this forces the traditional leaders and elders to be impartial. As both sides receive the decision after they have contributed to the discussion, it is felt that there is no winner and loser.

Finally, when compared to the state institutions, customary institutions are more easily accessible to local communities. Travelling to and staying in towns in order to access a state court is costly, while customary reconciliation takes place locally, on either the *dubusha* or *ayidama*.

State agents have duly recognized the local preference for customary law and have also noted that it is difficult to restore peace and ensure stability in the area if customary institutions are excluded. Understanding how much the customary institutions are integrated into the local culture and recognizing the importance of their social capital in peace-building processes, the state institutions collaborate with customary institutions in the resolution of conflict in general and homicide in particular.

(ii) Shared interest in resolving cases of homicide

Both state and customary institutions perceive the act of homicide as the violation of a norm. Views expressed by local elders and policemen revealed that neither the local culture among the Gamo nor state law tolerate homicide. As described above, among the Gamo the act of homicide is a violation that results in ritual pollution (*gome*) and endangers the whole community if it remains unresolved. The government rates homicide as a violation of state law and a disturbance of social order. As a result, both legal systems sanction any act of homicide on the basis of certain normative orders, although the kinds of sanctions imposed are different.

The numerous interviews I conducted with local elders and state agents show that, whenever homicide cases are reported, both customary and state institutions intervene in order to settle them. Representing government institutions, the police and local militia arrest the slayer and keep him at the police station until the court comes to a final verdict. Representing customary institutions, local leaders and elders get involved and engage in reconciliation efforts with the aim of healing the relationship between the families of slayer and deceased. One policeman expressed how working with local agents enables the police to be more effective:

> We [the police] are from Gamo and we understand that crime is not limited to an individual perpetrator. It is a matter of the family and the clan of the criminal. Therefore, the reconciliation process should address the needs of all stakeholders. In this context, elders and traditional leaders approach the crime to reconcile the family and their clan. Quite the opposite, in our context [government institutions and state law], crime is perceived as a matter of an individual criminal and thus we have to punish the individual. (Summary of an interview, 26 October 2017)

As can be seen, while sharing an interest in avoiding and resolving conflicts related to homicide, in practice the state and community deal with different aspects of the same problem. While state law deals with the individual criminal, the Gamo elders are concerned with healing the social ill that was caused by the slayer at the group level. Thus, when a case goes to court, the duty to reconcile and purify the family and the clan of the slayer and the deceased rests on the shoulder of the local actors. As the problem is thereby addressed both at the individual and the communal level, ideally, the two systems complement each other.[11] Although, it cannot be denied that in practice there can be tension and conflict over areas of responsibility.

Areas of cooperation in handling homicide

(i) Handover of the slayer

The cooperation between customary and state institutions in the handling of homicide can be observed at different stages from investigation to the conviction of a wrongdoer, and has been confirmed during interviews with local elders and traditional leaders, as well as policemen in Kamba town, who particularly appreciate the efforts of the traditional leaders. Adala, the *ogade* of Balta *dere* explained how – under pressure from the government side – he and others made the handover of a slayer to the police a precondition for the initiation of the reconciliation process:

11 See Lauth (2000) who emphasizes this positive impact of legal pluralism.

> In the past, after killing a person most of the time a slayer took refuge in the home of the *kawo* to escape revenge from the deceased person's relatives. Nowadays, the government is taking care of slayers by hiding them in prison, which is a safe place for them. We are working with the police in facilitating the handover of the slayer, and do not initiate the reconciliation before this.
>
> The police and other members of the peace forum have told us repeatedly that we [the traditional leaders] are not allowed to initiate reconciliation for serious criminal cases like homicide before the transfer of the slayer to the police or local militia. As a result, in collaboration with a slayer's family, we identify his whereabouts and facilitate his handover to the police in case he hides in order to initiate the reconciliation process. (Summary of an interview with Adala, 20 February 2017)

The following case illustrates such cooperation in the handover of a criminal.

> Seo[12] was a young man from Balta and aged 25. He was sentenced to seventeen years in prison by the Arba Minch Area High Court for killing a man from a neighbouring Kamba *dere*. During my interview he told me that he had already served four years in prison office in Arba Minch. After killing the man, he had sent word to his parents through a messenger about what he had done, in order to prevent a possible revenge attack by the family of the deceased person. He spent the whole night in the nearby forest and oversaw the on-going situation from there. After understanding that the situation was difficult, he decided to take shelter with relatives in a remoter place. However, after a week the police came and took him to the police station. (Summary of an interview with Seo, 29 April 2017)

Seo's father recounted the hardship the family underwent until things were settled:

> I don't want to remember those horrible months [referring to the six months he had to take refuge with his family far from his residence]. I lost everything, houses, cattle, sheep, horses, grain, everything I had accumulated since my childhood within less than an hour. A week after the killing happened, two policemen and militiamen visited me with the Balta *ogade*. We discussed and agreed on how to initiate the reconciliation process, so I told them where my son was hiding. The next day I heard that the police had taken him to the police station. Immediately, the *ogade* initiated the reconciliation process. Thanks to everyone involved, the policemen, the militia, the *ogades* and the *dere cima*, we managed to get back to our residence after six months and pick up our life there from scratch. Once he is released from jail, my son will also join and live with us [referring to his family, community and clan], and nothing will happen against him since we have already finalized everything. (Summary of an interview, 25 October 2017)

---

12 Pseudonym

The case illustrates how local actors – that is, the *ogade* and the family of the slayer – collaborate with state agents in identifying the whereabouts of the slayer and thereby help prevent the post-homicide conflict escalating. It also shows the great social pressure put on the family, whose members are ostracized along with the slayer and forced to leave their home until reconciliation is over. Transferring the murderer to the state institution is not really a matter of choice for them but a duty, as it has become a precondition for the reconciliation process to begin.

(ii) Identification of the criminal

Identification of the slayer is another area in which state institutions depend on the cooperation of the local community. By Gamo custom, people meet to take an oath (*chako*) at the *kawo's* public meeting place (*kawo dubusha*) in order to identify a slayer. Assuming that he is at the assembly, the traditional leaders and religious experts (*demutha*) instruct and advise the slayer to disclose himself. Most of the time, as I was told by my informant Adala, slayers disclose themselves, fearing that they might be cursed if they hide their identity. If no one gets up to admit their guilt, the clan leaders and elders to go back home for a few days to consult their respective clan members before they resort to performing a public curse at the meeting place. If it comes to that, all the suspected individuals are presented in front of the public. They are again strongly advised to speak the truth. This time, if no one admits the wrongdoing, the elders sit down in two rows opposite each other while the religious specialist speaks as follows:

> Look at the God in the universe, look at the *dubusha* where we are sitting, carry the spear and cross in between the public body sitting covering their faces in two rows.

With this speech, the expert is saying that, while no person may have seen what the slayer did, God in the universe and the ground on which the slayer moves have seen what he did and will judge him for it. The suspects are then asked to walk between the two lines of seated elders; the assumption is that the innocent will do so, while the real slayer will fear to pass between them and throw himself to the ground, asking forgiveness to avoid being cursed by passing through knowing their guilt.

This traditional way of identifying a culprit is now being used by state officials, who attend the oath-taking ceremonies. Policemen, local militia and security personnel document such events with photos and video, assuming that they lead a suspect to speak the truth.

(iii) Preventing revenge and further escalation

As seen in the above case, the family of a deceased person will seek to avenge the killing of one of their number. Sometimes, if the situation allows, revenge attacks even happen during the reconciliation process. This inevitably leads to further escalation, so the police, local militia, local people and the mediators (*maga, ogade*) work together to prevent this. The policeman who led the taskforce in Seo's case said that he often worked with traditional leaders and other potential stakeholders in resolving serious criminal cases like homicide. As he recounted:

> It happened four years ago. I was assigned to lead the taskforce established to investigate and resolve the case. We had learned from the local people that the killing happened around 7 pm. After collecting necessary evidence from the crime scene, the body of the deceased person was sent to Addis Ababa for medical investigations.
> At about an hour after midnight, we received the information that there was a security problem in the village of the slayer, and that his family was being attacked. Together with local people, we managed to control the situation and forced the relatives of the deceased to return to their village. Then I ordered all of the policemen in the taskforce and the local militia to arrest the slayer, but we could not find him.
> After one week, four members of the taskforce together with the *ogade* contacted Seo's father in the remote village where he had hidden. We offered to help initiate the reconciliation process through the *ogade* if he would tell us where his son was hiding. He agreed and on the basis of his genuine information we were able to arrest the slayer. As promised, the reconciliation process was initiated soon after that.
> From the very beginning the police officers concerned attended every step of the reconciliation process with three missions: the first mission was to collect additional information about the reasons behind the killing from the discussions held by participants: whether it was intentional or not and how it was actually done. The second mission was to ensure that the reconciliation process was undertaken only for the purpose of restoring the social peace between the families of the slayer and the deceased, rather than to punish the slayer. The third mission was to protect the family of the slayer from an unexpected attack during the ritual of re-integration that would take place in the presence of both the slayer's and deceased person's family.
> The whole process took more than six months until the final reconciliation and re-integration ritual marked the completion of my mission of restoring peace and order. (Summary of an interview, 26 October 2017)

The police officer's account shows the direct cooperation between his office and the traditional leaders, who – in combining government pressure and the ritual power of the *ogade* – are able to enforce the handover of a slayer as well as the start of the reconciliation process. Their common interest here is the re-establishment of social peace between the two families/clans, as well as the prevention of revenge attacks that would result in further killing and destruction of property.

Summary and conclusion

As in many non-western societies, among the Balta community in the Gamo highlands, customary law continues to be practised alongside state law, even in cases of homicide. The findings of this study show that, despite certain contradictions in the values and practices underlying customary and state laws, their relationship displays complementary and cooperative elements when it comes to their application.

Looking specifically at the case of homicide, it was shown that the cooperation between customary and state laws is based on a common view that intra-ethnic homicide[13] is a crime and should be sanctioned. While homicide is an individual matter demanding the punishment of the murderer according to state law, it is locally viewed as a crime that affects the wider social networks of slayer and victim, which makes a ritual restoration of their relationship indispensable. Putting their resources together, state and local community cooperate in identifying, arresting, sanctioning and protecting the slayer, and in preventing further escalation.

The cases shows that, at the local level, the resources of both legal systems can be used productively and in the interests of all the parties involved if enough space is given for flexibility, mutual understanding and tolerance of difference.

References

ABELES, Marc, 1981 "In search of the monarch: Introduction of the state among the Gamo Ethiopia", in: Donald Crummey and Charles Cameron Stewart (eds.) *Modes of production in Africa: The precolonial era*, 35–75. Beverly Hills, London: Sage

ALEMAYU Fentaw, 2004 *Legal pluralism in light of the federal and state constitutions of Ethiopia: A critical appraisal*. Addis Ababa: Addis Ababa University (MA Thesis)

ARTHUR, John W., 2013 "Transforming clay: Gamo caste, gender, and pottery of southwestern Ethiopia", *African Study Monographs*, Suppl. 46:5–25

AYALEW Getachew, 2012 *Customary laws in Ethiopia: A need for better recognition? A women's rights perspective*. Copenhagen: The Danish Institute for Human Rights

AYKE Asfaw and Mekonnen Feleke, 2008 "Customary dispute resolution in the SNNPRS: The case of Sidama", in: Alula Pankhurst and Getachew Assefa (eds.) *Grass-roots justice in Ethiopia*, 201–215. Addis Ababa: Centre Français d'Études Éthiopiennes

BOSHA Bombe, 2013 *Slavery in Gamo Highlands, Ethiopia*. Saarbrücken: Lambert Academic Publishing

13 Inter-ethnic homicide is entirely handled by state institutions.

BUREAU, Jacques, 1978 "Étude diachronique de deux titres Gamo (A diachronic survey of two Gamo titles)", *Cahiers d'Études Africaines*: 279–291.

2012 *The Gamo of Ethiopia: A study of their political system*. (translated from French by Dominique Lussier). Oxford: Bardwell

DEJENE Gemechu, 2002 *Some aspects of conflict and conflict resolution among the Waliso Oromo of eastern Macca, with particular emphasis on the Guma*. Addis Ababa: Addis Ababa University (MA Thesis)

DONOVAN, Dolores and Getachew Assefa, 2003 "Homicide in Ethiopia: Human rights, federalism and legal pluralism", *The American Journal of Comparative Law* 51 (3):505–552

ESAYAS Awash, 2015 *Indigenous conflict resolution institutions: A study among the Gofa people of the Demba Gofa district, SNNPR*. Addis Ababa: Addis Ababa University (MA Thesis)

FEDERAL DEMOCRATIC REPUBLIC OF ETHIOPIA (FDRE), 1995 *The Federal Democratic Republic of Ethiopia Constitution*. Addis Ababa: FDRE

FREEMAN, Dena and Alula PANKHURST (eds.), 2001 *Living on the edge: Marginalized minorities of craft-workers and hunters in southern Ethiopia*. Addis Ababa, Addis Ababa University

FREEMAN, Dena, 1999 *Transforming traditions: The dynamics of cultural variation in the Gamo*. London: London School of Economic (PhD thesis)

2004 *Initiating change in highland Ethiopia: Causes and consequences of cultural transformation*. Cambridge: Cambridge University Press

GAMO GOFA ZONE CULTURE AND INFORMATION DEPARTMENT, 2004 E.C. *The history of Gamo Gofa peoples up to 1974*. Addis Ababa: Bole Printing Enterprise

GEBRE Yntiso, FEKADE Azeze, ASSEFA Fisseha (eds.), 2011 *Customary dispute resolution mechanisms in Ethiopia*, Vol.1. Addis Ababa: The Ethiopian Arbitration and Conciliation Center

2012 *Customary dispute resolution in Ethiopia*, Vol 2. Addis Ababa: The Ethiopian Arbitration and Conciliation Center

GEBREYOHANHNES Tadla, 1993 E.C. *Gamoththo-Amharic middle dictionary*. Addis Ababa: Bole Printing Press

GETANEH Mehari, 2006 *The role of women in the household economy: The Dorze case*. Addis Ababa: Addis Ababa University (MA Thesis)

2014 *Betwixt and between? Culture and women's rights in the context of multiple legal and institutional settings: The Dorze case, south-western Ethiopia*. Addis Ababa: Addis Ababa University (PhD Dissertation)

GONFA Ebsa, 2014 *Customary conflict resolution among the Haro Limmu Oromo of northwest Wallaga: The case of the qaalluu institution*. Addis Ababa: Addis Ababa University (MA Thesis)

MAHE Bodda, 2013 *Promoting culture for local development in the Gamo highlands: The case of Chencha Woreda in Gamo Gofa Zone*. Addis Ababa: Ethiopian Civil Service University (MA Thesis)

MANN, Kristin and ROBERTS, Richard (eds.), 1991 *Law in colonial Africa: Social history of Africa*. London: Currey

OLMSTEAD, Judith, 1975 "Agricultural land and social stratification in the Gamo highlands of southern Ethiopia", in: Harold Marcus (ed.) *Proceedings of the first US conference on southern Ethiopian Studies, Michigan*. East Lansing: African Studies Centre

PANKHURST, Alula and GETACHEW Assefa (eds.), 2008 *Grass-roots justice in Ethiopia*. Addis Ababa: Centre Français d'Études Éthiopiennes

SNNPR COUNCIL OF NAITONALITIES, 2008 E.C *Shared values of Gamo, Gofa, Oyida, Zayse and Gidicho nationalities of Gamo Gofa Zone*. Addis Ababa: Birana Printing Press

WEEDMAN, Kathryn, 2013 "Material entanglements: Gender, ritual and politics among the Boroda of southern Ethiopia", *African Study Monographs*, suppl. 46:53–80

WONDIMU Gaga, 2010 Sociolinguistic facts about the Gamo area, South Ethiopia. Addis Ababa: Arccikl

WOODMAN, Gordon, 1996 "Legal pluralism and the search for justice", *Journal of African* Law 40 (2):152–167

ZELALEM Zewdie, 2016 *Woga: An ethnographic study of customary law among the Gamo of Ethiopia*. Addis Ababa: Addis Ababa University (MA Thesis)

ZENEBE Beyene, 2014 *Challenges of Gamo traditional leadership in conflict resolution: The case of Bonke Woreda, southern Ethiopia*. Hawassa: Hawassa University (MA Thesis)

6. The interplay of customary and formal legal systems among the Tulama Oromo
Cooperation and competition

Melaku Abera

Introduction

Prior to their incorporation into the modern Ethiopian state in the 1870s and 1880s, the Oromo had their own customary institutions that dealt with disputes under the framework of the *gadaa* age and generation system. Following the conquest by Menelik II at the end of the 19th century, the state law and other normative orders were introduced into the Oromo land, which gave rise to plural legal settings for dispute settlement (Mamo 2006). The aim of this paper is to examine the interplay between customary and formal legal systems in dispute settlement at the district and *kebele* levels in Jidda district, North Shewa, Oromia Regional State.[1]

There exist numerous studies in Ethiopia on customary law and conflict resolution, and some also tackle the question of how customary and formal law interact in dispute settlement.[2] However, most of these works have focused on the posi-

1 This paper is based mainly on a total of 12 months of ethnographic fieldwork conducted from May 2014 to April 2016 for my PhD dissertation presented to the Department of Social Anthropology, Addis Ababa University, in December 2017. It was conducted in Jidda district of North Shewa Zone, Oromia Regional State. Data was collected through participant observation of customary dispute settlement and the formal law. Interviews and FGDs were also held with elders, women, youth, *kebele* officials and legal practitioners of the formal law. Besides, case studies were employed to reveal the cooperative and problematic aspects of the relationships between the two legal systems. Furthermore, statistical reports of dispute cases found in the formal courts and legal documents were consulted to augment primary methods of data collection. For ethical reasons, the privacy of informants was kept anonymous. I am thankful to my advisors, Prof. Gebre Yntiso and Dr. Assefa Tolera, for their helpful comments and advice during my PhD project. My thanks also go to Addis Ababa University, German Academic Exchange Service (DAAD) and Association of African Universities (AAU) for their financial support of the fieldwork.

2 See, for example, Girma (2009), Mamo (2006), Melaku (2009), Meron (2010), Negash (2013), Yihunbelay (2010), almost all chapter contributors in Gebre *et al.* (2011, 2012); cases studies in Pankhurst and Getachew (2008), and Tarekegn and Hannah (2008).

tive aspects of the relationships between the two legal systems while studies on the competitive and problematic aspects are scarcer, especially in Oromo studies. As such, the present study is in line with recommendations of previous scholars who suggested a further investigation on the subject and appeal for a careful study of an interface between the customary mechanisms of dispute resolution and the formal structure (Pankhurst and Getachew 2008:271, Gebre *et al.* 2011:471). The present paper, therefore, aims at filling this gap about the state of legal pluralism in Ethiopia, specifically in Oromia.

The focus is on the time since 1991 because it is only after the end of the Derg regime that legal pluralism was officially recognized both in the 1995 Ethiopian Constitution and in the 2001 Revised Constitution of Oromia.[3] Since then, disputants can choose whether to appeal to a customary or a formal court in matters of concerning family or personal law while other cases still have to be handled by the state law. The recognition of legal pluralism was further extended by the 2004 Revised Criminal Code of Ethiopia, which seems to leave the choice to the disputants (mainly to the victims) to take crimes upon complaint to the forum of their own choice. However, serious civil and criminal cases continue to be under the exclusive jurisdiction of the formal law. In practice, as will be illustrated in this paper, customary law settles disputes covering a wider range of issues in addition to those stipulated in the constitutions and the Criminal Code.

This paper is divided into five sections. This introductory section briefly provides issues that need further research and the time of the analysis. Section two discusses the Tulama Oromo and their socio-political organization with particular focus on Jidda district, the study area. On the basis of what has been discovered in the fieldwork, section three and four deal with, in detail, the interplay between customary and formal legal systems among the Tulama Oromo of the study area. Section three examines the cooperation between customary and formal legal systems in dispute settlement while section four looks at the problematic areas and competition between the two. Finally, the paper summarizes and concludes with suggestions to improve the working relationships between customary and formal legal systems.

3 As a result of the federal system of the government in place in Ethiopia since 1995, the regional governments established their own constitutions in line with Art. 52(2) of the 1995 Ethiopian Constitution. Based on this, the Oromia Regional State established its own constitution in 1995, which was later revised in 2001.

The Tulama Oromo

The Oromo people are one of the largest ethnic groups in Eastern Africa (Asmarom 1973), constituting nearly 34.5% (a little over 25 million) of the Ethiopian population in 2007 (CSA 2008). Most of them reside in the Oromia National Regional State. The Oromia region is one of the nine regional states constituting the Federal Democratic Republic of Ethiopia. It is bordered with all the regions except Tigray. It is also the largest of all the regions in Ethiopia in terms of population and land size. Currently, the region is divided into 20 administrative zones, with North Shewa being one of them. Jidda, the study area, is one of the thirteen districts in North Shewa zone (see figure 1 below).

The Oromo are divided into two major groups: the Borana (senior) and the Barentu (junior) (Gada 1988:8). The descendants of these two main groups later formed major Oromo clans and sub-clans. The Borana section of the Oromo is divided into three main branches, namely the Southern Borana, the Guji and the Macha Tulama (Mohammed 1990:18). The settlement of the Tulama Oromo largely occupies the Shewan plateau extending over vast areas between Lake Zeway in the south and Wollo in the north, Macha lands in the west and the territory of Karayu in the east (Alemayehu *et al.* 2006:137–145). Thus, the Tulama Oromo who occupy the present day Jidda district are part of the Borana Oromo group.

Jidda district, the study area, is far from the main highway road connecting Addis Ababa with Bahir Dar and Dessie towns. Its administrative seat, Sirti, is located at about 110 km from Addis Ababa and 70 km from Fiche, the administrative capital of North Shewa zone of Oromia Region. The town is where the formal legal institutions like the district police, public prosecutor and court are found. In 2007, the total population of Jidda district was 53,658 with the overwhelming majority of the inhabitants being the followers of Orthodox Christianity (CSA 2008).[4] Almost all inhabitants of the district are Oromo and speak *Afaan* Oromo as their first language. According to the Jidda Agriculture office, the district is located at a high altitude ranging from 2600–3500 meter above sea level. Topographically, it is largely plain with some plateaus, mountains, valleys and rugged terrains. The same office disclosed that Jidda from North Shewa is the leading district in animal population such as cattle, sheep, horses, donkeys, and mules. Because of its altitude

4 Although the central statistics show that the majority of the Oromo of the area claim to be followers of Orthodox Christianity, most of them actually mix it with their indigenous faith, *waaqeffannaa*. In their everyday social life, they make oaths in the name of their traditional belief systems, calling upon the *qaalluu* instead of Christian Orthodox saints and the Ark of the Covenant (*tabot*). When they face serious difficulties such as lack of rain and natural disaster, they often go to their indigenous ritual sites (rivers and hills) to slaughter a bull, pray and make a pleading (*isgoota*).

and climate, wheat, barley, *teff*, beans, peas, and lentils are important crops grown in Jidda.

Figure 1: Map of Jidda District (CSA 2008)

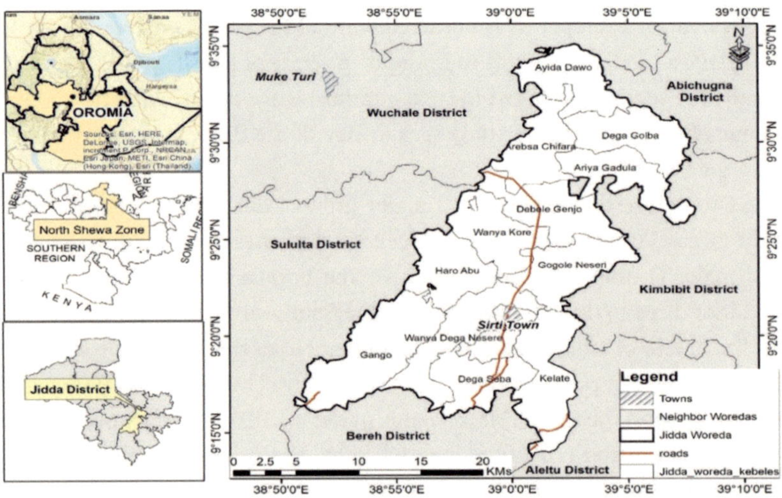

Social and political organization among the Tulama Oromo is structured and organized by their well-known age and generation system called *gadaa* (Blackhurst 1978, Knutsson 1967). Despite their inclusion into the Ethiopian nation-state, many Tulama groups have sustained the *gadaa* system, or at least elements of it, and activate it in religious, ritual social, economic and also legal contexts. In the study area (and among other Tulama groups), the *gadaa* system still survives though it is not strong as it was before. This paper confirms that the five class structure, the *gadaa* assembly, the ten *gadaa* grades and the eight-year *gadaa* period are features common to both the contemporary and the past systems of the Tulama. *Gadaa* symbols and some ritual practices such as the *foollee* institution (one of the stages in the *gadaa* grade) were recently reintroduced.

In the study area, there are two major customary legal institutions related to the *gadaa* system. The first is the *jaarsummaa*, which can be translated as the 'council of elders'. The most important task of the *jaarsummaa* is dispute settlement, besides other services.[5] The *jaarsummaa* is formed by males of different age groups, but it serves both sexes in the community. It is not a permanent council, but rather the

5 Elders play also important roles as go-betweens during marriage negotiations, and in times of drought, disease and other disasters.

elders meet on ad hoc basis whenever a certain dispute occurs. After achieving its mission of dispute settlement, the council is disbanded.

The *qaalluu*, often translated as 'ritual leader' as well as the religious institution, is another customary system involved in dispute settlement[6]. According to my observation, the *qaalluu* is divided into a court with three tiers. The first and the lowest level is the court run by the elders (*jaarsa*) of the institution. Most cases first appear before this court. Then, if disputants are not satisfied with the decision of this court, they can appeal to the second level court, which includes the elders and the *qaalluu* himself. If one of the disputed parties is not satisfied with the judgment of this court, he/she can appeal to the last and the highest level for ritual judgment. This third level court is sacred and run by the *qaalluu*, who is possessed by a spirit. The verdicts of the *qaalluu* are mostly accepted since he is believed to have the spiritual power to cause misfortune to the one that rejects his reconciliation. Compared to the *qaalluu* located in other districts of North Shewa, its role in dispute settlement is very limited in Jidda. Besides, its interaction and cooperation with the formal legal institutions within the context of dispute settlement are rather rare in the area.

Therefore, this study looks specifically at the council of elders (*jaarsummaa*), which is currently the main local forum in dealing with a variety of disputes ranging from civil to criminal matters. Besides, the council of elders frequently interacts with the formal legal system in the study area. The formal legal institutions[7] this study deals with include the district court,[8] the police and the public prosecutor that are located in Sirti town, the social courts[9] and the *kebele* administration councils[10] that exist in all villages (*kebeles*) of the study area. Thematically, the focus of

6 The *qaalluu* believes to be the intermediary between the people and supernatural power called *Waaqa*. He exercises considerable influence in the economic, political and social life of the Oromo people, as he is responsible for their spiritual well-being. The *qaalluu* institutions are centers of healing, worshipping and administration. They are also the place where children are given Oromo names.

7 District Administration, District Administration and Security, District Women and Children Affairs, District Land Administration and Environmental Protection are other offices that exist in Sirti town and that deal with disputes in the area.

8 The formal courts have original jurisdictions over civil cases (excluding issues related to the land boundary) which values exceed 1.500 ETB, as well as overall criminal cases and appeals coming from *kebele* social courts and *kebele* administration councils.

9 The social courts are run by the local judges, who are not legally trained and salaried but authorized by the Ethiopian law to provide justice to the local people free of charge. The court has jurisdiction over civil disputes relating to property claims and money, which values do not exceed 1.500 ETB (roughly 55.50 dollars) (see the 2001 Constitution of Oromia and 2007 Oromia Social Court Proclamation).

10 The *kebele* administration council together with elders has the original jurisdiction over land boundary disputes as stated in the 2007 Oromia Land Proclamation.

the analysis is both civil and criminal aspects of disputes, ranging from minor civil cases to homicide. In the following sections, the cooperative as well as the problematic and competitive aspects of the relationships between *jaarsummaa* and the formal legal system will be discussed.

Cooperation between customary and formal legal systems

This section will show the cooperative areas in the relationships between customary and formal legal systems including case transfer and notification of the decision of the transferred cases of settlement to one another's jurisdiction, joint dispute settlement, the elders' double role in both legal systems and collaboration in de-escalation of disputes and crime prevention. For this, court statistics and selected cases are used to illustrate the areas of the cooperation between the two legal systems.

Case transfer and notification of the transferred cases

One of the cooperative aspects between the two legal systems is case transfer and notification of the decision of the transferred cases to one another. Though in principle case transfer from one legal forum to the others happens in both directions, most often the formal institutions (court, police and public prosecutor) transfer cases to the *jaarsummaa*. This occurs in different contexts: when the disputed parties invited elders or when the elders convince the disputants to move the case from the formal legal system to the *jaarsummaa* and when the formal legal system lets the disputants settle their disputes outside the courtroom, or when the formal legal system itself transfers the case to the elders (see also Desalegn Amsalu, this volume). Table 1 presents a summary of the total number of criminal cases over five years reported to the prosecution office, those taken to the formal court by the office, those referred to elders, and those dismissed due to various reasons.

Table 1: Criminal cases reported to district public prosecutor from 2010/11 to 2014/15 (Jidda District Public Prosecutor's Office, 2016)

Years					
	2010/11[a]	2011/12[b]	2012/13[c]	2013/14[d]	2014/15[e]
Total cases	366	1685	903	713	809
Cases taken to court	223	231	210	221	250
Transferred cases to elders	92	271	293	67	115
Interrupted cases[f]	51	1183	400	425	444

a: [11], b: [12], c: [13], d: [14], e: [15], f: [16]

As can be seen from Table 1, a considerable number of criminal cases that were reported to public prosecutor's office were withdrawn. One factor for the withdrawal of the cases was case transfer by the prosecution office to the *jaarsummaa*. It should be noted that while Art. 212 of the 2004 Revised Criminal Code of Ethiopia seems to leave the choice for the disputants (mainly to the victims) to take crimes upon complaint to the forum of their own choice, there is no article in the criminal code that permits the court or prosecutors to transfer upon complaint crimes to the customary institutions including *jaarsummaa*. This means that public prosecutors transfer criminal cases informally to the *jaarsummaa*, but actually without any legal basis. The following example shows how a criminal case can be transferred from the public prosecutor to the local elders.

Case 1: Beating
The plaintiff, who was struck on his head with a big stick and bled on 12 September 2015, accused two individuals: father (the first defendant) and son (the second defendant) and took the case before the police, bypassing the customary institutions. The case appeared before the office of the public prosecutor on 9 November 2015. A public prosecutor and a policeman asked both defendants about the matter. The first defendant admitted having beaten the plaintiff as he had suspected

11 July 1, 2002 to June 30, 2003 E.C.
12 July 1, 2003 to June 30, 2004 E.C.
13 July 1, 2004 to June 30, 2005 E.C
14 July 1, 2005 to June 2006 E.C.
15 July 1, 2006 to June 30, 2007 E.C.
16 Cases were interrupted due to lack of supporting evidence, the disappearance of the defendants or time lapse.

> him of having a sexual affair with his wife. The second defendant refused to accept the charge against him saying that he was not involved. The public prosecutor asked the disputants to choose between the court of law and the local elders to settle their dispute. The disputants agreed to settle their differences through customary procedures and selected six elders to look at the issue. Then, the office sent the disputants with a stamped letter and a list of elders to deal with the matter locally, urging elders to report the results of their endeavour back to the office. The first meeting of the elders on the matter was on 15 November 2015, a few days after the referral. The injured person refused to accept the reconciliation proposal of the elders and took back the case to the prosecution office. However, elders solicited by the first defendant intervened. The public prosecutor agreed to withdraw and return the case to the *jaarsummaa*. In their second meeting on 10 February 2016, the same elders settled the issue and the plaintiff was compensated with 2,000 ETB (125 dollars) for his injury. He was also restricted from getting close to the house of the defendants. It was further agreed that in case one or both of the parties violate the agreement (*waligalte*) and take back the case to the court, the violator would have to pay 500 ETB (roughly 31 dollars) as a fine for the government and another 500 ETB (31 dollars) to the local saving association (*iddir*). A written agreement was made and a copy of reconciliation was sent to the office of the public prosecutor.

Case transfer and notification of the decision of transferred cases of settlement to one another's jurisdiction is one aspect of the cooperative relationship between the two systems. The above-mentioned case and those statistics shown in Table 1 demonstrate that in Jidda people use both legal forums: taking their disputes from one forum to another. The interviews made with several people in the study area showed that people take their cases to the formal law in order to give weight to their cases before the elders. Subsequently, solicited elders approach the plaintiffs to take the case out of the court of law and to settle through customary law.

Joint dispute settlement

The other area of interaction observable between *jaarsummaa* and the formal legal institutions in the area is joint dispute settlement. In Oromia Land Proclamation No. 130/2007, joint dispute settlement is described: when land dispute case arises, disputants should first submit their application to the local *kebele* administration council. Officials of the *kebele* then urge the disputants to elect the arbitral elders. A chairman of the elders is elected by the disputing parties or by the arbitral elders. If they cannot agree, a local *kebele* administrator shall assign the chairperson. One representative from the *kebele* administration council will be involved in the elders' meeting to record the result of the reconciliation. Once the case has been resolved, the result has to be documented and then given to the *kebele* administration by the elders for registration. The administration also gives a sealed copy to both disputed parties. Anyone dissatisfied with the result can submit his/her complaint to the district court (see Proclamation No. 130/2007, Art.16, No.1). This kind of joint dispute settlement exists also for other issues, not only for land disputes, as the following case of a dispute over water use illustrates.

> Case 2: Dispute over water use
> One of the few group disputes over resource I encountered during my field stay was associated with the usage of water from Aleltu River[17] for irrigation and watering of animals in February 2015. The dispute involved seven *kebeles* of Jidda district located along the river and thus a large group of people. The cause was over the share of the water as the flow of the river significantly decreases every year during the dry season in January, February, and March. At the same time, compared to the previous years, there was no rainfall during the season. Therefore, the peasants and *kebeles* living at the lower stream competed over the water with those living further upstream, accusing them of arresting the flow of the water.
> First, the Jidda elders tried to settle the matter. But, when they did not succeed, the case was taken to the district court by a public prosecutor. The court was, however, also not able to settle the water issue since it involved many *kebeles* located along the river. When the dispute approached the level of physical fighting with clubs and rifles, the court transferred the case to the district administration and the security office, recommending it to be settled together with the elders.
> Then, officials from the district administration and the security office together met with some respected elders and discussed the issue. I attended their final meeting held on the bank of the disputed river on 16 February 2015. After a long discussion, they were able to avoid the problem before it turned into violence. All parties in dispute agreed to equally share the water of the Aleltu River and elected a committee, which was assigned to supervise the activities and prevent future disagreements. The reconciliation result was positive. Since then, I did not hear any dispute related to the share of the water of the Aleltu River.

The major point we can draw from this case of joint dispute settlement is that officials from the state system involve local elders when they face serious problems to resolve a conflict, using them as an additional strategy to establish or keep peace. As such, joint dispute settlement is another example of positive interaction and cooperation between the local elders and the state system in the area.

17 Aleltu River is one of the tributaries of Abay (Blue Nile) that flows throughout the year. It originates from Mount Baraki located in Bereh district, south of Jidda.

The elders' double role

When a case is handled in *jaarsummaa* in the study area, many actors are involved, including elders, the disputants and their allies, guarantors, witnesses and community observers. Of all these, elders are the main actors. As will be shown in this subchapter, they may also take over important roles in the state systems.

Below the district level, there are three state-based institutions that deal with disputes at the *kebele*, the lowest administrative level in the area. These include the social court, community policing committee and the *kebele* administration council. Although the types of disputes, which found their way into these systems are not many, the role of elders is important here. The following case reveals how the elders can work in both systems in the capacity of dispute settlers.

Case 3: Dispute over grazing land

On Sunday, 24 January 2016, I attended a hearing of the social court at Siba Sirti *kebele*. It was related to civil disputes that fell under its mandate. One case was related to grazing land. An elderly couple, e.g. a husband of more than 70 years and his wife of around 65 years accused three men (one was a *kebele* official) whose cattle had destroyed their grazing land. In line with the 2007 Social Court Proclamation No. 128,[18] the judges of the court recommended the disputants to settle the matter through the *jaarsummaa*. All agreed and the parties in dispute selected five elders of their own choice who were in the *kebele* compound at the time of the hearing for their own matter. One of the judges of the social court himself became a member of the ad-hoc council of elders with the consent of the parties in dispute.

On the same day, the appointed elders met to discuss the matter. The meeting was held inside the compound of *kebele* administration council and began at 11 am. The first presenter of the case was the aggrieved couple. In her statement, the wife presented the case by accusing the three men of deliberately grazing their cattle on their land. The defendants responded to the case one after the other, all admitting that their cattle had accidentally entered the grazing land and asking for an apology. Following this, the elders fixed the amount of compensation to be paid by the defendants to the plaintiffs. Later on, however, they requested the couple not to accept it, saying, "For the sake of God (*Waqqaf jeedhi*), for the sake of earth (*lafaaf jeedhi*) and for the sake of elders (*jaarsaf jeedhi*), please not take the compensation!" The couple agreed to forgo the compensation, warning the defendants to not let their cattle enter the grazing field again, as otherwise, they would take the

18 Art. 24 and 34 of the proclamation say that the *kebele* court shall first push parties to solve their dispute through arbitration. If this is not possible, the court shall hear witnesses from both sides and decide the case accordingly. Otherwise, decisions that do not follow these procedures shall be null and void.

case back to the social court. With this, the meeting ended quickly with a mutual agreement at 12:30 pm.

In this case, one elder is acting in both systems in different capacities: being a judge at the social court and also became a member of the council of elders. It was he who had strongly pushed the disputing parties to settle their difference outside the social courtroom. As the member of the council of elders, his influence was also strong in convincing the disputants to come to the reconciliation. Playing such a double role in both legal systems is common in the area, as often local elders are chosen based on their experiences, age, knowledge, and impartiality to serve the two institutions at the same time. They work at the interface between the systems.

This case is also another example of case transfer from the social court to the elders. In this case, judges in the social court initiated the transfer and told the disputants to choose the elders. This practice, as discussed in the previous section, is common also in the area.

Cooperation in de-escalation of disputes and crime prevention

Both customary and state systems work in crime prevention and cooperate when crimes occur to avoid escalation, sometimes even in the context of serious crimes. The state law prescribes that elders report crimes in their locality to the community police centre or the police station, as such cases have to be dealt with in the court. The case of a girl's abduction, which led to her death demonstrates the cooperation between customary and formal legal systems.

Case 4: Abduction and related death
A young man with a disability was looking for a spouse. He had been without a partner while his age mates were already married. People suspect that he was annoyed that he had remained a bachelor for so long, probably due to his disability. One day, the boy observed a girl in a neighbouring village, while he was visiting his relatives. He decided to take her as his wife and told his relatives about his wish. His relatives tried to get the consent of the girl's family, but the latter rejected the marriage proposal. When his request was turned down, the boy resorted to abduction.

The teenage girl, by then 13 years old, was abducted on 11 April 2015 in Dega Golba *kebele*, some 30 km from Sirti town where the district police are located. The perpetrator chose a day when most local militias were in Sirti town for a training related to security issues. Taking the advantage of their absence, the boy secretly contacted five friends to help him. The men had the information that the girl had left home for the local mill. They waited for the girl to return home at 2 pm and when she came, they beat her with a stick, urging her to move when she resisted. The girl's family immediately heard about the abduction and reacted with anger.

> Together with relatives and neighbours, they followed the abductors who had taken refuge in one of their relative's houses. The girl's relatives surrounded the house, some threw stones and others shouted at the abductors. When the abductors noticed that they were being surrounded, they bolted the door from within, put a cloth in the mouth of the girl and sat on her head and face. Soon after, she died of suffocation.
>
> When the elders[19] who had also come to prevent an escalation of the dispute heard the rumour of the girl's death, they immediately called the police from Sirti town. Upon the arrival of the police and the local militia, together with the elders, they convinced the girl's relatives to leave, promising them to bring the abductors to the court of law. The parents learned about the death of their daughter only, after the police had taken the corpse and the criminals to Sirti town. People in Jidda and neighbouring districts were horrified by the girl's gruesome death.
>
> The following days, the police together with officials from the district administration, security and other offices visited Dega Golba, attended girl's funeral ceremony and held discussions with elders and relatives from the killers' and victim's families. Relatives of the killers also made cultural pleadings (*isgoota*)[20] to the family of the deceased on a nearby plateau. Their objective was to prevent revenge upon them by the deceased's sides and plead for peace talks. It was also aimed at future reconciliation upon the release of the criminals from the state prison. One year later, the abductor and his accomplices were formally prosecuted, found guilty and sentenced each to 14 years in jail by the High Court in Fiche for abduction and murder.

This case shows how the elders cooperate with the police when serious crimes occur. First, the elders reported the case to the police. They also prevented further escalation by closely working with the police and district officials to cool down the situation in the following days in order to prevent any revenge by the family of the victim on the relatives of the abductors. The interview with the police who investigated the case and FGD with the police revealed that had it not been for the elders' involvement, things would have gone in the wrong direction and further escalated.

19 Some of these elders are members of community policing committee.

20 When homicide happens deliberately or accidentally, the first step in Tulama Oromo culture is organizing the pleading ceremony by which the side of the killer plea for reconciliation. It lasts for several days until the family of the deceased shows a sign of their readiness for peace talks.

Problematic areas and competition

While the previous section showed various areas of cooperation, this section look at problems and competition between customary and formal legal systems and dispute settlement mechanisms focusing on five major areas though not exclusive ones: mutual undermining, confusion and dispute over jurisdiction, double jeopardy, lack of mutual trust and failure of both systems to settle certain disputes. Selected cases are used to illustrate the issue.

Mutual undermining

Despite their numerous areas of cooperation, the two legal systems also undermine each other in various ways and in both directions. The formal legal institutions hinder the activities of the *jaarsummaa* by disregarding the elders' decisions. Many cases have been reported in which disputants resorted to the state court after having been found guilty by the decisions of the elders. This was especially the case with disputants who allegedly did not have the truth on their side and hoped to win a case through corruption, as local informants told me. There were complaints by the elders who felt that dissatisfied parties could sometimes refuse to comply with their decisions. They also realized that at the end of the day it was the court, and not them, who make final and binding decisions (see also Desalegn Amsalu, this volume).

Complaints have been made especially in the context of land issues. As mentioned above, the Oromia Land Proclamation Art. 16, No.130/2007 gives an original jurisdiction for elders to deal with rural land disputes. Accordingly, elders selected by disputants should arbitrate the matter under the supervision of the *kebele* administration council. However, anyone dissatisfied with the results of the elder's decision can bring the case before the district court. During an interview with several elders, I was told that they were dissatisfied with the state court for repeatedly not taking their judgments into consideration, which affected their role in local dispute settlement. This was confirmed by an interview made with one of the judges of the district court, who stated that the decision of the elders had little or no value in the court's decision.

On the other hand, the customary court may also obstruct the activities of the formal court in many ways. As indicated above, many criminal cases reported to the police or court actually ends up in withdrawal. Elders use different techniques to intimidate disputants to withdraw their complaints before or even after investigations or prosecutions have started. The local people and elders know that for cases like rape and abduction, a wrongdoer would be sentenced to several years of imprisonment. As interviews with police officers and public prosecutors revealed, a considerable number of such cases are withdrawn or never reported after the family members of a victim reportedly have faced pressure from elders and the families of the perpetrators.

I was told and also observed situations in which the community made it difficult for the police and public prosecutors to collect evidence. When the formal institutions (police, public prosecutor and court) refuse to accept the withdrawal, elders may resort to other measures, such as pushing the parties in dispute to drop pursuing the case in the court, advising witnesses not to testify in the court, and stopping any support to the formal law enforcement agencies. This, as police officers and prosecutors told me, can occur at all stages of a court proceeding. Elders are also sometimes reluctant to handover serious criminal cases such as domestic violence against women and girls to the formal legal system, despite the clear obligation by law. The following case illustrates how the actions of elders undermine the activities of the police and public prosecutor to bring criminals before the state court.

> Case 5: Beating and injury
> A man lost one of his front teeth when a neighbour beat him with a club. After the victim reported the case to the police officer assigned to their area, the prosecution office opened a file against the offender. The victim also already brought a charge against the perpetrator. However, the elders intervened and forced the victim to withdraw the case. Thus, the process was interrupted without the consent of the public prosecutor, and the matter was settled locally in March 2015.
> After the reconciliation, the victim told me that he had been pressured several times by the elders to withdraw the case and to settle it locally, arguing that he would gain nothing by accusing the defendant before the court of law and making him get arrested. Finally, he agreed to withdraw the case from the prosecution.

This case reveals clearly how the elders involved in criminal matters, which are not under their jurisdiction by interfering with the formal legal system to exercise its mandate. During an interview with elders who participated in the reconciliation, they expressed their belief that if the case had been seen at the court, the result would have been different: the offenders would have been sent to prison.

Confusion and dispute over jurisdiction

There exist cases that neither the formal nor the customary legal system wish to deal with, as they are considered as trivial. As locals told me, plaintiffs have complained to the court that the police and public prosecutors do not accept cases that they consider unimportant, such as verbal insult, personal quarrels, minor assault, petty theft and petty damage to property. Instead of taking the plaintiffs' statements, they usually send them back to the community to have the case resolved by elders. The elders, however, are also sometimes reluctant to deal with such minor cases.

Disputes between spouses provide another kind of cases that both systems do not like to deal with. When, for example, women reported that they were insulted or harassed by their husbands or close relatives without being able to provide strong evidence, the offices of prosecution and women's affairs sometimes sends them to the elders, whom they consider better suited to settle private disputes. Elders, however, are sometimes reluctant to deal with marital and domestic disputes. One elderly informant told me that elders prefer to deal with homicide case rather than dispute that arises between husband and wife. He argued that husband and wife are sometimes unwilling to accept the decisions of the elders if they are not in his/her favour and then take their case to the formal court.

Another confusion is caused by the fact that aspects of the civil law fall into the sphere of personal and family law. The 1995 FDRE Constitution and the 2001 Constitution of Oromia have allowed customary laws to deal with personal and family matters, with the consent of the parties in dispute. They left particulars to be determined by law, but this issue has so far not been addressed by the concerned bodies. Thus, there is some uncertainty and confusion on the side of elders to clearly identify matters that fall within their jurisdiction.

Similarly, in the case of homicide, the handling is not clear. While such cases are usually handled in the state court and the killer is imprisoned, in order to avoid revenge, the family and close relatives of the killer additionally conduct a customary settling of the issue. Accordingly, the elders set certain rules to be respected by the families of the killer and the victim until blood price (*gumaa*) has been paid upon the release of the killer. One of the rules is preventing direct contact between the two families until the payment of *gumaa*. The prohibitions include avoiding drinking from the same bar, fetching water from the same spring and eating together in order to avoid any possible further hostilities between the two parties. The police and public prosecutors criticize the rule of avoidance, claiming that it is in conflict with the country's law. Elders, on the other hand, argue that the rule of avoidance prevents further disputes until customary reconciliation is held upon the release of the killer. Thus, they do not feel comfortable with the officials intervening in their affairs under the pretext of ensuring the observance of laws.

Double jeopardy

In the case of serious crimes (homicide, bodily injury, rape, and abduction), double jeopardy can be observed even though Art. 23 of the 1995 Ethiopian Constitution and the 2001 Revised Constitution of Oromia state that no one will be subjected to double jeopardy for the same offense if found guilty. At the same time, the Ethiopian law gives an exclusive jurisdiction over such criminal cases to the formal law. In response to this, elders deal with such cases after they have undergone through the formal law.

The findings of this study show that 'double jeopardy' is particularly common in homicide and serious physical injury when a victim has lost part of his body (teeth, eye or hand). Because of the exclusive jurisdiction of the court of law over homicide, the Tulama Oromo created their own way of dealing with such issues. The following homicide case reveals how a defendant was punished twice for the same crime: first by the court of law and then by the customary law (see also Aberra Degefa, this volume).

Case 6: Homicide

In 2003, a man killed his neighbour. The cause of their original dispute was associated with the land lease. The neighbour rented a plot of land belonging to the man's father. The man objected the land rent, which later led to the death of the lessee. When the killer was put in prison, his relatives and neighbours started a plea to the family of the deceased. However, the process of pleading was interrupted without any further negotiation when the killer told others to stop, arguing that the case had already been brought before the court of law. Sometime after his imprisonment, his wife left home, leaving her three children with her husband's father and mother.

The killer was released in 2009 after serving six years in prison. He then lived in town and visited his children and parents only occasionally. After his release, he was reluctant to agree to the elders' plea to reconcile with the family of the deceased, arguing that he had already been punished by the state system. When in 2013, his mother died, his wife returned home to take care of their common children and the children's grandfather though her relationship with her father-in-law was not good. On 12 December 2014, the killer's aged father was found dead in his home. When it came out that he died after he had been beaten on his head by a stick, she was suspected of having killed the man and was arrested, since no one else had been at home on that day. Jidda district police and public prosecutor who had investigated the case told me that the suspect later admitted the crime and was sent to the High Court at Fiche where found guilty and sentenced to 12 years in prison.

The local people argued that the death of the killer's mother, father and the imprisonment of his wife were signs of misfortune that occurred due to the killer's refusal to settle the matter according to the local culture. It is widely believed among the locals that receiving and paying blood compensation (*gumaa*) is mandatory in Oromo law and failure to do so may result in misfortune, as evidenced in what happened to this family. Fearing further future calamities, close and distant relatives of the first killer urged him to contact respected elders of Jidda. Then, the man asked the elders to reconcile him and his family with the family of the deceased. As a result, the process of pleading, which had been interrupted for 12 years, resumed.

> The local elders started the negotiation process. The elders later called an expert of customary law (*caffee ta'icha*)[21] to their meeting without whom they cannot handle serious crimes like this. A date and place for the reconciliation were fixed for 13 June 2015 in Gango *kebele*, at which both the killer's family and the family of the victim met after a long time. Various rituals were conducted on this day, including the slaughtering of a sheep, ritual hand holding in the sheep's stomach of the slayer and the deceased's relatives to symbolize reconciliation and a washing of hands between the slayer and the deceased families. Then, a pot was thrown to the ground by the killer, spilling the remaining water. Next, both sides took an oath under the leadership of the *caffee ta'icha*. The blood price was also given on this day. Lastly, the participants in attendance consumed food and drink prepared at the homes of the deceased and killer.

This homicide case illustrates that the formal and customary legal systems deal with different aspects of the same case. While the state court sentences the offenders to some years in prison with the intention of punishing him, the local community believes that true justice is only achieved through customary reconciliation with the aim of re-establishing social justice. The formal law focuses on the killer while the family of the victim is marginalized and the community is neglected. On the other hand, the Tulama customary law is more inclusive by involving many stakeholders including the family of the victim and the community at large.

The above case (as other similar cases) demonstrates that the criminal was subjected to double jeopardy for the same crime he had committed. The court sentenced him to six years in prison. After his release, he was punished locally again, underwent various ritual procedures and paid the necessary blood price necessary to reconcile with the family of the deceased before being fully accepted back to the society.

Lack of mutual trust

Mistrust is another aspect of the conflicting relationship between elders and the state officials. This mistrust is on both sides: actors in the formal legal system do not trust local elders because of the latter's involvement in disputes that do not

---

21 Caffee taa'icha, also called jaarsa caffee, is an Oromo judge and expert of customary law. He is from the ruling gadaa class. One can acquire this position after having participated in the Tulama caffee assembly at Odaa Nabee, East Shewa, which is held every eight years, where he acquires the necessary knowledge to judge over cases of homicide, serious injury and disputes between groups or lineages after listening to the caffee assembly meeting. His term of office lasts gadaa period that is eight years.

fall within their jurisdiction.[22] Similarly, the elders expressed disappointment that actors of the formal legal system violated the promises they made to them to the disputes they settled in a customary manner already.

During my fieldwork, I came across many instances when actors within the two legal systems were blaming each other and expressing their mistrust. The following case illustrates how the police arrested a criminal after his case had been settled by *jaarsummaa*, breaking their promise to let the case be resolved by the elders.

> Case 7: Theft
>
> Twenty years ago, a man had stolen a weight balance of another man from a mill house. The case had initially been brought before the police by the complainant. A suspect was arrested and brought before the court of law, but he denied having stolen the balance. The efforts of the police to further investigate failed since the crime had happened at night and there were no witnesses.
>
> When the elders approached the police to let them settle it locally, the suspect was released from police custody. Initially, the accused person denied the deed before the elders, but when they threatened they would make him an oath of innocence, the suspect admitted his guilt. They promised to keep him safe from any arrest related to this case and the stolen weight was returned to the owner. After he asked for forgiveness and paid compensation to the victim, the elders blessed him. When the elders reported to the police that the case had been settled, the police arrested the man again.

I was told about this case by the elders. One of them expressed his disappointment by the broken promise of the police. When the man was prosecuted, found guilty by the court and sent to prison, this angered the elders who had handled the case and who felt that they had been betrayed. The case further shows that the elders play an important role in investigating cases that are difficult for the police to handle for lack of evidence: had it not been for them, the truth may not have been revealed. Yet, their judgment was ignored by the court and actually led to double punishment for the same crime: first by the elders and then by the state court.

Failure of both systems to settle certain disputes

Nowadays, disagreements over land are one among the most significant sources of disputes in the area. They are often also the most contested and lengthy cases, as people neither accept decisions of the elders nor the lower state court if decisions are not in their favour. Rather, they take their cases through appeal to the next level court. While I was in the fieldwork, I gathered many cases in the context of

22 There are cases of elders who were criticized and even brought before the court of law for dealing with cases that were not under their jurisdiction.

land disputes. The following example shows a case both systems failed to settle and which has therefore been pending for decades.

Case 8: Borderland dispute between two *kebeles*

This dispute initially emerged during the final years of Emperor Haile Selassie's rule. During this time, the disputed land was under the control of the government. It was locally called the land of Empress Menen (*lafa etege*), the wife of the emperor, who had large tracts of her personal estate land in the area where a large number of imperial cattle used to graze.[23] However, two local notables claimed the land arguing that they had ancestral rights over it. The two notables not only disputed between themselves but also against the imperial government.

Following the fall of the imperial regime, the cattle were confiscated by the newly formed local administration and distributed to the local population. When the *kebele* administration was established by the Derg, the disputed cattle grazing land was left undivided because of the claim over the land by residents of the then two neighbouring *kebeles:* Qore Agabani and Abu Doye. The two individuals with their close associates who were already in dispute over the land continued their litigation before the state system. Later, other peasants who own adjacent land to the disputed land joined the litigation. Because of this, the boundary between the two *kebeles* along the disputed border was not demarcated.

The administrations of the two *kebeles* made several attempts to settle the matter and demarcate their boundaries. Jidda district administration, the responsible organ regarding land disputes at the time, also visited the area several times but their attempts did not end the dispute. The data I consulted from the district court shows that a committee was formed, representing officials from the district administration and agriculture office and the two *kebeles*. Finally, the committee gave the land to Abu Doye. That was on 10 February 1979. However, their decision was never implemented because of the resistance from the other *kebele*. Jidda senior elders also met several times to bring an end to the border dispute between the two *kebeles*.

After the fall of the Derg in 1991, two or more *kebeles* were merged for administrative purpose in Jidda. Accordingly, Qore Agabani was merged with other *kebeles* and called Wanya Qore, and Abu Doye was united with the neighbouring *kebeles* and took the present name Horo Abu. Since then, the disputed land became a boundary dispute between the two newly emerged *kebeles*: Horo Abu and Wanya Qore (see figure 1 above). When the land registration and certification started in 2005, many farmers from both *kebeles* included the disputed land into their certificates. This has contributed to further complication in the settlement of the

23 This cattle grazing land was allocated for the purpose of keeping dairy cows and beef cattle for the palace. The area was selected for its good climate, availability of sufficient fodder and geographical proximity to Addis Ababa.

dispute. Totally, over 70 people had claimed over the land and sometimes the disputed land is called the land of 70 people (*lafa abba torbbaatama*).

On 11 May 2015, a directive letter was written from the District Court to Jidda District Land Administration and Environmental Protection to search for a final solution. After visiting the area, the office replied to the court that it was beyond its capacity to deal with the matter alone and recommended the court to establish a special committee composed of different sectors. The court wrote letters to various offices to work with district land administration over the matter. Officials from the land administration and environmental protection together with other staffs representing district administration, district police, and district security offices visited the site where the disputed land was located. These officials together with representatives from local *kebele* administrations and local militia of Horo Abu and Wanya Qore as well as elders representing the two *kebeles* made a visit to the field and arranged several meetings. Totally, the committee was composed of 15 persons (nine government officials and six elders).

Finally, the office for Land Administration and Environmental Protection reported the decision of the committee by file No.1390/07 to the district court on July 3, 2015. In the letter, the office wrote that the boundary between the two *kebeles* (Wanya Qore and Horo Abu) was not known. It also reported that the dispute over the land started during the last years of Emperor Haile Selassie's rule. Besides, what many people included the disputed land into their certificate in 2005 and the investigated reality on the ground by the committee are contradictory.

Relying mainly on the report of the committee, the district court decided by file No.15399/07, contrary to the expectation of the parties in dispute, that the disputed land should be shared between the two *kebeles* and subsequently given to the landless youth. But, those people who have been claiming the land appealed and took the case to the high court. A final solution to the old disputed land has not yet given by the concerned bodies.

This particular case (and other many examples from my file of cases) illustrates the inherent weaknesses of customary and formal legal systems to settle land disputes, which involve a large group of people. The findings show that both systems tried to settle the case on a number of occasions, but each time the disputants refused to accept the proposed settlement. The case also demonstrates the failure of joint dispute settlement by representatives from customary and formal legal systems to find a satisfactory way of resolving it. Although this problem is not widespread, it, however, shows there is a need for the two systems to work closely.

Summary and conclusion

The paper showed that both customary and state laws and legal institutions have weaknesses and in some ways complement, in others contradict each other. The relationship between customary and formal legal systems in the research area has cooperative, competitive and problematic aspects.

The cooperative aspects include case transfer and notification of the decision of the transferred case of settlement to one another's jurisdiction, case transfer from the formal legal system to the customary one being more frequent. As could be shown, the two systems sometimes settle cases jointly such as when government officials face serious problems in resolving disputes in their own and seek support from local elders. Cooperation also occurs in the de-escalation of dispute and crime prevention. Elders can play double roles when serving as judges in state-based institutions at the village levels and at the same time serve as the main actors in *jaarsummaa*.

On the other hand, there are various competitive and problematic aspects. The first one is mutual undermining, e.g. when the activities of the customary legal system are undermined by the actors of the formal one and vice versa. The second problem is the unclear and incomplete jurisdiction, which causes among elders who fail to clearly identify matters of family or personal law that fall within their jurisdiction on one hand, and an unwillingness of the actors in both systems to deal with certain marital and minor crimes. In cases of homicide, even if handled in the court and the killer sent to prison, elders apply certain customary practices to make sure peace between the two parties is re-established, such as setting certain rules what the disputed families should and should not do until blood price (*gumaa*) is paid upon the release of the killer. Though the intent is to restore social harmony in the community, legal actors in the state system criticize elders for interfering in such cases, which leads to ambiguity and uncertainty on the side of the users of the systems. Third, in cases of homicide and some others, one can also observe double jeopardy, e.g. that the same case is dealt with in both systems and a perpetrator is punished twice for the same crime. Fourth, there exists mutual mistrust, e.g. elders and government officials do not trust each other, as when elders feel that police is violating the promise they had made to them. Finally, both legal systems fail to settle certain disputes and hence pending for years.

To minimize contradiction and confrontation and to productively make use of complementary aspects, the following suggestions are made:

1) Both Constitutions of Ethiopia and Oromia region in their Art. 34(5) did not provide the details of personal and family matters that fall within the remit of customary laws and left those particulars to be determined by law. To date, however, the House of People's Representatives and Oromia Regional State Council have not yet addressed these matters. Consequently, this has contributed to dispute and

confusion over jurisdiction between customary and formal legal systems in the area. This paper suggests that the legislatures should specify by law detailed lists of personal and family matters that fall under the customary legal system.

2) The current FDRE Constitution and the Constitution of Oromia give exclusive jurisdiction for the formal legal system in criminal cases and other aspects of the civil law that do not fall within the sphere of personal and family laws. However, the 2004 Revised Criminal Code of Ethiopia states the types of crimes that are prosecutable upon complaint and seems to leave the choice of the forum to the disputants. As discussed above, the police, public prosecutors, and judges in the study area informally transfer a considerable number of cases involving upon complaint crimes to the *jaarsummaa*. However, the Ethiopian law does not clearly give any legal basis for the formal legal system to do so. Therefore, a new law should be enacted by the House of People's Representatives and State Council of Oromia, which clearly governs the level of the working relationship between customary and formal legal systems over these crimes punishable upon complaint.

3) Under Ethiopian law, customary institutions have not yet been given official legal recognition to deal with serious criminal cases. Such cases continue to be under the exclusive jurisdiction of the formal legal system since the state regards them as offenses against the public interest. The Tulama Oromo of the study area wanted to deal by themselves with most serious criminal issues. They also felt that customary legal system should be legally allowed to be involved in such cases. For this reason, there is commonly a customary reconciliation after the cases have passed through the process of the state system in the area. This means the perpetrator is subjected to double punishment in reality since each system deals with different aspects of the same case. Thus, the paper suggests that Ethiopian legal system should officially recognize customary laws to deal with these customary matters, such as homicide, bodily injury (loss of body parts like eye, tooth, leg, hand, etc.) and arson as far as they are not in conflict with the country's constitution and international human right standards. For this, there should be clear guidelines on the operation of customary reconciliation ceremonies after cases have been dealt with by the formal court system. This paper further proposes that the formal court should take the future customary reconciliation into account while punishing the criminals. In other words, the court should pass a lesser sentence on the criminals. This view is supported by many elderly informants and discussants in focus groups who argued that the amount of punishment (including the prison sentence) by the court should be reduced considerably.

References

ALEMAYEHU Haile, BOSHI Gonfa, DANIEL Deresa, SENBATO Busha and UMER Nure, 2006 *History of the Oromo to the sixteenth century*. Finfinne: Oromia Culture and Tourism Bureau

ASMAROM Legesse, 1973 *Gada: Three approaches to the study of African society*. London: Free Press

BLACKHURST, Hector, 1978 "Continuity and change in the Shoa Galla gada system", in: Paul Trevor William Baxter and Uri Almagor (eds.) *Age, generation and time: Some features of East African age organisations*, 245–267. London: Hurst

CENTRAL STATISTICAL AGENCY (CSA), 2007 *The 2007population and housing censusofEthiopia:Results for Oromia region*. Addis Ababa: Berhanena Selam

FEDERAL DEMOCRATIC REPUBLIC OF ETHIOPIA (FDRE), 1995 *The Constitution of the Federal Democratic Republic of Ethiopia*. Addis Ababa: Procl. No.1, Federal Negarit Gazeta, Year 1, NO. 1

GADA Melba, 1988 *Oromia: An introduction*. Khartoum, Sudan: Gada Melba

GEBRE Yntiso, FEKADE Azeze and ASSEFA Fiseha (eds.), 2011 *Customary dispute resolution mechanisms in Ethiopia* Vol. 1. Addis Ababa: The Ethiopian Arbitration and Conciliation Center

2012 *Customary dispute resolution mechanisms in Ethiopia* Vol. 2. Addis Ababa: The Ethiopian Arbitration and Conciliation Center

GIRMA Hundessa, 2009 *Gadaa, qaalluu and elders: Customary settings for dispute settlement among the Torban Kutta'e Oromo*. Addis Ababa: Addis Ababa University (MA Thesis)

KNUTSSON, Karl Erik, 1967 *Authority and change: A study of the kallu institution among the Macha Galla of Ethiopia*. Gothenburg: Ethnografisca Museet

MAMO Hebo 2006, *Land, local custom and state policies: Land tenure, land disputes and dispute settlement among the Arsii Oromo of southern Ethiopia*. Kyoto: Shoukadoh

MELAKU Abera, 2009 *Land disputes and dispute settlement mechanisms among the Tulama Oromo of Sululta District, northern Shewa*. Addis Ababa: Addis Ababa University (MA Thesis)

MERON Zeleke, 2010 "*Ye shakoch chilot* (the court of the sheikhs): A traditional institution of conflict resolution in Oromiya zone of Amhara Regional State, Ethiopia", *African Journal on Conflict Resolution*, 10 (1):63–84

MOHAMMED Hassen, 1990 The *Oromo of Ethiopia: A history 1570–1860*. Cambridge: Cambridge University Press

NEGASH Abebe, 2013 *Indigenous mechanism of homicide reparation: The case of 'gumaa' among Tulama Oromo of Kuyu district, northern Shewa*. Addis Ababa: Addis Ababa University (MA Thesis)

OROMIA NATIONAL REGIONAL STATE, 2007 *Proclamation No.130/2007: Proclamation to amend the procl. No. 56/2002, 70/2003 & 103/2005 Oromia rural land use and administration*. Finfinne: n.p.

2007 *Proclamation No.128/2007: A proclamation to revise the proclamation for the re-establishment and determination of the powers of the social court No.66/2003 of the social courts*. Finfinne: Megeleta Oromia, 15th year, No. 10/2000

2001 *Proclamation No. 46/2001: Enforcement proclamation of the revised constitution of 2001 of Oromia region*. Finfinne: Megeleta Oromia Proc. No 46, year 8, No. 6

PANKHURST, Alula and GETACHEW Assefa (eds.), 2008 *Grass-roots justice in Ethiopia: The contribution of customary dispute resolution*. Addis Ababa: French Center of Ethiopian Studies

TAREKEGN Adebo and HANNAH Tsadik (eds.), 2008 *Making peace in Ethiopia: Five cases of traditional mechanisms for conflict resolution*. Addis Ababa: Peace and Development Committee

YIHUNBELAY Teshome, 2010 *Conflict and indigenous conflict management institutions: A case study of the Oromo of Arsi-Robe*. Addis Ababa: Addis Ababa University (MA Thesis)

7. Federal Sharia Courts in Addis Ababa
Their administration and the application of law in the light of recent developments

Mohammed Abdo

Introduction

Sharia-based law in Ethiopia gained greater political and legal prominence with the political liberalization that followed the regime change in 1991. However, almost two decades after they were formally constituted, Sharia courts have received limited academic attention and only a small number of research works focus on their jurisprudence and day-to-day operation. This chapter examines the nature of Sharia case law, litigants and the procedures for settling cases. Besides providing an analysis of the statistics of Sharia courts and a description of court proceedings, most importantly, it will look at two recent developments affecting the Muslim community: growing human rights and women's rights consciousness; and increasing Muslim demands for self-autonomy over religious matters, and their influence, if any, on Sharia court rulings. The research shows that, despite the fact that Sharia law prescribes a patriarchal tendency in marital ties and sanctions a sex-based differential treatment of divorce and post-divorce matters, young, educated and economically independent women form the overwhelming majority in suits brought before Sharia courts in Addis Ababa. It also shows that Sharia courts tend to apply civil procedure rules rather leniently but that their proceedings appear consistent. *Shafie* Islamic jurisprudence, which is said to be relatively less conservative over family and divorce matters than other schools of thought, guides their judgments. However, attempts by the Sharia courts to expand their jurisdiction to matters beyond those delineated by legislation has been kept in check by the state's judicial and quasi-judicial organs.

Islamic law in Ethiopia

Ethiopia's current legal system reflects the legacies of foreign laws (civil law and common law traditions), Christianity, authoritarian political heritages and the

Muslims' struggle for recognition. Long relegated to the status of second-class citizens, Muslims have struggled to gain recognition in public spheres but over time they have managed to win small concessions from successive regimes, including the first official recognition of Sharia courts in the 1940s.

A federal republic since the 1990s, Ethiopia is a multi-ethnic nation with a sizeable Muslim population and a constitution that established a parliamentary system and that guarantees fundamental rights and freedoms, including freedom of religion and the equality of all religious groups. While the current constitution emphasizes secularism, it includes customary and religious laws in the constitutional order. The recognition given to religious and customary dispute settlement mechanisms seems deliberately designed to accommodate religious autonomy and to promote diversity. This recognition does not, however, repudiate the secular nature of the nation and its constitutional dispensation.

While Sharia-based law gained *de jure* recognition in the early 1940s, it has experienced greater momentum since the regime change of the early 1990s and the adoption of multiculturalism and political liberalization. A distinct law setting up a separate Islamic judicial sector, based on constitutional provisions, was enacted in 1999 (Proclamation No. 188/1999) at the federal level and successively in all regions except Gambella.[1] The law implies that Islam is seen as an important source of legal, social and cultural values. Having been put in legal limbo by the 1960 Civil Code, which essentially repealed the 1944 proclamation on Sharia courts, Muslim personal and family law and the Islamic courts have been elevated by this new legal development, which symbolically gives Islamic law its due place in Ethiopian law.[2] The symbolism of official Islamic courts being implicitly anchored in the constitution and applying an Islamic law has proved appealing to the Muslim community.[3]

---

1 Article 34(5) of the Federal Constitution of Ethiopia (FDRE 1995): 'This Constitution shall not preclude the adjudication of disputes relating to personal and family laws in accordance with religious or customary laws, with the consent of the parties to the dispute. Particulars shall be determined by law.' Article 78(5): 'Pursuant to sub-Article 5 of Article 34 the House of Peoples' Representatives and State Councils can establish or give official recognition to religious and customary courts. Religious and customary courts that had state recognition and functioned prior to the adoption of the Constitution shall be organized on the basis of recognition accorded to them by this Constitution.'

2 Article 3347 of the 1960 Civil Code reads: 'Unless otherwise expressly provided, all rules whether written or customary previously in force concerning matters provided for in this Code shall be replaced by this Code and hereby repealed.' This provision is said to have repealed the 1944 proclamation setting up Sharia courts (see also Mustapha 1973:140, James and Clapham 1971:849).

3 In November 1994, before the current constitution was adopted, the Muslim community in Addis Ababa took to the streets demanding, among other things, the inclusion of Sharia law as one of the bases of the new constitution (Østebø 2007:3). The reference made in the FDRE constitution to religious dispute resolution and the subsequent promulgation of legislation

Non-state normative sources (customary and/or religious) are still influential in Ethiopia in settling disputes. They form a strong alternative to state institutions and may even be the first resort for justice for many people in rural areas. This chapter focuses on the Federal Sharia Courts in Addis Ababa and their function as dispensers of justice.[4] Studying the practices of the Federal Sharia Courts in applying Sharia law in Addis Ababa is significant for demographic, political, economic, and legal reasons. The Federal Sharia Courts in Addis Ababa were the first Sharia courts to be set up following the regime change in 1991. They serve the largest Muslim community in an urban setting in Ethiopia: Muslims account for more than 16 per cent of the total population of Addis Ababa. Many wealthy, prominent Muslim community figures and religious scholars, as well as relatively better-educated members of the Muslim community, live in the city. As Addis Ababa is the economic and political powerhouse of Ethiopia, studying the functioning of the Federal Sharia Courts casts light on their standing with the Muslim community in Ethiopia in general as well as on their relationship with the state. Moreover, studying their practices, uncovers the functioning of 'law in practice/action' rather than 'law in text', revealing the courts' inner workings and understanding of the jurisdiction granted to them.

Accordingly, this chapter examines the nature of cases, litigants and procedures for settling cases. The research is not merely an analysis of statistics on Sharia courts or a description of the courts' proceedings. It also looks at recent developments affecting the Muslim community, such as the push for an independent body to administrate religious affairs – manifested, among other events, in recent tensions relating to the *majlis* election – and the growing consciousness of human and women's rights and their influence, if any, on the proceedings and final rulings of the courts.[5]

---

establishing Sharia courts to some extent addressed Muslim concerns in that regard. In the past, Sharia courts were set up by secondary legislation and Muslims used to call for their establishment on the basis of primary legislation.

4 Sharia courts at the federal level are located in Addis Ababa and Dire Dawa city. Apart from housing the Federal Sharia Courts, Addis Ababa is also the seat of the Supreme Sharia Courts of Oromia National Regional State, since the city serves as the capital of the region as well.

5 Tensions have been simmering between Muslims and the government since December 2011. These tensions flared up following the closure of *awoliya* and a campaign launched by the Ethiopian Supreme Islamic Affairs Council (commonly known as *majlis*) to instil *Al-Ahbash* beliefs and undertaken with the alleged direct and/or indirect support of the government authorities. This resulted in a call for a free and fair election to an independent *majlis*. There are generally two opposing narratives on the problem. A considerable number of Muslims believe that they are contesting their constitutional rights, enabled by secularism and exercising their right to administer their own religious affairs. However, the government contends that extremism has been taking root in the country, forcing it to take legitimate measures to tackle it, and that it has not interfered in the freedom of religion in general and in the in-

Qualitative in nature, this study employed key informant interviews with the personnel of the Federal Sharia Courts (judges and Registrar) in Addis Ababa; interviews with randomly selected women who appeared before the courts on the dates set for interviews; literature review; review of the archive of Sharia courts; and analysis of relevant laws. Personal observation was also used to reflect on some of the issues that demanded explanation. To conduct meaningful interviews, a semi-structured list of key questions was prepared beforehand.

Historical perspective on Sharia courts in Ethiopia

Sharia as a normative system, along with customary norms and foreign laws, has impacted the Muslim community and influenced the development of state laws in Ethiopia. The unique legal position of Sharia courts is rooted in the Muslim community's on-going quest for self-governance in the personal matters intrinsically governed by Islamic law. To understand the existing jurisdiction of the Sharia courts and their relationship with state laws, it is important to understand their history.

The relationship between state laws and Sharia courts presents a challenge for states with a sizeable Muslim community. The political recognition of Sharia courts, the scope of their power and their relationship with state laws are intertwined with government attitudes and policy towards the Muslim community, which have often hinged on regime changes. The scope of Sharia-based law in Ethiopia has not, however, oscillated with regime changes as it has, for example, in Nigeria and Indonesia, where the power of Sharia courts has changed with shifting popular and government attitudes over the years ('Kola-Makinde 2007:186–190; Ostien and Dekker 2010:571–577; see also Huis 2015:8,45). That is to say, in Ethiopia the political discourse on the Sharia courts has followed a consistent trajectory in the sense that the subject-matter of Sharia courts' jurisdiction has remained the

---

ternal affairs of the religious community in particular. In some instances, the tensions led to violent protests that claimed lives and destroyed property. The prominent Muslim community figures, who spearheaded attempts to defuse the tensions were rounded up, charged and finally convicted of attempting to commit terrorist acts and forming an illegal committee to incite conflicts. They were eventually pardoned. The tension that flared up and the unprecedented perseverance of Muslim forces to have an independent *majlis* seems to have caught government officials by surprise and revealed the extent of the government's desire to keep religious institutions under its watch. On the other hand, there is a growing consciousness of human rights in general and women's rights in particular, ascribed to civic education and campaigns by government and NGOS. Although discriminatory attitudes and practices are still widespread in many rural parts, in urban areas women are becoming better educated and are thought to be in a better position to assert their rights and to demand equality in many spheres.

same and has not been significantly affected by regime changes in the years since their formal inception in 1942 (Mohammed 2011:86, 2012:273).

The Sharia courts gained official recognition and unprecedented support during Italy's brief occupation of Ethiopia (1936–1941) and flourished throughout the country during that period. They constituted part of a grand colonial scheme designed to attract the support of the marginalized Muslim community and thereby to enervate the Christian-dominated government (Markakis 1990:74, Trimingham 1965:77, Mohammed 1999:8).

Fearing a reversal of policy after the end of the occupation, the Muslim community pleaded with Emperor Haile Selassie to officially sanction the operation of the Sharia courts as before. The Emperor heeded their plea and introduced a law, enacted in 1942, which provided the basis for the creation and procedures of the first official Islamic courts.[6] These courts administered Sharia law in personal status cases and in litigation regarding pious foundations (*awqaf*). Their independent functioning was however compromised by the state's hand in appointing their judges (*qadis*). *Qadis* serving in Islamic courts during the imperial period were appointed according their allegiance to the government.[7]

Haile Selassie's fall from power in 1974 marked the demise of the privileged political position enjoyed by the Orthodox Church and Christian elites under his government and ushered in a new era for the Muslim community. The subsequent Derg regime made a pivotal move in relation to religious matters and in the political recognition of the Muslim community, rescinding the Orthodox Church's status as official state religion, declaring that all religions are equal and adding three Muslim holidays to the list of official holidays to be honoured. Also, an institution administering Muslim affairs (popularly known as *majlis*) – the first of its kind in the nation's history – was created in 1976, although it remained tightly supervised by the state authorities. Sharia courts were permitted to operate as before. Cognizant of the Ethiopian Muslims' long marginalization and in the wake of an unprecedented Muslim protest demanding recognition that occurred on 20 April 1974, the Derg sought legitimacy through reaching out to the Muslim community.[8] There was however no significant legal or institutional mechanism designed to advance Islamic normative principles introduced by the Derg. In other words, the Derg undertook no new legislative measures regarding Islamic personal law

6 The Proclamation to Establish Kadis' Courts, Proclamation No. 12/1942, Negarit Gazeta, No. 2/1942.

7 Miran 2005:211.

8 On 20 April 1974, Muslims in Addis Ababa took to the streets calling for changes to the status of Muslims and publicly demanding that the Imperial regime implement a series of actions, one of which was the establishment of Sharia courts by proclamation, as their legal status had been placed in limbo by the 1960 Civil Code (see Ahmedin 2015:272–273).

or Islamic courts because the regime retained its predecessor's policy as far as the status of Sharia courts was concerned.

The Derg's downfall in 1991 marked the revival of religious activism in Ethiopia. A combination of national and foreign factors, one of which is political liberalization, has enabled the resurgence of religion. In 1991, the country embarked on a new path, shifting away from earlier restrictive laws and policies and introducing a new legal and political discourse that underscored a democratic system and fundamental rights in general and religious equality and freedoms in particular. The rapid expansion of religious institutions (for example, mosques and seminaries) and the increasingly visible character of Muslims – manifested in dress codes and increasing representation in public sectors – are often offered as proof of religious resurgence following the regime change. Over the last two decades, Muslims in Ethiopia have thus attained, among other things, a symbolic language of identity and normative distinction that is implicit in, among other things, their assertiveness over religious self-administration and issues relating to the Sharia courts.[9] With regard to the Sharia courts, personal status law became a bone of contention and Muslim figures passionately debated the draft law that preceded the adoption in 1999 of the Sharia courts' establishment legislation.[10] So far, a law relating to personal and family matters is the only domain of legislation where Islamic legal norms are recognized for application by Sharia courts.

While the FDRE constitution emphasizes the secular character of the state as well as the equality of adherents of different religions before the law, it makes no reference to Islam or Sharia courts. However, Articles 34(5) and 78(5) of the Constitution set conditions for state-recognized and state-funded religious courts[11] that suggest that the provisions were designed specifically for Muslim courts. The

9 Aside from personal status law, another contentious issue between the Muslim community and state authorities is related to the administration of the Muslim community's internal affairs: that is, the establishment and running of the *majlis* and its powers. On efforts to free the *majlis* from alleged government control, see Jemal 2012:72–100. To counter the growing clout of Muslims, the government adopted a policy on management of religious issues fight against counter what it designated 'growing fundamentalism and extremism' taking root in the nation (see Ministry of Federal and Pastoralist Development Affairs 2015).

10 A committee set up by the *majlis* to study the status of Sharia courts and to come up with suggestions to strengthen them was chaired by a Muslim scholar. Other Muslim scholars took an active part in the debate to shape the draft law establishing Sharia courts. A conference on strengthening and consolidating Sharia courts was organized by the House of Peoples' Representatives and the Ethiopian Supreme Islamic Affairs Council (*majlis*) and took place from 12–14 September 1999. Five papers were presented for discussion by scholars, all of them were prominent Muslim figures. Also, most participants were knowledgeable Muslims, including *qadis*, lawyers, academics, elders, and well-known personalities (see Ethiopian Supreme Islamic Affairs Council 1999:35; see also Jemal 2012:39, note 13).

11 See note 1 on Articles 34(5) and 78(5) of the Federal Constitution of Ethiopia.

provisions offer legitimacy to courts that were in operation well before the current constitution and that had been recognised by the state in the past. The Sharia courts fulfilled these criteria and were thus reorganized and officially instituted by virtue of Articles 34(5) and 78 of the Constitution. By contrast, the Christian courts had been abolished in the 1960s and were therefore not in operation before the FDRE constitution. Thus, it seems that the government may not set up state-funded Christian courts within the meaning of the two provisions.

Contending principles relevant to the status of Sharia courts

The recognition accorded to Sharia courts involves the balancing of tricky legal and political issues, such as secularism, the equality of religious groups, civic citizenship, the accommodation of diversity and the relationship between state and religious courts. An understanding of the basic contending principles relating to the functioning of Sharia courts and their status in Ethiopia's legal system is important in casting light on the institutional structure of the courts and their standing as justice providers. This section does not, however, purport to offer an exhaustive list of these principles, but focuses rather on the crucial ones.

Sharia as a normative system incorporates rules that contradict state laws, especially around the notions of equality and non-discrimination on the basis of gender and religion. The recognition given to Sharia courts involves conflicts, real and perceived, with the government's mandate to ensure fundamental rights. The government's decision to grant the Sharia courts a specific mandate may be viewed as a political overture, and it is not subject to judicial review. This means that the government has come to terms with the fact that Sharia laws contradict certain state laws so that it can accommodate religious diversity and address the Muslim community's continuing quest to govern the personal matters that are intrinsically tied to their religious values. Weighted against this position is the perception of state endorsement or sanctioning of a particular religion at the expense of the equality of other religious groups.

Although one might marshal many legal justifications against the recognition of the Sharia courts, the very existence of such courts does not negate secularism nor amount to the adoption of a state religion within the meaning of Article 11 of the FDRE Constitution.[12] Article 11 does not in and of itself preclude a degree of accommodation of religious norms for dispute settlement, as long as individuals are guaranteed the freedom to choose a forum. Generally, as the courts function on

12 Article 11 of the Federal Constitution of Ethiopia reads: 'Separation of State and Religion: 1. The Ethiopian State is a secular state. 2. There shall be no state religion. 3. The State shall not interfere in religious affairs; neither shall religion interfere in the affairs of the State.'

a voluntary basis and are not intended to replace the ordinary courts of the country, their establishment does not affect the secular nature of the state.

The Sharia courts are composed of a three-tiered structure at both federal and regional levels, and administer Islamic law on matters falling within their jurisdiction. They function separately and independently of Ethiopia's ordinary courts, but function as 'state' courts in that they are subject to statutory law, accountable to the state judiciary and subject to review by the Supreme courts at both federal and state levels. While they are independent entities and apparently operate in parallel with the state courts of law, they lack inherent self-governing powers and rely, in terms of human and financial resources, on the ordinary courts of the land.[13] Unlike ordinary courts, the Sharia courts report to the Federal Supreme Court on their performance and utilization of budget and not to the parliament.

Regarding jurisdictional issues, Sharia courts have a defined mandate, which is specifically stated under Article 4 of the enabling legislation. This provides that the courts have common jurisdiction on any question regarding marriage, divorce, maintenance, guardianship of minors and family relations, provided that the marriage to which the question relates was concluded in accordance with Islamic law or the parties involved consent to be adjudicated in accordance with Islamic law. The Sharia courts can adjudicated over questions regarding *wakf*,[14] *hiba* and gift succession of wills provided the endower or donor is a Muslim or the deceased was a Muslim at the time of his death. If they exceed their jurisdiction, their decisions may be subject to review by state courts once they have passed through the Sharia court system and a final decision has been made by the Supreme Sharia Court.[15]

---

13 For the appointment of Sharia judges and hiring of other staff as well as funding, Sharia courts depend on the Federal Supreme Court. See Article 20 of Proclamation setting up Federal Sharia Courts, No. 188/1999.

14 *Wakf* is equivalent in meaning to mortmain property. It is an inalienable charitable endowment under Islamic law, involving, for instance, the donation of a property or a plot of land or other assets for Muslim religious or charitable purposes with no intention of reclaiming the asset.

15 Article 80(3) of the Federal constitution of Ethiopia: 'Federal Supreme Court has a power of cassation over any final court decision containing a basic error of law.' Accordingly, the final decision of the Sharia courts might be subject to review if they exceed their jurisdiction. Final decisions rendered by Sharia courts may be reviewed by the Federal Supreme Court only on procedural grounds, such as when they exceed their jurisdiction or when they decide cases without securing the consent of the defendants at the outset (see Mohammed 2011:19, note 8).

Federal Sharia Courts in Addis Ababa

Physical setting and overview of caseload

In 2015 the Federal Sharia Courts in Addis Ababa moved into their current building. Before that, they were housed in crammed and dilapidated buildings that created an environment unconducive to the work of the judges and other court personnel and was unpleasant for anyone who visited. The condition of these buildings was a cause for concern among Muslims, some of whom accused the government of deliberately housing the Sharia courts in a rundown building in order to tarnish the image of the courts and thereby diminish the Muslims' appetite for making use of them (Ahmedin 2015:230-231, note 12).

Today, the courts occupy a four-storey building, much larger than the previous rundown buildings. The new building is spacious and conducive for the successful conducting of proceedings. It has more amenities than the previous buildings and has waiting areas for clients, a separate room for each judge, a wide room for the Registrar, a room for old files and documents, and separate one for active ones. It is physically pleasant and the *qadis*, Registrar and clients have all openly expressed their happiness with the current building and its facilities, comparing it favourably with past conditions. All three levels of the Federal Sharia Courts are housed in the same building. The Federal First Instance Sharia Court has two benches, the High Court has one bench and the Supreme Court has three benches. There are ten *qadis* in Addis Ababa, including the chief *qadi*. The total annual budget for the July 2017–July 2018 fiscal year is about 13 million Birr.

For the last couple of years, the Sharia courts in Addis Ababa have handled more or less a similar volume of cases (Mohammed 2012:283): on average, a minimum of 7000 cases and a maximum of 8000 cases have been filed every year. Most cases relate to matrimonial issues, including *nikah* (the engagement that happens before the marriage ceremony) and permission to marry, marriage registration, divorce, custody of children and inheritance. Divorce makes up the lion's share of Sharia courts' caseload, while the number of cases relating to *wakf* is limited.

Practice in the application of subject-matter jurisdiction and substantive law

The jurisdiction of the Federal Sharia Courts is confined to personal and family matters. On matters involving marriage, divorce and the maintenance and guardianships of minors, Sharia courts are competent to hear suits when a marriage was concluded in accordance with Sharia law or when all the parties involved consent to having their suit adjudicated in accordance with Islamic law.[16] This rule

16 See Article 4(1) of Proclamation No. 188/99.

is highly significant as it not only limits the Sharia courts' scope of competence but also defines the nature of the parties over which they can preside. While it does not expressly demand that all parties be Muslim, it emphasizes the form of conclusion of marriage or consent of the parties at the time of the suit, rather than their religious background per se. The authority of the Sharia courts may thus be extended to non-Muslims, if they voluntarily subject themselves to Islamic law. This is in direct contrast to the 1942 proclamation setting up same courts, which stipulated that either all the parties should be Muslims or the marriage to which the question related had to have been concluded according to Islamic law.[17]

However, in practice, Federal Sharia Courts in Addis Ababa operate with the assumption that parties to family suits are Muslims or that the marriage was concluded as per Islamic form. The *qadis* take for granted that the parties are Muslims and feel they are not obliged to inquire into the reasons why some defendants refuse to have their cases heard by Sharia courts. Yet, the *qadis* are of the opinion that defendants' objections to their jurisdiction have little to do with religious background.

In other personal matters, Sharia law makes the religious background of a party a pre-condition, along with consent, for a hearing in the Sharia courts. As mentioned, in *wakf* (inalienable charitable endowment), *hiba* (gift), and succession of wills cases, the endower or donor has to be, or have been at the time of death, a Muslim for Sharia courts to hear the suit. According to a *qadi* from the First Instance Sharia Court in Addis Ababa, the question of who is/was a Muslim has not so far arisen in the Sharia courts.[18] Unless challenged and the contrary is proved, the court assumes that the endower or donor is/was a Muslim.

After securing the express consent of both of parties, Federal Sharia Courts apply normative Islamic law to decide the matter in hand. While there are primary and secondary sources of Islamic law, there is no express rule on the particular school of thought[19] that should be used for administering Sharia law in

---

17 See Article 2 of Proclamation to Establish Khadis' Courts, Proclamation No. 12/1942, Negarit Gazeta No. 2/1942.

18 Interview with Sheik Ali Mohammed, qadi of Federal First Instance Sharia Court in Addis Ababa, 25 November 2017, Addis Ababa.

19 The four schools of thought are: Shafie, Maliki, Hanbali, and Hanafi. The school chosen matters when it comes to personal and marriage matters. Of the four schools, the Hanbali school of jurisprudence is often considered the most restrictive when it comes to personal status issues. The Hanbali doctrine 'advocates a particularly patriarchal family structure. Among other things, it provides women with less justification for leaving a marriage. Accordingly, a wife can obtain a judicial divorce only on very limited grounds, namely the husband's incapacity to consummate the marriage, his apostasy, or in cases of a 'fraudulent marriage contracted prior to puberty'. The Shafie doctrine is said to be less conservative in comparison with other doctrines on personal and family matters (see Moussa 2005:11–13).

Ethiopia, unlike in Sudan[20], for instance. Nor is there a compilation of Islamic law that should be used as the main legal source for judgments. The absence of specific doctrine allows, in principle, parties to make use of the diverging opinions of the available schools of thought for litigation purposes. The heterogeneous nature of the Islamic community in Ethiopia in general and Addis Ababa in particular may be the rationale behind this non-specification of a particular school of thought. Consequently, Muslims make use of different schools of thought, often depending on their geographical location. In the northern part of Ethiopia (Wollo and Tigray areas), the Hanafi School is prevalent; in areas bordering Sudan and Eritrea, Malki is the dominant school; while Shafie is found across Ethiopia and is the influential doctrine in many well-known Islamic seminaries in the country (Abdella 2017:159). The *qadis* of the Federal Sharia Court in Addis Ababa tend to subscribe to the Shafie school of thought but occasionally resort to another doctrine if a particular issue justifies it, for instance, if another doctrine prescribes a lesser punishment than Shafie doctrine.[21]

The lack of a formally adopted Islamic doctrine to guide proceedings, in principle, paves the way for a reliance on the judges' discretion and puts the consistency of judgments at risk, which impacts upon predictability of judgments and legal certainty. However, if discretion-based interpretations are consistently applied over particular matters, they develop into case law and this mitigates the potential for unpredictability and uncertainty in judgments. Fortunately, the existing practice, which is tilted in favour of one doctrine, seems to have moderated the use of discretion and favours a degree of uniformity in judgments.

Cognizant of the interpretation problems that might arise from the Islamic law not being administered according to one particular school, a rule in the establishment proclamation gives the Chief *qadi* of the Federal Supreme Court of Sharia the power to form a temporary division, composed of at least five *qadis*, to look into cases involving fundamental differences between divisions of the Federal Supreme Court of Sharia with regard to interpretation of Islamic law. This measure helps to mitigate the use of discretion by the *qadis* and rein in divergent interpretations, thereby helping to maintain a uniform case law.

The personal and family matters that fall within the Sharia courts' ambit are open to interpretation and have implications for the scope of the courts' authority. Through adjudication, the Sharia courts provide interpretations of such open

---

20 The law governing the Sudanese Islamic courts, stipulates that the decisions of the courts should be in accordance with the authoritative doctrines of the Hanafiya Jurists unless directed otherwise by the grand *qadi* through a judicial circular or memorandum. In which case, the decisions should be in accordance with the doctrines of the Hanafiya or other Mohammedan Jurists as are set forth in the circular or memorandum (see Akolawi 1973:155).

21 Interview with Sheikh Ali Ahmed, Judge of Federal Sharia First Instance Court, 27 November 2017, Addis Ababa.

rules and when those interpretations are applied consistently in the court system, they become case law. In the following, an attempt is made to see how Federal Sharia Courts deal in practice with matters falling within their jurisdiction. Doing so sheds light on how Sharia courts go about defining the scope of their competence in adjudicating Islamic personal matters.

Article 4 of the Sharia courts' establishment legislation provides the list of matters Federal Sharia Courts are competent to deal with.[22] However, the provision is not clear on whether the list is exhaustive or merely indicative of major matrimonial and personal matters envisaged as subject to the jurisdiction of Sharia courts. The issue is: Do Sharia courts have full jurisdiction over all matrimonial and personal matters, for instance, over matrimonial and inheritance property, which are not explicitly specified under their subject-matter jurisdiction? To be more specific, do they have a mandate to hear cases involving the consensual division of marital property, and are they authorized to deal with the division of inheritances aside from determining who the inheritors are?

In practice, Federal Sharia Courts, while acknowledging the limits to their power, tend to assume jurisdiction over matrimonial property and division of inheritances if parties raise such issues in a particular suit. As long as the parties consent, the courts seem to believe they can legitimately take on these matters, even though they are not specifically outlined under their subject-matter jurisdiction as defined by the enabling legislation. However, some of their decisions in such cases have been challenged by parties who have lodged petitions before the cassation division of the Federal Supreme Court, alleging that the Sharia courts committed fundamental errors of law in expanding their jurisdiction. The Federal Supreme Court then rendered the decisions of Sharia Courts made while expanding their subject-matter jurisdiction to cover, for instance, ownership of property and division of inheritance, invalid on the grounds that they exceeded their jurisdiction.[23] The decisions of the Supreme Court set a precedent and are binding on any court . They demarcate the extent of Sharia courts' subject-matter jurisdiction and confine the provisions of the establishment law, purportedly creating room for widening the scope of the Sharia courts' competence in practice.

In general, based on the aforementioned case law of the Federal Supreme Court, Sharia courts are not entitled to expand the meaning of family and personal matters beyond that specified under Article 4 of the establishment legislation.

---

22 See Article 4 of the establishment proclamation mentioned earlier.

23 A case between Shamsi Yenus and Nuriya Mami over possession of a plot of land was heard first by the Federal Sharia Court in Dire Dawa city. It finally reached the Federal Supreme Court after the Federal Sharia Supreme Court had given a final ruling. The Federal Supreme Court held that Sharia courts could not expand their jurisdiction and hear cases not specifically indicated in their enabling legislation and they could not hear cases over possession of a plot of land. See Federal Supreme Court, Cassation File No. 36677, 2009.

The case law indicates that Article 4 is couched in exhaustive terms to preclude the expansion of subject-matter jurisdiction under the guise of interpretation and/or consent of parties, implying a strict limit to the scope of the Sharia courts' jurisdiction. This is in line with the intent of the Constitution's framers, who envisaged Sharia justice with competence limited to the matters specifically laid down in their legislation.[24]

Another interesting issue is whether regional states establishing Sharia courts can expand their reach to cover matters not specifically listed in the proclamation establishing Federal Sharia Courts. For instance, the legislation instituting Oromia regional state's Sharia courts envisaged competence to hear suits on matrimonial property.[25] To avoid expanding the discussion on this matter is important because, in addition to being a potential area of conflict between federal and state laws, it involves issues around the competence of the regions over personal matters in the federal setting.[26]

---

24 The minutes of constitutional assembly on Articles 34(5) indicate that Sharia courts would assume a strict mandate confined to those specified by law (Minutes of Constitutional Assembly 1994:10–26).

25 Article 5 of the Oromia Sharia Courts Establishment Proclamation, No. 53/2002, Magalata Oromiyya, 9th year, No. 2, 2002.

26 The question is: is a region justified in enlarging the jurisdiction of Sharia courts under the guise of competence to legislate on civil matters? If a region's attempt to widen Sharia courts' competence is found to be in conflict with the federal constitution and federal legislation, what is its legal effect? According to the division of power stipulated by the Federal Constitution of Ethiopia (Article 52(1)) residual powers belong to the units of the Federation. States as a result are competent to legislate on matters not included in the legislative list of matters that are exclusively reserved or concurrently granted to both federal government and the states. The matters falling under Sharia courts' power are obviously personal matters, and states are competent to legislate on personal matters as they are not expressly reserved for the federal government. However, it is unclear whether states can enlarge the Sharia courts' competence beyond the specific personal and family matters covered by the Federal Sharia Courts' enabling law. In Nigeria it was held that Sharia courts had restricted jurisdiction, confined to matters specified by the federal constitution (Ostien and Dekker 2010:581–582, note 3). Admittedly, while the Nigerian constitution gave the Sharia courts a specific mandate, the Ethiopian federal constitution failed to do so (see Article 262 of the Constitution of the Federal Republic of Nigeria of 1999). However, case law from the highest judicial body has cast light on the meaning of personal and family matters not only under the enabling law but also under the provisions of the federal constitution sanctioning the very establishment of Sharia courts. The FDRE constitution may not outline the scope of matters falling under the jurisdiction of the Sharia courts, but its framework seems to have intended Sharia courts to have limited competence to deal with the matters specifically falling within their power, as defined by legislators both at federal and state level (see the Minutes of Constitutional Assembly by the House of Peoples Representatives' 1994). States in Ethiopia, while competent to legislate on personal matters, may not therefore go beyond the personal matters defined

Federal Sharia Courts' case statistics and gender issues

Gender relations are undergoing changes in Ethiopia in urban settings, particularly in big cities like Addis Ababa. Women now tend to be educated and have jobs both in the public and private sectors, although their representation in the public space is not yet on a par with men. Education paves the way for an increasing awareness of the civic matters, especially regarding gender roles in society, espoused by government and human rights activists in general and women's rights activists in particular. Given that the law applied by the Sharia courts embodies patriarchal ideology and recognizes a sex-based preferential treatment regarding divorce and post-divorce issues, it is important to see what influence, if any, the assumed growing empowerment and awareness of Muslim women has had on case law in the Sharia courts.

A judicial divorce obtained through either the civil or Sharia courts is the only one recognized by Ethiopian law. The Sharia courts have thus been dealing with the issue of women's divorce and post-divorce rights, which are laden with gender sensitivity and involve normative differences and tensions between statutory rights and obligations on the one hand and religious norms and values on the other. The application by Sharia courts of religious norms in divorce and post-divorce proceedings thus attracts the attention of interest groups, researchers and activists. It is interesting to examine the practice of Addis Ababa-based Federal Sharia Courts in divorce and post-divorce claims in terms of gender, and question who resorts to these courts, given that women in Ethiopia tend to be economically dependent on their husbands.

Most of the suits filed to federal Sharia courts in Addis Ababa are related to marriage issues, including confirmation of consent for marriage, marriage registration, and divorce. Although the exact figure is difficult to come by, divorce accounts for up to 90 per cent of marriage suits.[27] Looking at their caseload, one could be justified in calling the courts 'divorce courts'. In the last years there has been a dramatic change that seems to have baffled the Sharia courts and currently around 85–90 per cent of divorce petitions are filed by women.[28] Most of the grounds for divorce include irreconcilable differences, abuse and violence, the husband's absence, and husbands marrying second wives without their first wives' consent. Most of the petitioners for divorce are young, employed, educated women. They tend to be economically independent and do not seem to encounter economic

---

by federal legislation and judicial bodies. Sharia court jurisdiction ought to be strictly construed as it forms an exceptional recognition of religious norms for dispute settlement.

27 Interview with Sheik Ali Mohamed and Registrar, 25 November 2017, Addis Ababa, Ethiopia.

28 *Ibid.*

hardship in sustaining their post-divorce lives. Such women are thought to be better informed and in a better position to assert their rights before the state courts, which could provide them better post-divorce terms, but they refrain from doing so.

According to female informants, seeking justice before the Sharia courts has more to do with religious conviction. They believe that the ruling of a civil court would not religiously end their marital ties. They also express that, from a religious point of view, it is not appropriate to submit claims for divorce to regular courts. As their entry into marriage in the first place was made according to a religious ethos, their exit from it, they believe, should be through the same route. Based on personal observation, the religious renaissance among Muslims seen in Ethiopia over the last two decades might underpin their decisions.

Sharia courts tend to mediate between the parties with the aim of reconciling them, in line with Islam's general decrial of divorce. According to the *qadis* and the Registrar of the Federal Sharia Courts in Addis Ababa, it is usually the women who insist on getting divorced, while the men often agree to reconcile or withdraw their cases after having filed an application for divorce. While the rationale is subject to speculation, better economic independence might explain women's insistence on divorce and their refusal to reconcile.

Should reconciliation fail, the courts issue a divorce verdict, the effect of which depends on the petitioner. If a women petitions for the divorce, it takes effect as soon as the presiding judge pronounces his verdict. If the husband is the petitioner, he has to come to the court in person to pronounce the *talak* (unilateral divorce or release of his wife from marriage) before the judge in order for the divorce to come into effect. After the divorce decree has been issued, women often make post-divorce claims for things such as spousal and child support and child custody. The courts make their decision based on Islamic law and husbands tend to comply with their rulings. Accordingly, the courts do not – in principle – award any spousal award if it was the woman who petitioned for the divorce. According to *qadis*, parties sometimes refrain from pursuing post-divorce claims, probably to avoid further confrontation and/or in the belief that ex-husbands will provide spousal and child support through their own volition. Parties also tend to make informal/private arrangements for post-divorce claims to avoid washing their dirty linen in public. Sharia court decisions settle such issues should informal arrangements fail to work out.

The *qadis* and the Registrar of the Federal Sharia Courts in Addis Ababa suggest that divorce has been shifting from the man's domain to become a women's practice. Indeed, several of the women I interviewed at the Federal First Instance Sharia Courts in Addis Ababa said they believed they had the right to divorce. They stated that they were neither afraid of the stigma attached to divorce nor were they be worried about their post-divorce life.[29]

Application of procedural laws

Generally, the Federal Sharia Courts in Addis Ababa, as a state institution, render justice based on laws. While they apply substantive Islamic law to settle cases, they are bound by state procedural rules that govern their proceedings.[30] By determining the procedures regulating the Sharia courts proceedings, the state seems to disengage religious law from its religious source and confine the scope of the laws to be applied by the courts. This seemingly strange combination of two distinct laws appears to be a mechanism designed to assert state control over religious law, probably with the intention of ensuring due process and fairness.

The *qadis* of the Federal First Instance Sharia Court in Addis Ababa state that they have no objection to using civil procedure rules for their proceedings, believing that it is somehow in line with Sharia rules on procedures. They apply a civil procedure with some necessary changes while acknowledging that they largely follow Sharia procedure, which they in turn believe is predominantly in line with the rules of civil procedure. The main procedural steps include confirmation of the presence of both parties, securing the consent of the defendants, reading the statement of claims followed by the statements for the defence, hearing the witnesses, securing the production of evidence if deemed necessary, and finally delivering judgment.

Sharia courts in practice seem to comply with the procedure of securing consent before hearing cases, as it is prescribed by the Constitution and the enabling legislation. Accordingly, they normally ask for confirmation of the defendant's consent at the opening of proceedings. However, after consent is secured, the procedure in use does not seem to strictly follow the rules prescribed by the civil procedure. Proceedings are somewhat less formal than in regular courts of law. However, the procedure in use in Sharia courts seems to be consistent and applied consistently. A breach of, or non-compliance with, civil procedure does not necessarily affect the outcome of the proceedings, and a decision may be rendered invalid only if the procedural irregularity committed is a substantial one.[31]

The full-fledged application of civil procedure by Addis Ababa's Federal Sharia Courts is hampered by at least two factors. One is the belief that Islamic procedure laws ought to govern the application of Islamic personal law administered by the courts. The other has to do with a lack of basic knowledge among the *qadis* of state

---

29 Four anonymous women were interviewed at the court compound, 26 November 2017, Addis Ababa, Ethiopia.

30 Article 6(2) of the enabling legislation (Proclamation No. 188/99).

31 On procedural irregularity and its effect, see Articles 201–211 of the Civil Procedure Code. See also Mohammed 2010:164–165.

law in general and procedural law in particular. This problem stems from a lack of training on basic state laws. In fact, the enabling legislation does not make knowledge of basic state procedural laws a pre-condition of appointment as a judge.

Pursuant to the establishment legislation, Sharia courts are supposed to ensure openness of proceedings.[32] However, most of the cases falling within the jurisdiction of the Sharia courts relate to private matters that often dictate a closed hearing.[33] Despite this, the Sharia courts hold open hearings whenever the parties do not object.

Evidence

Sharia law itself incorporates rules on evidence, the most important of which is the testimony of witnesses. However, there are normative differences between religious and state laws regarding witnesses, and the number of witnesses used by Islamic law in some cases is different for men and women.[34]

The proclamation establishing the Sharia courts is silent on the rules of evidence to be used by the courts. While they ask for witnesses and the production of written or other forms of evidence deemed necessary for particular cases, it seems that evidence production is regulated by the normative rules of Sharia law. The *qadis* seem to assume that, as matters within their jurisdiction are governed by religious norms, the relevant Sharia rules of evidence ought equally to apply to evidence issues.

Legal counsel

According to the *qadis* interviewed, in an overwhelming number of cases parties are not represented by lawyers. Most applicants to the Sharia courts handle cases by themselves or are assisted by family members and/or friends. Parties hire legal representatives in some instances, such as when appealing a decision made by the lower Sharia courts. There is no clear rule that governs legal counsel before Sharia courts. The establishment legislation is silent on this matter as well. However, the general rules governing legal counsel before civil courts might apply, with necessary changes having been made, to Sharia courts.

32 Article 15 of the Establishment Proclamation, Proclamation No. 188/99.

33 The Federal Courts Establishment Proclamation allows closed hearing for private matters. See Article 26 of Federal Courts Establishment Proclamation 25/1988.

34 For instance in financial transaction the Qur'an (2:282) says the following:'... and call in to witness from among your men two witnesses; but if there are not two men, then one man and two women from among those whom you choose to be witnesses, so that if one of the two errs, the second of the two may remind the other...'

As matters heard by Sharia courts are governed by Islamic laws per se, legal counsel is limited to procedural issues. Often, as one *qadi* from the First Instance Sharia Court told me, lawyers (mostly non-Muslims) who offer legal counsel encourage the defendants to rule out the Sharia court, and succeed in turning parties away from Sharia justice.[35]

The need for legal representation is apparently scuttled partly because Sharia court proceedings are not as formal, confrontational and complex as civil court proceedings. Another factor that may curtail the use of legal representation is a lack of lawyers with a sound knowledge of Islamic law, or their lack of interest in appearing before Sharia courts. Finally, the lack of representation might be simply because Sharia law does not encourage its use, especially in civil cases.

Administrative issues related to Federal Sharia Courts in Addis Ababa

As a state institution, Sharia courts are funded and staffed by the government. Recently, there has been an improvement in the management of the budget by Sharia courts. In the past, they had to apply to the Federal Supreme Court for operational costs on the basis of need, which often caused a delay in the procurement process. Nowadays, the Federal Supreme Sharia Court has its own account and managed the entire budget for the Sharia courts. This has significantly reduced the delays to payments to the courts. However, the Sharia courts continue to report to the Federal Supreme Court on the utilization of the budget.

Nevertheless, the remuneration for judges serving in the Sharia courts is lower than for those working in the regular courts, and Sharia judges do not receive any housing or transport allowance. There are no assistant judges and no training is available to the judges before they take the bench, unlike in the state courts. While the Sharia court *qadis* and Registrar are appreciative of the gradual improvements to their physical working environment and financial management, they still feel the courts are treated as inferior/second-class. To bolster this contention, they also point to a rule on contempt of court that is aimed at ensuring respect for the courts. Although in practice contempt of the court is uncommon. *Qadis* complain that the fine or punishment for it is lower in the Sharia courts than in the regular courts, and complain it suggests they are seen as less deserving of respect.[36]

The Addis Ababa-based Federal Sharia Courts do not seem to proactively seek to improve their image with the public. The reason for this, as a *qadi* at the First In-

---

35 Interview with Sheikh Ali Mohammed, 25 November 2017, Addis Ababa.

36 According to the establishment proclamation, any person who, in whatsoever manner, shows improper conduct in the course of any proceedings or who, without good cause, fails to comply with an order of the court shall be punishable with imprisonment of up to one month or to a fine of up to Birr 1.000 (One thousand Birr).

stance Sharia Court told me, may have to do with a general problem of leadership. The leadership of the Sharia Supreme Court is said to be unwilling and incapable of improving the courts' image.[37] While the leadership have arranged some seminars for *qadis* on particular issues, it has not taken the initiative to reach out to prominent Muslim community figures and scholars to conduct debates on issues affecting the courts' operation. The Sharia courts do not publish their cases in electronic or print form to generate debate or to ensure transparency. Nor is there a research unit that undertakes studies on the functioning of the courts in order to make suggestions for improvement. The Sharia courts remain, as a result, obscure.

Appointment procedure for qadis vs. Sharia courts' application of Islamic law

The qualifications for Sharia courts' *qadis* and the procedures for their appointment are set forth in the enabling legislation. Any Ethiopian may qualify for appointment as *qadi* if he has been trained in Islamic law in an Islamic educational institution or has acquired adequate experience and knowledge in Islamic law.[38] Other appointment criteria include personal qualities, consent, and age.[39] The same criteria are used for all levels of the Sharia courts, and thus any eligible candidate may be appointed at any level of the courts.[40]

Except for a training in Islamic law, the establishment law does not expressly require *qadis* to have any educational qualifications or credentials. It does not specify prerequisites to determine an applicant's knowledge or experience of Islamic law. The rationale for not insisting on any academic credentials or formal education/training might be in consideration of the reality in Ethiopia, where there exists only one Islamic higher academic institution offering formal training or education in Islamic law. Consequently, many would-be Islamic scholars travel abroad in search of formal religious education. The Awoliya College in Addis Ababa, which used to offer Islamic education, was accused by the government of being a breeding ground of '*Wahhabism*' or 'fundamentalism' (Jemal 2012:34–35, note 13).[41] It was sealed off by the *majlis*, with the alleged backing of the government, who dismissed

37 Anonymous *qadi* interview and personnel of the Federal Sharia Courts, 27 November 2017, Addis Ababa.

38 See Article 16(1) of Proclamation No. 188/99.

39 Diligence and good conduct, consent and a minimum age of 25 are required to become a *qadi* (see Article 16(2–4) of Proclamation 188/1999).

40 In other countries, for instance Malaysia, criteria for appointment might be different depending on the level of Sharia court, (see Zin 2012:119–120).

41 See also the Ministry of Federal and Pastoralist Development Affairs 2015: 211–215.

its teaching staff and banned its curriculum.[42] The closing of the college was one of several reasons for the recent confrontation (2011–2013), pitting government and large segments of the Muslim community. The college was reformed, with new teaching staff and a new curriculum that suits the *majlis*' interests and is aimed at producing students who will counter the so-called '*Wahhabi*' doctrine.[43]

In practice, most of the *qadis* currently serving in Sharia courts received Islamic 'training' or 'education' in traditional ways, attending traditional religious seminaries (*madrassas*) common in rural parts of Ethiopia. Except for three *qadis* in Addis Ababa, who secured formal credentials from foreign Islamic educational institutions, all of the sitting *qadis* do not have formal religious education.

The appointment procedure for *qadis* involves three bodies: the *majlis*, the Federal Supreme Court, and the Federal Judicial Administration Commission. The appointment of *qadis* is made by the Federal Judicial Commission, which follows the advice of the *majlis* and the recommendations of the Federal Supreme Court. In fact, the process is controlled by the *majlis*, which is in charge of recruiting the would-be *qadis* and submits the list to the Federal Supreme Court. Unlike state courts, the appointment of *qadis* does not involve the final approval of the House of Peoples' Representatives: the approval by the Judicial Administration Commission is sufficient.[44]

Historically, the appointment of *qadis* was manipulated by the state. The same seems to hold true today. People who have resisted the involvement of state authorities in Islamic affairs and in Sharia court business have faced reprisals, being either dismissed or systematically excluded from Muslim institutions in general. Sheik Khiyar Mohammed, a former President of the *majlis*, for example, was dismissed after publically detailing the direct interference of the government in Muslim affairs and manipulation of the *majlis* to advance government interests.[45]

As a result, candidates with a religious orientation other than the one approved by the *majlis* would not be allowed to assume any position in the *majlis* and impliedly in Sharia courts as well. This is particularly the case when candidates have credentials from 'Wahhabi' religious schools, including Awoliya College. The constraints of formal education and the *majlis*' control of the appointment process for *qadis* are said to have weakened the Sharia courts' capacity to fully apply Islamic law to cases (Abdella 2017:135–136, note 27). Consequently, some Muslim scholars and figures have challenged the dominance of *majlis* and called for the rescinding of its power in that regard (Jemal 2012:35, note 13).

---

42 Ministry of Federal and Pastoralist Development Affairs 2015: 214.

43 *Ibid*.

44 Article 17 of the enabling law.

45 For information on his interview see the weekly newspaper *Addis Admas* from 23 June 2018 and *Ghion Magazine*, 9 June 2018.

The *qadis* serving in Federal Sharia Courts in Addis Ababa seem to be circumspect of the Hanbali school of thought, which is said to be more conservative on many issues, including family and personal Islamic law. The existing orientation of Sharia courts inclined to Shafie jurisprudence which might have to do partly with the *majlis'* preference for Shafie-inclined traditional Islamic teaching prevalent at at many Muslim seminaries in Ethiopia or the requirements for appointment of *qadis* tend to downplay formal religious education and favours traditional Shafie-inclined nominees.

Concluding remarks

Although secularism is a fundamental constitutional principle in Ethiopia, the Sharia courts are recognized as the independent Islamic judicial body dealing with family and personal matters, and as forming an integral part of national law. Their establishment does not deviate from a secular constitutional order that is considered to be the most appropriate political and legal mechanism for multicultural and multi-confessional society.

The paper has shown that while the mandate of the Sharia courts is couched in general terms, their attempt to expand its scope as defined by law has been kept in check by the decisions of ordinary judicial and quasi-judicial bodies, which have held that Islamic law can only be applied to personal matters in the limited areas specifically designated to them.

Based on the case law of Sharia courts, divorce has today become a women's practice as opposed to being part of men's long-held sphere of influence over marital ties. Better economic conditions, religious conviction, and/or changing societal attitudes to divorce propel women to forgo the relatively better protection that may be afforded by state courts.

Influenced by substantive Islamic law and a lack of basic knowledge of state laws, Sharia courts apply civil procedure rules rather leniently. Nevertheless, their proceedings are largely consistent. Yet, a lack of visibility is the hallmark of Sharia courts, and this has, to a certain extent – prevented them from becoming subject of academic discourse. To rectify this lack of transparency, it is important to revisit the existing requirements for appointment to the courts, so that candidates with formal education could become judges. Issues arising from the *majlis'* control over the appointment process for *qadis* may be addressed if and when free and fair elections deliver an independent *majlis*.

The state courts also need to engage Sharia courts through platforms relevant to their functioning and to enhance their knowledge of basic state laws.

References

ABDELLA Kedir, 2017 *Islamawi sltane behabesha: Yetesfafabachew mengedochna yagatemu tedagrotoch* (Amharic, in English: Islamic civilization in *Ethiopia: Methods of expansion and challenges faced*). Addis Ababa: Altowaba

AKOLAWI, Natale Olwak, 1973 "Personal law in the Sudan: Trends and developments", *Journal of African Law* 17 (2):149–195

AHMEDIN Jebel, 2015a *Sostu Atsewoch ena Ethiopiyawuyan Muslimoch: Tgil ena Meswa'etnet* (in Amharic) (in English: *The three Emperors and Ethiopian Muslims: The struggle and sacrifice*). Addis Ababa: BBN Our Voice

2015b *Ministry of Federal and Pastoralist Development Affairs, the Federal Democratic Republic of Ethiopian Constitution and the management of religious diversity*. Addis Ababa: Berhanena Selam

ETHIOPIAN SUPREME ISLAMIC AFFAIRS COUNCIL, 1999 "News on Sharia Courts", *Hirja* 3 (2):35

FEDERAL DEMOCRATIC REPUBLIC OF ETHIOPIA (FDRE), 1995 *The Constitution of the Federal Democratic Republic of Ethiopia*. Addis Ababa: Procl. No.1, Federal Negarit Gazeta, Year 1, No. 1

1999 *Proclamation No. 188/199 Federal Courts of Sharia Consolidation*, Federal Negarit Gazeta 6th Year No. 10. Addis Ababa: Federal Negarit Gazeta

HOUSE OF PEOPLES' REPRESENTATIVES, 1994 *Minutes of constitutional assembly*. Addis Ababa: Berhanena Selam

HUIS, Stijn Cornelis van, 2015 *Islamic courts and women's divorce rights in Indonesia: The cases of Cianjur and Bulukumba*. Leiden: Leiden University

IMPERIAL GOVERNMENT OF ETHIOPIA, 1960 *Civil Procedural Code*. Addis Ababa: The Imperial Government of Ethiopia

JAMES, Paul C. N. and Christopher CLAPHAM, 1971 *Ethiopian constitutional development: A source book* II. Addis Ababa: Haile Selassie I University

JEMAL Hassen, 2012 YeEthiopia Mejlis Atadafi Chigrochu ina Amarach Meftihewoch, Bedr Ethiopia Alemaqef YeEthiopiawiyan Muslimoch Dirijit. Addis Ababa: Badr International

'KOLA-MAKINDE, Abdulfatah, 2007 *The institution of Shariah in Oyo and Osun States, Nigeria 1890–2005*. Ibadan: University of Ibadan (PhD thesis)

MARKAKIS, John, 1990 *National and class conflict in the Horn of Africa*. London: Zed Ministry of Federal and Pastoralist Development Affairs

2015 *The FDRE constitution and management of religious diversity*. Addis Ababa: Berhanena Selam

MIRAN, Jonathan, 2005 "A historical overview of Islam in Eritrea", *Die Welt des Islams* 45 (2):194–203

MOHAMMED Abdo, 2010 "Civil Procedure: CIVI 55 Ethiopia", *International Encyclopaedia of Laws*. Hague: Kluwer Law International

2011 "Legal pluralism, Sharia courts and constitutional issues in Ethiopia", *Mizan Law Review* 5 (1):72–104 (accessible online at https://biblio.ugent.be/publication/3160168/file/5874552.pdf, last accessed 11 July 2018)

2012 "Sharia courts as an alternative mechanism of dispute resolution in Ethiopia", in: Assefa Fiseha, Fekade Azeze and Gebre Yntiso (eds.) *Traditional dispute resolution mechanisms in Ethiopia*, 261–290. Addis Ababa: Eclipse

MOHAMMED Siraj, 1999 "The constitution of the FDRE and the application of Sharia law". Paper presented at the conference: *Reviewing the draft proclamation to strengthen and consolidate Sharia courts*, 12–14 September 1999, Addis Ababa

MOUSSA, Jasmine, 2005 "The reform of Shari'a-derived divorce legislation in Egypt: International standards and the cultural debate", *Human Rights Law Commentary* (accessible online at https://www.nottingham.ac.uk/hrlc/documents/publications/hrlcommentary2005/divorcelegislationegypt.pdf, last accessed, 11 July 2018)

MUSTAPHA, Zaki, 1973 "The substantive law to be applied by Muslim courts in Ethiopia", *Journal of Ethiopian Law* 9 (1):138–148

ØSTEBØ, Terje, 2007 "The question of becoming: Islamic reform-movements in contemporary Ethiopia", CMI Working Paper WP 8. Bergen: Christian Michelsen Institute

OSTIEN, Philip and Albert DEKKER, 2010 "Sharia and national law in Nigeria", in: Jan Michiel Otto (ed.) *Sharia incorporated: A comparative overview of the legal systems of twelve Muslim countries in past and present*, 553–612. Leiden: Leiden University Press

TRIMINGHAM, J. Spencer, 1965 *Islam in Ethiopia*. London: Frank Cass and Co

ZIN, Najibah M., 2012 "The training, appointment and supervision of Islamic judges in Malaysia", *Pacific Rim Law and Policy Journal* 21 (1):115–131

Legislations, proclamations and policies

"Proclamation to Establish Kadis' Courts", *Proclamation Negarit Gazeta* 1 No. 12/1942

Federal Supreme Court, Cassation File No. 36677, 2009

Oromiya Sharia Courts Establishment Proclamation, No. 53/2002, Magalata Oromiyaa, 9th year, No. 2, 2002

Federal Supreme Court, Cassation File No. 36677, 2009

Constitution of the Federal Republic of Nigeria of 1999

Federal Courts Establishment Proclamation 25/1988

Newspapers

Addis Admas, 23 June 2018
Ghion Magazine, 9 June 2018

8. Use and abuse of 'the right to consent'
Forum shopping between *shimgilinna* and state courts among the Amhara of Ankober, northcentral Ethiopia

Desalegn Amsalu

Introduction

This study examines how the local community in Ankober handles its right to consent to enter into customary court or switch to the formal one. The only condition attached to resolving disputes through customary court is that both parties in the conflict should agree to it. This sounds like a fair arrangement. But, as there are no laws that regulate how consent, already given, should be sustained or terminated, the right to choose and shift between courts is open to abuse.[1]

Article 34(5) of the 1995 Federal Democratic Republic of Ethiopia (FDRE 1995) Constitution stipulates that disputes relating to personal and family laws can be dealt with in accordance with customary or religious laws 'with the consent of parties to the dispute'. Article 34(5) of the 2001 Revised Constitution of the Amhara National Regional State (ANRS 2001) is a verbatim copy of the analogous provisions of the FDRE Constitution. However, neither the constitutions nor any of the subsidiary laws give any details on how to apply the constitutional notion of consent. Both constitutions stipulate that 'Particulars shall be determined by law', but this has not been done so far.

---

1 The idea for this paper came in February 2012 when I was doing a research in Ankober on traditional mechanisms of conflict resolution, with particular reference to *shimgilinna* (conflict resolution through elders). It is commonly known that local institutions enjoy respect among the Amhara people, but during my fieldwork, I noticed that people's obedience to *shimgilinna* had changed. What struck me was how people were manipulating the institution using the legal right of consent. After I received an offer to contribute a chapter to this book, I visited Ankober for a second time, from 12 June 2017 to 10 September 2017, to undertake more focused data collection. This time, I specifically looked at the use and abuse of consent in the community. I conducted several interviews with *shimagillés* (elders), disputants and judges at Ankober Woreda Court, women and youths. I attended court cases and organized focus group discussions with *shimagillés*. I also made use of my notes and interviews from my fieldwork in 2012.

Though there is an abundant literature relating to customary dispute resolution mechanisms (CDRMs) in Ethiopia since 1991, there is a dearth of research on the legal and practical role of 'consent' in CDRMs. Generally, the literature focuses on the legal framework for CDRMs (see for example, Tesfa 2009, Temesgen 2010, Tekle 2009) and case studies (see for example, Alemayehu 2009, Asnake 2010, Assefa 1995, Ayke and Mekonnen 2008, Pankhurst and Getachew 2008, Tarekegn and Tsadik 2008, Tolosa 2010, Wodisha 2010). An annotated bibliography edited by Fekade *et al.* (2011) listed 136 research outputs related to CDRMs, of which 19 were written in Amharic and 117 in English. Since the publication of this list, more researchers have written on the subject matter (Solomon 2014, Mekuanint 2015, Esayas 2015, Tasew 2016, Balew 2016). However, the relationship between customary law and formal law is not much discussed and no significant research is available on how 'consent' is being used to transfer a claim from one legal forum to another.

Conflict resolution among the Amhara of Ankober

Overview of the people and the area

In line with the state structure effective since 1995, most Amhara people live in Amhara National Regional State (ANRS), but many are found in other regions.[2] The Amhara of Ankober *Woreda*,[3] in particular, are found within a sub-regional division known as Semen Shewa Zone. The *woreda* (district) headquarters are in Gorebella town, some 172 kilometres away from Addis Ababa. The historic town of Ankober[4] lies three kilometres to the east of Gorebella.

According to the Ankober Woreda Government Communication Affairs Office (AWGCAO 2016), the population of Ankober *Woreda* in 2016 was 89,691. In its last census in 2007, the Central Statistics Agency determined that the population of Ankober was made up of Amhara people (92.77 per cent), the Argobba (7.04 per cent), and other ethnic groups (0.19 per cent). The census also shows that the Amhara are predominantly Orthodox Christians, while the Argobba and Afar are

2 According to the 2007 national census of Ethiopia, the Amhara numbered 19,867,817 individuals, comprising 26.9 per cent of Ethiopia's population.

3 *Woreda* (English pl. *woredas*) is the third level administrative unit in the current state structure of Ethiopia. 'District' is often used in the literature as an English equivalent. The *woredas* are subdivided into several smallest units, *kebele* (English pl. *kebeles*). Several *woredas* form higher-level units known as zones, which in turn form regions (*kilil*).

4 Today's Ankober town was chosen as the royal place of the Kingdom of Shewa in the late eighteenth century for its strategic position as a border station. It was the base from which Nigus Sahala Sellase (r.1813–47) stretched his control over Argobba, Afar and Oromo. It also served as the seat for Emperor Menelik II (r. 1889–1913) when he was the king of Shewa (1866–1889).

entirely Muslim (CSA 2008). The Amhara predominantly live to the west of Ankober town, in the Amhara community of Shewa. To the east live the Argobba and Afar ethnic groups. The Amhara settlement area lies in the highland climatic zone, the Argobba in the midlands, and the Afar in the lowlands. In terms of subsistence, the Amhara are ox-plough agriculturalists, who produce highland crops like barley, peas, and teff. The Argobba are also cultivators but they also weave and trade. The Afar are pastoralists.

Figure 1: Location of Ankober Woreda (Desalegn 2018) [5]

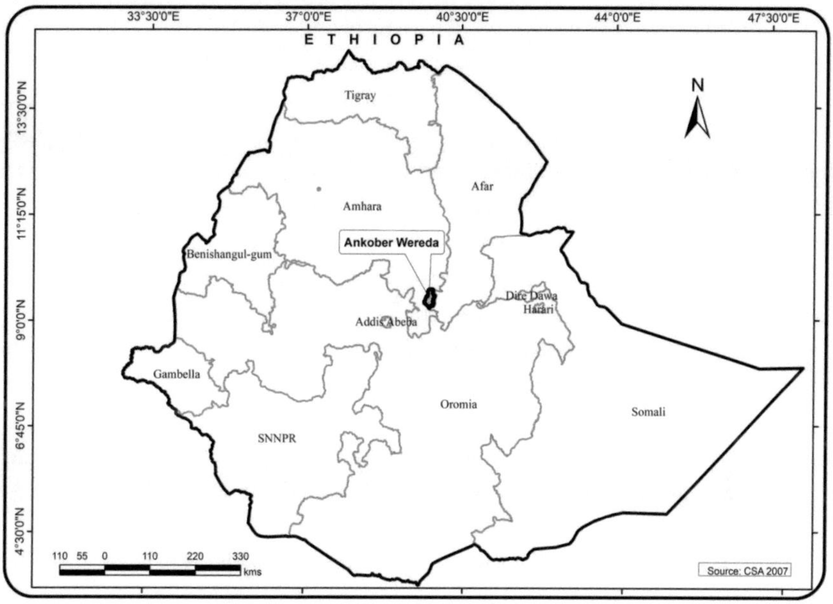

Shimgilinna

Shimgilinna is the 'most common' CDRM among the Amhara people (Pankhurst and Getachew 2008:14). However, the local practices relating to this institution seem to vary from one area to another, and there are institutions particular to certain

5 The Central Statistics Agency (CSA) of Ethiopia provided GIS data, collected in 2007, for this map. Bamlaku Amente, an expert in GIS at Addis Ababa University, assisted me with mapping the data.

Amhara groups. For example *abegar*, a conflict resolution mechanism employing elders who claim to have hereditary divine power, is practised among the Amhara of Wollo (see Uthman 2008). Among the Amhara of North Shewa, people seek remedies to conflict before a *wofa legesse*, a spirit medium (see Melaku and Wubshet 2008). These and other CDRMs are traditionally used to resolve conflicts varying from simple interpersonal disputes to the most serious cases of homicide.

The terms *shimgilinna* and *shimagillé* carry two different meanings: biological and cultural. In the biological sense, *shimgilinna* (lit. 'aging') refers to getting old, that is growing grey hair, getting wrinkles and becoming weak. The term *shimagillé* (lit. 'old') refers to an aged person. *Shimgilinna* in the cultural sense refers to a CDRM institution while *shimagillé* (Amharic pl. *shimgilinna woch*; English pl. *shimagillés*) refers to a council of elders tasked with resolving conflicts for free. In this latter sense, *shimgilinna* is a wider institution that includes *shimagillé*.

Shimgilinna as a CDRM has normative and procedural aspects. The normative aspect refers to the long-established system of beliefs, values, and norms used for promoting peace and resolving conflicts. In the Amhara community, they are known as *ye'abatader hig* (lit. 'the laws of the fathers') (Yohannis 1998). The procedural aspect refers to the steps taken in the process of conflict resolution. Traditionally, conflict resolution through *shimgilinna* followed a certain procedure that began with identifying the causes of conflict and ended with the restoration of an amicable relationship between the disputants. In most cases, members of the council of elders are elderly people, although age is not an exclusive requirement: younger people can also be called *shimagillé* and assume a role in conciliation, for they are the 'wise of the young'. *Shimagillés* need the respect of the society in which they live in, wisdom, the oratory skills to convince people, and a sense of fairness in arbitration.

There are different types of *shimgilinna*. *Yegiligil shimgilinna* is conciliation between parties in an on-going disagreement. *Erq* refers to conciliation between disputants whose relationship had already broken down in an earlier conflict. There is also *dem adreq shimgilinna*, which usually refers to conciliation aimed at stopping a lengthy conflict between families, involving a cycle of retaliatory killings, hence *dem adreq* (lit. 'to stop bloodshed'). Finally, there is *yebetezemed guba'e* (lit. 'family council'), which settles disputes that arise between husbands and wives.

Shimgilinna is integrated into different levels of societal organization in Ankober. If a conflict occurs in a neighbourhood or village and is small in magnitude or relatively uncomplicated, elders in the village will handle the case. This type of conciliation is called *yesefer* (lit. 'village') *shimgilinna*. On the other hand, larger and more complicated conflicts are resolved by more influential elders selected from the wider community in what is called *yehager* (lit. 'country level') *shimgilinna*. There is also a version of *shimgilinna* that resolves conflicts between subscribers to the informal insurance arrangements known as *iddir*. Similarly, *yesebeka guba'e shimgilinna* operates between church members. Each parish of the Ethiopian Orthodox Church has different committees, one of which is *yesebeka guba'e shimagillé* (lit. 'council of parish elders'), made up of respected members of the community and the Church. People sometimes prefer to bring disputes to the Church council of elders.

Shimgilinna in Ankober is and has always been male-dominated. First, there is no direct participation of women as *shimagillés*, since – as a well-known Amhara proverb says – 'Man (belongs to) to the public and woman to the kitchen'. Second, women's interests are suppressed when they are parties to a dispute. According to the head of Ankober Woreda Women's League, when a woman brings a case to *shimgilinna*, she will be told by the *shimagillés*: 'You are a woman, you need to tolerate this'; or 'You don't have to bring this case in public'; or, if a woman challenges a decision of *shimagillés*, 'You have to accept the decision because you are a woman'. In *shimgilinna*, conflict and its resolution is often seen from a male perspective.

Co-existence of *shimgilinna* and the formal justice system

For each tier of administration in Ethiopia's regional states, there is a corresponding tier of court. The regional states have a supreme court, the zonal administrations have high courts, and the *woredas* have a first instance court. This means that the entire *woreda* of Ankober has one *woreda* court. *Woreda* courts are located in towns that are usually administrative centres and are thus more accessible to urban than rural residents.

However, there are also *kebele* level social courts[6] that deliver justice at the lowest level of the community. In Ankober *Woreda*, there are twenty-two *kebeles*, each with a social court. The jurisdiction of the social courts in Amhara Region in August 2017, according to the presiding judge of a *kebele* social court in Gorebella town, was over civil matters whose value is not more than 1,500 Ethiopian Birr (ETB). The maximum punishment social courts can impose is 300 ETB or one month's imprisonment. The courts cover small-scale crime such as minor theft and insult, but they do not resolve disputes involving bodily injury or bleeding. Any party dissatisfied with the decision of the social courts can appeal to a committee of three *shimagillés*,

6 *Social courts* are *kebele*-level courts in Ethiopia that address minor claims at the grassroots level. Each of the nine regional states and the two city states (Addis Ababa and Dire Dawa) determine the jurisdiction of social courts, hence their competence differs slightly from state to state. For example, according to Article 9(3)(d) of Proclamation No. 361/2003 (The Addis Ababa City Government Revised Charter Proclamation), Addis Ababa City's social courts have jurisdiction over disputes whose monetary value is not over 5,000 ETB (Art. 50(1)), while the jurisdiction of Amhara Regional State social courts at the time of this research covered cases not over 1,500 ETB. A *kebele* social court has usually three judges, one presiding judge, one secretary and one member.

selected and appointed by the community. If they are then not satisfied with the committee's decision, they can file their claim with the *woreda* court.

As well as working with the courts, *shimagillés* work with the *kebeles* quasi-formal, state-initiated conflict resolution institutions known as *gichit aswegaj* committees (lit. 'conflict prevention/resolution committee'), which consist of approximately seven members.[7] The committees are a common platform for the community police, security and administration office, and the community. Members are drawn from *shimagillés* and representatives of government offices. After the community policing officers report a case to the *kebele* police, the latter determine which organ should handle the conflict. If it falls under their jurisdiction, cases are forwarded to the *gichit aswegaj* committee.

Manipulation of consent

Giving and withdrawing consent at different stages of dispute resolution

In Ankober, dispute resolution through *shimgilinna* can be initiated by the court, by the disputants, or by *shimagillés*. According to judges at Ankober Woreda Court, the court encourages parties to settle personal or family cases through *shimgilinna* because it reduces the burden on the court and also restores good relationships between the disputants. Disputants themselves may also direct their case to *shimgilinna* immediately, or after the case has been filed with the court. In the latter case, they simply have to inform the court of their decision and then the court authorizes the request. Finally, *shimagillés* themselves may initiate a dispute resolution by indicating their willingness to arbitrate either to the conflicting parties or to the court. In all cases, the results of the conciliation have to be reported to, and approved by, the court.

However, cases from Ankober show that the sustaining of consent for cases to be brought before the *shimagillé* is uncertain and slightly depends on who initiated a case. If the court initiates *shimgilinna*, either or both parties in a dispute can discontinue the process at any stage. Either party can also refuse to comply with any agreement reached. This means that there is no end to the use of consent to initiate or end a *shimgilinna* process and its outcome. The only limit is the formal submission of a decision in writing to the court, on the basis of which the court will give its judgment. Both parties then have to fill in and sign a form from the court, confirming that their dispute has been resolved. As a judge from Ankober

7 Directives of Operation of Committee of Peace, No. 001/2002, The Amhara National Regional State Administration and Security Affairs Office, Bahir Dar, document in Amharic.

Woreda Court explained, after the signed form has been submitted to the court, the parties cannot invoke consent to reverse the decision either jointly or severally.

When *shimgilinna* is invoked locally, without the prior authorization of the court, the situation is slightly different. Even though parties can revoke their consent at any stage of the conciliation process, they are obliged to abide to the agreed decision of the *shimagillé*, which can be fixed either orally or in writing. The decision is binding, without any form having to be signed and submitted to the court. However, the Ankober Woreda Court judges have different views on the legal enforceability of decisions of this type in cases where one of the parties disagrees with the outcome. Some judges apply principles of general contract (see Articles 1696–1710 of the 1960 Civil Code) and argue that, as long as the dispute resolution is duly made and consent for conciliation was given by both parties, the decisions of the *shimagillés* should be endorsed by the court. Any party who rejects the decision should be forced to comply. Other judges say that the validity of such contracts should be proved through new litigation if one of the parties denies its performance by withdrawing consent to an agreement already reached or refusing to give consent in the first place. There is no uniform practice among the judges in the Woreda Court and each judge follows what he or she believes is right.

Reasons for and mechanisms of giving or withdrawing 'consent'

Parties in a dispute use their right to give or withdraw consent to control the *shimgilinna*/court process and/or results: (1) for their own personal benefit; (2) for the benefit of others; (3) to harm others; or (4) to avoid a negative outcome when they are uncertain of the decision that will be made. In the following, some of the mechanisms of such an abuse are discussed.

Exploitation of chances from missing evidence

The principle of consent can be manipulated in order to take advantage of someone who is unable to produce the required evidence to prove their claim in court. This may occur when an agreement, such as a contract, has not been made in a valid form, or when one party has failed to preserve evidence relating to a given dispute. Let us consider the following case, obtained from an interview of two informants who were *shimagillés* in the case.

> Nesibu,[8] 65, hereafter creditor, gave a loan of 5000 ETB to his friend, Asaminew, 54, hereafter debtor, in May 2010. According to the creditor, the debtor borrowed the money from him to cover the wedding expenses of his two children, a son and a daughter, who got married in a joint ceremony. The debtor promised to return

8 The names mentioned in this paper are all pseudonyms.

> the money by the next harvest season. However, in the end, he refused to repay the loan, denying he had received any money at all from the creditor. The creditor approached *shimagillés* to resolve the case peacefully. The *shimagillés* managed to persuade the debtor to enter into arbitration. In the course of the arbitration, the debtor's statements varied. At first, he admitted to having received money, yet a smaller amount than the creditor claimed to have given him. At another time, he denied having received any money at all. In the end, the debtor withdrew his consent to be arbitrated by *shimagillés*. When the creditor took the case to court, the court required written contractual evidence to prove the loan, which the creditor did not have. Thus, in the end, the creditor lost the court case. According to the *shimagillés*, this kind of case has become common (summary of an interview with two elders, February 2012).

According to Article 2472 of the 1960 Civil Code, contracts for loans for sums over 500 ETB have to be made in writing. Moreover, Article 1727(1) provides that any contract required to be made in writing 'shall be of no effect unless it is attested by two witnesses', so that if the evidence is lost, witnesses to the written contract can testify to prove a claim. In the above case, however, as there was no written contract, no witness could be adduced to the court, including the *shimagillés* who had attempted to resolve the case and before whom the debtor had admitted taking the loan. In cases like the above, the involvement of *shimagillés* is often more successful as they do not rely only on evidence to prove a case. They use different techniques, such as oratorical skills of persuasion, demanding oaths and threatening with curses, to convince the conflicting parties to come to an agreement. Therefore, from the perspective of the debtor, it was to his advantage to have the case handled in the formal court, where disputes are won or lost on the basis of evidence.

Exploitation of chances from an adversary's level of social standing

Some disputants file their case with either the customary or formal court with the intention of hearing the case from their adversary's perspective in order to assess the level of evidence he or she can produce. Someone who sees that their adversary is more competent in the formal court may suggest moving the case to the customary court. They may lobby or even force, by exerting social pressure – as shown in the next paragraph – the other party to give consent for *shimgilinna*. If, on the other hand, an adversary's standing is strong in the customary court, the other party can thwart *shimgilinna* by withdrawing consent and moving the case to the formal court. The consent of both parties is required to enter *shimgilinna*, but the withdrawal of one is enough to end it.

As mentioned in the preceding paragraph, an adversary's level of social standing, by which I mean the ability to exert social pressure on an opponent, also determines the provision and maintenance of consent to a particular legal forum. One elder I interviewed remembered the following case, where one party maintained control over a dispute resolution.

> In June 2016, a dispute occurred between Sergew, 45, hereafter plaintiff, and Yihalem, 32, hereafter defendant, when the defendant damaged some of the plaintiff's crops while the latter was ploughing on a bordering land with the former. The plaintiff who had more family members than the defendant took the case to *shimgilinna*. He exaggerated the loss and demanded compensation from the defendant. Some of the shimagillés were the plaintiff's supporters and the defendant knew the decision would be made against him. Moreover, the defendant was scared of the opponent's aggressive family members. Thus, at first, he rejected the *shimgilinna* saying that the plaintiff can take the case to the court. However, the plaintiff pressurized the defendant to give his consent to the *shimgilinna*. As expected, the plaintiff was compensated with 1.200 ETB for his loss, a sum much higher than the damage he had incurred. (Summary of an interview with an elder, June 2017)

The above case illustrates that consent is used as a weapon by socially powerful disputants, who employ their local connections by taking the case to the *shimgilinna* at the expense of weaker adversaries. It shows that as much as socially powerful parties benefit from the right to give and withdraw consent, those in weaker positions may suffer through it.

Use and abuse of *shimagillés* as witnesses in the court

Some disputants enter *shimgilinna* intending to prepare the ground by using the *shimagillés* as witnesses when the case is later taken to court. This may happen with or without the knowledge of the *shimagillés*. Sometimes, one party may even bribe *shimagillés* and misuse their influence. Such *shimagillés* may misguide other *shimagillés* or the other party in the dispute during *shimgilinna,* and they may trick them into exposing issues that can be later used as evidence against them in the court. Though the *shimagillés* I talked to were not willing to give me concrete examples, they expressed a belief that it was becoming common for *shimagillés* to be partisan and to serve as false witnesses in court.

Breaking agreements on the choice of a forum

When two parties enter a contract, they sometimes agree on a legal forum to which they will turn if dispute arises. Sometimes, they agree to use *shimgilinna* only. However, one party may bring an action in the court, betraying the terms of the agreement and leaving the *shimgilinna* aside, if things turn out to be less favourable. In the existing practice, there are no ways to enforce parties to use the legal forum agreed beforehand. Many of the *shimagillés* I talked to stated that they had experienced this kind of cheating.

Effects on justice delivery and conflict resolution culture

The unrestricted freedom to use consent in forum shopping has consequences for justice delivery and the conflict resolution culture of the people. Dispensation of justice is often delayed as cases transfer to *shimgilinna* and return without resolution, or as they are transferred between the two forums more than once. Moreover, the manipulation of consent and the position of adversaries lead to unfair results, which in turn lead to secondary conflicts between disputants. It has also affected the values and procedures of *shimgilinna*.

Delay in justice delivery

An examination of Ankober Woreda Court records shows that the court transfers many cases to the *shimgilinna* whenever the parties involved agree. There are no restrictions on this and sending cases to the *shimgilinna* means that, in theory, the burden on the court is reduced. However, a major problem is that many cases return to the court without having been resolved. The *shimagillés'* efforts are rendered futile and become an extra burden on the court. As the table below shows, between 2011/2012 and 2016/2017, the number of cases transferred to the *shimagillés* increased, while the number of cases settled by them decreased. According to a judge in Ankober *Woreda*, despite the judges' efforts to keep disputes related to personal and family matters out of the court, many of them return without getting resolved.

Table 1: The transfer and resolution of cases between court and shimagillés, 2011–17 (Desalegn 2018) [9]

Year		Cases filed with the court	Cases transferred to *shimagillés*	%		Settled by *shimagillés*	Re-turned to court	%
2011/2012		693	28	4		28	-	0
2012/2013		592	145	24		95	50	35
2013/2014		791	221	28		67	154	70
2014/2015		779	104	13		69	35	34
2015/2016		1175	405	34		187	218	54
2016/2017		1377	475	34		120	355	75

9 Data was compiled from Ankober Woreda Court record management office.

Justice delivery is further prolonged since there is no limit, at least theoretically, to the number of times a case can be moved between the formal and customary courts. As one judge stated, the same case can move back and forth between the two fora up to ten times. A judge for over fifteen years, he had observed that the time needed to resolve certain cases had increased due to their movement between the two fora. There is no law that defines how many times a case can be transferred to *shimgilinna*. Judges send cases back to *shimgilinna* several times because of the right of the parties to give, refuse and withdraw their consent to have them handled through customary mechanisms. Judges may refer a case to *shimgilinna*, disregarding the number of times they have already done so, when they believe, for example, it is more just to do so, or when the nature of the case means it can be better resolved through *shimgilinna*. The following case over marital property division serves as a good example of a single case moving between the two legal forums several times.

Plaintiff: Mebrat Ayele, wife
Defendant: Asaminew Demisse, husband
On 18 June 2017, the plaintiff filed a claim over a partition of marital property. The court scheduled an appointment for both, the plaintiff and the defendant, to appear ten days later. The court examined both the claim and the defence. At this first appointment, the court advised the parties to end their dispute through *shimgilinna*. It selected five *shimagillés* (names omitted) and, if they proved successful in settling the dispute, ordered them to submit their decision in writing. The court scheduled another appointment after three weeks, when it anticipated it would receive the *shimagillés*' decision. But in that time, the parties failed to agree. Thus, at that second appointment, the court continued to hear the plaintiff's case.
The plaintiff's argument was as follows: 'Regarding the steel house mentioned in the suit, I have contributed 7.450 ETB from my own separate property. Our common property is 22.550 ETB. I ask the court to order the defendant to pay my share from this sum. We also have a hop garden. The defendant falsely said we used up the garden. But, the garden I am talking about is a different one. Even from the one he said we had used it up, our agreement was that he would give me 400 ETB since he sold the hops without my knowledge. Thirdly, he borrowed 2.100 ETB from me while we were still living together, so he should return the loan to me. Fourthly, the defendant claims to have a separate land of his own, which is true. But he 'sold' that land to a third party, and I bought it back. Now, I ask the court to

order the defendant to pay to me 1.000 ETB to cover the expenses I incurred when I reclaimed the land'.

The defendant's argument was as follows: 'Firstly, yes, when we constructed the house of corrugated iron sheets, the sheets were bought by the plaintiff's separate money of 7,450 ETB. The rest of the money was on an equal share. Thus, I will give her the 7,450 ETB and will equally share the common expenses. Secondly, regarding the hops, I sold the hops leaves for 800 ETB, and I agreed to pay the plaintiff 400 ETB. The other hop garden she mentioned was estimated to be worth 300 ETB and I already agreed to pay the plaintiff half of that, 150 ETB. Bringing this case to the court is not appropriate. Thirdly, she did not give me a loan of 2,100 ETB, that money was used for common marital matters, so she should not ask me to pay that back. Fourthly, it is true that she spent 1,000 ETB to reclaim the land I sold, but, after that, we used the land in common for three years, so she should not ask that money from me.

The court scheduled the next appointment for eleven days later, but when both of them appeared on that day, the court said the case had not yet been decided. The two parties then asked the court to authorize them for a second time to end their dispute through *shimgilinna*. The court allowed them to do so and authorized them to come with a decision two weeks later. When they came back to the court on the appointed day, the two parties reported that they had still been unable to agree, so the court gave them another appointment another two weeks later. By that day, again, they had not been able to resolve their dispute.

This time, the *shimagillés* themselves came and asked the court to extend their deadline for the third time; they were given one more week. When they came to that last appointment, the parties said they were not able to agree through *shimgilinna*, so the court dismissed the case for another two weeks so the judges could make a final judgment.

While the court was preparing its final decision, the parties involved were working on their own resolution to the dispute. On the day the judges expected to give their verdict, they were presented with a written agreement by the parties involved. The judge made sure the agreement was made with the full consent of both parties and that the decision did not contradict morality. With this, the case ended (Summary of interview with a judge from Ankober Woreda Court July 2017 and Ankober Woreda Court File Number 011/985).

Neither the case notes nor my informant spelled out the reasons behind the failure of the *shimagillés* to resolve the case, or the parties' motives for the case. However, when talked to the *shimagillés* involved, they told me that the two parties were not convinced of the need to dissolve their marriage. One of the *shimagillés* stated: 'We knew of this and we tried to repair their relationship. However, having agreed to our proposal in one moment, they refused in another.' According to the *shimagillé's* view, by changing their minds many times, the parties bought themselves time in which to decide whether or not they should divorce.

The Ankober Woreda Court does not keep records of the transfer history of each case, aside from the initial transfer. Even if a case is transferred to *shimgilinna* three or four times, this information is not recorded. An archivist in the court, who I interviewed in July 2017, told me that although they report the court's performance to the zonal court, the reporting format does not require the history of each case to be recorded. However, by investigating each record with the help of some assistants, I attempted to reconstruct the history of 475 cases that were transferred to *shimagillés* in 2016/2017 (see Table 1 above). The results are as follows.[10]

Figure 2: Transfer frequency of individual cases (2016/2017) (Desalegn 2018)

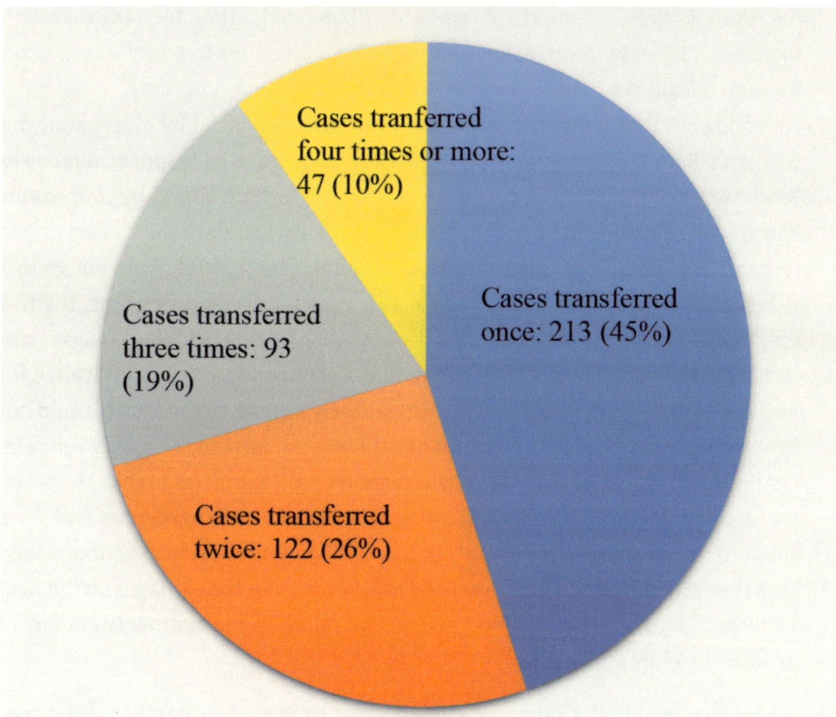

It was not possible to disaggregate cases for previous years in order to get a comparative insight because it was unfeasible to deal with all the files in the time

10 Data has been compiled from Ankober Woreda Court record management office.

available. However, the judges agreed that not only the number of cases transferred (as shown on Table 1) but also the number of times they are transferred is increasing.

Secondary conflicts

The number of secondary conflicts is recorded neither by the *woreda* nor the social courts. However, many informants, including *shimagillés*, disputants, and judges, believe that secondary disputes are often created or aggravated by the manipulation of the right to give or withdraw consent. The following case, narrated to me by one of the *shimagillé* involved in 2017, is an example of one such conflict.

> On 3 December 2015, the cattle of Taddesse had trespassed onto Gezmu's field and damaged some of his crops. Two weeks later, a *shimgilinna* was organized to bring the two parties to peace. After almost half a day of deliberations, the elders decided that Taddesse should pay 1,000 Birr for damage. Taddesse, unhappy with the result, withdrew from the *shimgilinna*. When Gezmu then filed the case with the court, Taddesse immediately expressed his willingness to end the case again through *shimgilinna*.
>
> Following this, another conciliation event was organized by elders almost a year later. Before the *shimgilinna* started, Gezmu is said to have spoken directly to Taddesse, saying: 'From the day of your birth, you are not bound by your words. You are not reliable and have the character of the wicked since the wicked do not respect *shimagillés*.' The situation changed and the two parties could not go to a *shimgilinna* at that day. After the conciliation was interrupted this time, the two men started to seek to physically attack each other. On one day when Tadesse was coming home from town late in the evening, Gezmu and some friends waited for him and beat him up. Taddesse, who was severely injured by the attack, could not take any legal action since he did not have witnesses. Instead, he took revenge by beating Gezmu almost to death. Again there were no witnesses to this. The situation escalated into a group dispute when each of them mobilized more and more supporters. The matter ended only in July 2017 when the *shimagillés* intervened for a third time. Then, Taddesse paid Gezmu 800 Birr for the damages on the field and loss of crops, and both men forgave each other for the beating (summary of an interview July 2017).

So, we see that manipulation of consent can lead to secondary conflict and sometimes to verbal and/or physical confrontation when one of the parties feels manipulated, betrayed, or unfairly treated by the other. Such conflicts can arise at the individual level or between groups. Some people also resort to sorcery to take revenge when they feel unfairly treated.[11]

Loss of the culture of respect for shimgilinna

Elders and judges also outlined their view that the lack of restrictions on consent in forum shopping has caused or exacerbated the loss of the conflict resolution culture among the youth and the community at large in Ankober. The elders characterize such changes as a 'dilution of culture' (*yebahil meberez*). The following section outlines the loss of the culture of respect toward *shimgilinna* and *shimagillés* in conflict resolution.

The youth

The youth's[12] loyalty to *shimgilinna* decreased as a result of the latter's attempts to resolve conflicts over resources, particularly land. The youth strive for access to land by every possible means. However, what used to work in more stable, peaceful, earlier times, many stated, no longer works. Elders also complained that the youth act selfishly in land disputes: they do not respect their parents and do not respect each other with other family members. A priest who is also a *shimagillé* told me: 'Nowadays, it is common to observe family members fighting with each other. We have even seen a youth who killed his father over a land dispute.' Other researchers (e.g. Balew 2016) have also shown that land is the leading cause of dispute among the Amhara today.

Many elders complained that the problem with the youth goes beyond the manipulation of consent in resource disputes, claiming that they are abandoning their culture. The change is so strong that families are not able to influence the youth anymore. Informants expressed their discontent with the modern education system, which does not teach children enough about respecting their own culture, including *shimgilinna*. Instead, students have an incomplete notion that being modern means disrespecting their own culture. The community is also critical of the influence of mass and social media. Elders also criticized modern law since it allows the youth to leave *shimgilinna* any time, thus rendering the elders powerless.

---

11 One informant told me how, after he had moved his own case between the court and the *shimagillés* and finally got a favourable decision from the court, his adversary threatened him. One day he found blood had been sprinkled over his cattle in the night. He was convinced that this was the work of the adversary who intended to kill his cattle or make them unproductive. He removed the alleged spell by sprinkling holy water over the animals.

12 The definition of 'young' and 'youth' differs based on who defines it. The Federal Ministry of Youth, Sport and Culture, 2004, used the term 'youth' for individuals between 15 and 29 years of age. The view of Ankober people suggests youth can also refer to a particular mind-set of being educated and having a different style of hairdo, dressing and the like.

Exploitation of the right to consent by other community members

Unreasonable exploitation of chances by giving and withdrawing consent can also be observed among other age groups. According to judges in Ankober Woreda Court, disputes often arise and are filed with the court over the dissolution of marriage, inheritance, and breaches of fraudulent contracts. Disputants in these matters enter a win–lose suit by using the freedom of consent to move cases between the two legal forums.

Corruption among elders

Some elders and members of the community complained about the *shimagillés* themselves. One elder with experience in *shimgilinna* since the regime of Haile Selassie I (r. 1931–1974) said that, in the past, there were many trustworthy *shimagillés* in every village who worked for free. Nowadays, he complained, the spirit of economic benefit is influencing *shimagillés*: less and less of them are willing to serve for free. There are even several rumours about *shimagillés* being bribed to influence the process or outcome of *shimgilinna* in favour of one of the parties. Corruption and nepotism are increasingly interfering with the fairness of *shimagillés*, and it is reported that unrestricted use of consent provides one loophole through which they can operate.

Loyalty towards elders in urban and rural communities
Disadvantage to women

Interviews with judges and *shimagillés* suggested that loyalty to *shimgilinna* varies between *urban* and *rural communities*. Rural people seem more likely to be loyal to *shimgilinna, while* urban and more educated disputants often give more value to economic rather than cultural issues. In Ankober Woreda, there are twenty-two rural *kebeles*, while Gorebella and Ankober are labelled as towns. People's loyalty to *shimgilinna* seems to increase the further away from the towns they live. Access to the Woreda Court also determines parties' loyalty to *shimgilinna*. As an elder informant who lives in a remote village said: 'The Woreda Court is very far from our village and *shimgilinna* is still our security.' Rural communities' preference for traditional institutions and urban communities' preference for the court is documented in several case studies though at various levels of emphasis (see for example, Meron 2010, Demissie 2005, Fekade *et al.* 2011, Pankhurst and Getachew 2008, and Tarekegn and Hannah 2008).

The disadvantage of women in *shimgilinna* has also been documented in many studies. The studies show that women are not allowed to be *shimagillés*, and that the decisions of *shimagillés* are more favourable to men (see for example Mekuanint

2015, Tarekegn and Hannah 2008).[13] What has not been discussed, however, is the role played by the right to give and withdraw consent on the ability to exert pressure on women and other weak members of the society. Interviews with the head of the Women's Office in Ankober and the heads of other women's associations in the area showed that, although women today are asserting their legal rights increasingly, they are still less influential than men. When men want to present a case to the *shimagillés*, they often force women to accept and give their consent to resolve the issue through customary law. In this way, there is an unfair treatment of cases, for example, between divorcees. The head of Ankober Woreda Women's Federation expressed her feeling that the government's enacted laws on equality for women have still not been fully implemented. According to her, 'You can discover many horrible things made to women in villages as the result of them being exploited in the name of consent!'

Changes in *shimgilinna*

The abuse of consent in *shimgilinna* has evoked changes in certain dimensions of the institution itself. *Shimagillés* have begun to follow traditional procedure a bit differently and some normative aspects of the process have become less accepted. In what follows, I will discuss selective acceptance of cases by *shimagillés*, changes in the mode of hearing parties during conflict resolution, and the role of guarantors, witnesses and coercive mechanisms in conflict resolution.

Selective acceptance of cases by *shimagillés*

When the parties in a dispute decide to resolve it through *shimgilinna*, they must, in the first place, choose *shimagillés* on whom they both agree. Some *shimagillés* have a better reputation in the community than others and thus receive more requests to sit for *shimgilinna*. However, they do not accept all invitations. They first collect information about any disputes they are requested to resolve, about the parties involved, and about their co-*shimagillés*. If they believe that there are bad motives behind the *shimgilinna*, they may reject the offer.

One *shimagillé* I interviewed in August 2017 claimed that, on average, he received five offers per month. Of these, he rejected about two per month on the basis that he suspected dishonest motives or felt that either or both parties would give up the arbitration at some stage if they feared an unwanted outcome. When he believed his efforts would be fruitful, he would follow the disputants into the court and suggest the latter send the case to *shimgilinna*, where he would serve as a *shimagillé*. Conflicting parties rejected by him either approached other *shimagillés*

13 Many case studies in the edited volume by Tarekegn and Hannah (2008) identified that women's participation in the CDRMs of different ethnic groups is not active.

or went to the court. As he stated, the selective acceptance of cases by elders is becoming common due to an increased risk of manipulation of consent.

Hearing parties separately

There are two procedures for hearing disputants' statements in *shimgilinna*: face to face and separately. In a face-to-face hearing, the oratorical and persuasive skills of the plaintiffs and respondents play a major role. The main characteristic of this procedure is its adversarial nature, so the ability to succeed depends on the ability to persuade the *shimagillés*. However, cautious *shimagillés* no longer follow, or follow carefully, this procedure since it may allow one disputant to make another expose evidence that may later be used in court. Hearing disputants separately is becoming more common, and the alleged wrongdoer is kept away until the victim's statements have been heard. The *shimagillés* weigh the two parties' statements and identify the relevant points, based on which they can resolve the dispute.

Another significant change is that the role of oral witnesses in *shimgilinna* is becoming unimportant. In the past, *shimagillés* required both parties to bring individuals who would testify in a case. However, the credibility of witnesses is declining nowadays. As one *shimagillé* said: 'Today, false witnesses are ruining the country.' Judges in Ankober Woreda Court also complained that it is a growing problem.

Lack or unimportance of guarantors

One stage of *shimgilinna* is when disputants choose *yezemed dagna* (lit. 'judge of the relatives'), who serves as a chairperson of the conflict resolution process. Though the name seems to imply this, a *yezemed dagna* need not be a blood relative of any of the parties or other *shimagillés*. The title has to be understood as a metaphor, referring to the hopefully positive outcome of the arbitration, which ideally transforms the hostile parties into relatives. A *yezemed dagna* is expected to be reputable, impartial, and considered as trustworthy by the other *shimagillés* involved in the case. If the parties do not reach a consensus with the *yezemed dagna*, the *shimagillés* themselves can choose one from amongst themselves.

Traditionally, a *yezemed dagna* asked each party to name a guarantor of their obedience to *shimgilinna*. But today, the *shimgilinna* functions only as long as the consent of parties exists, thus, there is neither a need to name a guarantor nor to penalize the parties if either breaches the agreed decision. People do not want to act as guarantors anymore since the disputants can withdraw from *shimgilinna*. The guarantors also know that they are responsible for ensuring payment of any fines arising from the conciliation. One informant, who acted as a guarantor in 2015, told me he was forced to buy five litres of local liquor (*araqé*) for the *shimagillés* and pay 1,000 ETB to the disputant who had remained loyal to *shimgilinna*. Once a guarantor enters an agreement, he explained, he remains bound by the obligation, while the original debtor can go free by invoking consent. He told me: 'It was my naivety to take the role as a guarantor. Now, people do not commit themselves to this obligation.'

Social pressure and supernatural forces becoming less important

In the past, *shimagillés* could impose various social, moral or religious sanctions on disputants and give weight to the conflict resolution through ritual ceremonies. For example, after an elaborate conflict resolution process, one final ceremony traditionally involved stepping over guns. A gun or guns, preferably ones used in a conflict, were placed on the ground and the disputants were made to jump over them while making an oath to end the dispute. The disputants would say: 'If I break the oath, let the guns not miss their target on me. If one misses, let another not!'

Such oath-taking ceremonies were common in conflicts between the Amhara and the Argobba/Afar, who follow different religions. If both disputants were Christians, a church ceremony was alternatively made. Disputants made an oath while carrying a cross or opening a church door; to break the oath would be a sin and meant being struck by an ailment called *mushro*. This disease begins as a tiny wound somewhere on the body, usually on a finger, and then expands rapidly to all parts and eventually kills the person. According to one *shimagillé*: 'This is the disease God created for oath breakers.'

However, neither the gun nor the church ceremonies are nowadays as effective as they used to be. One *shimagillé* explained: 'Nowadays, the notion of sanctity is decreasing; certain oaths said out loud during or at the end of a conflict resolution can be denied later when a disputant goes to court, rejecting progress made through *shimgilinna*.' *Shimagillés* cannot force parties to make an oath since they can discontinue the settlement process at any time or simply ignore its result.

Conclusion

Since 1995, when the Federal Constitution and state constitutions have outlined similar stipulations about consent as a pre-requisite for entering and staying in CDRMs, *shimgilinna* has turned into a consensual transaction. Consent plays a key role in a practical thinking of gain or loss that uses or abuses *shimgilinna,* impacting the prompt dispensation of justice and changing the customary dispute resolution culture of the people. This suggests the need for the regulative laws promised by the federal and regional constitution. Several questions need to be answered, including whether, once given, consent to dispute resolution through *shimgilinna* can be withdrawn and, if yes, at what level of the conflict resolution spectrum. What kind of test can we use to distinguish honest discontinuation of consent from dishonest? Should determination of whether consent has been given be left to the *shimgilinna* itself, or should there be detailed legal provision? The application of consent in the religious courts of Sharia could provide an example. Article 5(4) of Proclamation No. 188/1999 on Federal Courts of Sharia states that 'under no circumstance shall a case brought before a court of Sharia the jurisdiction of which has been consented to, be transferred to a regular court; nor shall a case before a regular court be transferred to a court of Sharia'. Parties dissatisfied with a decision can appeal to the next level of the Sharia Court, structured from lowest to highest: Federal First Instance Court of Sharia, Federal High Court of Sharia, and Federal Supreme Court of Sharia (see Article 3). The law also seems to create a hard line by which a party aggrieved by the decision of a Sharia Court cannot appeal to regular courts. Whether or not the Sharia courts can set a good example needs further investigation, but, one thing that clearly emerges from the experiences of the community among the Ankober Woreda is that there should be a law to reduce the negative effects associated with the arbitrary giving and withdrawal of consent to *shimgilinna* and perhaps other institutions in other parts of the country.

References

ALEMAYEHU Feyera, 2009 *The role of traditional conflict resolution methods in resolving cross-border community conflicts: The case of Borena-Gebra and Garri across the Ethio-Kenyan border*. Addis Ababa: Addis Ababa University (MA Thesis)

ASNAKE Menbere, 2010 *Inter-group conflicts in the Awash valley of Ethiopia: The case of Afar and Karrayu Oromo*. Addis Ababa: Addis Ababa University (MA Thesis)

ASSEFA Tolera, 1995 *Ethnic integration and conflict: The case of indigenous Oromo and Amhara settlers in Aaroo Addis Alem, Kiramo Area, North Eastern Wallaga*. Addis Ababa: Addis Ababa University (MA Thesis)

ANRS 2001, *The 2001 revised constitution of Amhara National Regional State*. Bahir Dar: ANRS

AYKE Asfaw and MEKONEN Feleke, 2008 "Customary dispute resolution in SNNPR: The case of Sidama", in: Alula Pankhurst and Getachew Assefa (eds.), *Grass-roots justice in Ethiopia. The contribution of customary dispute resolution*, 201–215. Addis Ababa: CFEE

AWGCAO, 2016 *Soreni: Ankober Woreda Government Communication Affairs Office Bulletin*. Ankober: AWGCAO

BALEW Baye 2016 *Traditional conflict resolution in Fogera Woreda: Documentation and analysis of the discourse*. Addis Ababa: Addis Ababa University (PhD Thesis)

CENTRAL STATISTICAL AGENCY (CSA), 2008 *Summary and statistical report of the 2007 population and housing census*. Addis Ababa: CSA

DEMISSIE Gudisa, 2005 *Social network, conflict and indigenous conflict resolution mechanisms among the Debra Oromo of North Shewa*. Addis Ababa: Addis Ababa University (MA Thesis)

ESAYAS Awash, 2015 *Indigenous conflict resolution institutions: A study among the Gofa people of the Demba Gofa district, SNNPR*. Addis Ababa: Addis Ababa University (MA Thesis)

FEDERAL DEOCRATIC REPUBLIC OF ETHIOPIA (FDRE), 1996 *Proclamation No. 25/1996, Federal Courts Proclamation 2nd Year No.13*, FDRE: Federal Negarit Gazeta

1995 *Constitution of the Federal Democratic Republic of Ethiopia*. Addis Ababa: FDRE

FEKADE Azeze, ASSEFA Fiseha, and GEBRE Yntiso (eds.), 2011 *Annotated bibliography of studies on customary dispute settlement mechanisms in Ethiopia*. Addis Ababa: The Ethiopian Arbitration and Conciliation Centre

IMPERIAL GOVERNMENT OF ETHIOPIA, 1960 *Civil Code of the Empire of Ethiopia*, Proclamation No. 165/1960, Negarit Gazeta Extraordinary Issue, 1960-05-05, Year 19, No. 2 (accessible online at http://www.ilo.org/dyn/natlex/natlex4.detail?p_lang=en&p_isn=52399)

MEKUANINT Tesfaw, 2015 "Ethiopian women: Agents and subjects in the Shimglna (a customary conflict resolution institution): Amharas' experience in Meket District, North Wollo Zone", *Sociology and Anthropology* 3 (2):95–103

MELAKU Abate and WUBISCHET Shiferaw, 2008 "Customary dispute resolution in Amhara Region: The case of Wofa Legesse in North Shewa", in: Alula Pankhurst and Getachew Assefa (eds.) *Grass-roots justice in Ethiopia: The contribution of customary dispute resolution*, 107–21. Addis Ababa: CFEE

MERON Zeleke, 2010 "Ye shakoch chilot (the court of the sheikhs): A traditional institution of conflict resolution in Oromiya Zone of Amhara Regional State, Ethiopia", *African Journal on Conflict Resolution* 10 (1):63–84

PANKHURST, Alula and GETACHEW Assefa, 2008 "Understanding customary dispute resolution in Ethiopia", in: Alula Pankhurst and Getachew Assefa (eds.) *Grass-roots justice in Ethiopia: The contribution of customary dispute resolution*, 1–76. Addis Ababa: CFEE

SOLOMON Berhane, 2014 "Indigenous democracy: alternative conflict management mechanisms among Tigray people: The experiences of Erob", *Community Journal of Science & Development* 2 (2):101–122

TASEW Tafese, 2016 "Conflict management through African indigenous institutions: A study of the Anyuaa community", *World Journal of Social Science* 3 (1):22–32

TAREKEGN Adebo and HANNAH Tsadik, 2008 *Making peace in Ethiopia: Five cases of traditional mechanisms for conflict resolution*. Addis Ababa: Peace and Development Committee

TESFA Bihonegn, 2009 *Ethnic conflict resolution by the Federal Government of Ethiopia: A study of institutions and mechanisms*. Addis Ababa: Addis Ababa University (MA Thesis)

TEMESGEN Thomas, 2010 *The quest for common ethnic identify and self-governance in southern regional state within the context of the Ethiopian federal system: The case of the Gawada-Dhobase (Ale) ethnic group*. Addis Ababa: Addis Ababa University (MA Thesis)

TEKLE Dideu, 2009 *Inter-ethnic conflict management under the Ethiopian federal system: A case study of the conflict between Sidama and Guji Oromo groups in Wondogenet Woreda*. Addis Ababa: Addis Ababa University (MA Thesis)

TOLOSA Mamuye, 2010 *The role of women-based institution (siiqee) in conflict resolution: The case of west Arsi Oromo*. Addis Ababa: Addis Ababa University (MA Thesis)

UTHMAN Hassen, 2008 "The role of abegar (divine father) in conflict resolution: The case of north Wollo Zone", in: Tarekegn Adebo and Hannah Tsadik (eds.) *Making peace in Ethiopia: Five cases of traditional mechanisms for conflict resolution*, 78–100. Addis Ababa: Peace and Development Committee

WODISHA Habtie, 2010 *'Neema' – Traditional conflict resolution mechanisms of the Boro-Šinaŝha people, northwestern Ethiopia: Challenges and prospects*. Addis Ababa: Addis Ababa University (MA Thesis)

YOHANNIS Brhanu, 1998 *Conflict and conflict resolution among the people of Chehara*. Addis Ababa: Addis Ababa University (MA Thesis)

Procalamations

Proclamation No. 361/2003 (The Addis Ababa City Government Revised Charter Proclamation),

Directives of Operation of Committee of Peace, No. 001/2002, The Amhara National Regional State Administration and Security Affairs Office, Bahir Dar, document in Amharic.

Proclamation No. 188/1999 on Federal Courts of Sharia

III.

Emerging hybridity of legal institutions and practices

9. Local strategies to maintain cultural integrity
The vernacularization of state law among the Bashada and Hamar of southern Ethiopia

Susanne Epple

Introduction

The Bashada and Hamar people, like many of their ethnic neighbours in the southern peripheries of the country, have continued to adhere to their customs, beliefs and lifestyle, and have a reputation for being rather resistant to change and development. Being agro-pastoralists, until recently they lived in relative isolation from the centre. Although encounters between the agro-pastoralists of South Omo Zone and the government occured also under earlier regimes, intensified and continuous interaction began only in the mid 1990s, when large-scale investment and development projects (such as the creation of sugarcane plantations and sugar factories, and commercial farming) were implemented.[1] Together with a modernized infrastructure (asphalt roads, mobile and internet networks, health centres, etc.), and

1 According to government documents, Ethiopia aims to become a middle-income country by 2025. It is focusing on 'rapid, broad-based and inclusive economic growth with the aim of eradicating poverty' (FDRE 2015:2). This is to be achieved through the implementation of four successive national development plans by the Ministry of Finance and Economic Development (MoFED, renamed the Ministry of Finance and Economic Cooperation in 2015). From 2002, the focus has been on the transformation and growth of the rural economy, and particularly the agricultural sector (FDRE 2002:iii); the development of the private sector and commercialization of agriculture, industry and urban development (MoFED 2007:1); and the improvement to both the quantity and quality of social services, especially education, health and other infrastructural developments. These initiatives have led to several mega development projects. In South Omo, these include the construction of the Gibe dams for hydroelectric power, the construction of sugar and cotton plantations as well as sugar factories (Yohannes forthcoming). The search for oil, which continued for several years, ultimately without success (see http://www.oilnewskenya.com/africa-oil-relinquishes-ethiopias-south-omo-block). In 2017, Jinka University was inaugurated, and there are plans to build a railway linking Ethiopia with Kenya in the near future. Throughout all these projects, the government has aimed to improve the standard of living of the agro-pastoral communities by integrating them into the mainstream national economy. The relocation of Bodi and Mursi communities

an expansion of the educational system (construction of schools and educational projects), there came also a stricter implementation and enforcement of state law.[2]

The government's efforts to integrate the southern communities culturally, economically and legally into the Ethiopian nation state have caused a wide range of local reactions. Many of these have been interpreted as signs of the resistance of local communities to development, modernity and cultural change. Little recognition has been given to the efforts made by indigenous communities to adapt to and make sense of the state law in ways that do not force them to completely abandon practices and values that lie at the hearts of their cultures. Many dynamics have remained unnoticed and/or under-appreciated, both with regard to the local communities who have to deal with the new realities on the ground, and also with regard to lower-level government officials.

The reorganization of the Ethiopian state into an ethnic-based federal structure in 1995 came with greater representation of the local communities in local and zonal administration, as well as in regional and national politics. Cultural diversity and local practices were officially acknowledged in the new constitution of 1995, and are celebrated during national, regional and local events. In the 1995 constitution, Ethiopia explicitly granted every ethno-linguistic community 'the right to express, to develop and to promote its culture' (Art 34:2), recognized customary laws and allowed their application in civil and family cases (Art 34:5). However, this has been accompanied by intensified state intrusion, even in the remotest areas, intensive awareness-raising activities designed to inform the population about national law, and stricter enforcement of the state law, with the aim of resolving all criminal matters through state law and eliminating cultural practices that contradict human rights and gender equality. These moves are part of the more general aim of promoting development and modernization, which are among the top priorities of the country.

The implementation of national and international law is leading to conflict and confrontation in many places of the world. Contradictions between local customs or values and human rights are proving difficult to resolve. What is central to a group's identity may not be easily understood from the outside, or may be contradictory to

---

to small irrigation farms along the Omo River can be seen as part of these efforts (Abbink 2012, Turton 2011).

2 While the number of children attending school has increased in the last two decades, so far only a few of them have completed higher education. The number of university or college graduates from Hamar differs from *kebele* to *kebele*. The first Bashada student graduated from university with a BA degree only in 2018. Generally speaking, the first generation of Hamar graduates (together with graduates from Arbore and Kara with whom they share the district) now dominates the district administration, while non-local officials are underrepresented.

the national law. Keeping the balance between integrating culturally diverse communities into a nation state and allowing them to maintain their cultural integrity is a major challenge. Today, it is internationally recognized that cultural values and the ways of life of indigenous peoples deserve to be protected – not only for the romantic reasons of preserving cultural diversity and cultural integrity, but out of a necessity to ensure the wellbeing of individuals, the survival of communities and, to some extent, even as a precondition for participation in other cultural contexts and change (Gilbert 2009, Tierney 1999). Hence, the protection of cultural rights has been included in the list of human rights, and has entered national constitutions in one way or the other. However, the protection of cultural rights is limited by the protection of the individual given by the Universal Declaration of Human Rights (UDHR), which has likewise entered into many constitutions.

This paper shows that people's efforts to maintain control over their values, beliefs and cultural practices are reflected in many adaptive strategies. To enable their cultures to survive through slow and partial adaptation, people reinterpret and use state institutions as they deem necessary and as suits them and their local context. Strategies to maintain group identity and integrity range from silent avoidance and circumvention of state institutions, to creative ways of adapting to or customizing state law, to open rejection and violent resistance. All are based on a fundamental wish to stay in control and maintain cultural integrity.

Cultural integrity and the vernacularization of law

> Cultural integrity or control over culture has become one of the key claims of indigenous peoples in their international efforts to gain recognition and accommodation of their interests in legal systems that have, in the past, ignored or excluded those interests.
> (Weatherall 2001:240)

As Karl-Heinz Kohl (this volume) notes, indigenous groups (especially in former colonies) are still suffering from disregard and neglect. And, on the African continent, smaller groups are particularly under threat. Many scholars working on the education of minorities (Tierney 1999, Deyhle 1995), rights over intellectual (Weatherall 2001) or common property (Amos 2004), cultural self-determination and land rights (Gilbert 2009) have emphasized that there is a need to protect minorities' right to determine their own way of life. Maintaining their cultural integrity, so the argument goes, not only helps ensure the survival of minorities as cultural groups, and the well-being of individual members, but also their successful participation in other cultural contexts.[3] In the United Nations Declaration on the Rights of Indigenous Peoples (UNDRIP), the need for cultural integrity is also emphasized:[4]

> States shall provide effective mechanisms for prevention of and redress for a) any action, which has the aim or effect of depriving them of their integrity as distinct peoples, or of their cultural values or ethnic identities (Art. 8:2a)

The protection of cultural integrity does not mean 'freezing' a culture to protect a kind of 'historical authenticity of certain cultural practices'. Rather it refers to the safeguarding of the 'distinct existence of a multi-dimensional culture' that is 'dynamic by nature and undergoing self-determined changes' (Weatherall 2001:225). This, as Gilbert (2009:13) has expressed, should lead to the formulation of a 'right to cultural integrity', which he defines as a right 'to subsistence, livelihood, cultural diversity and heritage', or, as Weatherall (2001:ibid.) puts it, the 'continued distinct existence of that culture without unwanted interference'. In short, in protecting cultural integrity, the emphasis is on the right of people to make decisions for themselves. This could involve the rejection, but also the (partial) acceptance of new values and practices, which are accommodated in the local context through a process of appropriation.

Cultural appropriation[5] is most often understood as a dominant group taking something from a subordinate group. Yet, appropriation also occurs in the opposite direction, for example, when less powerful groups adopt certain ideas or practices from a dominant group, and reinterpret and use them to their own advantage.

> Cultural appropriation means adopting a cultural product in terms of local meanings and practices. In its broadest sense the term means taking an existing cul-

---

3 Tierney (1999), for example, argues that enabling students of colour in the US to maintain their cultural integrity in college (as opposed to 'committing cultural suicide') will enable them not only to develop a sense of self and achieve an 'embodied and objectified capital' (Tierney 1999:89), but also to act as social agents and produce the conditions for change and improvements in opportunity (*ibid.*:85).

4 The Declaration was signed in September 2007 by 143 members of the UN General Assembly. Fourteen member states, including Nigeria and Kenya, abstained, and four (Australia, Canada, New Zealand, and the United States) voted against. Thirty-four countries did not participate in the vote at all. Out of these, fifteen were African states, including Ethiopia (see Kohl, this volume).

5 While the concept of cultural appropriation was originally developed in the field of intellectual property to refer to processes by which dominant groups take, and often profit from, the artistic, musical, and knowledge productions of subordinate groups, it actually encompasses a very broad and pervasive phenomenon, as cultural influences blend and merge in constantly layered ways.

> tural form from one social group and replaying it in another with different meanings or practices: perhaps taking the tune and playing it in a different key or at a different tempo so that it becomes something different, yet still the same (Merry 1998:585).

In the widest sense, this is what happened during the colonial period. As is known from various publications, the various norms and conflict resolution mechanisms and institutions on the African continent were greatly influenced by imported law and the colonial situation. So, what is today called 'customary law' is not the same as the law in use in precolonial times (Snyder 1981, Gordon and Meggitt 1985, Moore 1986). This change to local legal systems occurred not only by force and imposition, but also through the creative responses of local communities that had to adapt to the unavoidable. As such, it was to a limited extent led by the African people, who sought to secure their own interests and agency (Chanock 1985).

This process has continued, albeit in a different form. Today, the transnational flow of law is exerting a similar pressure to that of colonial law in its time on developing countries and local communities striving to keep pace with the international discourse of democracy and development (Merry 2003). In their study on the translation of global ideas about women's rights into local contexts, Levitt and Merry (2009) have shown how ordinary women in different cultural contexts understand and made sense of them. The vernacularization of the notions of women's rights, the authors argue, led to diverse social responses in the respective communities because, while some of the original formulations of women's rights were kept, local ideological and social attributes were also added. The local women were acting as *bricoleurs* (Levitt and Merry 2009:446), e.g. as creators of something new out of bits and pieces of what was available. This scrutinization and re-interpretation of external values and laws in their own logic allows local actors to create a sense of ownership over newly created 'custom(ary law)' (Scheele 2009, see also Beyer 2015 and her detailed study on elders' courts in Kyrgyzstan).

Besides creating a feeling of ownership, accepting and adapting state law into their own system can also be a way by which communities can present themselves to the outside world as 'modern'. As Franz von Benda-Beckmann (1989), for example, has reported, the Minankabau developed a legalistic version of their customary *adat* system, which they present and refer to when they communicate with state bureaucrats. By claiming that certain practices (such as land ownership or transfer) violated one of their customary laws, they could defend their interests against the dominant state in a convincing way. Had they simply claimed that land ownership did not exist or was disliked among the Minankabau, they would have appeared as backward and uncivilized.

Co-existence of state and local institutions in Bashada and Hamar

The Hamar people are one of the sixteen registered ethnic groups in South Omo Zone. The Bashada people are officially considered as a subsection of the Hamar, though they claim to have a slightly different history and identity.[6]

Most Bashada and Hamar local institutions continue to function today. Like many of their ethnic neighbours, the Bashada and Hamar do not have any political leaders or chiefs. Instead, they have ritual authorities who are responsible for the wellbeing of the people, land and animals. The most powerful ritual functionaries are the *bitta* (a ritual leader who blesses the community, animals and land) and the *parko* (a ritual expert who blesses the people, cattle and bees).[7] Though traditionally not endowed with political power, some of these ritual experts assumed a double role by adopting additional functions from the government, in the past,[8] and, more recently, by engaging with state politics (see below).

Public decisions are made through consensus by the *zarsi*, 'the community of competent adult men' (Strecker 1976).[9] Depending on the issue to be discussed or decided,[10] the *zarsi*'s gatherings range from small meetings (*assaua*) of the men of

6 Hamar Woreda (district) is one of nine districts in South Omo Zone, which is located in the very south of the Southern Nations Nationalities and Peoples Region (SNNPR). Three officially recognized ethnic groups share the thirty-eight *kebeles* of the district. These include the Hamar people – the largest in number – who have twenty-eight *kebeles*, the Arbore people who have four, and the Kara people who have three. The Bashada people have their own *kebele* in Hamar Woreda. Each of the three small towns in the district (Turmi and Dimeka in Hamar, and Tabia in Arbore) constitutes also its own *kebele*. In the 2007 report of the Central Statistical Agency (CSA) the total population in Hamar district was estimated to be 59,572 (CSA 2008:8). Out of this the Hamar number 46,129, the Kara 1,368, and the Arbore 5,926 (CSA 2008:135).

7 There are two *bittas* in Hamar, and one in Bashada; each has their own territory. There is a *parko* in Bashada, but there has not been one in office in Hamar for some time. Other ritual offices include the *gudili* (blesses the fields, earth priest), and the *k'ogo* (ritual fire maker, blesses the cattle). Seasonally, these ritual experts perform their rituals and bless the people, their animals and fields and protect them against disease and misfortune. In return, they receive gifts or communal work services (see Epple 2010).

8 Nakwa Dal'o, for example, was known not only to be a powerful ritual expert (Bashada *parko*) and diviner (*moara*), but also acted as a spokesman (*likamamber, ayo*) between the local population and the government.

9 In its widest sense, the term *zarsi* refers to all inhabitants, i.e. all men, women and children, of a neighbourhood, a settlement area, a territorial segment, or the whole population of Bashada, depending on the context in which it is used. Literally, *zarsi* is a patch of grass that has interconnected roots, just as the people of the community should ideally be connected with each other.

10 As the *zarsi* do not consist of a fixed group of elders, but is composed depending on the scope and kind of conflict (involving families, neighbours, a whole settlement area or the whole *kebele*), the term should not be translated as 'customary court'.

one neighbourhood, during which smaller conflicts are resolved or decisions concerning the settlement area are made, to large public meetings (*osh*), during which major conflicts are addressed or issues concerning the wider community decided. As the *zarsi* have the power to curse, bless, exclude and rehabilitate any members of the society, they are the most powerful institution of social control at the communal level. Seniority is important within the *zarsi*. It is expressed in the sitting order during meetings, coffee sessions in the house, and public dances. The most senior men have the right to bless and speak first at public meetings, and deserve the highest respect., Senior men are responsible for advising and guiding their juniors, have the right to give juniors orders and be served by them during meetings and festivities[11], and sanction wrongdoers and criminals. Age-mates also play a significant role in controlling and sanctioning men's behaviour: wrongdoers are advised, scolded and sanctioned by members of the same age-set or those of the age-set directly senior to them (see Epple 2010, 2014). Women do not attend the men's public meetings. However, as the men usually discuss things at length while sharing food and coffee at various houses before and after such meetings, women are usually well informed about what is going on in the community. Conflicts among women are often resolved by women, who constitute their own women's *zarsi* (*ma-zarsi*). Certain conflicts between men and women are also addressed by the *ma-zarsi*.[12]

Delinquents, both male and female, are locally called *d'abbi*, a term used for a wrongdoer whose relationship to the community has been disturbed. As a *d'abbi*, one is expected to submit to the *zarsi's* judgement and decisions. Depending on the case, sanctions range from giving advice and scolding to public whipping and demanding a goat, cow or beer as redress. Individuals who do not submit to the *zarsi* can be excluded from community activities or even cursed. To be re-included or healed from a curse, *d'abbi* have to approach the *zarsi* through a go-between (*motal*), ask for forgiveness, express the willingness to accept any fine imposed, and convincingly promise to improve in the future. The overall aim of sanctions is to 'guide and bless' the wrongdoer, that is, to bring him or her to the right behaviour and to re-establish social peace and understanding between conflicting parties (see Epple 2014). Therefore, any sanctioning usually ends with a blessing and the re-inclusion of the wrongdoer into the society.

11 In Bashada, the senior–junior relationships as well as those among age-mates are structured more formally than in Hamar: while in Hamar age-sets are said to have been given up a while ago, they continue to exist in Bashada (see Epple 2010).

12 This is the case, for example, when a woman has been insulted or treated disrespectfully by a man. In such a case, the *ma-zarsi*, i.e. the women of the neighborhood, may refuse to participate in rites of passage and thereby block the ritual's continuation until the wrongdoer has asked for forgiveness and given them compensation (see Epple 2010:51–52, 2018).

State institutions in Bashada and Hamar

The south of Ethiopia was included into the Ethiopian Empire at the end of the nineteenth century under Emperor Menelik II, and the people living there have been administered and dominated by the highland Ethiopian centre since then. It was only with the downfall of the socialist Derg regime in 1991, that the people were given the right to self-administration. Under previous regimes, both administrative personnel and legal practitioners belonged to ethnic groups from highland Ethiopia, and were either sent from the centre to the regions or were descendants of earlier migrants to the area.[13] Over the last decades, people from local communities have increasingly replaced these highland officials, and since the end of the Derg regime (1974–1991), all Hamar district administrators have been from Hamar, Banna, Bashada or Kara.[14] Because many more locals have undergone formal education with the intent of achieving ethnic self-administration since the introduction of 'ethnic federalism' in 1995, today most heads of the district sub-offices and the police, many of the legal practitioners at the *woreda* court and some of the staff at the police office are from Hamar, Bashada, Arbore or Kara.

Today, the small town of Dimeka is the administrative capital of Hamar Woreda, and the seat of the district administration and of various government offices, including the Justice Office, the Women and Children's Affairs Office, the Culture and Tourism Office, the Education Office, the Health Office and others. The district court is also located in Dimeka. In 2017, it had three judges and two prosecutors. The court handles civil and family cases as well as minor criminal cases, while major criminal cases, and all cases of homicide are sent to the zonal court at Jinka, the capital of South Omo Zone. The head office of the district police is also in Dimeka. It has three sub offices in Turmi/Hamar, Dus/Kara, and Tabia/Arbore. Minor conflict cases are sometimes handled in the police office, and sometimes sent back from there to be resolved at the village level.

Alongside the government institutions, Dimeka is home to the offices of several international NGOs.[15] These NGOs cooperate with the government in certain areas of legal concern (such as women and children's rights), in the improvement of social services such as education, health, food aid, and in various development activities.

---

13 There were mostly descended from *neftenya* (lit.: 'gunmen', Amharic), i.e. soldier-settlers assigned by Emperor Menelik II to administer the regions in southern Ethiopia after his armies had conquered them at the end of the nineteenth century. They were rewarded with legal rights to exploit the indigenous population inhabiting large parcels of land (Schaefer 2012:193–194).

14 Among the three administrators of what was by then called Hamar *Awraja* (province), there were two from the south of the country: one from Banna (son of a *bitta*, educated under Haile Selassie) and one from Basketto.

15 For example AMREF and Save the Children.

Customization of government institutions

The Hamar and Bashada people's customary institutions now co-exist with the state institutions, and the local understanding of state law is influenced by the local people's own values and practices. In the following, examples are given of how the community reinterprets and makes use of state law, and how state law is to some extent customized to the local needs and rationalities, customary structures, institutions, concepts and values.

Customization of government offices

Each *kebele*[16] has its own spokesman, locally called *ayo*. Officially, these representatives are called *likamenber* (Amharic: 'leader'), the local people pronounce it as *likamamber*. An *ayo* represents the interests of his locality during local public meetings and meetings with the government.[17]

In his own *kebele*, the *ayo* works with a group of assistants (the *kebele* speaker, his secretary, a *seraskaj*/manager),[18] several committees (such as the health committee, the education committee, and the development committee). In addition, the *ayo* keeps communication between the government and the local population alive. He informs and calls elders to meetings organized by the government, both in town and in the villages, attends government meetings at the zonal or sometimes regional level, and reports back to his people on what the government has to say. In cases of interethnic conflict, the *ayos* are also invited to act as a mediator during peace meetings organized by the government.[19]

Together with a groups of local men selected as *militias*, the *ayos* are also responsible for security and the application of state law in the communities: they must report on crimes and hand over wrongdoers to the police, and follow up cases

---

16 Smallest administrative unit.

17 Strecker (1976:60) translated the term the *ayo* as 'in the widest sense a kind of leader, but more specifically he is a spokesman'. The term *ayo* derives from the verb *aya*, 'to do', and the social symbol of an '*ayo*' in Hamar is his spear ' which signifies the right and duty to speak at a public meeting' (*ibid.*).

18 Most *ayos* are not formally educated and they therefore need educated assistants to help with formal communication with the government, as, for example, when letters have to be written or documents signed.

19 The members of these committees are respected (usually non-educated) individuals from the community who are made responsible for certain aspects of community life. Members of the education committee, for example, are there to motivate parents to send their children to school, to communicate with the teachers when there are problems, and to report to the government. The heath committee is there to follow up pregnancies and call the ambulance if necessary, to spread information on hygiene and modern health care, and to convince people to participate in vaccination campaigns or meetings on HIV prevention.

that the court or police have sent back to the villages to be resolved through customary mechanisms. Despite his close connection with government officials and his respected position within the community, the *ayo* cannot make any decisions without the consent of the community.

The *ayo* is chosen by the community on the basis of his reputation, but is officially appointed by the government. Although the *likamamber* is a government office, his appointment has been customized to local beliefs, and the community thereby has control over it: On the day of his appointment, he is given certain insignia, including a jacket, a spear and a cap, together with blessings by the outgoing office holder. The *likamamber's* cap has been an important item since Haile Selassie's reign, when the first *likamambers* were installed and received jackets and caps from government officials.[20] Originally simply a sign of recognition, the caps were locally bestowed with magic and only *likamambers* were allowed to wear them. Even today, a *likamamber*'s cap (together with a spear and a whipping wand)[21] can only be formally handed over to a successor on the *likamamber's* death or voluntary resignation, as it is believed that a *likamamber* is protected by his cap's magic. People claim that if taken without the consent of the previous owner, the cap would kill the new spokesman. Many of the government officials in Hamar Woreda are originally from Hamar or Bashada. They know about the strong belief in the cap's magic (and some of them share the belief), and they know that they cannot impose an unacceptable person on the community. As the former representative of the Hamar in the Ethiopian national parliament explained,

> It is like a monarchy (...). Someone might say, 'I will be an *ayo*! I want to have the cap!' But if the cap is given to him against the acting *ayo*'s will, that person will die! (...) Therefore, even if a new *likamamber* is appointed by the government, that person will not accept if the acting *likamamber* does not want to hand over the office to him. (Interview, 10 November 2016)

Similarly, candidates for the militia are recruited by the community on the basis of their reputation for trustworthiness and self-control. As for the office of the *ayo*, militiamen do not need to be formally educated. They are officially appointed during a public meeting, and given a uniform and a gun by the government as a sign of their position. The elders and the *ayo* bless them and thereby confirm their acceptance. If the elders and *ayo* reject a candidate, they withhold their blessing.

---

20 While the office of the *likamamber* was officially abandoned under the Derg regime (1974–1991), it continued to be active in Hamar Woreda. Under the Derg regime, the *likamambers* were also given pants, jackets and other clothes, so that wearing a cap has lost its symbolic weight and nowadays anyone can wear one. The belief in the cap's magic, however, has persisted until today.

21 Local insignia used for blessing and cursing during public meetings.

Both, the *likamamber* and the militia are government offices that have been to some extent customized to the local context. Just as the magic of the *ayo's* caps ensures that the local population retains ultimate control over who represents them before the government, the elders' blessing represents control over who can join the militia. Government officials have to respect the choices and the ritualization of these offices if they want to secure the cooperation of the local communities.

Prison and imprisonment re-interpreted

Conflict resolution in Bashada and Hamar, as indicated above, focuses on the restoration of social relations rather than on punishment. The common sanctions of scolding, whipping, fines, exclusion or cursing by age-mates and/or *zarsi* are meant to intimidate wrongdoers and are, along with the giving of advice, considered as elements of a learning process that will keep individuals 'on the right and straight track'.[22] Once a wrongdoer shows repentance, he is blessed by the elders or his age-mates and thereby fully rehabilitated and re-included into the community.

The state's imprisonment of wrongdoers emphasizes retribution and is, as such, alien to the local customs. People refer to prison as *daxe* (lit.: 'a place to tie up'). Until recently, to many in Bashada and Hamar, prison was a much-feared place, and the government an uncontrollable external power. Officials belonged to different ethnic groups and looked down upon the local communities, and many people in Bashada recall how, under previous regimes, prisoners were beaten up and sent to far-away places, where relatives could never visit and prisoners were not sure if and when they would return home. [23]

This situation has changed, as has the image of prison and imprisonment. Nowadays, most criminals are taken to Jinka prison (about 100 km north of Dimeka), which has become easy to reach with public transport in the last 10–15 years. Living conditions are much better than in the past and relatives can come to visit.

Although local communities still hide certain criminal cases from the police (see below), the pressure from government institutions to handle criminal cases in state courts has made prison to some extent inevitable. The Bashada and Hamar community has made efforts to reinterpret and customize the idea of prison and imprisonment so that it does not contradict and disturb local handling of conflicts, and in certain contexts even complements it. This has led to situation where, on the

22 See Epple 2012b on the meaning of whipping as 'guidance and blessing'.

23 People were sent to prison in Arbaminch (about 300 km from Hamar) and further away, and public transport was not available.

one hand, prison is talked about as something positive, as a place to learn and mature, and on the other hand it is used as a last resort, a place where uncontrollable individuals that the community does not want to deal with are sent.

Prison as a place of learning and maturing

The image of prison as an institution of *timirte* (Amharic: 'learning/education') emerged in the last couple of decades under the influence of the rhetoric used by the courts during awareness-raising campaigns on modern state law and sanctioning. However, it does relate to some practical realities and also to local ideas about sanctioning of wrongdoers.

First, Jinka prison has educational facilities where many prisoners attend school. Almost all learn to speak Amharic, read and write during their time in prison, and some receive vocational training in handcrafts or even attend the Jinka Industrial College.[24] For this reason, many people in Hamar joke that going to Jinka prison is comparable to securing a scholarship. Second, with regard to prison being a place where people mature, being imprisoned is intimidating and scary, and imprisonment leaves an imprint on those who are away from home for a long time. That means that the expectation is that many become better people after their return. Unlike in many western societies, there is no permanent stigma attached to a wrongdoer once he has admitted his mistake, accepted the sanction and ritually been re-included into society: any wrongdoing (even homicide) is forgiven and forgotten, at least socially if not emotionally, with the blessing given at the end of a reconciliation ritual. People who show remorse serve as living examples to the community. Thus, people returning from prison are also often fully integrated into society and live respected lives. However, there is an expectation that returnees will talk about their experiences in prison as a way to help keep others from making similar mistakes. Individuals who do so are locally appreciated, while those who return and play down the suffering they experience in prison are considered arrogant and those who do wrong repeatedly and never improve are despised.

24 Jinka prison was founded in 1950 (Ethiopian Calendar). In 2016, it had 1,721 prisoners, most of whom were men (only 82 were women). Among the prison facilities are a kindergarten for the children and a school that runs from 1st to 10th grade. As the head of the prison told me, almost all prisoners join the adult schooling programme. Some of the 10th grade graduates attend a college in Jinka. Others are interested in the woodwork and basketry workshops, which are part of the prisoners' cooperative. The cooperative also runs a shop and a cafeteria in the prison. With the income, the cooperative has recently purchased three vehicles (one four-wheel drive, one minibus, one large bus), which are used to take prisoners to court, college or the hospital (from fieldnotes after visiting Jinka prison, 14 November 2016). A new prison, which was under construction in 2016, has recently opened a few kilometres outside of Jinka. It occupies a large space and several modern buildings.

Prison as a last resort for obstinate wrongdoers

Many informants in Bashada and Hamar seemed to resent the fact that some young people are becoming disrespectful when it comes to listening to the elders. While this seems a common complaint among the senior generation worldwide, the prohibition of certain cultural practices in Ethiopia is believed to have contributed to the phenomenon. The traditional, rather authoritative socialization, which included physical punishment of children, assured a general respect towards senior people and their orders among them, but recent awareness-raising programmes have meant that whipping within the family has decreased, and whipping as a means of sanctioning wrongdoers has become less common. Many thus complain that the *zarsi's* authority has also been diminished, and that local mechanisms for controlling the youth and sanctioning wrongdoers sustainably have become ineffective. Consequently, sending wrongdoers to prison as a last resort has become acceptable,[25] as Shada, a young educated man from Bashada, explained:

> Nowadays, when the *zarsi* has exhausted its entire means [to deal with a wrongdoer], they call the police. (...) Maybe first the elders thought they could manage him, but if someone never stops and never listens to them, he is given to the police. They say, 'Let him get their kind of *timirte* (education) and see!' (21st September 2016)

A wrongdoer's refusal to give in to the *zarsi* is seen as a threat to the whole community, because it might lead to dangerous and harmful behaviour and community disruption. Imprisonment is therefore sometimes used as an additional threat or a way to get rid of an unrepentant individual.

While communities generally still prefer to handle conflicts locally, in urban contexts it has become more common to involve the police. On market days in town, the consumption of alcohol often leads to quarrels and physical encounters. While friends and age-mates prevent conflicts from escalating in the face-to-face context of rural life, in the towns, insults are easily taken seriously and end up in fights when people who do not know each other drink together. In the countryside, the re-establishment of friendship among age-mates after such quarrels is very important; in town, it has become important to provide financial recompense for damaged property or injuries incurred, and re-establishing a good relationship is not a priority.

---

25 I heard this complaint not only in Bashada and Hamar, but also by elders from other ethnic groups during a conference at the South Omo Research Center in 2017. During this conference, elder from almost all groups in South Omo participated. In discussions with government officials, the elders from the lowland pastoralist groups, especially, from Nyangatom, Arbore, Dassanech, Kara, Hamar and Bashada blamed the prohibition of whipping delinquents for the many wrongdoing of young men in the area.

Strategic interaction with state institutions

The Bashada and Hamar have developed certain strategies for dealing with government institutions and representatives. These strategic interactions include 'shopping' among state legal forums, limiting and controlling individuals' access to state institutions, delaying the apprehension of delinquents, negotiating and bargaining with officials, avoidance and hiding, pretending cooperation, and other more open forms of resistance. These strategies should not automatically be considered as opposition, but rather as variations of efforts to stay in control.

'Forum shopping' at government institutions

As elaborated above, the police and the courts are sometimes addressed in cases where local institutions have failed to sustainably improve a wrongdoer's behaviour. They are also increasingly being used to obtain financial compensation in cases of physical injury, especially in cases involving incidents in town. These are the locally acceptable contexts for making use of state law. For most other cases, it is preferred that they are handled locally or, at least, that the *zarsi* discuss such cases before handing them over to the police through the militia and *ayo*. The local communities strongly disapprove of, and will sanction, direct access to state institutions.

Limiting direct access to police and state court

While in principle everyone can choose which of the available legal forums they want to handle a case – the police, state court, government office or local system – in practice individuals are not that free to make the choice. Locally, it is considered inappropriate and disloyal to take a case outside the community, and it is expected that any issue should be taken to the *zarsi* first and then, if need be, through the *militia* or the *likamamber* to a government institution. Anyone who addresses the police or court directly risks being locally sanctioned and fined by the elders. Women who directly report abuse or mistreatment by their husbands to the police are commonly sanctioned by the other women in the neighbourhood.

A former court officer in Dimeka Woreda court confirmed that very few individuals address the police directly. Those who did, she said, were mostly individuals who were sure that their case would not be listened to locally because local customs were contradictory to their personal interests.[26] Such cases sometimes involve women who have decided to leave their husbands and the community and have moved to town. In most instances, they involve adolescent girls, who use the

26 Interview on 12 November 2016.

protection offered by the state to escape arranged or forced marriages. Claiming they want to gain a formal education, the girls enter the police stations from where, with the support of the Women and Children's Affairs Office, they are usually sent to school hostels. The government's protection of runaway girls has caused a lot of resistance among the Bashada, Banna, Hamar and Kara (see Epple 2012a, Masuda n.y., Maurus 2016, Niebling 2010, Yohannes this volume), especially because some of the girls involved have already been betrothed, and bride wealth been given. Parents are also concerned about the inadequate supervision of the girls in the town hostels, as unwanted pregnancies and sexually transmitted disease are not uncommon. Moreover, many of the girls, especially those who were already adolescents when they arrived, drop out of school after a few years; they do not usually return home, but stay in town, working in bars or restaurants.

Delaying the handover of criminals

In certain contexts, the local people delay the handover of perpetrators to the police in order to make time to make peace and perform reconciliatory rituals between the conflicting parties.

As among many other Ethiopian groups, intra-ethnic homicide in Bashada and Hamar is considered harmful to the victim, the perpetrator and their families: it affects the relationship between the families of killer and victim not only emotionally, but also metaphysically. It is believed that if members of the two families eat or drink together before peace has been re-established and ritually sealed, disease and a quick death will follow for anyone who consumed anything that was produced by the other party. If a killer is convicted by the court and goes to prison before reconciliation rituals can be held, members of the two families remain at risk for many years. As even distant relatives are said to die if they eat food provided by the other family, even unknowingly,[27] the performance of a reconciliation ritual is imperative. Therefore, the community usually holds back on handing over a killer to the police by pretending that they cannot find them.

When the police or the court hears of a serious crime in the villages, strong efforts are initially made to get hold of the perpetrator. However, as the Bashada and Hamar territory is a large and bushy area where people are armed with guns, the police cannot easily get hold of a criminal if the local community does not cooperate. Therefore, the police usually choose to follow up a case only occasionally.

27 During my stay in 2017, I was told about a herding boy who unknowingly drank milk from a cow belonging to a family with whom his own family had not made peace. The alleged reason for his death came out during a consultation with the sandal oracle. After this sad event, the reconciliation, which had been delayed for several decades as the two families lived far apart, was quickly enforced.

Furthermore, many government officials are now native to the area and know the local customs. Consequently, many people in Bashada are convinced that the police tolerate delayed handovers in order to give the community a chance to settle the case locally before formal law is enforced, as a young married Bashada man explained:

> The *woreda* administrator [originally from Bashada/Banna] and those working with him know our tradition. When people say, 'The culprit did not come to us, we have not heard anything, the guy did not come!', he knows that people are doing their rituals. (...) When everything has been finished, they will say to the government, 'Now we have heard about it, people came to us.' Then they say to the culprit, 'Now you have to go, everything is finished, go!' and send him. It is the *gal* (non-Hamar), who do not know.... (Interview, 21 November 2016)

What he describes seems to be a kind of silent agreement between the government and the locals, and so it is difficult to get a statement on the issue from legal practitioners, who officially must prosecute any case of homicide immediately. Many confirmed, however, that getting hold of and prosecuting anyone in the bush against the will of the community was impossible.

Negotiations with government officials on the application of state law

People in Bashada know that there is room for negotiation even after a case has been handed over to the police or court. This applies in less serious cases, such as quarrels, insults, family issues and minor criminal cases, when a case can officialy be returned to the local community for resolution with the agreement of all parties involved (following article 34(5) of the Constitution). The initiative for negotiation can come from the local people's side, but may also come from the government side. Sometimes, negotiations also take place in more serious contexts, when it seems more promising to resolve cases outside the courtroom. such as when adolescent girls run away from home to escape an unwanted marriage. Instead of punishing the families who may have forced a girl into marriage, other offices, such as the Women and Children's Affairs Office get involved in mediating between the parties. Social background of a perpetrator may also be taken into accunt. When a perpetrator comes from a poor background or has very few relatives, elders sometimes approach the court and plead for a fine for the wrongdoer rather than imprisonment, arguing that his family would suffer without him. As the former president of Hamar Woreda court explained, judges may use the legal room available in the law and decide on a fine or communal work instead of imprisonment in such contexts. They understand that the wife and children of a man who has no brothers to support his family during his absence would not be able to sustain themselves.[28] Generally, however, legal practitioners want to be seen to be loyal to state law. One of the prosecutors[29] at Hamar Woreda court emphasized,

> Wrongdoing is wrongdoing. The law treats all: whether someone steals a needle or a cow, both is theft and it is treated here. (...) The provision we have in the law is that when small problems, like insult or so, can be sent back and solved locally. But theft and murder, these are treated only in court. (...) If there is a theft, somewhere in the bush, and we don't hear about it, it might be solved there, that is fine. But when we hear about it, we have to follow up. (Interview 28 March 2017)

Keeping silent, avoiding and hiding

In the last couple of decades, representatives of the Bashada and Hamar people have been increasingly invited to meetings in town organized by NGOs or government offices to inform the population on issues such as health, education and development, but also gender equality, HTPs and state law in general. At the same time, government officials, NGO representatives, health officers, agricultural extension workers have been visiting the villages with the same agenda. In the early years of this education programme, certain individuals were appointed by the local government as members of committees (such as health committee, education committee) and taken to meetings in different parts of southern Ethiopia, where they met with members of other ethnic groups. Today, some of them remember that they enjoyed the free travel, the chance to see other places and other people, and the per diems and other incentives.

While such journeys have become less common, meetings in the villages or local towns (Dimeka and Turmi) have become so frequent that people complain they are a hindrance to their daily duties. While the *likamambers* and the members of their committees are expected to attend these village and town meetings, for others participation is voluntary. Nevertheless, meetings often start with the organizers complaining about low attendance, little change or improvement, and low motivation. Though participants are encouraged to express their views, opinions and complaints, most attendants keep silent when they disagree with what has been said, or when they are scolded for having been late or absent, or for not fulfilling

28 This could include working for the district administration for some months in construction, watering plants, cleaning offices and the like (interview 24 June 2017).

29 Originally from Kara.

what they promised to do during an earlier meeting.[30] Instead of airing their views during the meetings, as I observed, they discuss them when walking home.

The silence of participants during meetings is a common sign of withdrawal from a conversation that, from a local perspective, has taken an inappropriate turn; in this case, when the tone of government officials is perceived as paternalistic, dominant or arrogant. When discussions are held face to face, they are often quite lively and direct. The reasons for people's silence is common knowledge, as the head of the Education Office in Hamar Woreda, himself from Hamar, explained:

> When we explain things slowly, people listen. Especially, when they do not like the work of the government, we explain things again slowly... [means here also: 'we repeat things several times with patience']. If you tell them the hard way, people stay silent. That means that they have not accepted it, they don't speak it out loud. (interview 28 March 2017)

Government officials meet this passive behaviour with patience and continuous and repeated effort in the hope that their message will be accepted in time.

Hiding crimes

Minor offences, such as insult, physical injury or theft are often not reported to the police; if they are, they are sometimes sent back to be resolved locally. Serious offences such as forced marriage and abduction are not considered locally as crimes, but rather as part of local custom. Therefore, such cases are usually kept with the community, and the *zarsi* prevent victims reporting to the police, arguing that it is better to handle such things locally.

Fathers commonly complain when their daughters are forced into marriage or abducted. Relatives and elders usually calm such a father down. They remind him of the reciprocity between generations: though it might be painful now to let the daughter go, he himself may have abducted his own wife, and his own son might do so in the future. One Bashada elder recounted how a father is stopped from going to the police:

> 'It is our tradition. Yih, tomorrow you might also abduct a girl! Today, if you send this guy (the abductor) to prison, tomorrow, will you go to prison too then? What if tomorrow you will go to prison? What if your son is going to prison? Who would tomorrow talk in favour of you or your son? Don't do it!!' This is how the elders

30 The health officers, for example, have been urging the community to build pit latrines in their settlement areas. Many Bashada and Hamar people feel disgusted by the latrines in towns, which are usually very dirty and smelly. They prefer to use the bush where there is no smell and any remains usually disappear by themselves after a few days.

> talk and stop him from going to the police!' (...) [Then he will respond] 'Eh, if this is what the *zarsi* is saying, it is good. I will not go.' (25 January 2017)

Only when a girl decides to seek protection in town does abduction and forced marriage become a matter of law, most cases remain hidden.[31] This shows that with regard to marriage, custom is locally rated higher than state law.

Faking cooperation

The highest priority in combatting harmful traditional practices (HTPs) in Bashada and Hamar is to eliminate infanticide, the ritual whipping of girls and women during male initiation, and forced and early marriage and abduction. As many initiatives have proved unsuccessful, more recently, the *bittas* (ritual leaders) have been asked by the government to get involved with the hope that through the performance of a ritual of abandonment these practices could be given up.

After several meetings and lengthy discussions between government and local elders, the Hamar and Bashada *bittas* were convinced, albeit under pressure, to ritually curse and abandon whipping, abduction and infanticide. However, when these rituals were performed – in the presence of government officials and local elders – certain elements were changed so that the rituals were in fact non-binding.[32] While the situation was clear to the local participants, it was not to most of the officials who learned only later that the rituals had been incomplete and therefore ineffective.

Resistance through magic, curses, verbal and physical violence

The Bashada and Hamar also use magic and curses against individuals to protect their interests. Cursing is commonly used to sanction those who do not listen and submit to the *zarsi*. Locally, persistent wrongdoers, those who act disloyally or have angered senior relatives can be targets of curses, which affect the health and sometimes even the lives of the cursed through disease or accidents. The community has turned cursing on government officials in the past, as the following stories show.

In the early 1990s the first administrator of Bashada and Hamar was chosen from the local communities. He was known as someone who took state law very seriously, employed very strict measures whenever the law was broken, and ignored the needs and interests of his people. The Bashada vividly remember that this particular administrator, tasked with protecting the wildlife there, asked them and the Hamar to remove their cattle from Mago Park. As they had taken their

31 See also Epple (forthcoming) on details about forced marriage and abduction in Bashada and Hamar.

32 See Epple (this volume) for details on the handling of infanticide in Bashada and Hamar.

animals to the park to graze during a drought, the people refused to comply with the request for fear their animals would starve. The administrator then loaded the cows and calves onto trucks and moved them elsewhere. He also insulted the elders with whom he had discussed his request, and ordered that some of the small houses and cattle enclosures built by the herders be burnt down. This behaviour angered the community so much that they cursed him. As a result, people say, he turned crazy, lost his job and never recovered. Today, he lives in Dimeka, his mind still broken.[33]

His successor, also a Hamar, was also a strict supporter of government interests. He strongly supported the government's wish to get girls into education, and willingly accepted all runaway girls who came to town to go to school. At that time, many parents were set against their daughters being educated, and some even withdrew them from the hostels by force (see Masuda n.d.). People felt betrayed when the administrator helped girls to escape to Jinka without consulting their parents or any elders.[34] While he was on a visit to southern Hamar, an *edi arti* (magician) offered him a goat and fresh milk in a traditional container as a gift, as is common for honoured guests. Both milk and goat were bestowed with magic, and many people recount how the administrator became very sick when he ate the meat and drank the milk. He remained half paralyzed, unable to walk or talk properly. When after some years, he asked the elders for forgiveness, they performed a ritual for him and his health slightly improved. Later, however, he was said to have acted against the interests of the Hamar again, so the curse was renewed and he died.

All subsequent local administrators and other officials have heard about these curses and all educated Hamar – including those who have converted to Christianity – I talked to consider the magic and curses of Hamar elders as powerful and effective.

Open confrontation: Physical violence and revitalization of HTPs

Some court officials reported that they experienced verbal threats and intimidations by individuals who felt that the court had treated them unfairly. One of the administrators (in power from 2010 to 2014) who had gained a reputation for being rough and very disrespectful was in fact beaten so severely he almost died. This happened during a time of extreme tension between the Hamar and the government that ultimately lead to a violent and open conflict erupting in some Hamar *kebeles* and in was a reaction to continuous pressure from government officials on the local

33 From a scientific perspective he probably had a stroke, which may have damaged his brain.

34 During my research in the late 1990s one of the popular songs to which the youth danced in the night was about the first Bashada girl who ran away and escaped secretly by Dagne's car, defying the will of the elders.

communities. As Yohannes has shown (this volume), the main underlying reasons for the violence were the continuous demands to send more children (especially girls) to school, the prohibition on hunting wild game and the legal prosecution of hunters, and the efforts to end certain cultural practices labelled as harmful. The communities' usual strategies – of avoidance, partial acceptance and pretending to cooperate – had failed to stave off the pressure, so the situation escalated at the end of 2014: the Hamar physically attacked the district administrator, police and other government representatives, destroyed schools and health posts and thereby clearly demonstrated their rejection of government intervention. As a strong sign of their position, they even revived one of the HTPs that had been most strongly addressed by the government: the abortion or postnatal killing of allegedly impure children. Several allegedly impure children, who had grown up and were attending school, were killed (see Epple this volume).

Summary and conclusion

Local communities use a variety of strategies by to cope with changes – here in the form of the implementation of state law – offered by or imposed on them by the state. As the example of the Bashada and Hamar people has shown, these strategies range from customizing institutions and official positions and avoiding state institutions, to hiding crimes, pretending cooperation, trying to influence court decisions and – as a last resort – openly resisting.

In Hamar *Woreda*, both customary and state legal institutions are available and, in theory, individuals can freely decide which legal forum they want to address (except in criminal cases, which have to be dealt with by the state). In practice, individuals are not always free to choose, and the law is not always followed so clearly. Instead, the communities make many efforts to stay in control and preserve their cultural integrity.

First, individuals are not free to report crime to the police because they are expected to first address the elders, the *ayo* (spokesman) or the militia. These local representatives then discuss a case before deciding whether to report it to officials. Individuals who go directly to the police risk being considered disloyal to the community and face local sanctions. Usually, only individuals who are determined not to submit to cultural expectations – such as girls who want to escape an unwanted marriage – take that risk.

Second, certain government institutions have been customized and to some extent brought under local control. These include the office of the *ayo/likamamber* (the local representatives of each *kebele*) and the local militia. While the government created these positions to extend its control into the communities, they are indirectly controlled by the local communities through the ritualized installation of the office holders. To reach the communities more effectively, the government is also making use of local practices. For example, meetings between government officials and local elders begin and end with the elders' blessings. Additionally, the ritual leaders' influence is used to give more weight to decisions reached during such meetings, and 'harmful traditional practices' are not only combatted through awareness-raising and legal prosecution, but also by asking the ritual leaders to ritually ban them.

Third, it can be observed that while, in principle, individuals can 'shop', i.e. choose between legal forums, the communities selectively 'shop' elements of state law and institutions that are suitable to them, and strategically reinterpret, avoid, manipulate or reject and resist others that contradict local values. For example, although imprisonment is alien to the local culture, which favours reconciliation over punishment, it is nowadays used by the communities as a threat or to get rid of wrongdoers who can no longer be handled by traditional mechanisms. When the police hear of a crime and do get hold of the perpetrator, the community rhetorically changes the meaning of imprisonment. Rather than being a place of suffering far away from home, prison is reimagined as a place of learning and maturing (with actual offers of schooling and vocational training) from which wrongdoers return as better people. This image was promoted by the government and has been locally picked up, but it is only evoked when someone is convicted and imprisoned. In individual cases, elders try to influence court decisions with the intention of having imprisonment changed to a fine by reporting to the prosecutors or judges on family background, emphasizing that their family would suffer greatly if the person goes to prison. When communication fails and/or government pressure is high, people tend to pretend or fake their cooperation: when the elders or the militia are asked to hand over a criminal, they often claim they cannot get hold of him. When ritual leaders are pressurized into performing rituals to abandon certain cultural practices, they may do it wrongly, so that the ritual looks real to outsiders, but is locally ineffective. Open resistance and violence is the last resort to which people turn when the pressure gets too much, communication between government and communities is imbalanced and unsuccessful, and cultural key values are felt to be severely under threat. As the recent conflict in Hamar Woreda shows, people will not only defend themselves with weapons, but will also attack innocent government employees (such as teachers or nurses), and revitalize prohibited and formerly abandoned practices (such as infanticide) as an additional provocation.

Many of the local government officials are now native to the area and have a good knowledge of local customs and values. Having been through a modern education system, these officials may not share all the views of the local population, but most of them do have a good understanding of local needs related to the local culture and values. Therefore, many indirectly support the vernacularization of state law and institutions, and accept that people avoid or circumvent state law sometimes. The delayed handover of perpetrators in cases of homicide, for example, which gives communities time to perform reconciliation rituals, is informally tolerated, and pragmatic given that the vastness of the territory makes it practically impossible to get hold of any perpetrator without the cooperation of the community. When communicating with local elders, government officials – who are often much younger – display the expected respect. Most of them marry a local wife to achieve local acceptance, and they often take the threat of being cursed seriously. They also place great emphasis on information and awareness-raising about the state law, human rights and gender equality, and tolerate violations of state law in the hope that a gentler approach will slowly bring about cultural change. And indeed, it appears that the will to cooperate is much higher when people feel that the cultural integrity of their community is not violated.

References

ABBINK, Jon, 2012 "Dam controversies: Contested governance and developmental discourse on the Ethiopian Omo River dam", *Social Anthropology/Anthropologie Sociale* 20 (2):125–144

AMOS, Lourdes, 2004 "'Cultural integrity': Promoting cultural survival and decentralizing good forest governance in ancestral domains. The Agta-Dumagat people, province of Aurora, Philippines", Conference paper at *10th Biennial Conference of the International Association for the Study of Common Property* (IASCP), Oaxaca, Mexico, 9–13 August 2004 (accessible online at (https://dlc.dlib.indiana.edu/dlc/bitstream/handle/10535/1292/Amos_Cultural_040327_Paper565d.pdf?sequence=1, last accessed 13 March 2019)

BEYER, Judith, 2015 "Customizations of law: Courts of elders (aksakal courts) in rural and urban Kyrgyzstan", *Political and Legal Anthropology Review* 38 (1):53–71

BENDA-BECKMANN, Franz von, 1989 "Scape-goat and magic charm: Law in development theory and practice", *Journal of Legal Pluralism* 28:129–148

CENTRAL STATISTICAL AUTHORITY, 2008 *Census 2007 Report on SNNPR*. Addis Ababa: CSA (accessible online at http://www.csa.gov.et/census-report/complete-report/census-2007?start=10, last accessed 28 February 2018)

CHANOCK, Martin, 1985 *Law, custom and social order: The colonial experience in Malawi and Zambia*. Cambridge: Cambridge University Press

DEYHLE, Donna, 1995 "Navajo youth and Anglo racism: Cultural integrity and resistance", *Harvard Educational Review* 65 (3):403–445

EPPLE, Susanne, 2010 *The Bashada of southern Ethiopia: A study of age, gender and social discourse*. Köln: Köppe.

2012a "Selective resilience: Local responses to externally induced cultural change in southern Ethiopia", *Paideuma*: 197–212

2012b "Harmful practice or ritualized guidance? Reflections on physical punishment as part of socialization among the Bashada of Southern Ethiopia", *Rassegna di Studi Etiopici* 3:69–102

2014 "Marrying into an age-set: The redefinition of social relations and extension of social networks", *Paideuma* 60:171–185

2018 "Impeding rites, restoring rights: The refusal of ritual participation in Bashada, southern Ethiopia", in Felix Girke, Sophia Thubauville, Wolbert Smidt (eds.): *Anthropology as homage: Festschrift für Ivo Strecker*, 337–350. Köln: Köppe

2020 "Contested customs and normative pluralism: Forced marriage and abduction in Bashada, Southern Ethiopia", *Rassegna di Studi Etiopici*: 107-146

FEDERAL DEMOCRATIC REPUBLIC OF ETHIOPIA (FDRE), 2002 *Ethiopia: Sustainable development and poverty reduction program*. Addis Ababa: Ministry of Finance and Economic Development

2015 *The Second Growth and Transformation Plan* (GTP II) (1015/16 – 2019/20) (draft). Addis Ababa: Ministry of Finance and Economic Development

GILBERT, Jérémie, 2017 "Litigating indigenous peoples' rights in Africa: Potentials, challenges and limitations", *International and Comparative Law Quarterly* 66 (3): 657–686.

2009 "Custodians of the land: Indigenous peoples, human rights and cultural integrity", in: Michele Langfield, William Logan, Mairead Nic Craith (eds.) *Cultural diversity, heritage and human rights: Intersections in theory and practice*, 47–60. London: Routledge

GORDON, Robert J. and Mervyn J. MEGGITT, 1985 *Law and order in the New Guinea highlands: Encounters with Enga*. Hanover, N.H.: University Press of New England

LEVITT, Peggy and Sally Engle MERRY, 2009 "Vernacularization on the ground: Local uses of global women's rights in Peru, China, India and the United States", *Global Networks* 9 (4):441–461

MASUDA, Ken, n.d. *Education in conflict: The case of the Banna in Southern Ethiopia* (unpublished)

MAURUS, Sabrina, 2016 "Times of continuity and development: Visions of the future among agro-pastoral children and young people in southern Ethiopia", *Anthropochildren* 6:1–24

MERRY, Sally Engle, 1998 "Law, culture, and cultural appropriation", *Yale Journal of Law & the Humanities* 10 (2):575–603

2003 "From law and colonialism to law and globalization", *Law and Social Inquiry* 28 (29):569–590

MOORE, Sally Falk, 1986 *Social facts and fabrications: 'Customary' law on Kilimanjaro, 1880–1980*. Cambridge *et al.*: Cambridge University Press

NIEBLING, Maria, 2010 *Schulbildung bei den Hamar in Südwestäthiopien*. Leipzig: Leipzig University (MA Thesis)

SCHAEFER, Charles, 2012 "We say they are neftenya, they say we areOLF': A post-election assessment ofethnicity, politics and age-sets in Oromiya", in: Kjetil Tronvoll and Tobias Hagmann (eds.) *Contested power in Ethiopia: Traditional authorities and multi-party elections*, 193–219. Leiden, Boston: Brill

SCHEELE, Judith, 2009 *Village matters: Knowledge, politics and community in Kabylia, Algeria*. Woodbridge: Currey

SNYDER, Francis, 1981 "Colonialism and legal form: The creation of 'customary law' in Senegal", *Journal of Legal Pluralism* 19:49–90

STRECKER, Ivo, 1976 *Traditional life and prospects for socio-economic development in the Hamar administrative district of southern Gamo Gofa* (unpublished manuscript)

TIERNEY, William G. 1999 "Models of minority college-going and retention: Cultural integrity versus cultural suicide", *The Journal of Negro Education* 68 (1):80–91

TURTON, David, 2011 "Wilderness, wasteland or home? Three ways of imagining the Lower Omo Valley", *Journal of Eastern African Studies* 5 (1):158–176

UNITED NATIONS, 2007 *United Nations Declaration on the Rights of Indigenous Peoples* (UNDRIP) (accessible online at https://www.un.org/esa/socdev/unpfii/documents/DRIPS_en.pdf, last accessed, 13 March 2019)

WEATHERALL, Kimberley, 2001 "Culture, autonomy and Djulibinyamurr: Individual and community in the construction of rights to traditional designs", *The Modern Law Review* 64 (2):215–242

Webpages

http://www.oilnewskenya.com/africa-oil-relinquishes-ethiopias-south-omo-block

10. Legal pluralism and Protestant Christianity
From fine to forgiveness in an Aari community

Julian Sommerschuh

Introduction

For several years, the topic of legal pluralism in Ethiopia has been the subject of lively scholarly debate (e.g. Donovan and Getachew 2003, Pankhurst and Getachew 2008, Baker 2013, Girmachew 2015). In this chapter, I would like to contribute to this debate by offering a new perspective. My suggestion is that, at least in some parts of the country, there is a further actor in the legal arena that has hitherto been overlooked: Protestantism.

Legal pluralism is commonly defined as 'a situation in which two or more legal systems coexist in the same social field' (Merry 1988:870); with 'legal system' meaning both 'the system of courts and judges supported by the state as well as non legal forms of normative ordering' (Merry 1988:870, cf. Griffith 1986, Benda-Beckmann 2002, Berman 2009). In the Ethiopian case, interest in legal pluralism followed in the wake of the 1995 constitution, which provided 'a clear recognition of the jurisdiction of customary and religious laws and courts in family and personal matters' (Pankhurst and Getachew 2008b:6). So far, research has concentrated on examining the customary norms and legal procedures of the different ethno-cultural groups in Ethiopia, both as such and in their relation to the formal, state-organized legal system. In addition, some attention has been paid to Islamic jurisdiction, notably in the form of *Sharia* courts (Mohammed 2011, Berihun 2013, Girmachew 2018).

Protestantism, by contrast, has not yet received any attention. However, there are at least two reasons to think that Protestantism ought to be part of the debate. First, the number of Protestants in Ethiopia has increased massively over the past few decades, rising from 5.5 per cent in 1984 to 18.6 per cent (or 14 million people) in 2007. The majority of believers live in the Southern Nations, Nationalities and Peoples Region (SNNPR), where 55.5 per cent of the population (or 8.4 million people) are Protestant; followed by Oromia (4.8 million or 17.7 per cent). Indeed, with Ethiopia having 'one of the fastest growing evangelical churches in the world' (Anderson 2004:126), numbers are bound to increase even further. Second, Protestant Christianity, like Islam or Judaism, offers not only a set of substantive rules and norms, but also stipulates procedures through which believers should deal with conflicts.

Taken together, these points suggest the importance of including Protestantism in the study of legal pluralism in Ethiopia. In this chapter, I take a first step in this direction, offering an ethnographic case study of legal pluralism in a southwest Ethiopian community, with a particular focus on the role of Protestantism. I show that in my field site, the Protestant church offers an alternative approach to dispute resolution to that of the state, and that, in fact, the Protestant approach, which privileges forgiveness over retribution, is increasingly informing the functioning of local formal judicial institutions.

The chapter is based on twenty-two months of fieldwork conducted between 2014 and 2017 in a rural southwest Ethiopian community called Dell. Dell is a *kebele* of SNNPR's South Aari *woreda* (district), located at about four hours walk into the mountains north of Jinka, the zonal capital. The roughly 4,000 inhabitants of Dell are ethnic Aari and speak Aaraf (on Aari see Jensen 1959, Naty 1992, Gebre 1995). People are subsistence agriculturalists and live in dispersed homesteads. Since 2010 a small village has emerged in the western part of Dell, next to the *kebele's* administrative buildings; it has been accessible by a 40-minute motorbike ride from the *woreda* capital at Gob (also known as Gazer) since 2014.

At the time of my fieldwork, about 60 per cent of the population in Dell were Protestants and 40 per cent were traditional believers. Conversion to Protestantism began in the late 1980s, accelerated in the early 2000s and continues today. The vast majority of Protestants in Dell belong to one of the three local branches of Ethiopia's largest evangelical church, Kale Heywet. In recent years, two small Pentecostal churches have also emerged, although these do not differ in terms of dispute resolution and will therefore not be treated separately. The 40 per cent of the population that have not converted are locally referred to as *alem*, Amharic for 'world'.[1] The term was originally introduced by the Protestants to signify 'non-believer', and has over time been adopted as self-designation by the non-Protestants. It is perhaps best translated as 'traditionalist', since the people who call themselves *alem* self-consciously follow what they consider to be 'tradition' (*karta*) or 'the ways of the ancestors'.

Both traditionalists and Protestants have their own modes of dispute resolution. These two approaches and their respective institutions coexist with the judicial institutions of the state. Formal courts have existed in Dell since the administrative unit of the *kebele* was first established by the Derg in 1975. While people used the formal courts from the beginning, their importance has clearly increased

1 The Aaraf spoken by people in Dell features many Amharic loanwords. In this chapter, both Aaraf and Amharic terms appear in italics; but when using an Amharic word for the first time, I indicate this in brackets: (Amh.).

over time. Today, when faced with a conflict, every person in Dell has to decide between two ways of addressing it. The traditionalists have to choose between what, following Pankhurst and Getachew (2008a: viii), I will call the 'customary mode of dispute resolution' on one hand, and formal litigation on the other. The Protestants, in turn, have to choose between the Protestant mode of dispute resolution and formal litigation.

In what follows, I will discuss customary, formal and Protestant ways of dealing with conflicts. The largest part of the chapter deals with the Protestant way, since the chapter's main aim is to make a case for taking Protestantism into account as a hitherto overlooked player in Ethiopian legal pluralism. However, some knowledge of both the customary and the formal approach is required in order to understand the specificity of the Protestant approach to conflicts. My description of these approaches will be rather brief both because of the demands of limited space and because it seems justified since customary and formal legal institutions in Dell do not – in their broad logics – strongly differ from their counterparts elsewhere in Ethiopia, which have already been described quite extensively in the literature.

Legal forums in Dell

Customary dispute resolution

To understand the customary mode of dispute resolution, some knowledge of traditional social organization is required. Dell forms part of Baaka, one of nine Aari kingdoms. While Baaka lost its political independence with incorporation into the Ethiopian empire in the early twentieth century, it has retained its ritual significance. Baaka is headed by a hereditary ritual king (*babi*), who is assisted by a group of hereditary ritual specialists (*godmi*) in guaranteeing the fertility and well-being of the land and its people. There are two exogamous moieties, each of which is composed of numerous patrilineages; and each lineage is headed by a so-called *toidi*, who carries out rituals on behalf of his junior kin. Relations between seniors and juniors are strictly hierarchical; and those higher up in the hierarchy are thought to be able to bless or curse those further down. The hierarchy characteristic of traditional social organization also plays an important role in the customary mode of dispute resolution.

This customary mode of dispute resolution is called *k'esh*. *K'esh* refers to a process aimed at finding an agreement between conflicting parties and restoring peaceful relations among them. It is therefore best translated as 'reconciliation'. *K'esh* is done for conflicts of every magnitude, ranging from minor quarrels between spouses to land or property disputes to adultery and homicide. The men – and it is only men – charged with leading the negotiations are referred to as *galta* (elders) and are selected depending on the nature of the case. Conflicts between members of the same household or lineage are commonly dealt with by their lineage head, who may sometimes also call elders from related lineages considered as ritual helpers (*geta*). In case of conflict between people of different lineages, respected men unrelated to either of the opponents are usually chosen as *galta*. In more serious cases, such as adultery or where there has been bloodshed, cases are taken to the *zia*, the local representative of the ritual king, who will call upon other high-ranking elders to assist him with arbitrating. The most severe cases, especially homicide, may also see the involvement of a high-ranking *godmi* (ritual specialist).

In every case, the *galta* begin by hearing the two sides and then make further inquiries, sometimes among witnesses. The aim here is to gain a clear understanding of the offence (*dax'ilsi*) that has been committed. Sometimes, a perpetrator will openly and from the outset acknowledge (*buts*) his or her wrongdoing; in other cases such an acknowledgement is only obtained in the course of the hearing and under pressure from the elders. In all cases, an admission of guilt is necessary for *k'esh* to be possible;[2] only once it has been obtained does the work of reconciliation proper begin.

Here, it is useful to distinguish four techniques or practices through which the imbalance created by the offence is redressed: humiliation, compensation, purification and commensality. Each of these practices features in every instance of *k'esh*, taking on a more or less elaborate form depending on the magnitude of the conflict.

(1) The first key element of reconciliation is the humiliation of the offender; with 'humiliation' defined as 'rendering humble' (rather than 'shaming' or 'disgracing'). This needs to be understood against the background that people in Dell frame most transgressions in terms of disrespect – of one person 'belittling' (*toksi*) another by treating them as 'smaller' than they can rightfully expect to be treated. During *k'esh* this belittlement is redressed by way of inversion: the offender humbles himself before the victim by displaying signs of inferiority – being submissive, displaying fear (*bashi*), addressing the other with honorific titles, clutching the other's knee, putting grass on his own head etc. The victim, in turn, will participate in the humiliation of the offender by acting for a while as if unwilling to agree to a settlement. This forces the offender to beg (*miks*) more strongly by displaying even clearer signs of humility.

2 Where a defendant continues to deny the charge, the plaintiff can either take the case to the formal system or, remaining within the customary system, take the case to a *godmi* living on the eastern boundary of Dell. The *godmi* is able to bring out the truth by way of letting the disputants testify before making them drink water which is thought to make ill or kill anyone who has testified falsely.

(2) Compensation is the second key principle of *k'esh*. The plaintiff commonly requests a certain amount of compensation, but ultimately the elders decide the amount to be given. Compensation can range from a small sum of money or a litre of alcohol, to a sheep or several heads of cattle (or an equivalent sum of money). It is important to note that, while victims often do take compensation, they may also refuse it for the sake of social harmony. In one homicide case, for instance, the kin of the victim refused to take the virgin girl and ten heads of cattle that had been agreed as compensation. They argued that the two lineages had previously intermarried and that to normalize their affinal relations it would be better to be magnanimous and not take what was rightfully theirs. Similarly, there are instances – such as stray livestock damaging crops – where compensation is agreed but both sides work with the tacit understanding that it will not really be paid.

(3) Most conflicts and transgressions are thought to produce either pollution or a sort of heat in the disputants' stomach (*norti*, the locus of feelings), which will lead to harm if unremedied by purification. Purification can take numerous forms, ranging from small acts, such as a lineage head throwing grass into the granaries of a household where spouses have quarrelled over the distribution of grain, to large rituals, such as two lineages washing their hands in the blood of a bisected sheep to overcome enmity after homicide. But the most basic form of purification, used in almost every reconciliation, is the drinking of purifying water which washes away the pollution or heat and brings 'coolness' (*shimma*), and which, together with the pronunciation of 'forgiveness' (*negane*), marks the penultimate step in the reconciliation process.

(4) The final step is commensality between the disputants and the elders. Drink and food need to be provided by the offender, who thus incurs expenses even when the victim does not take compensation. In a very immediate way, commensality marks the end of hostility, since the parties in dispute refrain from eating together until reconciliation has been achieved – not least because eating together before reconciliation is thought to entail illness or even death.

Formal litigation

If *k'esh* denotes customary dispute resolution, *kisi* (Amharic 'lawsuit') is the term people in Dell use for the process of dealing with disputes through state institutions. Contrary to *k'esh*, which is about reconciliation, *kisi* is locally understood as being more antagonistic. Why this is the case and why people file lawsuits nonetheless is one of the questions addressed in this section.

There are two levels at which people can sue others in Dell: the level of the 'cell' (local people use the English term) and that of the *kebele*. Dell *kebele* is subdivided into sixteen so-called cells, each of which groups together between thirty-five and fifty households from one neighbourhood. The cells were first formed in

2006. Officially, they are party organizations of the EPRDF, Ethiopia's ruling political coalition. In practice, however, people consider the cells as part of the state apparatus – they belong to the realm of the *mengist* (Amharic 'government') no less than the *kebele* or the *woreda*.[3] As well as carrying out public works, the different cells assemble on one morning each week at their respective meeting grounds. At these meetings, court hearings take place, with the cell's three leaders acting as judges (*danya* [Amharic]). Issues commonly dealt with include domestic conflicts, petty theft, unreturned loans and disturbances. Usually cases concern members of the same cell, although it is possible to sue outsiders by going to their cell. Cases that remain unresolved in the cell or that fall outside its jurisdiction are referred to the *kebele*.

The *kebele* has two courts and one *komitee* (committee) for dealing with legal issues, all of which operate on Wednesdays and Fridays: the *meret komitee* (Amh.) for land disputes; the *mahberawi firdebet* (Amh.) or Social Court for property and monetary claims; and the *wana firdebet* (Amh.) or Main Court. The first two refer more serious cases to the Main Court, which also deals with matters like adultery, divorce and fights involving bloodshed. The Main Court, whose judges are the five main *kebele* leaders, is the highest court at the *kebele* level and it alone is able to refer cases upward to the *woreda*. No matter at which level litigation takes place, there are three possible outcomes: (i) the respective court passes its own judgement; (ii) the court asks people to deal with the case through *k'esh* and then notify it about the agreement reached; (iii) if neither of these works – for example, because one party does not consent to doing *k'esh* – the case can be referred to the next highest level.

Judgements are usually passed in those cases where the evidence is clear and where the damage done can be easily assessed. For instance, in one case, where a man had beaten up his wife, the cell ruled that he had to give her the money she had spent on going to hospital, and pay a fine to the cell. In another case, the judges of the Social Court ruled that a defaulting debtor had to repay his loan with interest. In a third case, where one man had sued another for injuring him with a stone while they carried out public works together, the Main Court found the accused not guilty, arguing that he had not hurt the other with intent.

In many cases, however, disputants are asked to solve their conflict by way of *k'esh*. There are two main reasons for this. First, cell and *kebele* courts lack the capacity to deal with every case presented to them; and asking people to do *k'esh* is a way of reducing caseload. Second, having no legal training whatsoever, cell and *kebele* judges are aware that they lack detailed knowledge of state law and therefore, in some cases, might not make adequate or legally binding judgements.

3 For similar observations from elsewhere in Ethiopia see Vaughan and Tronvoll 2003:41.

In one case, for instance, an unmarried woman who had become pregnant by a married man sued him for alimony. Her original demand had been that he marries her, but the Main Court judge told her that the law did not permit a man to take a second wife and that a monthly support should be paid instead. He went on to say that the *kebele* court was unable to decide the amount of alimony to be paid, and that the woman would have to go to the *woreda* court to get a decision. Pointing to the costs of this, the judge proposed *k'esh* as an alternative. For this, both sides selected elders, and negotiations took place outside the court building. After an hour, the disputants reported back to the judge that it had been agreed that the man would pay 50 Birr and 3 *tassa* (c. 2.5 kg) of grain each month. This agreement was written down by the judge, who also included a clause stipulating that the man would have to pay a 500 Birr fine to the *kebele* should he fail to stick to the agreement. The document was signed by thumbprint by both parties. Finally, the judge decreed that the man had to immediately pay a 150 Birr fine (*zera* [Amh.]) to the *kebele* for having failed to support the woman as had been agreed between them orally at the time of the child's birth.

As this example shows, people who sue others in court often end up being asked to deal with their conflict through out-of-court negotiations. These out-of-court negotiations are – like the customary mode of dispute resolution – referred to as *k'esh*. Contrary to customary *k'esh*, however, this latter kind of *k'esh* does little to diminish the antagonism between the disputants. This is for two reasons. Firstly, *k'esh* done on the recommendation of a judge commonly only deals with questions of compensation. It does not feature the other three elements of customary *k'esh* – humiliation, purification, commensality – and therefore is not as reconciliatory. As people often put it, this kind of *k'esh* is 'done just with the mouth' (*gurri afak*) and not 'truly from the stomach' (*dofen norti girank*). Secondly, the court is always notified about the agreement reached, which is written down and commonly includes a threat of punishment for repeated infringement. Beyond that, virtually every case ends with the offender having to pay a fine, which varies with the magnitude of the offence, from 50 Birr for minor cases to 5000 Birr for adultery.[4] Fines – often linked to one-day imprisonment – are the main punishments (*k'itat* [Amh.]) dealt out by local courts, and it is the inevitability of these fines that makes taking someone to court such an antagonistic move.[5]

4 The courts have a strong institutional interest in imposing fines because fines are the main source of income for the cells and the *kebele*. It is also true that, while one part of the fines is used to finance the operation of these institutions, another part goes to the judges, who – not receiving any remuneration for their work – take them in lieu of a salary.

5 As one reviewer has pointed out, in many other Ethiopian societies, rituals of reconciliation and purification may be done even after a case has been settled in court. In principle, this also applies for Dell, in particular for serious crimes like homicide, where it is felt that communal life would be impossible unless the punishment imposed by the court was complemented

Given that reconciliation and the restoration of peaceful relations have traditionally been important values in Dell, why do people sometimes take the antagonistic step of suing someone in court? There are several reasons. Firstly, there are cases where an offender refuses to do *k'esh* and openly challenges the claimant to sue him. Secondly, some groups in local society, especially women and craftworkers (*mana*), feel disadvantaged by the male-dominated customary mode of dispute resolution. Thirdly, for these groups in particular, but also more generally, it seems that one can get a higher compensation by going to court than by solving a case through customary *k'esh* because one has more bargaining power. A final reason relates to the fact that customary *k'esh* does not have any developed notion of punishment (*k'itat*), whereas punishment – in the form of fines and short-term imprisonment – is central to the formal system. When asked why they had taken someone to court, several people explained that they hoped that the punishment would deter the offender from repeating their offence. There also exist cases where the plaintiff's main desire is to see their opponent fined out of a belief that one's enemy's loss is one's own gain.

The perception locally is that people now use the formal judicial system much more frequently than in the past; and during my fieldwork I heard many complaints about the fact that 'these days' people even sue their parents, and brothers go to court. This assessment is not free of romanticism. On closer examination, it turns out that the purportedly better past also had its cases of litigation among kin. Yet, it would be wrong to simply dismiss the emic analysis. In a context of progressive land scarcity and intensified competition for economic 'growth' (*gabinti*), conflicts touching on money and property in particular have increased, and so have the perceived costs of peaceful reconciliation. It is not least against this background of increased litigation that the Protestant message of unconditional forgiveness needs to be understood.

Protestant dispute resolution

In Dell, the Protestant mode of dispute resolution is shaped by the key local Protestant value of forgiveness (*negane*). Protestants in Dell regularly make use of a number of Bible passages to promote this value; the most frequently cited one is Matthew 6:14-15:

> If you forgive others the wrongs they have done to you, your Father in heaven will also forgive you. But if you do not forgive others, then your Father will not forgive the wrongs you have done.

---

by reconciliation. In many other, less dramatic cases, however, rituals of reconciliation do not follow settlement in court and latent antagonism thus remains.

The Protestant logic of forgiveness stands in utmost contrast to the logic of formal litigation. And while *negane* is a concept that also plays a role in the customary mode of dispute resolution, the Protestant and the customary understandings of the concept differ starkly, as do the respective modes of dispute resolution, as I show in the following.

This section, then, explores the differences between customary, state and Protestant ways of dealing with conflicts by taking an in-depth look at the latter. Additionally, it looks at the personal, institutional and ideological factors that move people to employ the Protestant mode. As a way into my discussion, let me offer a case that exemplifies some key characteristics of Protestant dispute resolution.

> One day when passing by his field in the morning, Mathos[6] saw two large oxen belonging to his neighbour Elias. The oxen had broken free from where Elias had tethered them the previous evening, and had spent the night feeding on Mathos' ripening maize, causing considerable damage. Mathos dragged the oxen out of his field and tethered them securely by the wayside. Early the next morning, Elias went to Mathos house. He was accompanied by two Protestant men, whom he had asked to act as his *galta* (elders). One of the *galta* began with an apology for only coming after a whole day had elapsed. He explained that Elias had gone to town the previous day and had only heard about the troubles when he returned in the evening. Mathos calmly replied that it wasn't a problem at all, and that he had trusted Elias to come. Then, Elias spoke about how very sorry he was for what had happened, and how much it 'burnt inside his stomach' to see his neighbour's maize devastated. He also offered to bring Mathos some dried maize in compensation. At this point, however, Mathos gently interrupted him by clearing his throat to indicate that he would now speak himself. He began by asserting that they were all believers in God, and that the Bible demanded that you 'not make your brother pay' (*indapsi antam ay kashishka*).[7] He went on to say that he didn't doubt that God would find a way to feed his family, and that he was willing to forgive Elias freely and without further ado. Thereupon, one of the elders asked the two to 'take confession' (*nisah teykate*). Rising to his feet, Elias gave a condensed account of what had happened, stated that he had 'made his brother sad' and asked for God's and Mathos's forgiveness. In response, everyone including Mathos waved their hands over Elias, saying '*sabi an negane*!' ('May God forgive you!').

6 All personal names are pseudonyms.

7 The term 'brother' is part of an idiom of spiritual kinship; in reality Elias and Mathos are unrelated.

> Then Mathos himself got to his feet, gave a similarly condensed account, noted that he had become sad on first seeing the damaged crops, and asked God's forgiveness for this sadness. Like Elias before him, Mathos then bowed and everyone waved their hands over him, calling out 'May God forgive you!' The reconciliation was thus officially concluded and, after one of the elders had spoken a prayer, the elders and Elias left. (Summary of fieldnotes, 2 August 2016)

The case of Mathos and Elias exemplifies a number of characteristics of the Protestant mode of dispute resolution that, in the following, will be drawn out through a comparison with how a similar case would be handled in the formal or the customary mode.

To begin with, Mathos did not take the opportunity to take Elias' oxen to the *kebele*, that is, he decided not to use the formal system. This would have been a way of punishing Elias, since Elias would have had to pay money to the *kebele* to ransom his oxen. Such antagonistic moves are sometimes made by people in Dell, but they are prohibited to Protestants since they would violate the principle of not making others pay.

Secondly, it is noteworthy that no assessment of the damage was made, even though the damage was considerable. In the customary mode, such an assessment (*gemet* [Amh.]) is always made, and the elders subsequently state approximately how much grain has been lost. There is usually a tacit understanding that compensation will not really be paid, but people use the assessment for mental accounting, and might in a future conflict make use of this knowledge. Moreover, verbalizing how much has been lost helps in the humiliation of the offender, since it increases the pressure on the latter to submissively beg the injured party (see above).

In Mathos' case, humiliation is conspicuously absent; and this is a third key distinctive feature of Protestant dispute resolution. While Elias humbly apologizes for the damage done by his oxen, Mathos in no way exploits the fact that his property was damaged or that Elias only came to apologize one day after the event. Rather than blustering and being unconciliatory so as to force Elias into acting submissively, Mathos himself acts in a humble way. Behind this attitude is the local Protestant idea that the one who has been damaged or otherwise wronged is as much in need of forgiveness (and thus of humility) as the offender, because 'becoming sad' – for example, about losing crops – is no less sinful than 'making someone sad'. Hence, in the end, both Elias and Mathos ask God's forgiveness.

Finally, it is also characteristic of Protestant *k'esh* that the offender is not required to provide drink or food. Rather than engage in commensality, as would be done in the customary mode, Elias and the elders quickly leave once reconciliation has been achieved. The eschewal of demands for food and drink is partly motivated by the notion of 'not making others pay', but an idea of divine blessings is also at play. Protestants in Dell believe that God rewards people with blessings (*anje*) if they forgive freely or freely help others to solve their conflicts. Mathos and the elders would have lost their entitlement to divine blessings by asking Elias for food, since their forgiveness and help would no longer have qualified as 'free'.[8]

The requirement to forgive freely applies in all cases where damage is caused involuntarily – no matter how great the damage. For instance, during my time in the field, one man lost two of his four oxen when they were gored to death by another man's bull. The enormity of the loss notwithstanding, church leaders urged the man not to ask compensation and, after some inner struggle, he agreed to this.

At this point it is important to note that, where damage was caused involuntarily, forgiveness is not merely a recommendation. Rather, it is a duty backed up by a threat of divine punishment (*sabite gami*) – a threat, which is very real to Protestants in Dell. Protestants frequently cite the case of Angri's horse to illustrate the reality of this threat. Some years ago, Angri's horse died after being kicked by another man's horse. Angri, despite being Protestant, did what would be done in the customary mode: he took the other man's horse as compensation. Soon after, however, Angri's hut was destroyed by fire, and a little later he suffered the death of a child. These troubles were interpreted as divine punishment for having taken compensation. It was only when he returned the horse and asked God's forgiveness – or so people in Dell say – that Angri's luck improved.

Cases where damage was caused involuntarily are distinguished from conflicts resulting from intentional action. While forgiveness is mandatory in the former case, it is virtuous but not strictly required in the latter case, as can be seen in the following case. The case at the same time allows me to introduce a second Protestant setting for dispute resolution: taking a case to the church leaders rather than gathering elders and going to another person's house for *k'esh*.

> Every Tuesday evening, the leaders of Dell *Kale Heywet* church assemble for their weekly meeting. The evening begins with a service, celebrated in the intimacy of the leaders' assembly room. Afterwards, church business is conducted, and then the leaders turn to dealing with conflicts brought to them by church members. On one evening in May 2017, two men – Mangi and Ali – turned up and asked the leaders for help with solving a conflict that had been smouldering for weeks.
>
> The two men had share-cropped together for several years. Using a common type of share-cropping arrangement (called *kotsa*), Mangi provided the field and Ali

8 Note also that Protestantism in Dell does not place high value on commensality. Contrary to what traditionalists assume, local Protestantism does not consider commensality necessary for (re)producing relations. Rather, it is thought that believers are already related in and through Christ, and that this relatedness is more profound than any relatedness that could be produced by worldly means like commensality.

provided seeds and the bulk of the labour, and each year they divided the harvest equally. Recently, however, Mangi had announced that he would stop working *kotsa* with Ali because he needed the field for his own purposes. Ali was unhappy about this decision and asked Mangi to give him 300 Birr. He reasoned that he had a right to this money because, when they first negotiated their share-cropping arrangement, Mangi (who at that time was in need of money) had asked Ali to pay 300 Birr as a sort of entry fee and had promised to pay back the money once their cooperation ended. Now, however, Mangi refused to return the money to Ali, arguing that they had worked together for several years, and that Ali (who had very little land of his own) had greatly benefited from their partnership, so that the money had effectively already been repaid.

After each side had presented its point of view, one of the church leaders rose to speak. In a way typical of Protestant dispute resolutions, he began in very general terms: 'God's Holy Word tells us to not fight with each other. So abandon your fight and live together in peace and love... What is dividing you, are but things of the flesh – things that will remain behind on earth [i.e. cannot be taken to Heaven]... God blesses the one who forgives.' As these exhortations moved neither of the disputants to give in, another of the leaders then started to gently urge them to compromise. Both of them had a point, he asserted. Ali was right to claim back the money if that was what had originally been agreed. But Mangi was also right to observe that Ali had profited a lot from their cooperation. These days, he noted, it was not uncommon for field-owners to terminate share-cropping agreements after only a year or two, at a point when the partner had hardly recovered his original investment in seeds. Mangi, by contrast, had worked faithfully with Ali for several years, and so Ali had gained more than he could initially have hoped for. After the leader had gone on in this way for some minutes, Mangi – adopting a conciliatory attitude – said that Ali had been a good partner, that he was grateful for the economic success they had had together, that he did not want there to be any resentment between them and that he therefore offered to give Ali 150 Birr. Thanking him for this offer, the church leader turned to Ali and urged him to content himself with this offer rather than to take the case to the *kebele* court to sue for the full 300 Birr. Still somewhat disgruntled, but bowing to the leader's authority, Ali agreed to this. The two disputants were then asked to take confession (*nisah* [Amh.]) and to speak 'truly from their stomach' if they harboured any other ill feelings.

As it turned out, there was another issue. In his *nisah*, which followed Mangi's, Ali recounted how, two or three years ago, the onions had not grown well and Mangi's wife had hinted that someone with the 'evil eye' (*afi*) might be responsible for the poor growth. She had said this in a way that made Ali feel that she suspected him. 'No one has ever accused me of being *aish* [person with the evil eye]', Ali told the church leaders, 'but this woman [pointing to Mangi's wife, who

> had come along to the dispute resolution] is always belittling me because I am poor.' After Ali had finished his confession, asking forgiveness for having become sad about both Mangi and his wife, the latter was asked by a church leader to take confession herself since she was also implicated in the conflict. She did so, saying that she had not meant to imply Ali had given the onions the evil eye, that she was sorry if it had come across that way and that she asked Ali's forgiveness. With this apology the confessions ended; and Mangi and Ali, as well as Ali and Mangi's wife, were asked to hug each other. With a prayer the case was then laid to rest, and the church leaders called in the next two disputants. (Summary of fieldnotes, 23 May 2017)

The conflict between Mangi and Ali differs from that between Mathos and Elias inasmuch as there is no clear-cut requirement for either of them to freely forgive the other. As one of the church leaders points out, forgiving would be virtuous and divinely rewarded; and it is imaginable that more committed believers might have solved the issue that way, with one paying the 300 Birr or the other abandoning his claim. But in Mangi and Ali's case, neither of the two was ready to back down so the church leaders had to negotiate a compromise between them.

Given their initial unwillingness to give in, one may well ask why they did not take their conflict to a formal court. Addressing this question allows us to take a closer look at the factors that move people to solve their conflicts through Protestant rather than through state institutions, and also brings to light further specifics of the Protestant mode of dispute resolution.

The first, straightforward answer to why Mangi and Ali avoided court is that the church in Dell prohibits its members from going to court. Given that courts inevitably impose fines (see above), filing a lawsuit against someone is seen as equivalent to 'making him pay', which is impermissible for a Protestant. As one church leader put it to me: 'The Bible tells us to not give our brother to the hyena; but the government will always make you pay.' Hence, the church's prohibition. Moreover, drawing inspiration from 1 Corinthians 6:1–6, the church holds that believers suing each other would set a poor example for outsiders. By solving their conflicts through the church, Protestants can instead impress unbelievers with the peacefulness of their religion.

Under certain conditions the church will give permission for someone to go to court.[9] But anyone who goes to court without having first asked permission will

9 Among others, this may happen in the case of a conflict between a Protestant and a non-Protestant, if the latter does not agree that the case can be handled by the church. Note, however, that non-Protestants do sometimes agree to the church handling a conflict, because church leaders have a reputation for being excellent at reconciling people. According to my informants, the only cases that would not be handled by the church, but would directly be referred to the formal system, are homicide cases.

be punished with *dakri*. Literally translatable as 'tying' (the same term, indeed, as the one used for 'imprisonment' in the *kebele* prison), *dakri* means that a person is banned from active religious participation (praying out loud, singing in a choir etc.) for a specified number of months. Should the person die without first having been 'untied' (*bul*), i.e. absolved, their soul is believed to go to hell.

On top of the church's threat of disciplinary action, there is the threat of social disapproval. As I have said above, forgiveness and peacefulness are key values for Protestants in Dell, and the violation of these values elicits much gossip and disapprobation. Therefore, those who care about being considered good Protestants have to solve their conflicts without recourse to the formal system.

Alongside these negative incentives that deter Protestants from going to court, there are also positive aspects of the religious mode of dispute resolution that Protestants in Dell find attractive. To begin with, solving a case through the church has economic advantages. For both parties it saves a lot of time, since formal lawsuits often drag on for several weeks, with people spending hours waiting in front of the court house, or being asked by judges to return the following week. In church, by contrast, cases are usually solved in one evening. For the offender – or the one who is more likely to be found guilty – it is also financially advantageous to settle the case in church. Although, as we have seen in Mangi's case, Protestant dispute resolution may involve compensation payments, these are usually lower than those agreed in the context of litigation. This is because there is a moral expectation – embodied by the church leaders – that the claimant compromise at least a little bit. Thus, in the above case, Ali agreed to content himself with 150 Birr rather than to demand the full 300 Birr originally requested.

More importantly, the church unlike the formal courts – does not levy any fees or fines. This, of course, is hugely advantageous to the offender. But the absence of fees also means cost benefits for the claimant, since filing a lawsuit in the *kebele* requires paying a fee for 'opening a dossier' (*dosi potsh*) and, in some cases, for sending a *militia* (auxiliary policeman) to seize the defendant.[10] The church's refusal to levy fees and fines is not only a matter of religious principle. Unlike the *kebele*, which is financially dependent on collecting fines (see footnote 4), the church is financed through members' tithes. Hence, the operational costs of the church's forum for dispute resolution – notably the food served to church leaders after a long evening of arbitration – need not be covered by the disputants. Likewise, the church leaders have no personal interest in imposing fines, even though they are unpaid volunteers. They conceive of their work as a service to God (*sabite woni*), which will be rewarded with divine blessings if carried out freely.

10 Note also that costs of litigation increase massively for the claimant should the case be referred to the *woreda*: according to people in Dell, *woreda* judges do not consider cases without first having been bribed.

Aside from the locally perceived cost and time-saving advantages of solving conflicts through the church, another – even more meaningful – advantage relates to social harmony. It is true that there is a culture in Dell of exhibiting one's greatness or 'heaviness' (*detsmi*) through self-assertive and feisty behaviour, with litigation being one means to this end. At the same time, however, many people also have a genuine interest in maintaining respectful and harmonious relationships with their surroundings. As was often explained to me, life in a small place like Dell becomes awkward and unbearable if one has to avoid someone. Thus, the Protestant mode of dispute resolution's peacefulness and capacity to repair damaged relations makes it attractive. This concern with overcoming hostility and recreating harmony is readily perceptible in the atmosphere of Protestant *k'esh*. Both church leaders and disputants speak softly, often with humbly downcast eyes, and there is none of the yelling and cursing typical of cell or *kebele* court hearings. Furthermore, as Ali's confession in the case above exemplifies, the Protestant principle that people may only ask or grant forgiveness after having confessed *all* the ill feelings they harbour toward their opponent, even though these may not directly relate to the case, can bring to light further conflicts, which then become the subject of reconciliation efforts. In this way, the Protestant mode of dispute resolution is able to repair social relationships in a very comprehensive way. And this, I would suggest, is one of the key things people cherish about it.

Protestantism's impact on the formal system

In the previous section, we encountered the church's demand that conflicts be solved through the Protestant mode of dispute resolution, rather than by the formal judicial system. Not every church member, of course, follows this rule: cases exist where Protestants have demanded compensation where they ought to have forgiven freely or have gone to court without the church's permission. Yet, even though they may sometimes fail, and even though it may not always feel easy, most Protestants in Dell do genuinely try to forgive or compromise most of the time. With 60 per cent of the population in Dell currently Protestant, the church is clearly an important player in the local legal arena, providing a much-used alternative mode for dealing with conflicts. However, Protestantism's impact on legal life in Dell goes even further. Beyond offering a mere 'alternative', there is an observable tendency for Protestantism to also affect the way in which the local formal system operates. In short, one could speak of a 'Protestantization' or – to use a slightly less awkward term – 'Christianization' of local courts.

To spell out this point, I need to begin by explaining how local state institutions, including cell and *kebele* courts are staffed. All people who work in state institutions in Dell are locals. They do not get a salary, and work is quite time-consuming.

Consequently, hardly anyone is keen to work in these institutions. However, once appointed to office,[11] one is obliged to do the job. Starting in the early 2000s, when a Protestant was appointed as *kebele* chairperson for the first time, the number of Protestants working in local state institutions has increased rapidly. Indeed, since around 2013, all *kebele* staff have been Protestant. At cell level, too, Protestants are clearly over-represented, although there remain a few cells in which the leaders are predominantly 'traditionalist'. The over-representation of Protestants in local state institutions is due to the understanding – shared by 'traditionalists' – that Protestants are better suited to these kinds of job because they don't drink alcohol, do subscribe to ideals like punctuality and industriousness, and are often literate.

The observation that almost all local officials are Protestant raises an important question. Given that the Protestant mode of dispute resolution is deeply opposed to the formal approach, how do Protestant cell or *kebele* staff deal with this contradiction? How, that is, do Protestant officials reconcile belonging to a religion that demands forgiveness with working in judicial institutions that convict and punish people?

More than an anthropologist's musing, this is a burning question for at least some of the local judges. As one of my interlocutors, a middle-aged man by the name of Simon, who had recently ended his term as judge in the *kebele* Social Court, told me:

> On us Protestants, work in the *kebele* weighs very heavily. God says 'Do not judge!' (*ay berimka*), but the government says 'Beat!'[12] Fine! Imprison!' (*gika, kashka, dakerka*) ... After my election, I pleaded with God. I told Him that this work [as judge] clashed with His Word, and I prayed and prayed that God would relieve me from my office. I also asked the church leaders to pray on my behalf, and now, finally [after five years], my prayer has been answered and God has removed me from this heathen work (*aysafte woni*). (Interview, 4 March 2017)
>
> Having told me how God had extricated him, Simon went on to talk in more detail about the dilemmas he had faced in his work. One issue was beating suspects to extort a confession, as Simon explained: 'The Bible does not give us authority to beat others. All people have been created by God and one may not beat God's creatures. So when acting as a judge, I did not permit beatings.' Oaths were another problematic point. Courts in Dell frequently make disputants or witnesses testify under oath (*tsha'x'a*), on the assumption that false testimonies may result in supernatural punishment, including death. But, as Simon asserted:

11 Appointment is either through the '*kebele* parliament' (composed of 200 local people) or by higher-level officials.

12 Note that Ethiopian law does not allow suspects to be beaten. In reality, however, beatings do happen and thus local people may come to the understanding that beating is an officially sanctioned practice.

> God says, 'Don't make others swear oaths'. I had read that in Matthew's Gospel. I was very afraid. You know, these oaths have the power to kill people. But if someone died after I had made him swear, God would punish me. So I said I wouldn't make people swear. Although this may be the way of the government, I will not follow it. The government rules over the flesh, but as a Protestant I need to look after my soul. I need to save my soul – I need salvation for myself, do I not? (Interview, 4 March 2017)

Simon's account shows two things. First, it reveals how seriously he had reflected on what it meant to work as a Protestant in state institutions. The problem, as he sees it, is that by using certain procedures typical of the local formal system (e.g. requiring people to swear oaths), he may be committing sin. This means nothing less than to imperil the salvation of his soul. Second, it is clear that Simon had not only reflected on this problem but had taken practical steps to mitigate against it. Driven by anxiety over salvation, he decided that he would conduct court business without recourse to beating or oath-taking. In other words, Simon introduced a small change to how the Social Court worked in order to make it less opposed to Protestant values. Of course, the change was not very substantial and may not be adopted by other judges. Yet, it is noteworthy because it fits into a broader pattern, composed of similar subtle changes, introduced by other Protestant officials. Some further examples will help to substantiate this point. The first example concerns a case that occurred some years prior to my fieldwork. It was related to me by Petrus, who was vice-chairperson of the *kebele* at the time of the case.

> The *kebele* Main Court at that time had repeatedly dealt with a man who regularly beat his wife. The man was a drunkard and the beatings always happened when he was intoxicated. An agreement was signed that he would pay a 200 Birr fine to the *kebele* should he repeat his offence. Before long, however, his battered wife once again appeared before the Main Court. A *militia* was sent out to seize the man who admitted to the offence. Petrus, who was presiding over the court that day, pointed out to the man that he would never stop beating his wife and paying fines to the *kebele* if he did not give up alcohol. He then proposed to him that he should become Protestant (which is locally deemed the best way to stop drinking); and proposed that he would not have to pay the infringement fine of 200 Birr if he converted. The man agreed to convert on the spot; and it was the judge Petrus who then went with him through the declaration of faith required to become a Protestant. Indeed, eager to demonstrate to the new convert the brotherliness that reigns among believers, Petrus not only did not impose a fine but actually paid the 20 Birr fee that the man would have had to pay to the *militia* who had gone to fetch him. 'You are a child of God, now', Petrus recounted having

> said to the man, 'so I will pay for you.' Ever since – and to the satisfaction of his wife – the man has been a Protestant. (Summary of an interview, 12 July 2017)

This example, like the previous one, shows how a Protestant logic is introduced into the formal system. Rather than imposing a fine, Petrus dealt with the violent drunkard by way of forgiveness. Indeed, by making conversion a precondition for forgiveness, Petrus – from his point of view – not only respected God's command to not make others pay but also realized the Protestant value of making converts. In this example, too, then, personal religious convictions find their way into the mode of operation of public institutions.

This colouring of public institutions by religion can be seen in the cells too. In some areas of the *kebele* – namely in those located at some distance from a church – the concentration of Protestants is lower than in other areas. Therefore, since cells bring together people from one area, some cells are – both in terms of members and leadership – predominantly Protestant while others are predominantly traditionalist (although no cell is entirely homogeneous). It is commonly understood among people in Dell that this difference is reflected in the legal life of the respective cells. As people repeatedly pointed out to me, and as I observed myself, 'there is not a lot of fines' (*kashi beday*) in Protestant-majority cells; whereas in traditionalist cells fines are common. The reason for this is that Protestant cell leaders, when acting as judges in the cell court, urge disputants to solve their conflicts peacefully through confession (*nisah*) and forgiveness, and without payment. By contrast, in traditionalist cells there is a stronger impulse to impose fines. This is because such cells lack the Protestant concern with 'not making others pay', but also because they believe that commensality is an important part of dispute resolution. Consequently, it is common in traditionalist cells for parts of the fines imposed on the offender to go towards *hisbint dassken*. Roughly translatable as 'helping people up', *hisbint dassken* means that the offender has to provide food and drink for all cell members, who will not leave the cell's meeting ground until they have eaten.

One way in which Protestant logic is introduced into the cell, then, is through the judges' personal religious convictions. However, I have also observed cases, such as the following one, where the church directly influenced proceedings.

> One Wednesday morning in March 2017, the cell, the meeting of which I regularly attended, dealt with the case of Doba's dog. Some days before, a sheep belonging to a man called Gizo, had been found dead, torn apart by what was suspected to have been a dog. Gizo had then set a trap and, a day later, had indeed found a dog caught in the trap – Doba's dog. Bigger than any other dog in the area, and known for its voracity, everyone agreed that this must have been the dog that had killed Gizo's sheep. After some discussion, the cell leaders granted Gizo's claim for compensation. Doba's own sheep had recently given birth to twins, and it was decided that – after raising them for a while – Doba was to give the two lambs

> to Gizo. A couple of weeks later, during another cell meeting, Gizo angrily told the cell leaders that, according to Doba, one of the lambs had died. However, no one had seen the carcass, which Doba claimed to have buried quickly, so Gizo alleged that Doba had secretly sold the lamb. The cell judges once again sided with Gizo, ordering Doba to pay 300 Birr to Gizo as a substitute for the lamb. Doba was deeply angered by this decision and exclaimed before the whole cell, 'Oh, God! How is it that my nephew deceitfully makes me pay?' (Gizo and Doba were indeed not only members of the same Protestant church, but Gizo was also Doba's sister's son.) Soon after the meeting at which Doba had to pay 300 Birr, Gizo fell very ill, and this illness coincided with the sudden death of two of his sheep. He called the church leaders to pray for his healing. As is normal on such occasions, the leaders asked him to reflect on possible sins, and Gizo mentioned the issue with Doba. For the church leaders, Gizo's illness was a clear case of divine punishment for having sued Doba in the cell rather than having solved the issue the Protestant way – an offence aggravated by the fact that Doba was Gizo's mother's brother (*irki*), and thus someone to be treated with special respect. Two of the church leaders therefore decided that they would personally go to the next cell meeting to rectify things.
>
> At that meeting, speaking to the assembled cell members, one of the two began by reminding everyone that while there was, of course, the law of the government (*mengiste higi* [Amh.]) and while God wanted his people to obey that law, ultimately everyone was subject to God's law (*sabite higi*). And God's law was clear that believers should not take each other to court. It had thus been a first mistake for Gizo and Doba to deal with their case through the cell rather than through the church. The decision of the (Protestant) cell leaders in favour of compensation was problematic too, since this was the type of case where damage had been done involuntarily and free forgiveness would have been the right and necessary response. Even worse, the church leader claimed, was that Gizo had accused his uncle of lying and had pressed for the 300 Birr. Even if Doba had been lying, didn't the Bible say (at 1 Corinthians 6:7) that it is better to be wronged and cheated than to take a fellow believer to court? To rectify things, the church leader ended, Gizo should return the money to Doba and renounce his claim to the remaining lamb. Gizo agreed to this, and there followed the standard Protestant ritual of confession and forgiveness. (Summary of fieldnotes, March and April 2017)

The church leaders' intervention in the affairs of the cell is a clear case of the church exercising direct influence on local judicial state institutions: by making Gizo return the money and relinquish his claim to the lamb, they effectively overruled the cell judges' earlier decision.

By way of closing, I would like to note two conditions that make this 'Christianization of the local judiciary' possible. First, there exists no developed notion of 'secularism' in Dell, that is, no real sense of the division between state and religion. While people do conceptualize the two as distinct realms, they also assume there is a clear hierarchy between them, with God ranking above the state. From their perspective, therefore, there is nothing unusual or critique-worthy in church leaders intervening in state affairs. Second, the particular nature of state institutions at the grass-roots level permits the kind of religious influence seen here. Unlike at higher levels of the state, the *kebele* has very little in the way of clear procedural rules. To a large extent, the local *kebele* staffs have to decide how they are going to run the local state institutions, and this relative absence of strict procedural rules allows the religious background of the local officials to influence their work.

Conclusion

This chapter has investigated legal pluralism in a southwest Ethiopian community. It has brought to light three coexistent modes of dealing with conflicts: customary, formal and Protestant. The customary mode aims at reconciliation, and draws on the key practices of humiliation of the offender, compensation of the victim, purification of both disputants, and commensality. Formal litigation is antagonistic rather than reconciliatory. Though sometimes requiring disputants to find a solution through out-of-court negotiation, local courts in the end always impose fines and often sentence offenders to short-term imprisonment. Protestant dispute resolution shares with customary dispute resolution a concern with reconciliation and restoring peaceful relationships, but it also differs in some profound ways: it does not allow for the humiliation of the offender, but asks humility of the victim, too; it does not permit compensation claims where damage has been done involuntarily, and requires compromise where conflicts are the result of intentional action; and it does not require the offender to provide food or drink for commensality. In positive terms, the key principle of Protestant dispute resolution is forgiveness.

Over the past few decades, 60 per cent of the population of Dell have converted to Protestantism. This means that an ever greater number of people has started to use the Protestant rather than the customary mode of dispute resolution. This is a first reason for considering Protestantism an important player in the legal arena in Dell. A second reason became visible through a closer inspection of the relation between the Protestant and the formal system. Protestantism, as I have shown, is deeply opposed to the antagonistic logic of litigation and the imposition of punishments. Believers are not only prohibited from going to court (at least, without having previously obtained the church's permission), but Protestants working as judges in the *kebele* or cell courts also bring to bear Protestant principles on these institutions. Driven by anxieties over salvation and enabled both by Protestantism's moral authority and a relative lack of clear procedural rules, these Protestant officials sometimes draw on the logic of forgiveness rather than on that of punishment. Clearly, this tendency is still in a nascent stage. Yet, it does not seem unlikely that if the number of Protestants in Dell grows even further, Protestantism's influence on the functioning of local formal institutions will also increase. All in all, this shows that Protestantism in Dell is a legal player to be reckoned with.

Whether or not this is true in other places in Ethiopia could well be the object of further inquiry. In advancing the study of legal pluralism in this direction, the following questions could be of help. What role does Protestantism play in urban settings, as opposed to rural areas? What differences are there between places where Protestants are in the majority and where they are in the minority? Can Protestant influence on state institutions also be observed at higher levels, such as *woreda* or zone? To what extent are there differences with regard to legal matters between different types of Protestants, such as Evangelicals and Pentecostals? And is forgiveness also a key principle elsewhere, or do other Protestants in Ethiopia emphasize different principles and parts of the Bible? Considering these and other questions, I hope, would help broaden what is already a very rich and lively debate on legal pluralism in Ethiopia.

References

ANDERSON, Allen, 2004 *An introduction to Pentecostalism: Global charismatic Christianity* (2nd edition). Cambridge: Cambridge University Press

BAKER, Bruce, 2013 "Where formal and informal justice meet: Ethiopia's justice pluralism", *African Journal of International and Comparative Law* 21 (2):202–18

BENDA-BECKMANN, Franz von, 2002 "Who's afraid of legal pluralism?", *The Journal of Legal Pluralism and Unofficial Law* 34 (47):37–82

BERIHUN Adugna Gebeye, 2013 "Women's rights and legal pluralism: A case study of the Ethiopian Somali Regional State", *Women in Society Journal* 6 (2):5–42

BERMAN, Paul Schiff, 2009 "The new legal pluralism", *Annual Review of Law and Social Science* 5 (1):225–242

DONOVAN, Dolores and Getachew ASSEFA, 2003 "Homicide in Ethiopia: Human rights, federalism, and legal pluralism", *American Journal of Comparative Law* 51:505–552

GEBRE Yntiso, 1995 *The Ari of southwestern Ethiopia: An exploratory study of production practices*. Addis Ababa: Addis Ababa University

GIRMACHEW Alemu Aneme, 2015 "Ethiopia: Legal and judicial plurality and the incorporation of traditional dispute resolution mechanisms within the state justice system", in: Matthias Kötter, Tilmann J. Röder, Gunnar F. Schuppert, and Rüdiger Wolfrum (eds.): *Non-state justice institutions and the law: Decision-*

making at the interface of tradition, religion and the state, 80–98. Basingstoke: Palgrave Macmillan.

2018 *The coupling of state and sharia justice systems in a secular state: The case of Ethiopia*. SFB-Governance Working Paper Series 75. Berlin: Freie Universität Berlin

GRIFFITHS, John, 1986 "What is legal pluralism?", *The Journal of Legal Pluralism and Unofficial Law* 18 (24):1–55

JENSEN, Adolf Ellegard, 1959 "Die Baka", in: Adolf Ellegard Jensen (ed.) *Altvölker Süd-Äthiopiens*, 29–86. Stuttgart: Kohlhammer

MERRY, Sally Engle, 1988 "Legal pluralism", *Law & Society Review* 22 (5):869–896

MOHAMMED Abdo, 2011 "Legal pluralism, Sharia courts and constitutional issues in Ethiopia", *Mizan Law Rev* 5 (1):72–104

NATY, Alexander, 1992 *The culture of powerlessness and the spirit of rebellion among the Aari people of southwest Ethiopia*. Stanford: Stanford University (PhD Thesis)

PANKHURST, Alula and GETACHEW Assefa (eds.), 2008 *Grass-roots justice in Ethiopia: The contribution of customary dispute resolution*. Addis Ababa: Centre Français d'Études Éthiopiennes

2008a "Preface", in: Alula Pankhurst und Getachew Assefa (eds.) *Grass-roots justice in Ethiopia: The contribution of customary dispute resolution*, v–ix. Addis Ababa: Centre Français d'Études Éthiopiennes

2008b "Understanding customary dispute resolution in Ethiopia", in: Alula Pankhurst und Getachew Assefa (eds.) *Grass-roots justice in Ethiopia: The contribution of customary dispute resolution*, 1–76. Addis Ababa: Centre Français d'Études Éthiopiennes

VAUGHAN, Sarah and Kjetil TRONVOLL, 2003 *The culture of power in contemporary Ethiopian political life*. Stockholm: Swedish International Development Cooperation Agency

11. Kontract: A hybrid form of law among the Sidama

Muradu Abdo

Introduction

Three legal regimes govern the Sidama's land. These partly support and partly compete with and contradict each other, leading recently to the emergence of new disputes and concerns.

The three legal systems are *utuwa* (customary land law), state land laws and *kontract* (a new hybrid form of land law). *Utuwa* refers to Sidama customary norms and institutions, under which individual farmers enjoy usufruct rights over agricultural land while the ownership rights reside with the clans. State land laws, including the 1995 Federal Constitution of Ethiopia (FDRE 1995), stipulate that the right to ownership of rural and urban land is exclusively vested in the state and in the peoples of Ethiopia. The statutory land laws further guarantee the rural masses usufruct rights over agricultural land, and prohibit the sale or exchange of such land. *Kontract* – the main focus of this chapter – straddles state land laws and *utuwa,* and exhibits hybrid characteristics. It is enshrined in written agreements concluded between an *akonatari* (transferor) and a *tekonatari* (transferee) regarding the permanent transfer of agricultural land by the former to the latter. The use of the written form and attempts to inject validity into it through both authentication and reference to state law give *kontract* a semblance of modernity. Yet, *kontract* is clothed with components of Sidama customary land tenure: it involves elders as witnesses, it ends with a *fenter* (special feast to mark the conclusion of a *kontract*), it imposes hefty fines should parties break their promise, and it makes elders responsible for reconciling the parties should they disagree on the *kontract* and ostracizing those who resort to invalidation.

Being a mixture of modernity and tradition, one would expect *kontract* to be an interesting case of cooperation and harmonization of state law and customary law. However, as will be shown in this chapter, in practice *kontract* often results in land alienation.

Informal land transfers have been observed in other peri-urban and cash-crop growing sections of southern Ethiopia and beyond. In parts of the study area where the value of land is high, they have also become common, whether designated as *kontract* or given another name. The proliferation of *kontract* has triggered disputes. For example, a local court administrator estimated that 70 per cent of court cases in the research site related to land disputes, one-third of which concerned *kontract*.[1] Though there are studies on large-scale formal land transfers (Dessalegn 2011, Makki 2014), only marginal attention has been paid to the widespread micro-land transfer schemes; and the extent and prevalence of informal land alienations, as well as their dispossessing consequences for the poor, has been neglected.

This chapter examines the nature of *kontract*: how it is viewed by various actors, and its implications for agricultural land alienation, which results in smallholders losing their livelihoods, and for rural land reform.[2] It is arranged as follows: after giving a brief profile of the Sidama land and people, I will provide some theoretical and comparative discussions with respect to informal land transfer practices before moving on to the main part of this contribution. First, I will sketch out the fundamentals of Sidama traditional land rights, land rights under the contemporary formal land laws of Ethiopia, and the concept and practice of *kontract* as a hybrid form of land law. Next, I will describe and analyse *kontract* from the perspective of Ethiopian lawmakers, the local people and regular courts. Then, I will single out factors that contribute to or correlate with the emergence and prevalence of *kontract* in the Sidama area and beyond. Finally I will investigate the existence of power imbalances between *akonatari* and *tekonatari*. In the final section, discussions and conclusion, I look at the practice of *kontract* from three perspectives – those of an economist, a legal positivist, and a legal pluralist – before concluding with a reflection on *kontract* and its wider effects, and how these could be addressed through land reform.

Sidama Zone and people

The Sidama people are speakers of the Cushitic Sidama language. They live in Sidama Zone, which is located in the Southern Nations, Nationalities and Peo-

1 Interview 14 September 2012.

2 The chapter is mainly based on qualitative data collected through interviews and focus group discussions with farmers, elders, policymakers, judges, researchers, public servants and legal practitioners, as well as observation in the study area for a total of two months, between September and December 2012, in April and June 2013, and in November 2015, 2016 and 2017. It builds on literature, relevant federal and regional constitutional provisions and legislative frameworks, court cases and comparative experience.

ples Regional State (SNNPRS) in the south central plateau of Ethiopia, about 265 kilometres south of Addis Ababa.[3]

Sidama Zone has a total of 6,972.1 square kilometres. According to the 2007 national population census, its population 3 million people in 2006, 90 per cent of which lived in rural areas, and its annual population growth rate was 2.9 per cent (CSA 2010). It is one of the most populous areas in southern Ethiopia, with a density of 451 people per square kilometre (CSA 2010). The Sidama land features diverse agro-ecologies including semi-arid and arid areas inhabited by pastoralists. With its beneficial climatic conditions, land fertility, economically valuable land and cash-crop production, Sidama can be seen as representative of the productive part of Ethiopia.

The Sidama predominately practise sedentary agriculture. They produce *ensete* (false banana), a highly drought-resistant staple food crop, cereals and legumes, and they also rear livestock. Small farmers in Sidama are also known for growing a type of organic *Coffea Arabica*. At present, around 70,000 hectares of good agricultural land is given over to coffee production, the sales of which bolster Ethiopia's foreign currency funds, and which formally links the Sidama to the global economy. The area also supplies animal skins and hides, and *khat* (a stimulant plant) for export nationally. The average farmland holding in the area is 0.3 hectare per household; this is smaller than both the national and regional averages, which are 0.8 ha and 1.01 hectare per family, respectively (SNNPRS Report n.d.). While cities and towns house only 10 per cent of the population of the Sidama Zone, there is a high degree of urbanization, as reflected in the urban population growth rate of 5 per cent and in the proliferation of towns (CSA 2010).

The Sidama people were incorporated into greater Ethiopia in the second half of the nineteenth century. The Sidama territory is divided between nine sub-clans, each of which controls its own sub-territory. There are various degrees of hostility and alliance amongst the sub-clans and with neighbouring ethnic groups (Hamer 2002, Aadland 2002).

Land rights and legal pluralism

Legal pluralism and its disempowering effects

There are several commonalities in the literature on legal pluralism. Firstly, legal pluralism pervades human society. Thus, the state is no longer the exclusive source

3 The SNNPRS is one of the nine regional states recognized by the Constitution. Administratively, the SNNPRS is broken down into more than a dozen zones and several special districts. Each zone is divided into *woredas* (districts), which in turn are split into *kebeles* (sub-districts).

of law since multiple legal orders co-exist in the same social field and same space at the same time. Secondly, such multiple legal orders may exist at international, national and local levels (Helfand 2015). Thirdly, legal pluralism appears to regard social justice as being of 'prime importance to legal validity' (Barzilai 2008:402).

Legal pluralism has been addressed by two theoretical approaches: relationalism and consequentialism. Relationalism focuses on the nature of plural legal orders as well as on the competition, conflict and cooperation between them, and their influence on each another. Consequentialism, which is the focus here, asserts that the effect of a plural legal order may be empowering or disempowering, depending on an actor's capacity to negotiate. On the one hand, when legal pluralism produces empowerment, it offers a greater scope for human agency as there is negotiability of interests in the course of re/making laws, through the access to different legal forums, and thus availability of normative and institutional choice (forum shopping) and the potential for procedural and institutional innovation or rule adaptation (Meingzen-Dick and Pradhan 2002: 27). This means legal pluralism can have an empowering effect provided that 'communities and households are able to better adapt themselves to change and retain their entitlements...to negotiate, bargain and reorganize relationships of production and exchange' (Parthasathy 2002:22). On the other hand, legal pluralism can bring about disempowerment where there are power imbalances among actors – due to impoverishment, gender and other vulnerabilities – that adversely affect the legitimate interests of the weak.

Prevalence of informal land transfer practices in other African countries

Land in Africa is governed by pluralistic legal regimes, as evidenced by the informal land transfer practices that are not uncommon in many areas of the Continent. Land alienation practices, for example, in Nigeria, Ghana, Burkina Faso and Tanzania exhibit some shared features. The practices are prominently observed in peri-urban and cash-crop growing parts, and are disguised as rent, mortgages, or the sale of perennial plants and fixtures. Such deals occur in times of financial distress and use a mix of customary and statutory norms and institutions (Lund 2000). Government officials recognize the practices through attestation, authentication and registration. Such recognition is not necessarily compatible with state law and may, in fact, at times conflict with or undermine age-old customs and legislation that proscribe land sales (Lund 2000). State recognition of informal land transfers makes it impossible for a transferee to get their land restituted. Land recovery is also made unfeasible by economic power imbalances, which tend to tilt in favour of the buyers: 'land is often irredeemable as a goat sold on the market place' (Lund 2000:7–8). These land transfer practices are seen to generate conflicts and disputes, which arise in the course of attempts to recover land (Shivji 2009).

Informal land transfer practices in Ethiopia

Informal land deals are prevalent in several parts of Ethiopia. In Oromia National Regional State (ONRS), for example, small farmers in Western Wollega, Ilubabor and Jimma have been displaced by urban elites who bought their coffee plants (Pausewang 2000). This forced policy makers in ONRS to conduct diagnostic research, which revealed that many peasants had become victims of *kontract* (Gudeta 2009:125). In particular, peasants in coffee and *khat*-growing areas of ONRS have been evicted from their land as a result of the sale of the coffee and *khat* to unscrupulous urban bourgeoisie,[4] a practice which has caused social problems, according to Gudeta Seifu (2009:135):

> The sale transactions usually take place when the landholders are in distress and in dire need of finance to meet their basic needs. The farmers who have already alienated their holdings are now financially in a precarious position... for they lost their livelihood. In effect, this has brought devastating ...[social] effects.

Land deals under the rubric of *kontract* are also taking place in other parts of Oromia. The most well known example occurred in Meki, a small town located along the road from Addis Ababa to Hawassa and close to the Awash River plains, which makes it suitable for horticulture. The local authorities ascertained in early 2012 that a total of 700 small farmers had lost their land to either individual or commercial farmers with urban origins – who began growing vegetables and fruits – under *kontract*, the terms of which sometimes extended to 99 years, violating the legal limit of 5–15 years for a lease. Some of these commercial farmers rented land for 1,000 to 1,400 ETB per hectare per season, with advance payments covering several years (The Ethiopian Reporter, 6 January 2012).

As discussed below, one force driving small farmers to engage in these deals is the lack of agricultural support systems, such as loans, to enable them to benefit from their land. Commercial farms are resource intensive – requiring irrigation, water pumps, fuel, seed selection, fertilizers, shades and labour – and the costs of these inputs cannot be covered by smallholders. Moreover, as one local official noted, 'those who acquire land from smallholder farmers are much more organized and networked than we expect" (quoted in *The Ethiopian Reporter*, 6 January 2012). According to Gudeta (2009:140), it is not possible to stop investors from acquiring land from small landholders for commercial ends via enforcement of the formal law alone. As will be considered in later in this chapter, small farmers are selling out their land to rich people as such farmers do not have the ability to utilize their land. Some of the purchasers are rewarded for using such land apparently efficiently. For instance, one investor who had accumulated more than 20 million Birr by growing

4 Interview with judges 29 April 2013.

vegetables on several hectares of land acquired through *kontract*, resulting in the displacement of about fifty households[5], was given a prize for being a model farmer by both the regional authorities and the Ministry of Agriculture.[6]

Three kinds of land rights in Sidama

Sidama traditional land rights

The Sidama people recognize two types of land tenure: *dannawa* (communal land) and *utuwa* (private land). The underlying principle behind both *dannawa and utuwa* is that land is the common property of a clan (*gosa*), but that individuals have access to and can use the land on the basis of clan membership (Markos *et al.* 2011).

Dannawa is composed of roughly demarcated pasture lands belonging to sub-clans and forests outside *utuwa* dedicated to the use of members of the particular sub-clan, or of several sub-clans in common, for grazing, hunting, beekeeping, extraction of forest resources (e.g. firewood and wild fruits), social and cultural sites and market places (Markos *et al.* 2011). *Dannawa* can, under exceptional situations, be distributed to individual members of a sub-clan. This could happen when a household is facing a shortage of farmland because of changes in demography or in order to accommodate outsiders. Otherwise no one is allowed to privately appropriate *dannawa*. Historically, *dannawa* was placed under the administrative and judicial jurisdiction of the highest clan council (*songo*), who determined the use rights of this communal land and settled disputes relating to it. Both *utuwa* and *dannawa* could not be subject to alienation. Access to and use of the two land tenure types has traditionally enabled Sidama households to make an adequate living (Markos *et al.* 2011).

Utuwa is the more prominent kind of customary land tenure among the Sidama (Markos *et al.* 2011:71). The *utuwa* is said to have been inherited from a distant ancestor who occupied and developed it and then passed it on to his descendants. As such, today *utuwa* is privately held agricultural land expected to be passed on to male descendants, and every male has the customary right to receive a plot of farmland from his father's *utuwa* when he comes of age and gets married. The underlying principle is that land is an inalienable common property of a clan, but with individual access based essentially on clan membership (Hamer 2002). As a local youth leader expressed it:

5 Interview with Daniel Behailu, researcher from the School of Law Hawassa University on land policy and law, 26 November 2012.

6 Recently renamed the Ministry of Agriculture and Natural Resources.

> *Utuwa* means 'tomb'. It is the ancestors' burial ground. It is also land, which you till, you drive your living from, which is passed onto you by your father who received it from his father, which you have to hand over to your descendants. It is a taboo to sell land; it is even prohibited to mention the word 'sale' in regard to land. If you dare sell part of your land, you will be cursed by the ancestors' spirit. There is a belief that once you sell a part of your plot, you do not stop short of selling out your entire land, and if you happen to sell your land as a whole, you are deemed to be a cursed person and as such you must disappear from the area as you did a shameful thing and are not worthy to be member of your locality. Sale of one`s ancestral ground makes one a social outcast as he who does that must leave the village for fear of being burnt by the eyes of ancestors. (Interview, 12 October 2012)

Land alienation to non-clan members occurs rarely. When it does, it is preceded by collective deliberation and consultation among the clan members of the man selling the land, and only after close family members and the sub-clan have been given first refusal on buying the land in question. In addition, the potential buyer must be welcomed by the seller's clan.[7] The entire process of land alienation is therefore a collective decision, and is as good as accepting the person who acquires the land into the sub-clan: by virtue of the transaction, the buyer changes his clan membership and becomes one of them.

National law and land rights

The 1995 Federal Constitution of Ethiopia tacitly classifies rights over land into two categories: ownership and subordinate rights (Art. 40), stipulating that 'the right to ownership of rural and urban land is ... exclusively vested in the state and in the peoples of Ethiopia' (Art. 40[3]). Subordinate rights over land, which may be termed as usufruct rights, have several dimensions and have been further elaborated in the Constitution and state land legislation.

First, the Constitution bestows usufruct rights over agricultural land to all Ethiopian peasants and pastoralists without payment (Art. 40 [4 & 5]). These rights have been extended by offering agricultural land for an indefinite period of time to 'any citizen of the country ... who wants to engage in agriculture for a living' and who has no other adequate means of earning a livelihood.[8] Second, usufruct rights accorded to peasants are not given to the head of a farming family or any particular member therein; the right is bestowed on the farming family as a unit

7 Interview with a local elder, 12 October 2012, and with a legal practitioner, 8 June 2013.

8 The Federal Rural Land Administration and Use Proclamation No. 456, 2005 (hereinafter Proclamation No 456, 2005), Art. 5; The Rural Lands Proclamation No. 31, 1975 (hereinafter Proc. No 31, 1975), Art. 4.

and as a going concern.[9] It remains the right of the current and future members of such families considered collectively and inter-generationally so long as one of them continues farming. Hence, it is a right given to the living and the yet to be born members of such rural households.[10] The main legal implication for the joint nature of usufruct rights is that no member of a household, in particular the head, can validly transfer the rights without the free consent of all the other members.[11] Finally, the Constitution enshrines the principle of non-eviction of peasants and herders from their land.[12] One of the top priorities of the Ethiopian Government is 'to protect the rural poor from the risk of losing their land' (De Schutter 2011:532). The constitutional commitment to protect peasants from eviction from their land refers to the state itself as well as to non-state forces, such as investors or community authorities. Article 40(3) also protects peasants from their own folly by ruling out any meaningful transfer of land rights through the formal market channels, stating that: 'Land...shall not be subject to sale or to other means of exchange'. Peasants are only allowed to rent out part of their land, for a short period of time, with the consent of concerned family members and the prior approval of local authorities.[13] These restrictions on the marketability of land usufruct rights are linked with the overriding essence of the existing rural land law of Ethiopia, which views land as a subsistence asset for peasants and pastoralists.[14]

Concept and practice of kontract: a hybrid form of law

The etymology of the term '*kontract*'[15] is obscure. It seems that it originated in the English term 'contract', which is pronounced in Amharic as " (*kontract*) and in Sidama language it as '*kontracta*'. The Sidama people's inclination to use the term *kontract* instead of *kontracta* lies in the fact that Amharic, as the lingua franca of Ethiopia, is widely spoken there. It is also used interchangeably with the Amharic translation of the English term 'contract', which is (*wule*). There is, however, a fundamental difference between the two terms. While the term '*wule*' does not necessarily imply the existence of a definite term in a given agreement, the notion of *kontract* suggests the existence of a fixed period in a transaction. The practice

9 Proc No. 31, 1975, Article 4; Proc No 456, 2005, Art 8(2).

10 The Federal Constitution, 1995, Art. 40 (7); Proc No. 456, 2005, Art 2 (4).

11 Proc No 456, 2005, Art. 8.

12 The Federal Constitution, Art. 40 (6); and Art. 40 (4&5).

13 Proc No 456, 2005, Art. 8.

14 *Rural Development Policies and Strategies of Ethiopia* (Ministry of Information 2001)

15 Nomenclature-wise, local people use the words '*kontract*' and '*kontrata*' as synonyms to describe the practice. However, during my fieldwork for this chapter, I realized that the inhabitants use the former much more frequently than the latter both in their day-to-day conversations and in written documents relating to these transactions, so I have chosen to follow their example here.

among the Sidama people shows that by *kontract* they mean a written agreement concerning a plot of agricultural land, concluded between *akonatari* (transferor) and *tekonatari* (transferee) with a view to permanently transferring the land from the former to the latter. In short, it is a sale agreement.

Kontract is a Janus-faced transaction. On the one hand, parties to a *kontract* incorporate into it elements of the modern notion of 'contract'. For example, they reduce *kontract* to a written statement, affix their signatures to it, have it attested by witnesses and even sometimes have it authenticated by relevant government offices. In addition, *kontract* is clothed with modernity by the inclusion, in cross-references, of some of the provisions of the Country's Civil Code. On the other hand, *kontract* embodies components of the Sidama customary land tenure. For instance, in most cases elders help the parties reach an agreement and serve as witnesses. Other elements of Sidama custom which are made part of *kontract* include the organization of a feast (*fenter*) to mark the conclusion of the agreement[16], the indication of hefty fines (monetary and customary visitations) should a party break their word, and the elders' obligation to reconcile the parties in the event of a dispute or to ostracize or even curse anyone who breaks the *kontract*.

It should nevertheless be noted that parties to a *kontract* never openly call it a land sale agreement; instead they disguise the transaction as a sale of coffee or *khat* bushes, fruit trees or other types of immovable property. This implies the eventual restitution of the land related to the transaction and suggests that *kontract* is a land rental agreement, a temporary transfer of land use rights. As such, it would seem to lead to a landlord – tenant relationship. However, in reality, this immovable property rarely exists on the transferred land and *kontract* does not relate to the sale of property on the land but simply involves the transfer of a piece of bare farmland. If some crops, fruit trees, ground works or huts on the land are transferred with the land, this is merely incidental. As one community leader/farmer expressed it, *kontract* 'is a twisted form of an ordinary land rental transaction'.[17]

During imperial times, such land deals were not disguised, but were openly labelled '*kontract* for the sale of farmland' as land sales were legal. The change in nomenclature began to occur in the mid 1990s, when the parties involved and the land deal facilitators, such as agricultural extension workers and lawyers, realized that the law prohibited land sales. From then on, the term 'sale' was avoided; it was replaced by terms such as sharecropping, *kontract* and rental, used to pretend that only immovable property on the land or land use rights were being transferred.[18]

---

16 A *fenter* may consist in having some local drinks or just paying some money to the elders who helped them make the deal and ultimately served as witnesses.

17 Interview, 18 September 2012.

18 Interview with a local farmer, 22 December 2012.

Therefore, *kontract* embodies a rejection of a fundamental common tenet of both the present state land tenure and Sidama custom: the inalienability of land. Moreover, as will be shown below, *kontract* is a blend of state land tenure and Sidama customary land tenure.

Different views on kontract

Kontract and formal law

As mentioned above, under the 1995 Constitution of Ethiopia and as reiterated in various subordinate laws, land cannot be subject to sale or any other means of exchange, and any practice or decision that authorizes transfer of ownership over rural land is of no effect. Specifically, it is unlawful for an informal land seller to assume an obligation to deliver ownership or even usufruct over rural land to a land buyer. Similarly, it is illegal for a purchaser to assume an obligation to pay for the transfer of ownership or usufruct in regard to rural land. So, from the standpoint of the formal land law, land alienation deals – regardless of their age – should be struck down for transgressing the supreme law of the land. A joint reading of Article 1845 and Article 1810(1) of the Civil Code sends the message that contracts tainted with unlawful objects are not subject to prescription. This is because the phrase 'Unless otherwise provided by law…' in Article 1854 suggests so. Thus, any deal relating to land sale remains invalid under the state law.

Local views on kontract

Many land deals are made with *kontract*, even though the local people are well aware of its risks and disadvantages.

A model farmer and community leader residing in Sidama Zone compared *kontract* deals with 'a black market for the sale of a farmland', stating that he had never seen such land being restituted to the landholder.[19] During a focus group discussion, a land administration expert described the situation as follows:

> They sell the land, claiming that the land is rented out for any period between 40 and 99 years or even for life. According to the law in force, the maximum period for which a peasant can rent out their land is 25 years when dealing with an investor, 10 years when the deal is between peasants. They do it between those who trust each other. It is a deal based on trust. We cannot do anything about informal land deals. The seller is not benefiting out of it. It is a puzzle for us. The

19 Interview, 14 September 2012.

> peasant is selling land by using the language of state land law, which permits land rentals, but for completely different purpose. (Interview, 14 September 2012)

As indicated by a focus group discussion with female-headed households, an *akonatari* – often a household head – enters into a land deal with the *tekonatari* without securing the consent of his family members, contrary to what is required by state land laws.[20] In addition, the *kontract* is not submitted to the relevant authorities for registration and approval in the initial stage because they might hamper the transfer process, even though they might know about the transaction informally and even cooperate. As several different informants – farmers, officials and the police – told me, land-related corruption has become common. Stein Holden (2012:10), who has undertaken research in the Sidama area, observed:

> … the courts favour the wealthy who can afford to pay for decisions in their favour. If people do not pay, the cases may take a very long time… cases [land related] are decided through mobile phones, meaning that the wealthy and influential have mobile phones and communicate easily with the court judges while the poor have to travel and wait for long time for their cases to be handled and for communicating their situation. Decisions may also be based on family ties.

The *tekonatari* is often a member of the rural elite or a trader with urban roots deemed to be a 'model farmer' by national and local politicians.[21] They are people capable of paying for the land and investing in it; they may invoke tradition to shame an *akonatari* that demands the return of the land; and they can litigate all the way from the sub-district land administration committee right up to the Federal Supreme Court. The *tekonatari* makes use of a mixture of elements of state law and of Sidama traditional land tenure rules and processes to make his land deal secure, then uses his influence and connections to register the land subject to the *kontract* in his name.[22]

As one judge told me, most cases (80 per cent) dealt with in the district courts are rural land disputes, out of which 30 per cent relate to *kontract*.[23] As I was told by several lawyers and judges,[24] practising lawyers play an important role in the legalization process of *kontract* – they draft *kontracts*, have them authenticated and defend them in court – despite the fact that they are fully aware of the nature and negative consequences of *kontract*.[25]

---

20 Focus group discussion with local farmers, 16 September 2012.

21 Interview with a Sidama elder, 18 September 2012.

22 Interviews with local farmers, 14 and 18 September 2012.

23 Interview, 17 September 2012.

24 Interview, 14 September 2012.

25 Ambreena Manji (2012:467) describes lawyers playing a similar role in Kenya, facilitating small-scale land grabs: 'the legal profession, far from upholding the rule of law, has played

The increasing use of *kontract* is, in part, the result of changes to *koota*, a sharecropping arrangement used to match land with labour and/or other inputs. *Koota* has served as a social safety net for those who have land but are unable to work it for various reasons, including ill health, old age, absence from the land while working elsewhere, or destitution. Land left in the care of widows may also be left untended as cultural barriers prevent widows working on the land. In such cases, sharecropping arrangements – usually lasting for one or two seasons – traditionally came into play. Under this arrangement, the net profits from the harvest would go to the landholder. These could range from a quarter to three-quarters of the harvest after the deduction of expenses, depending on the nature and size of the contribution of the landholders and sharecroppers. Recently, *koota* has become a kind of precursor to *kontract*. Sharecroppers usually grow permanent crops such as coffee, *khat* and sugar cane and would, therefore, prefer to keep the land. To achieve this, having first become a sharecropper, a potential *tekonatari* extends loan after loan to the landholder until they are heavily indebted. This gives the sharecropper a bargaining chip with which to pressurize the landholder to enter into *kontract*.[26]

Kontract in the courts

When disputes emanating from *kontract* reach the regular courts, they are challenged, as the courts must handle such disputes in the context of opposing constitutional provisions, subsidiary land laws and Sidama custom.

Pre-empting court litigation

A *tekonatari* who foresees and endeavours to pre-empt court litigation by the *akonatari* will use elements of customary and state law selectively. To this end, as mentioned above, the *kontract* is made in writing with the attestation of three to seven elders. The written *kontract* indicates, *inter alia*, that hefty fines will be levied on any party who opts to invalidate the *kontract*, stating therein that part of the fine will go to the state treasury and part to the elders. Coupled with this is the obligation on the part of the *akonatari* to repay the entire sale price should he demand restitution.

Should an *akonatari* move to attack a deal, among the sanctions based on customary law that can be read into the *kontract* is ostracism; this means that the *akonatari* is cut off from his vital day-to-day social relations. As one informant put

a central role in (…) using its professional skills and networks to accumulate personal wealth for itself and others'.

26 As explained to in interviews with a local farmer, 12 September 2012 and with a Sidama farmer, 14 September 2012.

it: 'A person who is excluded from society in this way is regarded as a dead person.' John Hamer (1998:151), who studied the Sidama extensively, expressed it this way: 'To seek to escape normative pressure is to invite social isolation and ultimately destruction by the Creator.' Elders, who are indicated as witnesses in the *kontract* will, therefore, try to dissuade the *akonatari* from seeking to invalidate the deal, threatening him with exclusion from society, customary visitations, and ultimately cursing – the most feared sanction.[27] If the *akonatari* yields to the elders' demands, he is compelled to abandon his intention to file a lawsuit, or withdraw it if he has already filed it, and reconcile with the buyer. Even in this scenario, he may be ordered to pay a fine, usually slaughtering an animal to mark the end of the reconciliation. The heavy fine indicated in the *kontract* might be reduced or waived altogether depending on the circumstances of the case.

All these tactics, especially the use of traditional sanctions, tip such lands deals in favour of the *tekonatari,* and run counter to the fundamental tenets of *utuwa,* as well as state land laws. To suit the interests of elites it seems that new practices are being grafted onto traditional elements.[28]

Overcoming pre-emptory measures

Some *akonatari* refuse to be cowed by tradition, and show signs of breaking away from it. For example, some use a family member who did not sign the *kontract* to complain to the court that the *kontract* is invalid as it was done without their consent.[29] Finding a family member who was not part of a *kontract* is not a problem because land transfers in the locality are mostly done unilaterally by the family heads, as permitted by Sidama patriarchy. When the prompted family member goes to court to seek the invalidation of the *kontract,* the instigator (i.e. the *akonatari*) plays the role of Good Samaritan, pretending to dissuade their relative from dragging the *tekonatari* into court.[30] In some cases, the person seeking to battle it out in the court genuinely opposes the *akonatari's* unilateral act; either way *kontract* cases end up in the regular courts.

---

27 Interview with Daniel Behailu, researcher from the School of Law Hawassa University on land policy and law, 22 December 2012; see also Seyoum (2006:96).

28 My fieldwork reveals that the Sidama categorize their elders into two: 'people's elders' and 'government elders'. The former are conservative, authentic, fear the sceptre of the spirit of ancestors, incorrupt, faithful to custom and rarely involved in *kontract*. When *kontract* cases are submitted to them, they tend to decide in favour of the *akonatari*, invoking *utuwa*. Government elders act to the contrary. In particular, they offer services related to dispute resolution for money, are regarded as corrupt and facilitate *kontract* much more frequently and in favour of the *tekonatari*. This taxonomy warrants a separate study.

29 Interview with a lawyer, 22 December 2012.

30 Interview with a judge, 14 September 2012, and interview with Daniel Behailu, researcher from the School of Law Hawassa University on land policy and law, 8 June 2013.

Invalidating kontract

The *akonatari* invokes the concept of contract invalidation on the grounds that the land deal was unlawful, claiming that the agreement was underpinned by a promise to deliver land ownership or land use rights contrary to the law of the land. The pleading is based on cumulative reading of the constitutional provisions, which ban land alienation, and Article 1808(2) of the Civil Code, which provides that

> A contract whose object is unlawful...may be invalidated at the request of *any contracting party or interested third party* (because) obligations to convey rights on things, if the latter are not in *commercio*, that is, are made non-transferable (non-conveyable) by law, the obligation is clearly unlawful (Krzeczunowic 1983:64–65).

Before September 2011, the decisions of the state courts (i.e. district and zonal courts) in the Sidama area on such *kontract* cases lacked uniformity, varying from court to court, from judge to judge in the same court, and even from case to case heard by the same judge. As an SNNPRS Supreme Court judge explained, in some cases, the *kontract* was invalidated and the *tekonatari* ordered to return the land. In others, judgments went in favour of the *tekonatari*, who retained the land. While in others, judges applied a ten-year period of limitation relating to contracts in general embodied in Article 1845 of the Civil Code, which provided that 'actions for the invalidation of a contract shall be barred if not brought within ten years'. This meant that, if ten years had lapsed from of the effective date of the *kontract*, the *akonatari's* claim would be rejected; if less than ten years had elapsed, then the *tekonatari* was required to restitute the land. This variation in the handling of *kontract* cases was widely witnessed in state courts in the Sidama Zone, and the lack of uniformity in the decisions of regular courts on the matter also prevailed elsewhere in the SNNPRS, where areas given over to cash crops frequently witnessed – and continue to see – deals made under the rubric of *kontract*.[31]

In September 2011, concerned with the inconsistencies around how *kontract* disputes were being handled, the SNNPR Supreme Court adopted a uniform position on the disposition of *kontract* cases through a Circular, which was approved by a forum that brought together all the court presidents in the region. The Circular stated that *kontract* should be treated like any other ordinary agreement and, as such, those legal rules governing contracts in general should apply to these deals as well. According to the Circular, one of these stipulations was the aforementioned Article 1845 of the Civil Code. The Circular also assumed that the intention of the parties at the time of the conclusion of a *kontract* was clearly to transfer ownership over land: there was no intention on the part of the parties to restitute the land at a certain point in the future. Under the Circular, land subject to *kontract* was assumed to have gone out of the hands of the *akonatari* forever. Based on this assumption,

31 Interview with SNNPRS Supreme Court judge, 25 September 2012.

the Circular divided *kontract* agreements into two types: those for which ten years or more had elapsed between the date of conclusion and that of filing for invalidation; and those for which less than ten years had elapsed. The former were to be barred from the courts by the period of limitation; the latter were to be be struck down, leading to the restitution of the disputed land to the *akonatari*.

The standard justification for the application of the period of limitation is that it is difficult to find evidence for deals that are over ten years old, much having been destroyed or witnesses having died.[32] Providing certainty around investment activities and discouraging people from sleeping on their rights for an intolerable amount of time are further cited as justifications for the ten-year limitation. However, the underlying reason for the courts not to evict a *tekonatari* is that they are regarded as 'land improvers'. As one judge observed:

> Declaring *kontract* illegal and consequent land restitution amount to evicting the developer. We judges have to consider the prevailing interest in the society, which is not to restitute the land to the seller. (Interview, 21 September 2012)

A *woreda* (district) court judge also told me:

> We currently decide in favour of the 'developer', the one who is currently working on the land. (...). There is a need to prevent a socio-economic crisis, as such transactions are rife. People genuinely thought that the transactions they have undertaken are legitimate and hence have been using the land for a longer period of time. (Interview, 17 September 2012)

In 2015, the SNNPRS Supreme Court turned round and annulled the conditional recognition of *kontract*, deciding that all *kontracts* are illegal and therefore invalid and that the passage of time should not save a *kontract* from invalidation, so all land subject to *kontract* must be restituted to the *akonatari*.[33] However, the Federal Supreme Court Cassation Division, whose decisions are binding at all levels of federal and regional courts[34], has taken two positions with regard to the practice of *kontract*: the first is the invalidation of agreements that expressly transfer land[35];

32 SNNPRS Supreme Court Cassation Division Case, File No. 36888, October 2010.

33 SNNPRS Supreme Court Cassation Division File No. 64745, May 16, 2015.

34 Federal Courts Proclamation Amendment Proc. No 454, 2005, Art. 2(1).

35 This is reflected in the decision to nullify a farmland sale agreement that was explicitly designated as such. In this case, the court also decided that a period of limitation was inapplicable (Federal Supreme Court Cassation File No, 110549, February 2016). The position was further applied in the court's decision to invalidate a land mortgage agreement given in the form of security for a loan (Federal Supreme Court Cassation File No 79394, September, 2012). The court has also applied the same approach by invalidating an agreement to transfer rural land in consideration of settlement of a debt (Federal Supreme Court Cassation File No 49200, November, 2010).

the second is to turn down petitions seeking the invalidation of disguised land sales. This means that a *kontract* whose true character is concealed – as commonly happens through the deliberate avoidance of any explicit reference to sale of land – escapes court nullification and is thus saved.

The story of *kontract* in the courts does not end here, however, because some *kontract* cases have landed in the House of Federation, which is entrusted to adjudicate constitutional disputes. The House of Federation has repeatedly struck down land sales of any kind – be they direct or indirect – based on their violation of the Constitution, and has required land restitution.[36] The House of Federation invariably invokes the constitutional principle of small farmers' immunity from eviction as a key justification. On the same grounds, it has nullified sale and mortgage agreements concerning land, and attacked rental agreements that purport to transfer agricultural land for an indefinite duration or for a period that exceeds the limit set by the law.[37]

Kontract and the local government administration

Apart from the courts, as one land administration expert indicated, other local state actors also have a role to play in the practice of *contract*, in particular by giving legal cover to such land alienation deals.[38] The entire local government administration may be implicated in supporting *kontract*, and agricultural development agents, land administration and use committees and trade and industry offices contribute conspicuously.

Firstly, agricultural development agents working for the local government administration use their knowledge of the financial vulnerability of peasants to broker land deals when potential *tekonatari* ask them to 'find land' for them.[39] Secondly, members of the local land administration committee 'write support letters' to the local agriculture office, asking for a land certificate to be issued in the name of the *tekonatari*. The committee members extort money from the *tekonatari* transferor, threatening him by saying: 'Land sale is illegal. The *kontract* is unlawful. It is even against the Federal Constitution. The committee is going to issue a land certificate in the name of the *akonatari*, not in your name!'[40] With this message they communicate to the *tekonatari* that he should give a 'good sum of money' to the committee members, who will then issue a land certificate in his name. Based on the 'support

36 Decisions of the House of Federation rendered on 26 June 2015 and 12 March 2016.

37 Decisions of the House of Federation rendered on 12 March 2016.

38 Interview with a land administration expert, 21 September 2012).

39 Interviews with Yidnekachew Ayele, Director of Legal Aid Clinics at the School of Law, Hawassa University, and researcher on family law and land rights, 12 October 2012; and with a lawyer, 8 June 2013.

40 Interview with a land administration expert, 12 October 2012.

letter', the agriculture office '(...) puts a signature on an already printed certificate and awards the certificate to the *tekonatari*'.[41] Thirdly, the agriculture office often also plays a role in overvaluing the property on a plot of land that the courts have ordered to be restituted, thus rendering restitution ineffective as most peasants are unable to pay the required compensation.[42] Fourthly, some land *tekonatari* use their *kontract* to obtain an agricultural investment license and investment incentives from the local trade and industry office. One expert working in the local trade and industry office told me:

> ... some agricultural investors get land for their investment through the device of *kontract*. When such investors bring documents such as a *kontract* proving that they have secured land, we provide them with the required license and investment incentives, including loans, for which they are eligible. (Interview, 24 September 2012)

The treatment of the *tekonatari* as an agricultural investor eligible for investment incentives opens a door for him to collateralize the land subject to *kontract* – as currently happens with land acquired for coffee-processing purposes. Government-owned micro-finance institutions also take land acquired via *kontract* as security for loans.[43]

Factors driving small farmers into kontract

Several factors contribute to the prevalence of *kontract* among the Sidama. Among them are the historical experience of land alienation in the area, demographic pressure and a lack of significant out-migration from the rural population, whose consequent increase in the value of land might have contributed to the revival of land deals such as those considered here. The *akonatari* are also often driven into *kontract* by a lack of money to cover expenses such as those for customary weddings, medical treatment, education or old age (see Berhutesfa 1999). However, two factors stand out from the others as contributors to the rise of *kontract*: the lack of agricultural support schemes and the provisions of state land laws.

The unavailability of agricultural support to peasants in the area is not without historical antecedents. During the Empire (prior to 1974), agricultural support schemes were directed at commercial coffee farmers. The pursuit of socialist modernity during the Derg period (1974–1991) skewed resource allocation towards producers' cooperatives and state farms, which led to the small farmers be-

---

41 Interview with a local public servant, 8 June 2013.

42 Interview with a lawyer, 14 September 2012.

43 Interview with a public servant, 25 September 2012.

ing given little agricultural support. This bias has been continued since 1991, as Ethiopia has adopted and implemented an agricultural policy founded on market principles that, thus, focuses on peasant production for the market. For the Sidama smallholders, this post-1991 liberalization has meant a lack of any meaningful agricultural complementary support – such as loans and access to affordable fertilizers or quality government extension advisors – escalating input prices and market volatility, all of which have contributed to an inability to get fair prices for their produce and, consequently, to the emergence of *kontract*. The *akonatari* alienates his land because he is unable to work the land because, at present, there are no agricultural support schemes open to him.

For example, peasants are expected to purchase fertilizers and seeds from the market on a cash basis. Some time ago, the government authorities in the Sidama area briefly introduced a programme by which peasants with land could get a 50 per cent short-term loan for the purchase of fertilizers through local government bureaucracy. However, the arrangement was abused by local officials, local militia men, elders on the government payroll, unemployed youth and other people with political affiliations, who purchased more fertilizer than they were able to use and sold them back to the market, having recognized that there was no effective mechanism for enforcing the repayment of the fertilizer loans. One farmer recounted:

> I went to the chairman of my neighbourhood to find out that his house had been converted into a fertilizer store... He took fertilizers in the name of dead residents, those who left the area, children and the elderly with the intent to sell it out to retailers... (Interview, 26 September 2012)

Such corrupt practices resulted in poor collection of fertilizer debts (SNNPR Report 2011), and the scheme was discontinued, leaving small farmers to purchase fertilizers at market price.[44]

There are also problems with the government's agricultural extension service, whereby farmers who are able to purchase agricultural inputs get free advice from government deployed agricultural extension workers. At present, there is at least one government agricultural extension worker stationed in each neighbourhood in Sidama Zone. They are supposed to counsel peasants on how to till land vulnerable to erosion, how to use fertilizers and seeds, conserve land, avoid wastage during harvest and generally employ modern techniques to raise agricultural productivity. However, many peasants have questioned the relevance of the advice given to them by the often young, inexperienced extension agents, especially given the complexity of the local agro-ecology. Some are, at best, contemptuous about the quality of services given by these workers, which also include land certification, census, political agitation and work as election facilitators. As one peasant told me:

44 Interview with a local administrator, 19 September 2012.

> The government's extension program is to be valued more for creating job opportunity for the youth than for the quality of agricultural services to be gained from it. (26 September 2012)

All in all, informants claim that giving them a piece of land without the ability to use it themselves drives them to engage in *kontract*, which has the effect of reducing the size of their landholding or rendering them landless.[45]

The second overarching factor contributing to the rise of *kontract* is a set of legal rules that implies the possibility that the government authorities can confiscate land that they believe to be improperly cultivated or that has been left uncultivated for a certain period of time. This rule, which is part of the rural land laws of five major regional states, arises from the duty of the peasant to continuously till his land or risk government dispossession: 'A holder of rural land shall be obliged to properly use and protect his land. When the land gets damaged the user of the land shall lose his use right.'[46] This general provision is amplified by a regulation, which provides that:

> An individual loses land use right when he fails to implement soil conservation techniques, and leave the soil to erode, when he does not plant trees suitable to the environment, and the concerned official ascertains such failure with evidence. ... The landholder shall be evicted by the concerned legal body after notifying the land holder as well as a higher body... Any rural land user who is evicted from his possession is obliged to return the land use right certificate within in a month after the decision.[47]

In practice, this means that no rural land user may negligently let his land lay fallow for more than two consecutive years. After the *kebele* administration ascertains that the land has not been ploughed, it gives an oral warning to the land user in the presence of the *kebele* land administration and use committee and local elders. If the land is not ploughed within six months of this warning, the *kebele* administration gives a written warning to the land user within a month. If the land is still not tilled even after this written warning, he loses his usufruct rights.[48]

These stipulations give unchecked discretion to local administrators to evict peasants for misuse use of the land or failure to use the land for two consecutive years. When these provisions are seen in the context of the Sidama area's

---

45 Focus group discussions with local farmers, 21 September 2012 and 12 October 2012; and interview with Yidnekachew Ayele, Director of Legal Aid Clinics at the School of Law, Hawassa University, and researcher on family law and land rights, 10 December 2012.

46 SNNPRS Rural Land Administration and Use Proc. No 110, 2007, Art. 10 (1).

47 SNNPRS Rural Land Administration and Use Reg. No. 66, 2007, Art. 13 (4, a, c and d).

48 SNNPRS Rural Land Administration and Use Reg. No. 66, 2007, Art. 13 (5); SNNPRS Rural Land Administration and Use Proc No 53, 2003, Art. 9 (6) & 7).

longstanding association with the state in relation to land, people are quite legitimately suspicious, even though there is no evidence that the authorities have actually invoked these provisions. In summary, the above accounts show that the ability of small farmer to use their land has been incrementally diminished by several decades of government inaction concerning agricultural support services and the introduction of land laws that increase the insecurity of tenure.

Winners and losers under kontract

There is a distinct imbalance in the economic positions of the *akonatari* and *tekonatari*. In most cases the *tekonatari* has urban roots and his livelihood does not depend on farming but comes rather from non-agricultural sources, often he is either a model farmer or trader or local public servant. He makes permanent improvements on the land acquired immediately, to foreclose any possibility of land recovery in the event of litigation. He further possesses the capacity to cover the costs associated with land certification and successfully defend himself from land recovery suits. He also has the ability to invoke Sidama tradition to foreclose any land restitution claim. *Kontract* cases entertained by the House of Federation, on the other hand, reveal the weak financial status of the *akonatari*. In one case, an *akonatari* mortgaged her land to cover the expenses for searching for her lost children; the mortgage led eventually to sale. In another case, a litigant mortgaged her land to provide money for food, and ended up selling her farmland.[49] Moreover, a review of the decisions of the federal and regional supreme courts with regard to *kontract* reveals that many *akonatari*, being indigent, are only able to pursue their cases in the courts with the support of free legal aid.

The relative weakness of the *akonatari* is also manifested in the likelihood that his land will be restituted even after a decision is made in his favour by the federal and regional supreme courts or House of Federation. The current position taken by the federal and regional supreme courts, including that of the House of Federation, indicates that land will be restituted. However, in practice, the land is often not recovered by the *akonatari* because immediately after securing a decision invalidating the *kontract*, the *tekonatari* may file another suit demanding compensation for the property on the land on the basis of Article 1815 of the Civil Code, which states: 'Where a contract is invalidated...the parties shall as far as possible be reinstated in the position which would have existed, had the contract not been made.' Such suits are routinely accompanied by a stay of execution order aimed at retaining possession of the land in the hands of the *tekonatari* until the litigation on compensation is finally settled. The second round litigation is long and protracted. The court order,

49 Decisions of the House of Federation rendered on 26 June 2015 and 12 March 2016.

which delays the execution of land restitution to the *akonatari*, allows the *tekonatari* to continue investing in the land and, in the end, to use the experts from the local agricultural office to secure an overvaluation of the property.[50] Property overvaluation is often exacerbated by corruption, the lack of a national property valuation formula and experts. Even if property appraisement is carried out properly, it is difficult for the *akonatari* to pay compensation to the *tekonatari*, because the latter has usually made significant improvements to the land since the conclusion of the *kontract*, with a view to 'buying tenure security' and hence forestalling any future possibility of land restitution. Under such circumstances, it is virtually impossible for an *akonatari* to actually get their land back.

Peasants who transfer their landholding as a whole via the *kontract* scheme tend to lose their farming skills, first during periods of *koota* (sharecropping arrangements) and then during the long period of *kontract*.[51] And the increasing trend for commercially driven *kontract* transactions is one of the reasons for a noticeable shift away from production of food crops to the production of cash crops – particularly coffee, *khat* and sugarcane. The revival of *kontract*, together with the lack of seed and fertilizer subsidies for poor farmers, has contributed to food insecurity in the study area. As one local farmer put it:

> We used to produce pretty much most of what we ate on our own farms in the old days; now we buy food items from the markets at higher prices, like those who live in towns. Those who purchase land through kontract grow cash crops, mainly sugar cane, khat and eucalyptus trees, all destined primarily for urban people. (Interview, 23 September 2012)

Thus, evidence suggests that rural households in the area are experiencing food insecurity in which land alienation through *kontract* plays a part, even if the degree of its contribution in this regard requires further empirical investigation.

Discussion, conclusion and suggestions

Analytical perspectives from economics, legal positivism, and legal pluralism

Kontract may be seen through the lenses of economists, lawyers, or legal pluralists. Economists view *kontract* as a simple land rental agreement, with land to be restituted on a specific agreed upon date. More broadly, the economists also regard *kontract* as a free juridical expression of the peasants' demand for restrictions on

---

50 Interviews with a judge and a practising lawyer, 24 September 2012.

51 Interview with an elder, 14 September 2012 and interview with a local public servant, 18 September 2012.

the transferability of land use rights imposed by the state law to be lifted (Tesfaye 2004, McClung 2012). To such economists, a degree of differentiation in the size of landholdings is necessary in rural Ethiopia, where too much equality in land allocation prevails, to enhance the productivity of the land. For them, *kontract* is a useful tool in replacing the miniscule and uneconomical farm plots (also called starving plots) common in rural Ethiopia with relatively larger farmlands, since it transfers land from those who cannot use it to those who can. These medium and large farms improve agricultural productivity, which in turn leads to economic development, with its supposed trickledown effect on the poor (Deininger *et al.* 2008). Thus, they argue, policy should let these 'people-driven land rental practices' evolve and be prudently governed by land laws and institutions. State courts should nurture, not nullify, grassroots practices concerning land transactions.

The economic efficiency oriented view outlined above can be attributed to international organisations such as the World Bank and United States Agency for International Development (USAID). A study conducted by the World Bank has argued that:

> Most farmers would rather rent their land during stressful periods compared with any other alternative, such as selling it. In other words, in addition to all the other benefits of rental markets suggested in the literature, the availability of formal land rental markets will serve as a caution to enable farmers to withstand unfavourable circumstances by temporarily renting their land rather than selling it. Small farmers are driven into informal land deals by state land laws that impose restrictions on land use rights of small farmers; remove the restrictions to make them beneficial for the poor (Haddis 2013:9).

It has also been claimed that 'unofficial transaction may negatively affect women and other vulnerable people because it does not provide effective legal backing when local land grabbers snatch their holdings' (Haddis 2013:10). Thus, the solution is to liberalize land markets, among others, to solve the problem of shortage of land and capital, to encourage the movement of people towards off-farm activities, and to increase land tenure security. Research done under the auspices of USAID presents *kontract* as an ordinary 'land rental', that is, as, a contractual arrangement for a defined duration with land restitution in the end (Gizachew and Solomon 2011:7, McClung 2012). The same research classifies land transactions in Sidama area simply as land rental and sharecropping arrangements, discounting out *kontract* in the sense understood here (Gizachew and Solomon 2011, McClung 2012).

Lawyers with a legal positivist orientation (i.e., those who assume that the state is the exclusive source of law) would see *kontract* in terms of a violation of state land law. Under *kontract*, the intention of the parties is to transfer land rights over rural land permanently in favour of the *tekonatari*. The legal positivist approach is in line with the stance taken by the House of Federation, as well as with the position adopted by the Federal Supreme Court Cassation Division and the latest judgments of the SNNRS Supreme Court. To positivist lawyers, the prevalence of *kontract* is due to a lack of clarity, the existence of loopholes in the state land laws, their weak enforcement, and an absence of clear sanctions against those who enter into land sales. As *kontract* is a legal problem, therefore, they recommend the introduction of additional laws that are specific, complete, clear, effectively communicated to the right people and properly enforced upon transgression.

Legal pluralists, on the other hand, view *kontract* as constituting a third layer of the land tenure regime, lying somewhere between *utuwa* and state land law. Unlike for the legal positivists, the accent here is not on mere legality or economic efficiency, but rather on the recognition of a different set of land norms and institutions, including *kontract*, whose validity and legitimacy emanates from the grassroots, that is, the local people.

However *kontract* is viewed, one point is clear: the prevalence of *kontract* in rural Sidama is weakening the professed protective purpose of the current land policy of Ethiopia, which is meant to ensure that land remains in the hands of peasants as a survival asset. Allan Hoben (2000:30) has observed:

> The present tenure system with state ownership of land...could not prevent land sales and mortgaging but made them take place where the sellers are at a disadvantage, could not prevent land transfer from rural communities to commercial farmers and urban dwellers... could not slow rural–urban migration...

Summary and conclusion

Kontract is a practice of disguised permanent transfer of farmland encapsulated in an agreement concluded between *akonatari* (transferor) and *tekonatari* (transferee). It is a hybrid of state law and Sidama customary law, for it takes elements from both. At the same time, it is opposed to both. *Kontract* conflicts with the Constitution's clearly stated tenet that agricultural land held by the rural masses is a survival asset and is *ex-commercium*. And it is inconsistent with time-honoured egalitarian, though not inclusive, principles embodied in Sidama custom.

Despite this, *kontract* has gained some kind of legitimacy from the state apparatus. The position of the federal and regional highest courts towards *kontract* has been contradictory and lacks uniformity: where the courts repudiate *kontract*, their decisions are not effective because of power imbalances; and from the point of view of the *akonatari*, court decisions in this regard are not worth the paper they are written on. Legitimacy is also given to *kontract* by land administration agencies, which accept the *tekonatari*'s annual land use fee and register land subject to *kontract* in the *tekonatari*'s name. Hence, to some degree, *kontract* is a state-sanctioned land deal, which allows those with financial clout to undertake what might be called small-scale land grabs.

The subtext in the practice of *kontract* favours those deemed 'improvers' of the land, and has adverse consequences for economically vulnerable sellers. Thus, the diagnosis of *kontract* undertaken here suggests that the egalitarian principle behind Ethiopia's land policy is being undermined. This indicates the need for a rural land reform, which should have twin pillars: it should grant the poor access to both agricultural land and to meaningful agricultural support. Such a land reform should be augmented by a system of good land administration that, among other things, includes a mechanism for minimizing or eliminating land-related corruption. The implication of all this is that the debate surrounding negotiated legal pluralism should consider critically its outcome, which is rooted in a significant power imbalance, instead of merely valorising it as a potent tool for providing flexibility and human agency. In other words, there should be critical scrutiny of who is negotiating with whom, under what circumstances and with what impact.

References

AADLAND, Øyvind, 2002 "Sera: Traditionalism or living democratic values: Case study among the Sidama in southern Ethiopia", in: Bahru Zewde (ed.) *The challenges of democracy from below*, 29–44. Uppsala: Nordiska Afrikainstitutet

2008 "Beyond relativism: Where is political power in legal pluralism?" *Theoretical Inquiries in Law* 9 (2):395–416

BERHUTESFA Costantinos, 1999 *Natural resource competition, conflicts and their managements: Case study from Wondo Genet, south-central Ethiopia* (accessible online at www.costantinos.net/NRMbased Conflict–South Ethiopia.pdf, last accessed 7 December 7 2013)

CENTRAL STATISTICAL AGENCY (CSA), 2010 *Population and Housing Census Report – Country* 2007 (accessible online at www.Doc/Reports/National Statstical.pdf, last accessed 7 December 2013)

DE SCHUTTER, Olivier, 2011 "The green rush: The global race for farmland and the rights of land users", *Harvard International Law Journal* 52 (2):504–559

DESSALEGN Rahmato, 2011 *Land to investors: Large-scale land transfers in Ethiopia*. Addis Ababa: Forum for Social Studies (accessible online at http://www.landgovernance.org/system/files/Ethiopia_Rahmato_FSS_0.pdf, last accessed 7 December 2013)

FEDERAL DEMOCRATIC REPUBLIC OF ETHIOPIA (FDRE), 1995 *The Constitution of the Federal Democratic Republic of Ethiopia*, Proclamation No.1, Federal Negarit Gazeta, Year 1, No. 1. Addis Ababa: Berhanena Selam

GIZACHEW Abegaz and SOLOMON Bekure (eds.), 2009 *Proceedings of a consultative meeting on rural land transactions and agricultural investment*, (Addis Ababa: Ethiopia – Strengthening Land Administration Program, 2009); Ethiopia: Strengthening Land Administration Program Annual Report (1 August 2010–30 September 2011) (December 2011). Addis Ababa: USAID

GUDETA Seifu, 2009 "Rural land tenure security in the Oromia National Regional State", in: Muradu Abdo (ed.) *Land, law and policy in Ethiopia since 1991: Continuities and changes*, 109–146. Addis Ababa: Addis Ababa University

HADDIS Zemen, 2013 "Towards improved transactions of land use rights in Ethiopia", paper presented at the *Annual World Bank Conference on Land and Poverty*, The World Bank-Washington DC, 8–11 April 2013 (accessible online at https://www.usaid.gov/sites/default/files/documents/1860/Towards%20Improved%20Transactions%20Land%20Rights %20Ethiopia.pdf, last accessed 23 May 23 2018)

HAMER, John, 2002 "The religious conversion process among the Sidama of northeast Africa", *Journal of the International African Institute* 72 (4):598–627

1998 "The Sidāma of Ethiopia and rational communication action in policy and dispute settlement", *Anthropos* 93 (H.1/3):137–153

HELFAND, Michael, 2015 "Introduction" in: Michael Helfand (ed.) *Negotiating state and non-state law: The challenge of global and local legal pluralism*, 1–11. Cambridge: Cambridge University Press

HOBEN, Alan, 2000 "Ethiopian rural land tenure policy revisited." Paper presented at the *Symposium for reviewing Ethiopia's economic performance 1991–1999*, organized by Inter Africa Group. Addis Ababa, 26–29 April

HOLDEN, Stein, 2012 "Findings in the research project 'Joint Certification and Household Land Allocation: Towards Empowerment or Marginalization?'" (accessible online at http://iloapp.steinholden.com/blog/ajoint?Home &category=0, last accessed, 19 March 2012)

IMPERIAL GOVERNMENT OF ETHIOPIA, 1960 *Civil Code of the Empire of Ethiopia*, Proclamation No. 165/1960, Negarit Gazeta Extraordinary Issue, 1960-05-05, Year 19, No. 2 (accessible online at http://www.ilo.org/dyn/natlex/natlex4.detail?p_lang=en&p_isn=52399)

JOIREMAN, Sandra, 1996 "Contracting for land: Lessons from litigation in a communal tenure area of Ethiopia", *CJAS* 30 (3):214–232

2000 *Property rights and political development in Ethiopia and Eritrea* (1941–74). Oxford: Currey

KRZECZUNOWIC, George, 1983 *Formation and effects of contracts in Ethiopian law*. Addis Ababa: Addis Ababa University

LEFORT, Rene, 2012 "Free market economy, 'developmental state' and party state hegemony in Ethiopia: The case of the 'model farmers'", *Journal of Modern African Studies* 50 (4):681–706

LUND, Christian, 2000 "African land tenure: Questioning basic assumptions" (accessible online at www.hubrural.org/IMG/pdf/iied_dry_ip100eng.pdf (last accessed 7 December 2013)

MAKKI, Fouad, 2014 "Development by dispossession: Terra nullius and the socio-ecology of new enclosures in Ethiopia", *Rural Sociology* 79 (1):79–103

MANJI, Ambreena, 2012 "The grabbed state: Lawyers, politics and public land in Kenya", *The Journal of Modern Africa* 50 (3):467–492

MARKOS Tekle *et al.*, 2011 *The Sidama nation: History and culture*. Hawassa: Sidama Zone Tourism and Communications Division

MCCLUNG, Margi, 2012 "Making land rental markets work for Ethiopia's rural poor" (accessible online at www.focusonland.com/download/51fa3aee39f84, last accessed 7 December 2017)

MEINZEN-DICK, Ruth and Rajendra PRADHAN, 2002 "Legal pluralism and dynamic property rights", *CAPRI Working Paper No 22*. Washington: IFPRI (accessible online at http://ageconsearch.umn.edu/bitstream/55442/2/capriwp22.pdf, last accessed 6 March 2018)

PARTHASATHY, Devanathan, 2002 "Law, property rights, and social exclusion: A capabilities and entitlements approach to legal pluralism", Paper presented at the *XIIIth International Congress of the Commission on Folk Law and Legal Pluralism* 7–10 April 2002, Chiang Mai, Thailand (accessible online at http://www.eldis.org/document/A12459)

PAUSEWANG, Siegfried, 2000 "The need for a third alternative: The amputated debate on land tenure in Ethiopia" (accessible online at www.irsa-world.org/prior/XI/papers/4-8pdf)

SEYOUM Hameso, 2006 "The Sidama Nation", in: Seyoum Hameso and Mohammed Hassen (eds) *Arrested development in Ethiopia: Essays on underdevelopment, democracy and self-determination*, 57–75. Trenton, New Jersey: Red Sea Press

SHIVJI, Issa, 2009 Where is Uhuru? Reflections on the struggle for democracy in Africa. Cape Town: Fahamu Books

SNNPR REPORT, n.d. (accessible online at www.snnprs.gov.et/Regional Statistical Abstract.pdf, last accessed 7 November 2017)

Newspapers

THE ETHIOPIAN REPORTER

2012 "Leasee–Leasor Confusion over Commercial Farms", (accessible online at http://www.ethiopianreporter.com/business-and-economy/296-business-and-economy/4754-2012-01-06-07-32-57.html, last accessed 20 February 2012)

Legislations and proclamations

Federal Rural Land Administration and Land Use Proclamation No. 456/2005
Rural Lands Proclamation No. 31, 1975
SNNPRS Rural Land Administration and Use Proclamation No 53/2003
SNNPRS Rural Land Administration and Use Regulation No. 66/2007
SNNPRS Rural Land Administration and Use Proclamation No. 110/2007
SNNPRS Supreme Court Cassation Division Case, File No. 36888, October 2010.
SNNPRS Supreme Court Cassation Division File No. 64745, May 16, 2015
Federal Supreme Court Cassation File No 79394
Federal Supreme Court Cassation File No, 110549, February 2016
Federal Supreme Court Cassation File No 79394, September, 2012
Federal Supreme Court Cassation File No 49200, November, 2010

Case files

Abdella Ibrahim vs. Uso Abdi, Federal Supreme Court Cassation File No 79394, September 2012 in: Decisions of the Federal Supreme Court Cassation Division, Vol. 14, September 2013, Federal Supreme Court, Addis Ababa: 199–201

Alemitu Gebre vs. Chane Desalgn, House of Federation 5th Year 2nd Regular Meeting, 12 March 2016 (unpublished, on file with the author)

Aliye Dawe vs. Muhammed Adem, House of Federation 5th Year 2nd Regular Meeting, 26 June 2015 (unpublished, on file with the author)

Demekech Nera vs. Galeme Rebso, Federal Supreme Court Cassation File No 110549, February 2016 in: Decisions of the Federal Supreme Court Cassation Division, vol. 19, August 2016, Federal Supreme Court, Addis Ababa: 352–356

Emahoye Banchiamlak Dersolign vs Abebawu Molla, House of Federation 1st Year 2nd Regular Meeting, 12 March 2016 (unpublished, on file with the author)

Feto Dangura vs. Dubala Feto, SNNPRS Supreme Court Cassation Division File No. 64745, 16 May 2015 (unpublished)

Hasay Doye vs. Tinsae Kutale and others, House of Federation 5th Year 2nd Regular Meeting, 12 March 2016 (unpublished, on file with the author)

Jemal Aman vs. Tewabech Ferede, Federal Supreme Court Cassation File No 49200, November 2010, in: Decisions of the Federal Supreme Court Cassation Division, vol. 13, September 2012, Federal Supreme Court, Addis Ababa: 423–425

Tilahun Wondo vs. Tadesse Shalo, SNNPRS Supreme Court Cassation Division Case, File No. 36888, October 2010 (unpublished)

12. Legal pluralism and emerging legal hybridity

Interactions between the customary, state and religious law among the Siltie of southern Ethiopia

Kairedin Tezera

Introduction

Examining the versatile relationship between the customary, state and Sharia legal systems, and focusing on Siltie people in southern Ethiopia, this paper provides an anthropological understanding of the legal dynamics of state–society relations. Based on the experiences of dispute settlers and disputants, the paper investigates how the three legal systems interact in the area, and explores why and how disputants show a preference for one form of conflict resolution over another. It also looks into how dispute settlers use dispute settlement forums not only to end conflicts, but also to protect the custom and the language of the people and preserve and promote Siltie identity.[1]

The situation in Siltie is especially interesting because of the great complexity of legal institutions. The Siltie legal landscape consists of three normative systems: the state law, the customary law and the religious (Sharia) law. The complexity of the legal sphere is also observable in the intra-plural nature of these three legal systems. The religious legal system, for example, is comprised of Sharia courts, courts of local *mashayik* or *waliye*,[2] courts of local sheiks such as Abdul Qadir Jailani and Sheik Hussein of Bale, and the Salafi Social Committee, which was set up by Siltie-educated Muslim youth in the 1990s (Zerihun 2013:141).

1 This paper is the result of the research done for my PhD, which was conducted between August 2014 and March 2017. It was funded by the Bayreuth International Graduate School of African Study (BIGSAS) at Bayreuth University in Germany. I conducted several months of ethnographic fieldwork and mostly used qualitative methods, but also included some archival sources to substantiate the empirical data. Being from Siltie Zone myself, I was able to use my native language skills and prior knowledge of the local culture of Siltie to easily integrate with the local community.

2 A *waliye or* a *mashayik* is a human religious figure, dead or alive, popularly recognized as honourable Islamic symbols by the majority Muslims. It is usually represented by a tomb, and in some cases by a mosque, and is associated with a shrine.

While customary law has the longest history in the area, state law was introduced in the late-nineteenth century and Sharia law has been used since the 1950s. Since 1995, all three legal systems have been recognized and have a constitutional right to function and offer their services to the public, and parties in a conflict can choose which legal forum they want to hear their case. However, the customary and Sharia courts are constitutionally mandated to deliver legal services only in civil and family cases. Yet, the findings of this study show that customary courts deal with all forms of conflict – including those that are the preserve of state law – at the grassroots level in the study area. They also show that the relationship between the different institutions is both cooperative and competitive since the courts exchange some cases while contend also over the others when they handle some cases like murder cases. Additionally, not only do the clients to the courts choose the forum that seems to best represent their interests, but some of the legal practitioners from the various courts also pursue their personal interests when dealing with conflicting parties. While state legal actors, often rely on non-state actors in dispute cases that the state legal system cannot adjudicate. In addition, the interactions of the legal systems reveal contradictory perspectives and crossings into territories claimed by the other. Religious dispute settlers, for instance, borrow ideas and legal norms from the state and customary legal systems whenever they handle dispute cases. In turn, customary legal actors use Islamic legal precepts and at times state legal norms to settle disputes. This hints at the porousness of the boundaries between the various legal systems.

The empirical data presented here further indicates that some dispute cases do not remain in one court, as disputants often take their cases from one legal system to another. Marital disputes in particular are often moved between state and customary courts, and some disputes are moved from one customary court to another, all of which indicates that 'forum shopping' exists not only between the various legal systems but also within the same legal system. This is partly because many state and Sharia court judges favour the customary courts for their efficiency in handling legal cases, and this has greatly increased their legitimacy in the area and has affected disputants' choice of forum.

Islam plays a key role in Siltie and has been important in the construction of the Siltie people's identity (Markakis 1998:130–33). Islam also plays an important role in the area of dispute settlement and as a control mechanism that regulates social and moral aberrations among the Siltie and their neighbours. The Sharia courts, which have been in place since the1950s, thus play a paramount role as faith-based dispute settlement institutions, though nowadays some of the younger Muslims accuse the *qadis* (Sharia court judges) of being acquiescent to the state agenda.

My findings indicate that, despite the fact that the constitution of the Federal Democratic Republic of Ethiopia (henceforth FDRE) recognizes both customary and religious institutions of dispute settlement (FDRE 1995 Articles 34(5) and 78(5)), the customary legal system delivers justice to the grassroots level more frequently than other tribunals, and that Sharia courts cannot do so to the same extent due to a number of internal and external factors. These factors include not only competition with the other legal systems, but also the plurality within the Islamic legal system itself, as represented by the Salafi Social Committees that have developed since the 1990s and the local Sufi shrines.

There is also a kind of competition between individual actors within these systems. I found that elders and religious figures (sheiks and imams) use their mediation services not only to settle conflicts, but also to acquire and consolidate their power and influence in the area. The competition between legal actors is accelerated by a shortage of trained manpower in both the state and Sharia courts that negatively affects the courts' ability to deliver justice to the community. There are reportedly only thirty state judges and seven *qadis* serving about one million Siltie people. This has the effect of rendering these courts irrelevant in the eyes of many local people, who often question their legitimacy and jurisdiction. This is also evidenced by the high number of people who prefer to take their cases through the local religious and customary modes of dispute settlement rather than to the *Sharia* and state courts.

Yet, there exists also cooperation between the legal systems. For instance, the customary courts' handling of a large number of civil cases helps the state courts reduce their caseload. Elders likewise seek the assistance of state court judges in certain contexts, such as when they handle cases of domestic violence. Nevertheless, since the customary legal system has normative proximity to the community, it enjoys a wider legitimacy and hence resolves disputes in restorative ways.

Finally, the fact that dispute settlers from the three courts borrow norms and legal concepts from each other to handle dispute cases in their respective courts points to the emergence of hybridized legal practices in the area.

The Siltie Zone and people

Geo-political setting, social and political organization

Siltie Zone is located in the Southern Nations, Nationalities, and People's Regional State (SNNPRS) of Ethiopia. The Siltie people mainly live in the Siltie Zone,[3] although quite a large number of them are also found in various urban centres in the country. Although historical documents clearly indicate that the Siltie are a separate ethnic group (e.g. Markakis 1998, Braukämper 2002, Abdulfeta 2002, Kairedin 2012), the Siltie were incorporated into the administrative zones of

3 Zone is the second administrative division after Regional State in the contemporary federal structure of Ethiopia.

Hadiyya, Gurage, and the then Hallaba Kambata in the early 1990s. In the early days of the post-Mengistu regime, they felt neglected both economically and politically. The urban youth and entrepreneurs, as well as rural self-help organizations, initiated an ethnic identity movement called 'The Siltie Movement' that lasted for ten years (1991–2001). Its aim was to define Siltie ethnicity and to develop the socio-economic conditions of the society. According to Bustorf (2011:457), the Siltie activists' first important political goal was 'to assert their ethnic unity and to realize equality with neighbouring ethnic groups by acquiring their own administrative zone'.

Their political struggle resulted in a referendum on1 April 2001, when they regained the ethnic and administrative independence that they had lost following the incorporation of Siltie land by the forces of Emperor Menelik II in 1889 (Bustorf 2011:457–458). Based on the 2007 national population census, the total population of the Siltie was projected to be more than one million in 2017 (CSA 2008). Agriculture is the mainstay of the local economy. Muslims make up 97.6 per cent of the population, while 2.03 per cent belong to various Christian denominations (Siltie Zone Finance Abstract 2016). Some works (e.g. Abdulfeta 2002, Braukämper 2001, Kairedin 2013, 2017, 2018) indicate that the Siltie were one of the societies that came into contact with Islam very early, probably as early as the ninth century. There has been some erosion of cultural norms and practices due to the influence of reformist strains of Islam imported from the Gulf region over the last 25 years. However, the Siltie have maintained their customs, local beliefs and values, including the faith-based and customary modes of dispute settlement.

Siltie society is internally differentiated and consists of several stratified descent-based subgroups. These include the dominant majority of farmers and traders (*woleba*) and the marginalized craft workers (*awneya*), including blacksmiths, tanners and potters. People also differentiate between believers in Islam and non-believers. Believers are further differentiated into higher and lower classes. High-class individuals are called *sharafic* and belong to a group of people who trace their genealogy to the Hashemite and the Prophet Mohammed's family and who migrated to the Siltie area in three different exoduses after the ninth century. Low-class individuals are called *yeafer seb*, are of non-*sharafic* descent and are believed to be native to the area, having lived there long before the coming of the new settlers led by the legendary Siltie father Hajji Aliye from eastern Ethiopia during the sixteenth century. Finally, believers distinguish between Siltie highlanders (*ansewa*) and lowlanders (*qalla*).

Craft workers have no right to own land or local titles. They are socially marginalized, not allowed to intermarry with farmers and traders, and cannot be chosen to serve as dispute settlers. They are also treated differently in the elders' councils. For this reason, as my informants indicated, members of minority groups prefer the state legal system over the customary courts, since the latter are said to favour members of the dominant majorities.[4]

Recently, another form of social stratification has emerged. Due to the expansion of development and education in the area, Siltie are now categorized as urban or rural, as well as elite or ordinary people. Resulting from the recent economic progress in the area, one can also see a middle class emerging in the space between lower and upper class Silties. Furthermore, there is gender segregation in the social life of the Siltie. Women are predominantly housewives who control their household's economy, while men work in the fields as farmers or as traders. However, in urban centres, Siltie women have begun to participate in new activities, including business. Rural women prefer customary courts for handling marital disputes than urban ones who mostly resort to State courts. But due to the patrilineal nature of the customary courts, rural women prefer property cases to be handled by the state courts. This is because the state courts take cases involving women seriously as part of the government's commitment to redressing the general imbalances in society. In the urban areas, more-educated women prefer both the Sharia and state courts, rather than customary courts, to handle property disputes.

Legal pluralism and hybridity

Some conceptual notes

Conflict transformation, conflict management, and conflict resolution have been distinguished in the existing literature. Appleby (2012:212) defines conflict transformation as the transformation from violent to non-violent means of dispute settlement, while conflict management entails the prevention of conflict from becoming violent or expanding to other areas. Conflict resolution refers to the removal, as far as is possible, of the inequalities between disputants through the use of mediation, negotiation, advocacy and testimony.

In complex industrial societies, the formal law is usually retributive and consistently employed, indicating the social distance between members of the societies (Lewellen 2003). In 'traditional' societies, restorative justice – that is, the conciliation between conflicting parties – is the main purpose. For this, techniques that involve mediation, conciliation or even forgiveness are commonly used to handle

4 The reason behind this is that the craft workers are said to have 'impure blood' (*deme keleb*). If a craftworker kills a farmer, the victim's family will not prosecute him/her in the customary court, because at the end of the dispute settlement the families of the perpetrator and the victim have to forge a new form of kinship. To avoid this social tie, the families of such victims usually deliberately drop the case.

disputes. The modalities by which disputes can be settled are divided into violent and peaceful. Violent modes include duel or combat, self-help and warfare, while peaceful modes include avoidance, negotiation, mediation and adjudication (Gulliver 1979:11).

With the growing interconnectivity of the world, contemporary conflict resolution entails the involvement of different legal systems even in remote areas. This challenges the hitherto alleged monopoly of the state legal system as a dominant dispute resolution mechanism (F. von Benda-Beckmann and K. von Benda-Beckmann 2006:9) and leads us to definitions of legal pluralism. Authors have attempted to define pluralistic socio-legal structures at least since the 1930s. However, due to its cross-disciplinary nature, scholars have struggled to come up with a universally agreed definition of legal pluralism (Griffiths 1986:9, Tamanaha 2008:376, Twinning 2010:11). In an attempt to resolve the intellectual battle over the concept of legal pluralism, Tamanaha (2008:396) introduced what he calls a 'simple approach', stating that, 'legal pluralism exists whenever social actors identify more than one source of "law" within a social arena'. He further defines legal pluralism as multiple uncoordinated, coexisting or overlapping bodies of law that may make competing claims to authority (Tamanaha 2008:375). Taking ideas from Moore's 'semi-autonomous social field', Griffiths (1986:38) asserts that, since 'law is present in every semi-autonomous social field, and since every society contains many such fields, legal pluralism is a universal feature of the social organization'. In this way, legal pluralism challenges the assumed state monopoly of making, administering, imposing and sanctioning the law. If one closely inspects the various definitions of legal pluralism, one notes that they imply that law covers a continuum from the state law to the informal social controls mechanisms of the customary legal spheres (Moore 1978, Woodman 1998, F. von Benda-Beckmann and K. von Benda-Beckmann 2006, Twinning 2010).

A number of authors (for example, Santos de Sousa 2006, F. von Benda-Beckmann and K. von Benda-Beckmann 2006) point to the fact that law is increasingly becoming hybridized. This hybridization, or mutual influencing among coexisting legal systems, is not a recent phenomenon. It could be observed during the colonization period (Tamanaha 2008:384), where the customary law and the colonizers' law influenced each other in various ways, with each exchanging or recognizing the other's norms. Nevertheless, the increasing economic and social pressures that have accompanied globalization and that surpass national boundaries (Santos de Sousa 2006, Tamanaha 2008:386) have further accelerated the porosity of legal systems' boundaries. This has led to the coming of what Griffiths (1998:134) calls 'cross-fertilization', a process whereby rules in one system are shaped by those of another, and are also shaping those of the other. Legal hybridism underpins the existence of multidirectional interactions rather than hierarchical relationships among legal systems, whereby an actor from the state legal system, for instance, borrows legal ideas from religious or customary legal systems and vice versa, as is witnessed among the Siltie people. The form of legal hybridism that is currently emerging indicates that each legal system influences the practices of the others whenever legal practitioners handle dispute cases. In this regard, we can see the birth of a 'hybrid legal system' among the Siltie in which each legal system incorporates elements of the other two, yet still stands by itself.

Ethiopias experiences of legal pluralism

Ethiopia's historical and political milieu is particularly rich, for the country is one of the oldest independent political entities in the world, having existed as such for more than two thousand years (Bahru 2000, Pankhurst and Getachew 2008:2). It is a legally plural state not only because it hosts different ethnic groups that have various coexisting normative orders, but also because the country has embraced constitutionally sanctioned federal and state laws that co-exist with other normative orders – including customary and religious ones – that have been formally recognized since 1995.

The current legal system reflects Ethiopia's history and politics, including the various doctrines – be they religious or ideological institutions the country has passed through since at least the nineteenth century. Many studies indicate that the customary legal systems serve as alternative institutions of dispute resolution in Ethiopia, where the state legal system is failing to fully provide the judiciary needs of the nation (see for example Meron 2010). Pankhurst and Getachew (2008:2) go further, saying that the various customary systems are the dominant legal systems delivering justice at the grassroots level in the country. Even though the religious and customary legal systems have long existed in Ethiopia, it was only in 1995 that the country officially embraced legal pluralism, in its Constitution. In the Constitution, Article 34 – entitled 'legal pluralism' – and Article 78(5) specifically contemplate the linkages between statutory courts, religious courts, and non-state dispute resolution forums. Article 34(5), for example, stipulates that the Constitution 'shall not preclude adjudication of disputes relating to personal and family laws in accordance with religious or customary laws, with the consent of the parties to the disputes.' Article 78(5) underlines that 'pursuant to sub-article 5 of Article 34, the House of People's Representatives and state councils can set or give official recognition to religious and customary courts.' Article 78(5) goes on to say that 'religious and customary courts that had state recognition and functioned before the adoption of the Constitution shall be organized on the basis of recognition accorded to them by this Constitution.' Following the national constitution, regional constitutions have also provided room for religious and customary laws to operate in their communities.

Following the arguments of Griffith (1986), Ethiopia could be understood as having 'weak legal pluralism' (Griffith 1986:6), since the state legal system accords supreme status to the Constitution, as seen in Article 9(1) of the 1995 Constitution: 'The Constitution is a supreme law of the land. Any law, customary practice or decision of an organ of state or a public official which contravenes this Constitution shall be of no effect.' Indirectly, however, it empowers the state law to validate the activities of other laws and legal forums. In this regard, although the government recognizes the customary and the Sharia courts, they are given a limited mandate (e.g. to handle family and civil matters) so long as both parties give their consents. Yet, the courts do not have a means by which to enforce their decisions. However, as will be shown in this chapter, even though the greatest power lies with the state law, when it comes to daily practices, the different legal systems have been influencing each other.

The Siltie legal world
A descriptive analysis of three legal systems

The state legal system

The late-nineteenth century marked a turning point in the modern history of Ethiopia as much of today's South was then incorporated into the Ethiopian empire under Emperor Menelik II, ushering in the beginnings of the modern Ethiopian state. At the same time, the foundations for legal pluralism in the country were laid. It was then that the state introduced its legal system in Siltie and many other places as a way of strengthening its grip on power and building state processes (Bustorf 2011:468). Since then, new forms of land tenure, the modern centralized state bureaucracy, a new judiciary system and economic order have grown up.

Most of my respondents indicated that, during both the Imperial (1931–1974) and the Derg regimes (1974–1991), the capacity of the state judiciary systems to deliver justice to the Siltie community was limited to the urban areas of neighbouring ethnic groups. This was because the Siltie area was broken up into adjacent areas following its fierce resistance to Menelik's expansion that led the area not to have an administrative centre of its own. This situation continued during the early days of the EPRDF regime: between 1991–2001 there were, for instance, only three state courts of first instance with a small number of trained judges in Silti, Dalocha and Lanfuro Woredas. This forced many people to travel long distances to get justice since there were not state justice offices in Siltie-settled areas.

After the establishment of Siltie Zone in 2001, the Siltie people set up nine first instance courts plus a High Court in Worabe town. There are now also more than

Figure 1: Meeting of clan courts in Lanfuro Woreda, Edeneba Kebele to handle both murder and civil cases (Kairedin 2015)

150 social courts in 181 *kebeles*. Most of the social courts were established by the state after 2001, with the intention that they would handle minor cases, for example, civil cases up to 500 ETB. However, their roles and functions have declined because of various legal reforms made in response to competition from customary courts in the country. The state system also exhibits some intra-plurality, as customs and revenue sections and the Good Governance and Appeal Office are also involved in dispute resolution processes.

According to the president[5] of Siltie Zone High Court, there are only thirty judges working in ten courts, including the High Court, in the whole zone. This clearly shows that the state court still cannot effectively serve the more than one million Siltie people. Appointment to the position of president in the state courts' is a political decision since it is the zone officials who propose candidates and the Regional Council that approves them. State court judges are trained lawyers. The

5 Interview with Akmel Ahmedin, Siltie Zone High Court President on 7 April 2015 in Worabe town.

dearth of qualified judges in the study area seems to be one of the factors contributing to the decline in demand for the state courts in the area,[6] alongside the problem of accessibility, the normative distance and the perception of state judges as more corrupt than those of customary and Sharia courts.

The religious legal system: Plurality of intra-faith institutions and modes of dispute settlement

Local religious institutions also have a bearing on dispute settlement processes. In the following section, I will look into the plurality of intra-faith-based institutions of dispute settlement and how they interact and compete with each other over dispute cases.

According to my key informants,[7] the first Sharia court was set up in the 1950s. During the Imperial period, the Siltie people were categorized under Haikochina Butajira, Chebona Gurage and Kembata and Hadiyya *Awrajas*.[8] With no *woreda*-level administration, the *awraja* (Provincial) *qadi*s appointed one or two *qadis* within a given area of a *balaba*t (landlord). Informants mentioned that the *qadis* were very respected by the society, as they were considered to be fair and committed to serving the community. During the Derg regime, the Siltie were categorized under the southern Shoa administrative structure and had access to the Dalocha-Lanfuro Awraja Sharia Court, which persisted until the demise of the Derg in 1991. The Islamic Affairs Council and the Sharia courts had been set up in Dalocha and Lanfuro areas, while the majority of the Siltie were living in Gurage Zone from 1991 to 2001. It was after the establishment of Siltie Zone in 2001, that the Siltie established an independent Islamic Council and their own Sharia courts. The Siltie High Sharia Court handles cases not only from the six first instance Sharia courts in the zone, but also from those in the neighbouring Hadiyya and Gurage zones. The proximity of the areas as well as the cost-effectiveness of servicing several zones are the main factors behind this development.

---

6 Baker (2013:202) indicates that political interference in the judiciary system in Ethiopia is meant to bring local development. The lack of enough qualified human resources in the state legal system and a low retention rate is a result of low salaries in the state system driving many judges leaving to join the private sector as legal representatives. This is less observable at lower administrative tiers, e.g. regional and zonal levels.

7 These were Kaire Sule, an important informant who has a deep knowledge about Siltie culture and history, and Shifa Seid, who worked in the Islamic Affairs offices including as Secretary of Siltie's Islamic Affairs and Sharia courts at different levels between 1970s to early 1990s in Lanfuro and Dalocha Woredas.

8 *Awraja* was the third administrative tier below the province/region during the Imperial (1931–1974) and the Socialist Derg (1974–1991) regimes.

The Sharia Courts handle issues such as marriage contracts (*nikah*), inheritance and divorce cases. They also examine civil cases up to 5000 ETB (approximately 350 USD in 2018), wills (*wesiya*), gifts (*hadiya*), endowments (*waqf*) and family Maintenance cases. My research has shown that the Siltie Sharia courts are very much occupied with marriage contracts as well as divorce and inheritance cases. According to several interviewed *qadis*,[9] the number of cases referred to Sharia courts has decreased since the introduction of the Revised Southern Family Law in 2008, which prohibits courts from handling inheritance cases

According to my informants, the Sharia courts have rather little legitimacy in the community, as their establishment is attributed to the political agenda of the state rather than to a true commitment to Sharia law. Besides, like customary courts, Sharia courts do not have the power to enforce their decisions, but depend on the agreement of the involved parties to any proposed resolution to their cases. The local community also mentioned the fact that young Salafis consider the *qadi*s as ignorant of Islamic knowledge (*jahil*) and as more loyal to the political interests of the state than to Islamic values.

Some of the *qadis* I talked to during my research also expressed frustration that they were not practising the Sharia in its true spirit. Besides which, even the limited rights granted to the Sharia court could not be fully implemented due to a meagre budget, which is not even enough to cover purchases of basic office equipment, such as computers or copy machines. The *qadis* interpreted the small budget allocation as a manifestation of the government's lack of regard for Sharia law.

The president of the Siltie Sharia High Court[10], on the other hand, argued that many Muslims lacked of awareness about the Sharia courts for dispute settlement. As one *qadi* confirmed, many do not know the extent to which the Hanafi School of teaching gives an equal share of property to husband and wife upon divorce. He argued that if Muslims better understood the Hanafi School's teaching on gender equality, more Muslims would go to the Sharia court. This provides an indication of intra-faith competition among Muslims, since the *qadi* in this case was a follower of the Hanafi School, which is less dominant among the Siltie, who mainly follow Shafie teachings.

While most of the *qadis* I interviewed complained about the lack of state support – both financial and constitutional – for Sharia law, some appreciated the financial support of the government that allowed them to hire *qadis* in different Siltie *woredas* and provide training for them.

---

9 Interview with Hajji Siraj, Silti Wereda Qadi and Hajji Shemsu, Dalocha Wereda Qadi in April 2016.

10 Interview with Hajji Mifta Seid, President of Siltie Zone Sharia High Court on 18 July 2017.

Local religious dispute resolutions

Dispute settlement entails not only the material interests of disputants, but also reintegration and the restoration of relationships. Faiths play a pivotal role in achieving these goals by connecting disputants under one identity as well as promising them rewards such as eternal peace in the hereafter, in addition to the internal and external peace they can get in the social world. Moreover, religious actors can also admonish disputants if they reject a peace proposal, threatening them with not only divine punishment but also failure in the social world. In Siltie, local religious actors play an important role as dispute settlers, and religious centres like mosques are centres of dispute settlement. Zerihun (2013:139) notes that there are three forms of local holy man (*waliye*)-based institutions of dispute settlements among the Siltie: *mawlid, liqa*, and *warrie.*[11] *Mawlid* is categorized into two: the Prophet Mohammed's *mawlid* (*mawlid-un-nabi*) and *mashayik's mawlid* (*mawlid al-mashayik*). Veneration of *waliyes*[12] has a central place in the religious as well as communal lives of the Siltie (Kairedin 2012:180).

The Siltie revere the local religious leaders (*mashayik*) because of the role they played in bringing about the social order and in expanding Islam in the area. The religious leaders are called among the Siltie as sheiks. Those religious leaders who play an important role for expansion of Islam and are also involved in dispute settlement are known as *mashayik*. The most celebrated Sufi shrines are Alkeso, Dangeye, and Hajji Aliye mosques. The local community attend the sheiks' mosques daily for prayer, to strengthen social solidarity and to resolve disputes among themselves and the neighbouring ethnic groups. The mosques are used to resolving interfaith, inter-ethnic and minor disputes, which do not involve blood cases. However, some informants[13] told me that said that these local religious forums do not handle dispute cases directly but instead indirectly play a role in peace-building as faith leaders advise their followers to give priority to forgiveness and peace rather than retaliation.[14]

Since the 1990s, there has been another religious institution for dispute settlement – the Salafi Social Committee. Some Siltie youth formed these forums to consider disputes within their own socio-religious groups. The formation of

11 *Warrie, liqa* and *mawlid* are local people's gatherings to revere the *waliyes* (religious figure) and handle dispute cases in the study area.

12 A *waliye or* a *mashayik* refers to a human religious figure, dead or alive, popularly recognized as honourable Islamic symbols by the majority Muslims. It is usually represented by a tomb, and in some cases by a mosque, and is associated with a shrine.

13 Interview with Sheik Mohammed, Ato Bahredin and Ato Usman on 23 February 2016 in Werabe.

14 The local community also resorts to the religious centres during natural calamities like drought and earthquakes, believing that these disasters can be averted by the intercession of the *waliyes*, whose prayers (*du'aa*) may be accepted by the Almighty.

the Committee seems to have emanated from a rejection of the customary courts and Sufi-oriented social gatherings on one hand, and the perceived failure of the Sharia courts to deliver justice according to Sharia law on the other. The Salafi Social Committee informally considers marriage contracts, disputes between husband and wife, and supports the needy. The group does not have a fixed structure, but gathers whenever the need arises. It is led by young university graduates and civil servants and is widely preferred by youths in the emerging Siltie elite. Siltie elders and old religious scholars, however, state that the youths' form of dispute settlement should be viewed in the context of the struggle between Sufi-oriented teaching and the more textual and puritanical Islamic teachings that have been introduced in the area since 1980s. The competition or clash between the young and old indicates the existence of a generation conflict between the classic Sheiks and the younger generation in the area.

The customary legal system

The Siltie customary legal system is rooted in Siltie *ada* or culture. It is influenced by some Islamic values. It employs local values and beliefs – namely, *berche, tur* and *fero* – as enforcing mechanisms. *Berche, tur,* and *fero* are local notions of the right to justice and, if one refuses to fairly treat others – including animals – it is believed that *berche, tur* and *fero* can bring bad repercussions in later life. It is believed that *berche* is inherited, so if someone cannot address a grievance or tries to hide a crime – even if it was committed by someone else – the repercussions will affect up to seven generations of that person's family. Being highly embedded in local values and norms, the customary legal system enjoys a wide legitimacy among the community.

Both, the political and social organization of the Siltie are characterized by plurality. The Siltie people are subdivided into several exogamous patrilineal clans, and the highly respected clan leaders have both social and political power at the local level. Despite the fact that the Siltie are a patriarchal society, they also value the female lineage: while the father's lineage (*abotgae*) is superior to the mother's lineage (*ummegae*) in various aspects, women's role and involvement can be observed in dispute settlement sessions, where people recognize female descent.

The Siltie call their local mode of governance *yesiltie serra*. *Yesiltie serra* has two forms of administrative structures: lineage and territorial based systems. Siltie elders work at various levels of the *yesiltie serra* as local leaders and mediators. *Gote,*[15] the smallest customary local administration level comparable to the state's administration level is known as *yeburda baliqe shengo* (hamlet elders assembly). At the next level, we find *yeazegag baliqe shengo* (village assembly), followed by *yemewta baliqe*

15 *Gote* is the smallest state administrative level below *kebele*; it consists of less than 500 people.

(supra-village assembly). *Yebad baliqe shengo/chale* (local chiefs' assembly) functions at the apex of the Siltie territorial level.

The customary courts consist of the elders' court, the clan court and the *raga* (local legal expert) court. The elders' court mainly deals with marital cases and local boundary disputes, while the clan court handles inter-clan disputes and crime cases committed by members of the clans. The *raga* court resolves mainly homicide cases. Despite the allocation of responsibilities among the courts, actors in the customary courts converge to handle dispute cases and to avoid communal disputes. In addition, all homicide cases resort to the *raga* courts for final resolution since it is believed that the *ragas*' decisions are binding. But the customary courts may also contest the authority of another customary court to resolve some cases involving many actors, such as murder cases.

Local assemblies comprise the offices of the local leadership and the customary courts. According to key informants,[16] local actors such as the *mesaki* (family head), *murra* (representative of many interrelated households), *moro* (head of sub clan), and *gerad* (leader of a clan) exercise local political power, while the *maga, raga and ferezagegne* (local cassation court judges) are local legal actors working in the customary courts. As one clan leader[17] explained, the traditional elder assemblies oversee the cases in their respective localities. However, their organization is based on clan groups and not on territory.[18] These assemblies come together once or twice a year to discuss issues of common concern, such as how to keep the norms and values of *yesiltie serra* alive. They also hand over criminal suspects who have tried to avoid punishment by moving to another locality to their respective clan leaders. As I observed during my research, local dispute settlers handle all kinds of dispute cases including homicide.

Informants stated that one could become a *raga* (local legal expert) on the basis of one's maturity, marital status (married), knowledge of handling issues and social acceptability. The position is also often passed from father to son. The value and belief systems of the people serve as powerful enforcing modes for the decisions of elders. In addition to their role in ending disputes, such local dispute settlement sessions are stages for strengthening Siltie identity and channels for exchanging information about local developments.

---

16 This relies on FGD that was conducted with eight informants, namely Hajji Hussein Hassan, Hajji Hussein Bussera, Sheik Yusuf, Hajji Mifta, Gerad Kedir, Kaire Sule, and Hamid Azma Hassan in May 2016 at the annual Siltie History, Culture and Language Symposium in Werabe.

17 Interview with Girazmach Hussein Bussera on 3 April 2016 in Dalocha Woreda. He is the leader of the Chiro-Dilapa clan in Dalocha and Hulbareg Woredas, and is at the same time a customary dispute settler.

18 These are *Yechiro Dilapa Serra*, *Yemelga Serra*, *YeSumm Silti Serra* and *YeAlicho Serra*. These are the names of the clan councils, which are named after the communities they represent.

Although revived since 1990s, the customary justice system is currently in decline because of the competition it faces from the two other legal systems. First, the Islamic justice system promoted by the youth has labelled the customary justice system as an 'unwanted innovation' (*bida'a*) and an adulteration of the principles of Islamic justice. Second, it faces strong pressure from the state legal system and the government in general, which fears the creation of space for a 'state within a state' that might instigate a kind of power struggle between traditional authorities and local government officials. Due to the growing monetization of the customary courts in the area, some elders are also blamed for an increase in the prevalence of bribery.

Interactions of the various legal systems: Duality of cooperation and contestation

As has been indicated above, the interaction between the three legal systems is characterized by both cooperation and contestation. On the other hand, the fact that the three courts borrow local norms and legal concepts from each other indicates the emergence of a hybridized legal practice in the area, and possibly beyond. In this section, I discuss this issue in some detail. The judges of the customary justice system, for instance, operate pragmatically, borrowing from or referring to legal norms from other legal systems, in particular from the Islamic justice system.

While the local politico-legal system of the Siltie has continued to operate side by side with the new regimes, the state system has also brought changes in the application of the customary law. In the case of homicide, for example, previously, a person who committed homicide was thrown into a big gully by his relatives to end the feud and avert revenge. Since the late-nineteenth century, the customary practice of 'killing the murderer' – which is believed to have been taken from Sharia law – was replaced by the payment of blood money (*gumma*) to the victim's family.[19] Some informants said that the Siltie practised *gumma* even earlier, giving compensation in kind (such as cattle) rather than money to the victim's family. Hajji Kemal Barsebo, a 62-year-old elder and customary court dispute settler gave this account of his experiences in the area:

> We have asserted the right to self-administration, albeit late, in federalist Ethiopia. We paid every price to get recognized by the central government. As an independent ethnic group, we have our ways to settle disputes (e.g. *yesiltie serra*). We have employed the system for long to resolve disputes, including murder

19 Some informants stated that compensation payments were also common before Siltie was incorporated into Ethiopia, especially in cases of intentional murder. While such compensation was given in kind (e.g. in the form of cattle) before the late-nineteenth century, today is given in cash.

> cases. We also know that the government has set up its judiciary systems at the grassroots level. Alhamduli-Allah our Din (Islam) also acknowledges our role as elders to use our culture. It even recognizes *berche* (lit.: 'fairness').
> Ironically, the public prosecutors do not drop the dispute the cases we are handling and thereby affect our credibility as elders in the community. In fact, we do cooperate with the state legal system in those cases for which the police could not easily find evidence. The state has got prisons, yet we have got *berche*, which can keep inflicting harms on up to seven generations of the disputing parties as well as on the dispute settlers if not well addressed. Where is article 39 of the FDRE constitution? Why does the state not allow us to fully involve our elders in resolving disputes like our neighbouring ethnic groups? (Interview, 27 August 2014, Silti Woreda)

Barsebo recounts the cooperation he witnessed among different legal systems on the one hand, and the competition that characterized the interactions of legal actors on the other.

The various mechanisms that the state has developed since the 1990s indicate that the government has tried to expand the state judiciary system in the country. Yet the system seems to have remained ineffective. In this regard, the consolidation of state power and its legal system has two severe consequences for legal pluralism: it prevents religious and customary laws having an equal status as state laws; it changes the role of law from enforcing social norms, which is the typical characteristic of the religious and customary courts, to achieving the political and economic objectives of government (Tamanaha 2008). With the challenges the state legal system faces at the grassroots level, pluralism is at a crossroads in Siltie.

Summary and conclusion

The paper has shown that in Siltie today, the customary law and courts, the state (formal) legal system and Islamic institutions and courts operate side by side. While the customary and the religious legal systems have faced challenges from the state since the late-nineteenth century, they have survived because of the people's strong attachment to local values and norms on one hand and the agency of actors who have used their social legitimacy to deliver justice to the community on the other. Moreover, the state institutions' inability to provide sufficient and satisfactory services to all Siltie, as well as the community's lack of trust of the state, and partly of Sharia courts, have also contributed to the continued existence of the customary legal systems.

The study has also demonstrated that all three legal systems are marked by intra-plurality. The legal plurality of the customary justice system, for instance, is characterized by the various territorial or lineage-based institutions of dispute settlement. The Islamic legal institutions in the community use not only the Sharia court but also other institutions of dispute settlement, such as the Social Committee created by members of the Islamic reform movement (the Salafis). Its plurality also emanates from the plurality of Islamic jurisprudence itself, which is based on four legal schools that differ on various issues, particularly on the gender dimension of property rights: while most of the Islamic legal schools have a male bias, the Hanafi School stipulates equal shares of property between husband and wife upon divorce. There is also plurality within the state legal system, manifested in the existence of various laws and institutions such as municipality laws, custom law, and the Good Governance and Appeal Office, which is in charge of hearing cases that are handled by the state courts.

The paper has also revealed that the formal legal system, the Islamic institutions and the customary institutions interact in such a way that they complement one another and cooperate with each other in many instances. In this regard, the state courts rely on customary courts to solve cases that the formal courts cannot adjudicate due to a lack of evidence, which the customary courts can more easily obtain. The customary courts employ local means of investigation involving ritual oaths to find evidence of crimes with no witnesses. Customary courts also promote restitutive approaches to disputes as opposed to the retributive approach of the state courts and formal law, which are culturally disconnected from the communities where the disputes are processed. While the legal systems cooperate in particular in handling marital cases, there is competition and conflict in other areas, notably over homicide cases.

The study has revealed that the different realms of state, customary and religious law not only interact but also adopt elements from each other, which points to the emergence of hybridized legal practices in the area and even possibly beyond. State court judges, for example, use local notions of justice, such as *berche*, when they handle marital disputes, while customary court judges refer to and promote gender equality when they handle family cases, which is contradictory to the dominant patriarchal relations prevailing in Siltie.

To conclude, one can state that the interactions between the various legal traditions in the area are characterized not only by cooperation but also by competition. And that we are seeing the emergence of the hybridization of legal practices in the contemporary world that is challenging the prevailing definitions of legal pluralism as the coexistence of more than one legal system in a given social setting.

References

ABDULFETA Huldar, 2002 *Siltie's nationality expressions and its contribution to Ethiopia's existence and development* (in Amharic). Addis Ababa: Pan African Centre

APPLEBY, R. Scott, 2000 *The ambivalence of the sacred: Religion, violence and reconciliation*. USA: Carnegie Corporation of New York

BAKER, Bruce, 2013 "Where formal and informal justice meet: Ethiopia's justice pluralism", *African Journal of International and Comparative Law* 21 (2):202–218

BENDA-BECKMANN, Franz von and Keebet von BENDA-BECKMANN (eds.), 2006 "Dynamics of plural legal orders", *The Journal of Legal Pluralism and Unofficial Law* 53–54:1–270

BRAUMKÄMPER, Ulrich (ed.), 2002 *Islamic history and culture in southern Ethiopia: Collected essays*. Münster: Lit

BUSTORF, Dirk, 2011 *Lebendige Überlieferung: Geschichte und Erinnerung der muslimischen Silt'e Äthiopiens*. Wiesbaden: Harrassowitz

CENTRAL STATISTICAL AUTHORITY (CSA), 2008 *The 2007 population census of Ethiopia*. Addis Ababa: Central Statistical Authority

DINBERU Alemu *et al.*, 1995 *Gogot: History, culture and language of the Gurage people*. Welkite Town: Department of Culture & Sport

FEDERAL DEMOCRATIC REPUBLIC OF ETHIOPIA (FDRE), 1995 *The constitution of the federal democratic republic of Ethiopia*. Proclamation No.1, Federal Negarit Gazeta, Year 1, No. 1. Addis Ababa: Berhanena Selam

GRIFFITHS, John, 1986 "What is legal pluralism?", *Journal of Legal Pluralism and Unofficial Law* 24:1–55

GULLIVER, Philipp H., 1979 *Disputes and negotiations: A cross-cultural perspective*. London: Academic Press

KAIREDIN Tezera, 2012 *Serra: History, culture and language of the Siltie people*. Addis Ababa: Eclipse Printing Press

2013 *Ye Siltie Serra: Local governance system of the Siltie*. Berlin: Lambert

2017 "The unexplored assets: Religious approach for peace making among the Siltie people in southern Ethiopia", *Religion, Peace and Conflict in Contemporary Africa* (e-Journal for the Study of the Religions of Africa and its Diaspora) (ASSR) 3 (2):139–154

2018 *Dynamics of identity formation and legal pluralism: The case of customary, religious and state dispute resolutions among the Siltie people, southern Ethiopia*. Bayreuth: Bayreuth University (PhD Thesis)

LEWELLEN, Ted, 2003 *Political anthropology: An introduction* (3rd edition). Westport, CT: Praeger

MARAKAKIS, John, 1998 "The politics of identity: The case of the Gurage in Ethiopia", *Workshop on ethnicity and the State in Eastern Africa*, 127–146. Distributor in North America: Transaction Publishers

MERON Zeleke, 2010 "Ye Shekoch Chilot (The Courts of the Sheiks)", in: Siegbert Uhlig (ed.) *Encyclopedia Aethiopica* Vol 4, 63–84. Wiesbaden: Harrassowitz

MOORE, Sally Falk 1978 "Law and social change. The semi-autonomous field as an appropriate field of study", in: Sally Falk Moore (ed.) *Law as process. An anthropological approach*, 54–81. Hamburg and London: LIT & Currey

PANKHURST, Alula and GETACHEW Assefa (eds.) 2008a *Grassroots justice in Ethiopia: The contribution of customary dispute resolution*. Addis Ababa: CFEE

SANTOS, Boaventura de Sousa, 2006 "The heterogeneous state and legal pluralism in Mozambique", *Law and Society Review* 40 (1): 39–75

TAMANAHA, Brian Z., 2008 "Understanding legal pluralism: Past to present local to global", *Sydney Law Journal* 30:375–411

TWINNING, William, 2010 "Normative and legal pluralism: A global perspective", *Duke Journal of Comparative and International Law* 20:473–517

WOODMAN, Gordon, 1996 "Legal pluralism and the search for justice", *Journal of African Law* 40 (2):152–167

ZERIHUN Abebe Woldeselassie, 2007 "Contested popular Islamic practices among Ethiopian Muslims: The case of warrie among the Siltie", *Journal on Moving Communities* 7 (1):73–94

2013 "Wali venerating practices, identity politics, and Islamic reformism among the Siltie", in: Patrick Desplat and Terje Østebø (eds.) *Muslim Ethiopia: The Christian legacy, identity politics, and Islamic reformism*, 139–161. New York: Palgrave Macmillan

13. A matter perspective: Of transfers, switching, and cross-cutting legal procedures

Juridical processes among Oromo and Amhara, East Shewa

Andrea Nicolas

Introduction

The discussion about legal pluralism is often framed by the state's perspective. From this point of view, the state is in the centre and has to deal with the 'problem' of other legal systems, often subsumed under the generalizing term 'customary law' (e.g. Donovan and Getachew 2003:505), acting in 'its realm' (Griffiths 1986:1–7). Yet, these non-state legal systems often preceded state law historically, and may represent locally the legitimate heir of a legal tradition that used to be termed not 'customary law' but simply 'the law'.[1] Looking from the perspective of a local elder, senior lineage representative or individual affected by an on-going case rather than that of the court judge, advocate or government agent, state law may not be the primary focus or obvious choice for appeals; rather it represents one of several options or procedural variants 'out there' in an arena comprising both diverse regional institutions and authorities created by strangers (see Larcom 2013:205). So, when it comes to conceptions of the legal spheres, we always need to ask through whose eyes are they being perceived.

Such an understanding also implies that state law cannot be taken to be the sole reference point for defining legal pluralism. In fact, legal pluralism is more than a binary situation of 'state versus custom' since there is rarely just one 'custom' at work, particularly in inter-ethnic settings and in settings comprising different religious traditions (see Pankhurst and Getachew 2008). Instead, there is a complex

1 Although the 'making of' customary law by colonial forces has often been stressed (Snyder 1981:49, Tamanaha 2008:384), clearly not all of these legal traditions were invented by the state (K. von Benda-Beckmann and Turner 2018:261). Various local legal systems, including several orally transmitted law corpora, preceded and prevailed the coming of the nation state, even if in partially altered form.

arena comprising different institutions that may compete or cooperate, closely interact or (officially) ignore each other. Seen in this light, state institutions and their affiliates constitute just one out of several 'players in the game', albeit often powerful ones. This raises the question of what methodology should be used in describing and analysing instances where actors navigate through a plurality of legal options.

From an anthropological perspective, there are several ways of looking at legal processes. The actor-oriented approach, which focuses mainly on disputants (as well as other involved parties) and their diverging goals and interests, has long been a leading paradigm in anthropology (K. von Benda-Beckmann and Turner 2018:260). However, the approach has been challenged by recent global developments that have driven an increasing focus on state law and 'official' standards.

To take the state's perspective often means to look through the 'institutional eye': to look at corporate bodies and institutions, and their rules and staffing. Particularly in heterogeneous settings, one might find the emergence of networks, the involvement of hierarchies, and the interplay of competition and cooperation between different institutional bodies. In such settings, often called 'polycentric', 'problems of sovereignty (or sovereignties)' are frequently involved (Lange 1995:113). A particular case's cross-cutting of institutional boundaries appears to be an anomaly when seen from the standpoint of institutions that make exclusive claims on decision-making. Cross-cutting cases must then be described in terms of 'transfer' or 'switching' that require explanation as well as legitimate justification. However, another scenario emerges when tracing such cases with a 'processual view'. This involves following a case along its path, through its ups and downs and sideways turns. Thus, one may find some cases remaining, by and large, within one dominant institutional setting, while others pass through different instances or are dealt with by different institutions over a period of time. Actors make choices and switch the settings, appealing to different authorities in order to change the outcome of their cases. From an institutional, 'one-case-one-justice' standpoint, this is often branded 'forum-shopping', and is likely to be accompanied by a negative evaluation, since affected parties are seen as taking too active a role in shaping the outcome of their case – even though some authorities do the same (K. von Benda-Beckmann 1981). From a processual perspective, and in realist terms, however, this could be taken as no more or less than a legal and social reality.

The 'procedural' perspective provides another approach, and combines characteristics of both the 'institutional eye' and 'processual view': while some cases may be treated in formal ways that remain in the framework of a particular institutional setting, like the state court or a church council, other forms of conflict settlement, like mediations by elders, may regularly cross-cut different institutional settings, and even make this 'crossing' a standard procedure, without participants losing sight of their different personal and institutional backgrounds (Nicolas 2011:63–67).

In the following, it is argued that, depending on which perspective is chosen and which methodology is taken as a base, different conclusions on the analytical and theoretical level may follow from the empirical description of cases. The chapter draws on research on the different legal institutions and procedures that are commonly in use among the Oromo and the Amhara living in East Shewa Zone of Oromiyaa region, central Ethiopia.[2]

A history of change: Legal frameworks and pluralist settings

The rural areas of East Shewa Zone of central Ethiopia are inhabited mainly by Tuulama-Oromo and members of the Amhara ethnic group. The historical sources for the area mostly describe changes in the power relations between the two groups, among which processes of integration and exchange seem to have been strong. The period of Oromo predominance can be associated with the rule of *gadaa*, an age- and generation system introduced into the area in the sixteenth century by northward-migrating Boorana-Oromo (Bahrey 1954 [1593]:116–125; Mohammed 1990:18–27). Amharic rule, on the other hand, is marked by the exercise of power through the Shewan kings, who – after a period of 'insular' existence in settlement clusters surrounded by Oromo territory – expanded their domains outward from the Manz area in northern Shewa from the beginning of the eighteenth century (Asfa-Wossen 1980:23–35). Through successive military campaigns, they gained control of the area discussed here in the nineteenth century (Ege 1996:192–220).

The Imperial era in Ethiopia lasted until the reign of Emperor Haile Selassie (1930–1974, interrupted by the Italian occupation of 1936–1941) and was violently ended by the socialist Derg (1974–1991).[3] When the EPRDF government took power in Ethiopia in 1991, it divided the country into ethnic regions and East Shewa became part of Oromiyaa region.

Under Emperor Menelik II (1889–1913), the Tuulama-Oromo of Shewa were converted to Christianity (Aṣma 1987 [1901–13]:688–695). Today, the majority of the

2 This paper is based on 25 months of fieldwork conducted between 1995 and 2002, which led to the publication of a dissertation on mediation by Oromo and Amhara elders (Nicolas 2011), as well as to 8 months further fieldwork between 2003 and 2017. The case examples quoted here stem from the village of Qaallittii in the Ada'a Liiban district, where I lived for some time. Most of the interviews refer to a time period stretching back to 1999, but I would hold that their characteristics are still significant. I would like to thank Felekke Zewde for his help in translating from Amharic to English during interviews with Amhara elders. I conducted most of the other interviews in the Oromo language.

3 Amh. *därg* ('committee').

rural population are Orthodox Christians. Oromo religious prayer and ritual practices co-exist alongside Orthodox Christianity. The religious framework is supplemented by the widespread practice of spirit possession in the wider region.

Local ways and cross-cuts: Mediation by elders

In East Shewan rural society, where ethnic 'borders' are regularly crossed by intermarriage between Oromo and Amhara, and by the fact that the two groups live in joint settlements, old men possess a high status. They settle conflicts and arrange marriages for the members of the junior generations in a procedure called *jaarsummaa* in Oromo, and *shimgilinna* in Amharic. They deal not only with cases that one might assume to be too 'unimportant' for state courts or other juridical institutions, such as personal insults and intra-familial disputes, but also with aggravated cases, like physical injury and homicide, and cases that may affect the wider group or that have inter-ethnic dimensions. Special procedures and rituals are used to bring about reconciliation between conflicting parties, many of which are families clashing over cases involving insults, brawls, disputes about property, bride abduction or killing. The prescribed procedures differ according to the type of case, and are suited to the gravity and possible consequences of the incident involved. The rituals and courses of action already hold appeasing potential in their form and language (Nicolas 2011). For instance, in serious cases involving quarrels and bloodshed, throughout the mediation process, time is set aside to allow the quarrelling parties to calm down. The procedure also stipulates that go-betweens contact the victim's family and enter into negotiations with its elders. This helps avoid acts of revenge and an immediate face-to-face confrontation between the families involved in the conflict. The aim of mediation is not primarily to punish guilty persons but to reconcile the families or groups involved.

A shared complex: Elders and ethnicities

The need to solve conflicts between members of different ethnic groups led to the emergence of a shared institution of conflict resolution among Oromo and Amhara elders.[4] Amhara individuals who are adopted by Oromo families obtain the right to be integrated into the dia-paying and reconciliation system, which

4 The development of a joint institution of reconciliation was facilitated by the fact that both groups already shared some basic characteristics. Both Oromo and Amhara relied on reconciliation by elders. In Amhara, as in Oromo settings, elders have arranged marriages and been responsible for decision-making in particular community affairs. Evidence of such settlements and arrangements can be found, for instance, in Messing (1957) and Reminick (1973) for the Amhara, and in Abas (1982) and Abdurahman (1991) for the Oromo.

shields them from possible Oromo enmities. Vice-versa, Oromo who get into trouble with Amhara and are then threatened with revenge are in need of a mechanism of peace-making that is acceptable to their persecutors.

It is open to question whether Amhara elders in earlier times reconciled cases involving blood-fee payments in their communities. However, today members of both groups share the view that Amhara traditionally do 'not know' blood-fee payments, making them very difficult reconciliation partners who tend to turn to revenge or state prosecution if they are victims, while Oromo do 'know' it and therefore more easily yield to appeals for peace.[5] In cases where an Amhara has killed an Oromo, it is likely that the Amhara would fall back on the Oromo way of paying the blood-fee in order to calm down his Oromo pursuers. Amhara, in such instances, often trust their case to exclusively Oromo elders, who are of better help under these conditions.

Which procedural norm is followed, the Oromo or the Amhara 'way', and which law is applied depends not least on the individual composition of the group of elders in a given case, and on the ethnic, religious and biographical background of the parties involved. Indeed, although each case is arranged and prepared according to a common 'recipe', slight modifications are always made according to the individual needs of the people involved, and the ethnic background of the participants is one factor that affects any changes.

Higher-level standards: Oromo law and jurisprudence

Since the change of government in 1991, which put an end to the socialist era and introduced an ethnic-federal system in Ethiopia, there has been a resurgence of the *gadaa* generation system throughout the wider Oromo region. Every eight years, just before a new generation class takes power in the country, the ruling 'fathers of the land' (the *gadaa*) hold large regional meetings (Nicolas 2006, Alemayehu 2009; cf. Blackhurst 1978). The members of the ruling class then gather near the tree of *Odaa Nabee*, which serves as the regional assembly place for the Tuulama-Oromo, as well as at other open air locations, such as the places where laws are proclaimed (*caffee*). During these meetings the *gadaa* carry out rituals, decide on matters of public concern, and deal with disputes, particularly cases of homicide. The *gadaa* leaders invite legal experts from previous generations to come and recite for them the laws of the country at these meetings (Huntingford 1955:47, Nicolas 2006:172).

The Oromo law (*seera*) is not written in books but is preserved and orally transmitted by a relatively small number of legal experts (sing. *abbaa seeraa*). Usually

5 It is probable that the Amhara practised, at least in part, blood-fee payments. See Ibrahim (1990) and Kassa (1967).

two, but sometimes three, of them perform the ritualized proclamation of the laws of the country together. Depending on the way in which the experts memorize it, the body of law consists of about thirty sections, each with four to eight or more subsections. The recitation is performed in a question–answer form. Paragraph by paragraph, the law experts list what is respected and sanctified in Oromo society (Haberland 1963:226, 476–481, Nicolas 2010:592). The paragraphs list lineage seniorities, name sacred waters, trees and mountains, legitimate different kinds of marriages, recite rules for atonement and compensation for killings, injuries, insults and theft, and clarify the legal status of animals and property. The listeners, male adults who are members of the currently ruling generation class, are expected to memorize the content of the laws. They will need this knowledge in their subsequent stages of life, when they perform their duties as elders, mediators and judges in their various home areas.

Each of the five *gadaa* classes has a number of hereditary families in which titles and offices are handed down from father to eldest son. Thus, the offices of the 'fathers of the sceptre' (*abbaa bokkuu*), attached to senior positions in the Oromo lineage system and responsible for decision-making, as well as the most senior 'judges' (*hayyuu*) at their head, are repeated in all five *gadaa* classes (Nicolas 2006:170). They usually belong to the most respected families in their areas.

The mediation by Oromo elders does not represent an alternative to formal Oromo law, but is itself a part of the legally prescribed procedure. In cases of serious injury or murder, an expert and judge (*caffee taa'icha*) is usually called in during the protracted negotiations. In accordance with the law, he must determine the amount of compensation to be paid and give instructions for the reconciliation rituals. A *caffee taa'icha* (literally, '[he] who was at [the place of] the law gathering') has successfully passed the stage of *gadaa*, and has thus heard the proclamation of the Oromo law several times.

The Oromo 'law' (*seera*), however, does not cover the full spectrum of disputes and problems that people experience. Particularly in multi-ethnic and predominantly Orthodox Christian settings, where different legal conceptions are present, 'custom' (*aadaa*) and situationally accommodated practice provide more flexibility for individual decision-making.

Religious interventions, institutional diversity and plurality of law

For centuries, Amhara law was a codified state law, confirmed and protected by the Shewan rulers, and written down in a book called the 'law of the kings' (*fetha nagast*).[6] This law contained a number of draconian measures against wrongdoers, such as flogging, the amputation of a hand for theft, and the death penalty for killing. We can only speculate on whether these measures were actually and regularly applied among the Amhara population of Shewa, or whether many cases were instead settled with the help of local elders.[7] However, we know that the *fetha nagast* also included some articles on theft and (unintended) homicide that resemble regulations about compensation and reconciliation rather than punishment.[8]

Orthodox priests continue to refer frequently to this ancient law of the kings, even though it has been replaced by modern state law. Priests are also regularly involved in the mediation procedures of local Oromo elders, albeit only through the frequent participation of individual priests in local mediations rather than through any official institutional Church involvement.

Cooperation among elders, priests and Oromo lineage seniors is a regular feature in East Shewan conflict settlement, yet there seems to be a ranking in the right to make decisions. Priests might take a leading role in advising councils of devout Oromo and Amhara elders, but their role often diminishes when a group of tradition-oriented Oromo elders gathers to discuss a case. Particularly when a *caffee taa'icha* is present, the *seera*, not the *fetha nagast*, forms the basis of decision-making. In such circumstances, priests often have to relinquish their preference for the old law of the kings, which is much closer to Church teachings, and accept that the case will be settled according to Oromo law. The priests' readiness to handle such cases 'according to the local culture' (*ye-akkababi bahil*), as they term it, reflects the demographic givens and specific power configurations of the region they live in.

Church procedures

In general, the Church itself has no independent mediation procedures that might supersede the proceedings of elders. The Church's particular type of religious marriage, defined as being indissoluble, is confined to a few, rather rare, instances; and the institution where parishioners and priests carrying the cross and wearing

6 According to Messing (1957:309), this law code was 'a blend of Canons of the Coptic church councils, the Justinian Code and the Bible'. Compiled in Egypt, the code was later introduced to Abyssinia, and superimposed by kings and clerics on the older Amhara 'customary law'. According to Ibrahim (1990:29), the code was written in the early fourteenth century by the Coptic Egyptian writer Ibu al-Assal. However, authors disagree about the time of its introduction to Ethiopia. The work was translated from Arabic into Ge'ez and Amharic, and copies in these languages can still be purchased in clerical bookstores in Ethiopia.

7 On this issue, see Kassa (1967) and Ibrahim (1990). The same issue has been discussed with reference to Oromo law (see Dinsa 1975:86 and Bassi 1992).

8 For the different regulations mentioned here, see *Fetha Nagast*, Art. 24, no. 826–963; Art. 47, no. 1655–1717 and Art. 49, no. 1759–1770.

festive clothing gather to pray together, is almost exclusively done for the reconciliation of man with God. It might complement the reconciliation between perpetrator and victim (or their families) provided by the elders' procedure but it is not a substitute.

The Church, however, does offer some alternative to the elders' proceedings. Instead of following the Oromo peace-making rituals of promise-making in the victim's compound or at a gorge, participants may choose to perform their vows in the Orthodox way, within the church compound. Likewise, in some places, gatherings for collective pleading to God in the open air is not bound to the occurrence of exceptional, heaven-caused catastrophes such as droughts or famines, but is organized at more or less regular intervals to beg God for forgiveness for the sins of the parishioners accumulated in the interim. At these occasions, reconciliations among people may be carried out by priests and pious elders at the church compound, by way of a piece-by-piece handling of the many cases to be dealt with on a single day. Though this parochial form of reconciliation is usually preceded by traditional mediation through local elders, it is nevertheless evident that a Church reconciliation provides a possible alternative to the elders' procedures. Some parishes have also launched an independent platform for reconciliations by Church elders, founding a council of 'assembly delegates' (*mele'ata guba'e*) consisting of twenty elders chosen from the surroundings, who make the decisions. Their appointment, however, is highly selective and based on their devotion to the Christian Orthodox Church. The council's proceedings are guided by Church teachings, and are not under the direction of the traditional laws and practices of Oromo title-holders. Since this institution is still somewhat rare in the area, it does not influence customary mediation procedures on a large scale. Nevertheless, it undoubtedly constitutes a potential alternative to which people who are dissatisfied with other elders' ways can turn.

Courts of spirit followers

Similar courts are run by some influential spirit mediums at their temple compounds. A particular cult's leader, who acts as the spirit's medium, will carefully select loyal and devout followers to act as the 'elders of God' (sing. *jaarsa Waaqaa*) and hold these councils. These elders number three or more. Spirit cults, even without such councils of elders, offer mechanisms of conflict resolution and reconciliation to their members. For instance, reconciliations are regularly carried out at holidays or during the regular possession rituals held at the spirit's temple door. Via his medium, the spirit orders certain participants to end their quarrels; reconciliation is then sealed using grass and through the ritual performance of spitting and mutual hand-kissing of the former adversaries. A spirit medium described to me the reconciliation procedures at a spirit's temple in the following way:

> If, for instance, a thief has stolen money from me, I go to [the temple of] the *oogliya* (spirit), [and complain to him]: 'Someone has stolen from me. I want my money back.' The thief then gets sick.[9] He goes elsewhere to another *oogliya* and asks him why he fell sick. That *oogliya* answers: 'You have stolen money from someone. Give the money back to him!' The thief now goes to [the temple of] the first spirit medium, in the area where the person that was stolen from lives [and begs]: 'I have stolen from him, please reconcile us!' The *qaalluu* (spirit medium) now sends someone to the person that was stolen from, and has him come for reconciliation [at the temple]. The *oogliya* (spirit) then speaks to both, and the thief gives the money back. The money is swathed in some grass, and some money, 1–3 Birr, lay upon it. The person that was stolen from now spits three times on it, as well as three times towards the sky. Thereby, the [curse] ends and the sickness of the thief goes away. The thief and the person he stole from kiss each other's hands. This shows that peace has been made again.[10]

In general, only followers of the spirit cult involved attend the reconciliation proceedings. Since only small and a few medium-size cults have spread in the area, and are often competing with each other, not all the inhabitants are integrated into the same network of worship. Consequently, spirit mediations do not have the capacity to replace the elders' well-established procedures. Mediating elders, however, often have to pay a visit to the spirits' temples in cases of marriage, bride abduction or cursing. They may also occasionally ask a spirit medium to join mediation in order to gain support for their peace-making efforts.

The mediatory principles of spirit mediums and mediating elders are not unlike each other. Both exercise rituals for the good of the wider community and both share an explicit ideology of peace in their prayers and advice. It is true that some spirit mediums see their own reconciliations as the only 'true' ones, since a spirit is said to know everything, and reconciliations made before him have to be committed full-heartedly. From this point of view, elders' reconciliations are just made for the sake of the maintenance of order and do not come 'from the stomach' (that is, from the heart).[11] Inversely, not every elder might be a follower of a given spirit's cult, so that only elders who have no objections or are believers themselves are chosen for the task of visiting the spirits' temples. However, as a rule, spirit mediums and elders cooperate well with one another: spirit mediums often recommend that

9 The sickness is induced by the spirit as a punishment. The term *oogliya* derives from Arabic 'awliya, the plural form of 'saint' or 'guardian'. Many people in the area also use the term *ayyaana*. Both terms refer to spirits that speak to people and give them advice through the mouths of their human mediums, the *qaalluu*.

10 Interview Buzunesh Kormee, Qaallittii,13 October 1999.

11 Words of a spirit medium. Interview Buzunesh Kormee, Qaallittii, 1999.

their followers have their case settled by the local elders; and elders pay tribute to the spiritual authorities of their surroundings.

Shared know-how: Burial associations, NGOs and new/old clan assemblies

New 'intermediate forms' of legal activity between different social and legal institutions also exist. Among them is the 'clan assembly' founded in 1992 by the sub-lineage of Illuu, near the village of Hiddii in Ada'a, which has been given the task of teaching traditional Oromo law, of settling conflicts among the people of the surrounding area, of calling troublemakers to order, and of securing the locality's growth and prosperity. Moreover, it is involved in the collection of money from its members, which is used for blood-fee payments in cases of homicide (Nicolas 2007:486).

The assembly – called in Oromo *walygayii gosaa* (assembly of the clan) – is not just based on old clan and lineage ties, as its name would imply. Rather it has adopted the organizational structure of the *iddir*, a form of burial association commonly found in the area among both Oromo and Amhara.[12] At the same time, the assembly pursues a policy of monetary investment that closely resembles the activities of local NGOs. A special sub-committee of the assembly is responsible for buying and selling grain at the local markets in order to make profit from the transaction. In the case of the *walygayii gosaa*, legal activity is thus closely tied to capital-raising entrepreneurship.

Legal governance and state administrative units

State law claims precedence over all these forms of legal aggregates and procedures. Today's state law, referred to in Oromo as *seera mootummaa* and in Amharic as *hegg*, was mainly designed on a Western model. It was finally enacted by the last Ethiopian emperor in 1957, following a juridical reform of the first Ethiopian penal code, which had already officially replaced the 'law of the kings' (the *fetha nagast*) in 1930.[13] The penal code of 1957 largely remains in force today; it deals, among other things, with theft, beating and injury, abduction, robbery and killing, and gives as punishment – depending on the gravity of the offence – a fine, arrest, or 'rigorous' incarceration up to life-long imprisonment. In severe cases, the death penalty can also be applied. In cases of assault, beating and injury, the law further provides for compensation to the victim's side.[14]

---

12 The institution actually might be of Soddo 'Gurage' origin, having spread from urban contexts to the countryside (Pankhurst 2002:6, 8).

13 See Ibrahim (1990:29) and Aberra (2000:195).

14 For these regulations, see the Penal Code of 1957, of the Empire of Ethiopia.

Peasant associations

On the village level, state law is represented mainly by local militias and the work of village administrators. Peasants associations (PA) have administered the land since the time of the socialist land reform of 1975. Although, following the overthrow of the socialist government in 1991, profound changes have been made at the level of local politics, every peasant who wants to plough land still has to be a member of a peasant association and is subject to its local jurisdiction.

Within the wider administrative setting, all districts are subdivided into smaller administrative units called *ganda* (the Oromo equivalent to Amharic *kebele*), consisting of between one and three villages or settlement concentrations situated near each other. This administrative division is basically congruent with the division of the land into peasant associations (*waldaa qottoota*)[15] and, in fact, the village administration (*bulchiinsa gandaa*) and the peasant association's leadership are mostly one and the same body (Nicolas 2011:50, 291). The village administration consists of a chairman, a secretary, an overseer and four more members, all of whom receive no salary and must fulfil their duties in addition to their usual work. The whole village administration usually only comes together if there is a particular problem or need to address. Otherwise, it is considered enough if the secretary and two members meet once a week. As for the militia, a specified number of men keep a weapon at their homes and only gather if they are called together.

The leadership of a village can at any time call together the PA assembly to announce or discuss issues of concern. However, it is at the monthly meetings of the burial associations (*iddir*) where one can actually find most household-heads gathered. Each village has at least one or two *iddir*, and every household-head is a member of one. *Iddir* meetings are therefore where most issues of concern in the village are discussed, and are the most important platform for public life in the village.[16] The monthly *iddir* meetings may also deal with problems and conflict; otherwise, these cases are dealt with by a village tribunal.

The village tribunal

The village committee (*koree*) responsible for settling disputes consists of three people: a chairman, a secretary and a further member without specific designation. They work closely together with the leadership of the local peasant association, and

15 Also: *waldaa qoteebulaa*. Amh. ye-gabarewoch mahber, or in short form, gabare mahber.

16 Other forms of voluntary associations are the Church *mahber*, the local saving associations known as *eqqub*, as well as temporary working groups called *daboo*, in which people rotationally work in each other's fields.

actually constitute part of the PA's administration, having been elected though the same voting procedure. Accordingly, the PA and *koree* cooperate closely. If someone wants to make a complaint about wrongdoing, they must initially contact the committee of the community administration, which will try to solve the case. If unsuccessful, the community administration will refer the case to the village tribunal (*firdi shango*),[17] which is entitled to judge cases of petty theft and beatings – except those involving serious injury – and can impose fines or detention for up to a month, to be served in the prison of the nearest town.

The members of the tribunal are not full-time bureaucrats, and are usually fully integrated into 'ordinary' village life as well as in the procedures of elders' mediation. The institution they run nevertheless differs significantly in certain respects from other elders' proceedings. Unlike in the typical mediation procedure, where the offender – who regrets his wrongdoing – sends his elders to apologize, in a village tribunal, the victim initiates the juridical process by accusing his offender before the administration. The judicial process is thus not primarily aimed at reconciliation, but at identifying the culprit and punishing him.

The tribunal members draw their judicial knowledge from law workshops that are held by government officials at irregular intervals in the nearby towns. Sometimes, they are able to obtain typed documents that list the rules and procedures they are expected to follow. Consequently, the tribunal members are considered to be representatives of the state law in their local communities. In many respects, however, they are tied to the 'local way' of elders' mediation, and may consider a case solved if the culprit can prove that elders have already settled his case. Sometimes, tribunal members themselves act as 'traditional' elders. They thus work at the interface of state law and 'customary' procedure.

Town courts and police

Cases that surpass the level of petty crime cannot be dealt with by the village tribunals and are left to the state court (*mana murtii*) in town. In such cases, the victim will go directly to the police and accuse the offender. If he can produce three witnesses to prove that his accusation is true, the police and local militia search for the culprit, arrest him and bring him before a court. While the District Court (which for the district of Ada'a Liiban is found in Bishooftuu, also called Debre Zeyt) sees cases of significant theft, bride abduction, assault and beating, aggravated cases in the same categories, as well as cases of robbery and homicide, exceed its competence and are dealt with by the High Court in Adaama (also called Nazret).

17 It is also called *shanacha*.

Moving between different legal institutions

Many cases move between different legal institutions. An Oromo elder, who himself later became a village administrator, gave me the following example of such institutional cooperation:

> A man in a village in Ada'a was stolen some property. He had a suspicion who had done it, and it was a person living in the same village. So the man who was stolen something went to the police to press charges against the suspect. The police now came into the village and took the suspect with them to the police station in town and interrogated him. The man that was stolen from now went to court. When the thief heard about it, he got scared. He sent six elders to the compound of the victim, himself remaining behind. The elders sat in front of the victim's yard-gate, waiting for the victim to come out. The victim finally came out and agreed to discuss the case with them. They agreed that they would settle the case in mutual conciliation. The worth of the property, which the thief meanwhile had sold, was discussed. The elders of the offender rather quickly agreed to the victim's demands, as they were glad that he was ready to come to an agreement. It was consented that the thief would have to reimburse the worth of the loss, without any penalizing fee being added. Somewhat later, another meeting was arranged. This time, the elders came together with the thief. As at the first time, they all remained outside the yard-gate. The victim went out to them. The money was handed over to him, and all six elders, as well as the victim and the thief, signed a paper. On the paper it was written that the offender admitted to the wrongdoing, but that the case had been settled amicably. Also the sum that had been repaid was noted on the paper. The paper was afterwards presented to the police. The police read it and then closed the case. Therewith, the case was settled.[18]

Such transfers of cases between institutions occur not only between state courts and elders, but also between elders and other institutions, such as spirit cults. A young woman, for instance, told me what happened after her husband had beaten her after drinking and quarrelling. The woman's father did not live in the village and was also unsupportive of his former family, since he had divorced her mother, so the woman went back to her grandparents' home, where she had grown up, to search for shelter and protection. Her grandfather, an Amhara, was a respected elder in the village and had settled cases of conflict on many occasions. The woman's husband, an Oromo, sent two elders to try to convince the old man to begin reconciliation. The woman provided me with a memory account of the exchange, reproducing the elders' speech in the way that she remembered it:

---

18 Interview Siyyum Ketema, with Felleke Siyyum, Qaallittii, 6 November 1999.

> Both elders were Oromo but spoke Amharic on the occasion.[19] They were neighbours from the surroundings, and my grandfather came to the yard-gate to greet them: 'Peace be with you! How are you? Come in, come in', inviting them into the house. They then discussed the case.
> Grandfather: What is your problem? Why did you come?
> Elder: So-and-so [name of the husband] sent us.
> Grandfather: What did he say?
> Elder: So-and-so [name of the wife] shall return home [to her husband].
> Grandfather: She has a problem there.
> Elder: Well, wait, when she has a problem, then just call us [and we will intervene]!
> Other elder (addressing the woman): What is your problem?
> Woman: My problem is, why does he drink? Every evening he drinks in my house. He gets drunk [and is behaving badly].[20]

The woman also complained that her husband's father did not support the young couple when they got into financial problems. The husband's elders showed their understanding but tried to convince the grandfather to send the woman back home to her husband. The grandfather, however, left the decision to her:

> Grandfather: She does as she wants to. I don't know [what is the right thing to do].
> Elder: What is it? Please! She shall return home, please! We will also strongly advise [the husband to behave correctly]!
> Woman: My problem shall not be solved by elders. I want a solution by the *ayyaana* (spirit).
> Elder: What can we do about it?
> The elders now returned to the house of my husband, to bring him the news.
> Husband's father: What problem is there? What was the problem when you asked the old man?
> Elder: He [the grandfather] said, she [the wife] can do as she likes. But when we asked her, she had many problems. She said, 'I don't want the elders. The *ayyaana* (spirit) is better for us, truth will come from there for me.'Husband's mother: Her [the wife] and her grandmother will come to the temple of the spirit. She comes to the *ayyaana* (spirit), so we will do the same. We agree.
> Husband: We will reconcile through the spirit. I will go with my mother, and she will go with her mother.

19 They did so because Amharic was the mother tongue of the woman's grandfather.
20 Interview Seble Getaneh, Qaallittii, 11 October 1999.

> Woman: At the temple of the spirit, after coffee had been made, the *ayyaana* (spirit) approached [and gave advice]. The reconciliation took place. Afterwards, they accompanied me home [to my husband]. Now, everything is fine.[21]

The woman seemed pleased with the outcome of the reconciliation. Her strategy to involve the spirit worked in her favour. In fact, her decision to appeal to the spirit was not a spur of the moment one; she had planned it beforehand. The spirit medium whose spirit was invoked during the reconciliation recalled how the wife had contacted the temple some time before the elders gathered to attempt mediation:

> When the couple quarrelled, first the wife came here [to the temple]. She came alone. She cried and told me everything. On another day, the husband came here and told everything as he had seen it.[22] He also was alone. Then they both came to a *wadaaja* (ritual session for the spirit at the temple). The *oogliya* (spirit) spoke, and they both did reconcile.[23]

Thereafter, the wife was reassured by the belief that she would be guarded and revenged by a higher spiritual force if her husband should mistreat her again. What is interesting is that the case was put in the hands of the elders but they left it to be solved by another institution: the spirit and its medium at the temple. The transfer of the case, in fact, was a more powerful option for the wife than relying on the mediation of the elders.

Transfers of conjugal disputes not only occur between elders and spirit mediums, but also between state courts and the elders. An Amhara elder provided me with the following example of the divorce of a couple from a local village:

> A farmer and his wife were quarrelling. She loved another man, who was employed in the household. They both left the farmstead and started living together in a rented house in the nearby town. At that time the woman brought charges against her husband at the police station in town. She had asked her husband to divorce and share their joint property, but he had refused: 'Because you [his wife] left me with my employee!' The police sent a summons (*matriya*) to the husband, and he immediately accused his wife of leaving the house with his employee. The police asked whether he had a witness (*misikkir*) for that. He brought three witnesses for his side to the court.
>
> On the day of the court hearing, the wife did not come. The judge heard the three witnesses, who affirmed that they had seen her leaving with her lover for town.

---

21 *Ibid.*

22 The spirit medium had sent for him to come to her temple.

23 Interview Buzunesh Kormee, Qaallittii, 13 October 1999.

At a second hearing at court, the wife attended. The judge asked her: 'You have committed a wrong, is it true?' At first, she did not admit to it, saying it was not true. But the judge told her that they had heard three witnesses stating the opposite. A third court meeting was set. Both husband and wife were present that day. The court decided that the wife had to pay 800 Ethiopian Birr to her husband for leaving her home with a lover.[24] Then the court decided to give the case into the hands of the village elders. The court representatives said, 'It is above us', and entrusted the sharing of the couple's property to the elders. They said to the couple, 'You [each] have to select your own elders.' Both had to sign a paper wherein they promised that they would accept all that their elders decided on their behalf.

Both wife and husband now each chose two elders from the village to be their representatives, opting for people who knew them well and who might possibly speak in their favour. A week after the court proceedings (which had stretched over several months) the elders met at the house of the husband. Two people sent from court also attended the meeting. They did not interfere in the elders' work but oversaw their doings, and presented them with a paper carrying the signatures of both husband and wife stating that they truly wanted to divorce. The elders counted the cattle, the crops, the farmland and any other property, like cow dung and the like, and estimated the value of the house. While as a rule, property should be shared equally after a divorce, because of the wife's 'wrongdoing', her husband was given two thirds of the share, and she was given only one third. From that sum, the 800 Ethiopian Birr that the court had set as a fine were further subtracted. Finally, the woman got one oxen, 'half of the house', which amounted to 600 Birr (after the 800 had been subtracted),[25] and some farmland that she could rent out for lease (*kontrat*), along with 64 eucalyptus trees, which were growing on the land that remained with her husband. The woman took the oxen and the other property on the very same day but left the eucalyptus trees standing. The elders had made a mark on the trees, and she was told that if she would later come to catch them, and the husband refused, the elders would help her take her share.

The whole meeting had taken some five hours, and afterwards the elders and court attendants got invited for food and drink to the house of the husband's father, and later on the same day to the home of the wife's sister to ceremonially confirm the legal act. However, no blessing was given by the elders at the end, as

24 Ca. 28 USD at that time.

25 About 21 USD.

> is usual during legal affirmation acts overseen by the elders. A divorce was not considered a lucky occasion.[26]

A question arises: whether state court decisions are always the better option for women who aim to contest male prerogatives in decision-making, since judges may also adhere, to a considerable degree, to similar moral values and grounds for decisions as many village elders.

Legal compatibility, overlapping, tensions

Although the functionaries of state courts and elders may share moral ground, there are some significant differences between state court and elders' procedures. As western-designed criminal law, the Ethiopian Penal Code and its accompanying procedures do not officially acknowledge agreements made by elders that would result in a relinquishment of criminal persecution. This offers a potential way out for people who hope to escape the elders' mediation or want to shape the outcome of the process in their favour. Indeed, appealing to the courts is one of the most effective means of 'pulling the rug' from under the petitioning side's 'feet': the case is taken out of the hands of locals and the threat of state-punishment becomes immediate for the offender. The question is whether consecutive appeals to different legal institutions indeed constitutes – as an example of 'forum-shopping' – a problem to the efficacy and legitimacy of the legal process, or whether the cross-cutting of institutional settings could also be seen, from the point of view of users, as a legitimate choice. For women, the possibility of appealing to court in addition to elders or spirit courts can significantly enhance their standing in negotiations, even if they actually wish to have the case solved through local mediation.

Documents for legal transfer and transmittance

Written documents play a special role at the interface between mediating elders and legal institutions of the state. An elder outlined for me the procedure in cases of homicide:

> The victim's side beforehand in the discussions use state law as a threat: 'If we don't get the money, we go to the police station and accuse the killer.' After an agreement has been reached during the peace negotiations and an appointment been set for the killer's family to raise and hand over the blood-money, the elders of the victim's side sign a paper for safeguarding the killer's side. If he [the closest relative of the victim] goes to the police station before the appointment day,

26 Interview Getaneh Wolde-Maryam, with Felleke Zewde, Qaallittii, November 1999.

> he can be punished by up to 1000 Ethiopian Birr to be paid to the government administration, and by up to 500 Ethiopian Birr to be given to the elders.[27]

Such papers are meant as a safeguard for the offender's side. There is legal insecurity in the time between when the terms of peace making and amount to be paid are agreed and when the offender's relatives have raised enough money to actually pay the required sum. On the handover day, another document is written that states that the parties have reconciled and records the amount of blood-money paid. Both the victim's and the offender's parties sign the document. A delegation of elders from the killer's side then goes to town and presents the signed document at the police station. Even though this is not an officially recognised document, it can still be enough to secure the case's dismissal, as the elder elaborated:

> First, the killer disappears from the area. His father promises to the police: 'I will bring you my child. Give me two months for finding him.' He may also name a guarantor (*was*) who will take responsibility for bringing in the son. The police does wait for it. In the meantime, the father uses the time to initiate a *gumaa* (blood-fee payment/reconciliation) process. When the *gumaa* process has started and the police come to ask, the father tells them: 'We are on the way of the *gumaa* process.' Before the deadline for the compensation payment, both sides and their elders sign a paper that states that they are on their way to making peace. If they are asked in the meantime, they can show it. On the appointment day [when the money is handed over], they get another paper, with statements of both sides that peace has been made. If the police now asks the father, he shows them the paper. The police then put a copy of this paper in the police station and drop the case. According to law, the killer would have to appear at court. But if he has killed unknowingly, he will have to pay only a smaller fee. [28]

It is rare, however, for people who committed homicide to easily evade a prison sentence. Certainly, if an offender succeeds in hiding from the police for long enough that compensation has been paid to the family of the deceased, his prosecution will most probably be silently dropped. However, a killer who has already been apprehended and sentenced to jail is rarely released from prison after the two families reconcile. A case of homicide cannot be as easily overlooked by the administration as, for instance, cases of bride abduction, which are often dismissed on grounds that the families have already reconciled. However, a killer can hope to have his sentence mitigated at court, his efforts for reconciliation having proved his serious regret, or to get amnesty before the end of his prison sentence, in consideration of his good conduct and if the community elders vouch for him.

27 Interview Alemu Wube, with Felleke Zewde, 24 October 1999, in Qaallittii.

28 Interview Alemu Wube, with Felleke Zewde, Qaallittii, 24 October 1999.

A question arises with regard to 'double punishment' in cases where both state courts and elders give a verdict, for example, in cases of homicide. From the point of view of mediating elders, the payment of a blood-fee may be intended not as a punishment but as compensation for the loss of the bereaved family. While state courts work on punishing trespassers, elders aim to re-integrate perpetrators and reconcile their families. The question is then, whose procedures could be considered redundant and be dispensed with – the state's or the elders'?

Separate bodies, combined strengths: Emergent joint procedures

Elders, *gadaa* representatives, priests and spirit mediums agree on the value of reconciliation. This can lead to the building of mutual alliances and the emergence of joint procedures in conflict settlement. The following account of the settlement of a homicide case, given by the elder mentioned above, who participated, illustrates the point:

> It was in the early morning, in the dark. The victim was on his way somewhere. The killer had had a quarrel with another man, and wanted to kill him. So he laid in wait, with a gun, and when he saw the victim approaching, he thought it was his opponent, and shot. The victim was dead immediately.
>
> The killer went into hiding. The family of the deceased called the police, who came from the nearby town of Debre Zeyt. The very same day, family members and police brought the body to Menelik Hospital in Addis Ababa to be examined. Later that day, the family of the deceased returned to the village. The killer, meanwhile, having become aware that he shot the wrong person, told his family what had happened. They immediately took action and urgently sent messengers to near and distant relatives in other settlements to warn them and to quickly start the reconciliation efforts. The killer's relatives contacted elders, and these elders contacted other elders, and so forth, to organize most urgent precautions to prevent further violence. A whole chain of uproar took place, word of the killing making the rounds among neighbours and in the surrounding villages.
>
> Two or three days later, more than a hundred elders from five surrounding villages gathered in the morning on a plateau at the riverside, at some distance from the dwelling of the bereaved family. They gathered for an *isgoota*, a ritual apology and call for peace. All the children of the killer went with the pleading elders, as did the killer's father, mother and whole family (the killer himself had to remain in hiding). The people stood in line and shouted '*isgoo*' and '*abet*' for long, their voices being carried far through the landscape, so that they could be heard by the family of the victim. In the first line, along with the most respected elders of the area, there stood two Orthodox priests, who had come from a nearby

> church. They wore their full festive clothes and attire, and carried a cross. Each of them was accompanied by a deacon who held a brocade umbrella for them. The elders, furthermore, had brought a saddled horse with them that had no rider. They had also invited a respected elder from a neighbouring village, who was a bearer of *kallachaa caaccuu* (ritual object[s] of special power).[29] He had brought the holy item(s), covered under a cloth, with him, and stood somewhat apart. The gathered elders and family members called *isgoo* and *abet* for quite a while, standing on the plateau, and waited for a response from the victim's side that might show willingness for peace. But no one showed up. After a while, people gave up and went home.
>
> Two days later, they all gathered again on the plateau, carrying out precisely the same procedure. Again, there were the priests in their outfits, the horse and over a hundred elders shouting *isgoo* and *abet*. Again, no messenger showed up. Some days later, they made a third attempt. This time, an elder sent by the victim's side approached, and asked what they wanted. The killer's father and elders said that the victim was killed by mistake, and they wanted to reconcile. The messenger returned to the victim's family to bring them the message.[30]

The example above illustrates part of a standard procedure applied in most mediations over homicide cases all over the wider region. Oromo Orthodox Christians now mostly understand the involvement of Orthodox priests in the mediation procedures to be part of their own cultural repertoire. The way in which the *isgoo* pleading is undertaken is close to Christian Orthodox pleas to God in times of disaster. At the same time, the saddled horse, the elder carrying the *kallacha* object and other parts of the procedure hint at an Oromo background. Here, mediation is practised as a meta-procedure whose details are adjusted according to the need for a joint venture among the elders of the land. The different authorities involved in a case all keep their distinct identities: priests remain religious representatives of the Church, and *caffee taa'icha* remain titleholders loyal to the laws of the *gadaa*. Yet, for the purposes of peace-making, they all partake in the same legal process and comply with the same rules. For the elders, who invite them to join, both priests and *caffee taa'icha* are helpful allies, whose presence might convince reluctant parties to submit to reconciliation. This implies that we need to change our perspective when

29 The *kallacha* is a metal object said to have fallen from the sky in ancient times, while the *caaccuu* is a leather strip embroidered with cowry shells. At the occasion of *isgoota*, the ritual objects imply the threat of divine sanction if the plea for reconciliation is rejected by the petitioned side. Both objects are usually brought at the same time for reconciliation purposes, and the two terms are often blended together into a single term: *kallachaa caaccuu* (Nicolas 2011:196–199; see also Shewa 2011:57–58).

30 Interview Alemu Wube, with Felleke Zewde, Qaallittii, 24 October 1999.

analysing legal procedures, and move away from emphasizing the separateness and autonomy of the different institutions towards analysing a common procedure.

In the above case, both the victim and his killer were Oromo. The proceedings were mainly organized by Oromo elders. Amhara elders also participated in the *isgoota* pleading, as well as in the following meetings. An Amhara man who had attended the meetings as an elder on the offender's side, and who had twice before participated in Oromo homicide proceedings, gave me the following account:

> A meeting was arranged somewhat later at another place, under a tree, between elders and family representatives of both sides. The father of the victim insisted that his son was killed knowingly, while the killer's side emphasized that it all was just a terrible mistake, and the killer had killed him unknowingly. The victim's side also found the money offered to them as compensation too little. People discussed over three hours without coming to an agreement, so they left for the day and made another appointment.
>
> A week later, they met under the same tree. Altogether, there were now sixteen people attending, elders of both sides and the two fathers of victim and killer. The killer's side had brought one more special attendee, who sat the top of the elders of both sides and advised them in finding a solution. He said, 'The child was killed unknowingly!' and urged the victim's side to yield to the reconciliation. In the end, all the elders decided together that the blood-money would be fixed at a sum of 9000 Ethiopian Birr,[31] a smaller part of which would constitute the 'money for the soul' proper, and the larger part would compensate the victim's family for their expenses for the hospital, for police, and transport etc. The killer's family would pay the money to the family of the bereaved, and no further punishment should be set.
>
> Two weeks later, the money was handed over to the victim's family. A ritual reconciliation took place, which was attended by both families, including the killer, and the witnessing elders.[32]

According to my informant, the police did not then prosecute the killer. No priest was present during the negotiations at the meetings described above. In other cases, the elder told me, priests may be present at the negotiations. They, however, would usually not attend the same meetings as other traditional authorities, such as the guest who decided the amount of the blood-fee in the above account. The elder referred to the man counselling the other elders as a *qaalluu*, i.e. as a spirit medium. It is not unlikely, however, that the advisor in fact was a *caffee taa'icha*, i.e., an Oromo judge. The *caffee taa'icha*, who I later met and who the Oromo elders regularly used to invite to give judgement in homicide cases in the area, usually

31 About 320 USD at that time.

32 *Ibid.*

wore a headscarf and an earring and held a whip in his hand on such occasions. All these were symbols of his membership in the *yuba* grade, and of his authority within the *gadaa* organization. This symbolism, however, was not widely known to non-initiates, and so he could have easily been taken for a spirit medium by observers unfamiliar with his background. If this interpretation is right, it also raises the question of how well different participants in a process actually need to be informed about each other's institutional backgrounds in order to partake in a common legal procedure.

Conclusion

The relation between elders, state, Church, and other institutions is altogether ambivalent. On the one hand, there exist close correlations, connections and mutually supportive arrangements, ranging from silent agreements to regular 'referrals' of clients to each other's jurisdictions. The institution of elders' mediation often benefits from the presence of government institutions, since the threat of persecution by the law regularly leads culprits to admit their guilt and to seek reconciliation with the offended party. On the other hand, there are significant differences, both in substance and procedure, among the different institutions' laws and ways, as well as some competition for supremacy between them.

However, provided here is also evidence of standardized cooperative procedures emerging between different institutions; for example, in cases of homicide. Here, representatives of different institutions, such as Amhara priests and Oromo legal experts, may jointly participate in common legal procedures. These undertakings represent a sort of 'meta-procedure', where the cross-cutting of different institutions is not an exception but the standard. From a 'procedural perspective', different legal institutions thus become elements of one and the same legal procedure, and their joint involvement can no longer be seen as a 'switching' or 'transfer' between different legal bodies.

The question is, whether differences in the institutional backgrounds and questions of belonging of judges, priests, administrators and elders are the sole and only points for analysing legal processes on the ground. Changing the perspective from the 'institutional perspective' to the point of view of actors, and focussing on the procedural aims they might jointly pursue, another picture emerges. From that perspective, the non-linear course of cases, their 'march through the institutions', or their conglomerate appearance when looking at the varied institutional backgrounds of participants in the procedure, appear to follow a distinctive logic. They happen to be systematic markers of legal diversity, yet they do not prevent processes of standardization. The methodological implications of such a change of perspective for a theory of legal pluralism still need to be further explored.

References

ABAS Haji, 1982 *The history of Arssi (1880–1935)*. Addis Ababa: Addis Ababa University (BA Thesis)

ABDURAHMAN Kabeto, 1991 *Allo Arssi: The institution of customary laws in the Upper Wabe Shebele region*. Addis Ababa: Addis Ababa University (BA Thesis)

ABERRA Jembere, 2000 *An introduction to the legal history of Ethiopia, 1434–1974*. Münster: Lit

ALEMAYEHU Haile, 2009 *Gada system: The politics of Tulama Oromo*. Finfinne [Addis Ababa]: Oromia Culture and Tourism Bureau

ASFA-WOSSEN Asserate, 1980 *Die Geschichte von Šawā (Äthiopien) 1700–1865, nach dem Tārika nagaśt des Belāttén Gétā Heruy Walda Śellāsé*. Wiesbaden: Steiner

AṢMA Giyorgis, 1987 [1901–13] "Yä-galla Tarik [History of the Galla]", in: Bairu Tafla (ed.) *Aṣma Giyorgis and his work: History of the Gāllā and the kingdom of Šawā*. Wiesbaden: Steiner

BAHREY, 1954 [1593] "History of the Galla", in: Charles F. Beckingham and George W.B. Huntingford (eds.) *Some records of Ethiopia 1593–1646, Being extracts from the history of High Ethiopia or Abassia by Manoel de Almeida, together with Bahrey's History of the Galla*, 111–129. London: Haklyut Society

BASSI, Marco, 1992 "Institutional forgiveness in Borana assemblies", *Sociology Ethnology Bulletin* (Addis Ababa) 1 (2):50–54

BENDA-BECKMANN, Keebet von and Bertram TURNER, 2018 "Legal pluralism, social theory, and the state", *Journal of Legal Pluralism and Unofficial Law* 50 (3):255–274

BLACKHURST, Hector 1978 "Continuity and change in the Shoa Galla Gada system", in: Paul T.W. Baxter and Uri Almagor (eds.): *Age, generation and time: Some features of East African age organisations*, 245–267. London: Hurst

DINSA Lepisa Aba Jobir, 1975 *The Gada system of government and Sera Caffee Oromo*. Addis Ababa: National University of Addis Ababa (Senior Paper in Law)

DONOVAN, Dolores A. and GETACHEW Assefa, 2003 "Homicide in Ethiopia: Human rights, federalism, and legal pluralism", *The American Journal of Comparative Law* 51 (3):505–552

EGE, Svein, 1996 *Class, state and power in Africa: A case study of the kingdom of Shäwa (Ethiopia) about 1840*. Wiesbaden: Harrassowitz

FETHA NAGAST, 1997/98 [n.d.] *Fetha nagast. Nebabunna tergwamewu. Addis Ababa 1990 A. M. ["The law of the kings: Reading and its meaning"*, Addis Ababa 1997/98*]* (in Ge'ez and Amharic)

GRIFFITHS, John, 1986 "What is legal pluralism?", *Journal of Legal Pluralism and Unofficial Law* 1 (24):1–55

HABERLAND, Eike, 1963 *Galla Süd-Äthiopiens. Völker Süd-Äthiopiens. Ergebnisse der Frobenius Expeditionen 1950–52, 1954–56, Teil 2*. Stuttgart: Kohlhammer

HUNTINGFORD, George W.B., 1955 *The Galla of Ethiopia: The kingdoms of Kafa and Janjero*. London: International African Institute

IBRAHIM Idris, 1990 "Capital punishment and blood-money as options of the victim's relatives to requite homicide in the traditional Ethiopian administration of justice", in: Richard Pankhurst, Ahmed Zekaria and Taddese Beyene (eds.) *Proceedings of the first national conference of Ethiopian studies*. Addis Ababa, April 11–12, 1990, 29–37. Addis Ababa: Institute of Ethiopian Studies, Addis Ababa University

KASSA Beyene, 1967 *Blood-money problems in Ethiopian traditional and modern law*. Addis Ababa: Haile-Sellassie I University (Senior Thesis)

LANGE, Roel de, 1995 "Divergence, fragmentation, and pluralism. Notes on polycentricity and unity in law", in: Hanne Petersen and Henrik Zahle (eds.) *Legal polycentricity: Consequences of pluralism in law*, 103–126. Aldershot/Brookfield: Dartmouth Publishing Company

LARCOM, Shaun, 2013 "Taking customary law seriously: A case of legal re-ordering in Kieta", *Journal of Legal Pluralism and Unofficial Law* 45 (2):190–208

MESSING, Simon D., 1957 *The Highland-Plateau Amhara of Ethiopia*. Philadelphia: University of Pennsylvania, (PhD Thesis, reprinted in Dissertation Abstracts, Ann Arbor, MI 1957 17:12.21)

MOHAMMED Hassen, 1990 *The Oromo of Ethiopia: A history 1570–1860*. Cambridge: Cambridge University Press

NICOLAS, Andrea, 2006 "Governance, ritual and law: Tulama Oromo gadaa assemblies", in: Siegbert Uhlig (ed.) *Proceedings of the XVth international conference of Ethiopian studies, Hamburg July 20–25, 2003*, 168–176. Wiesbaden: Harrassowitz

2007 "Founded in memory of the 'good old times': The clan assembly of Hiddii, in Eastern Shewa, Ethiopia", *Journal of Eastern African Studies* 1 (3):484–497

2010 "Seera", in: Siegbert Uhlig (ed.) *Encyclopaedia Aethiopica* 4, 592. Wiesbaden: Harrassowitz

2011 *From process to procedure: Elders' mediation and formality in central Ethiopia*. Wiesbaden: Harrassowitz

PANKHURST, Alula, 2002 *The role and space for iddirs to participate in the development of Ethiopia*. Addis Ababa: Addis Ababa University (unpublished manuscript)

PANKHURST, Alula and GETACHEW Assefa (ed.), 2008 *Grass-roots justice in Ethiopia: The Contribution of customary dispute resolution*. Addis Ababa: French Centre of Ethiopian Studies

IMPERIAL GOVERNMENT OF ETHIOPIA, 1957 *Penal Code of the Empire of Ethiopia of 1957. Proclamation No. 158 of 1957*, Gazette Extraordinary, No. 1, 23rd July 1957. Addis Ababa: The Imperial Government of Ethiopia

REMINICK, Ronald A., 1973 *The Manze Amhara of Ethiopia: a study of authority, masculinity and sociality*. Chicago: University of Chicago (PhD Thesis)

SHEWA Tafa, 2011 *The pragmatic analysis of arbitration among relatives of murderer and murdered: With reference to gumaa tradition.* Addis Ababa: Addis Ababa University (MA Thesis)

SNYDER, Francis G., 1981 "Colonialism and legal form: The creation of 'customary law' in Senegal", *Journal of Legal Pluralism and Unofficial Law* 13 (19):49–90

TAMANAHA, Brian Z., 2008 "Understanding legal pluralism: past to present, local to global", *Sydney Law Review* 30 (3):375–411

IV.

Incompatibilities and conflict

14. When parallel justice systems lack mutual recognition

Negative impacts on the resolution of criminal cases among the Borana Oromo

Aberra Degefa

Introduction

In Ethiopia, the formal criminal justice system holds exclusive control over all criminal disputes. While civil and family cases can be handled in the legal forum of the conflicting parties' choice, the system bars customary justice systems from handling criminal matters, although in practice, they continue to be widely used for all kinds of cases in several parts of rural Ethiopia (Pankhurst and Getachew 2008). However, the lack of formal recognition for customary systems in the area of criminal justice is creating problems for justice seekers, perpetrators and legal practitioners. While there are numerous studies on customary conflict resolution in Ethiopia (see for example Dejene 2007, Donovan and Getachew 2003, Pankhurst and Getachew 2008, Gebre *et al.* 2012), not much has been written on the normative and institutional relationship between customary and state law in the settlement of criminal disputes. As this paper will argue, the two systems lack mutual recognition.

Among the Borana Oromo of southern Ethiopia, both customary and state law coexist side by side and assert their authorities. Their coexistence has undesirable effects for their users; for example, by subjecting offenders to sanctions imposed by both systems for the same crime. This paper explores the nature of the relationship between the state and customary legal systems with particular emphasis on the handling of criminal matters. It attempts to show the impacts of their coexistence on the Borana people, and to propose possible ways to improve the situation. By revealing the nature of the problematic relationship between the formal and the customary criminal justice systems in Borana, it will contribute to the growing literature on legal pluralism in Ethiopia, and hopefully serve to inform the Ethiopian government as it endeavours to reform the criminal justice system. The victims of crime, offenders and the communities who often are subjected to two justice systems may also benefit from the findings of the research.[1]

Over the last years, the idea of engaging with and making productive use of customary justice systems has gained ground globally (Penal Reform International 2000, Wojkowska 2006). Thus, by showing the available but untapped potential of customary law to address the shortcomings of the formal criminal justice system, the research has practical relevance. Of course, all the diverse customary justice systems in Ethiopia and beyond are not equally user-friendly. In view of this, this study mainly focuses on exploring the possible ways of making use of the strengths of the Borana customary justice system.-

Conceptual Framework

Legal Pluralism

The term 'legal pluralism' is used to refer to the co-existence of two or more legal systems within the same geographical space or jurisdiction (Twinning 2010). In almost all parts of the world, legal pluralism is a reality that includes the formal justice system (national law, international law) and informal justice systems (customary law, religious law, and other normative orders).

The relationship between formal and informal justice systems may be harmonious and cooperative, or antagonistic, with divergent effects on the users of the systems. Where the systems compete with or undermine each other, the setting is usually unfavourable to the users, especially if there is a lack of clear guidelines about which system should deal with which criminal cases, as this often results in people being punished twice. But where the two systems operate in a regulated and mutually supportive way, users have no difficulty in knowing when and how to make use of each of the systems (Forsyth 2007, Penal Reform International 2000, Wojkowska 2006).

1 The study is based on extensive and mostly qualitative ethnographic fieldwork undertaken from February 2012 to May 2014. It was conducted in Borana Zone of Oromia National Regional State, where the indigenous justice system is prevalent and in competition with the formal criminal justice system. Data for this paper was mostly collected during interviews and focus group discussions with individuals living in the study area and who were involved in the customary criminal justice processes, or affected by the rivalry between the two. They included prisoners, victims or relatives of victims, clan elders and others familiar with the justice systems like the police, judges and prosecutors. For some of the informants I used pseudo names to protect their identity. Wherever that has been the case I marked it in the text.

Forsyth (2007:70) described seven models of relationships between the non-state and state justice systems:

i) repression of non-state justice system by the state system;
ii) tacit acceptance of the non-state justice system by the state without formal recognition;
iii) active encouragement of the non-state justice system by the state without formal recognition;
iv) limited formal recognition by the state of the exercise of jurisdiction by a non-state justice system;
v) formal recognition of exclusive jurisdiction in a defined area;
vi) formal recognition of the non-state justice system to exercise jurisdiction by the state, which lends its coercive powers;
vii) complete incorporation of the non-state justice system into the state system.

In this continuum of relationships, there are two extremes. At one end, the non-state justice system is outlawed and suppressed; at the other end, the informal justice system is totally integrated into the formal justice system. In between, along the spectrum, there are different models of relationships (Forsyth 2007:69).

Restorative versus retributive justice

The notion of restorative justice is underpinned by a worldview that places much more emphasis on post-crime communal harmony than on the particular criminal act in question. It refers to a process whereby parties with a stake in a specific offence collectively deal with the aftermath of the offence and its implications for the future (Marshall 1999:5). The central tenet of restorative justice is that damage caused to the victim of a crime is healed. It aims to restore the relationship between the victim, the offender and their communities, which has been disrupted by the wrongful act.

Retributive justice defines a crime as an act that violates state rules. The state is a victim against whom the wrongful act is committed. Retributive justice mainly aims to establish guilt and punish the offender. Zehr (1990) described the salient differences between restorative and retributive justice as follows:

Table 1: Crime viewed through retributive and restorative lenses (Zehr 1990 184–185)

Retributive	**Restorative**
Crime defined by violation of rules (i.e. broken rules)	Crime defined by harm to people and relationships (i.e. broken relationships)
Harm defined abstractly	Crime defined concretely
Crime seen as categorically different from other harms	Crime recognized as related to other harms and conflicts
State as victim	People and relationships as victims
State and offender seen as primary parties	Victim and offender seen as primary parties
Victims' needs and rights ignored	Victims' needs and rights central
Interpersonal dimensions irrelevant	Interpersonal dimensions central
Conflictual nature of crime obscured	Conflictual nature of crime recognized
Wounds of offender peripheral	Wounds of offender important
Offence defined in technical, legal terms	Offence defined in systemic terms: moral, social, economic, political

The traditional African view of crime is quite different from that of the western-based formal justice system. The traditional African perspective explains crime not as a violation of a state rule, but as a disruption of the spiritual harmony of the community. It offers a more communal approach in which priority is given to the community rather than the individuals involved in the criminal dispute (Jenkins 2004): crime 'consists in the disturbance of individual or communal equilibrium, and the law seeks to restore the pre-existing balance' (Driberg 1934:231). As it disturbs and harms both individual and social relationships, crime is not a mere act of law breaking. In indigenous and tribal societies, the dominant philosophy is that crime is a problem that causes harm to the society, which requires that members of the society be involved in seeking a solution to the problem (Melton 2004:1).

While Africa is a vast continent of diverse peoples with distinct histories, traditions and justice systems (Malan 1997:8), the restorative aspect of their justice system is an important commonality of many African societies. Particularly in rural areas, many African societies are characterized by strong social ties. As disputes and conflicts are often viewed as concerning the entire community, customary justice systems give more weight to the restoration of social harmony in line with the beliefs, customs and traditions of the local people. In most societies, the customary justice process is not backed up by state coercion and relies on social pressure to secure attendance and compliance with a decision. In line with the principles of restorative justice, the procedures employed are informal and participatory. Decisions are based on compromise rather than strict rules of law, and the disputants and their supporters play a central role in the decision-making process (Penal Reform International 2000:15).

There are, however, a number of constraints to the value of African indigenous justice systems within contemporary society. The lack of predictability and coherency in decision-making is one such constraint. As there are no fixed standards to guide the elders, judgments are based on the decision makers' knowledge and moral values. The flexibility of the rules and procedures of customary justice systems may result in unpredictable and arbitrary decisions (Harper 2011:22, Wojkowska 2006:20).

In Ethiopia, the formal justice system and the various customary justice systems operate side by side, often competing instead of supporting and enriching each other (Macfarlane 2007:501, Tsegaye *et al.* 2008:64). The relationship between the systems is "co-existence and collaboration without mutual recognition (Pankhurst and Getachew 2008:258). Many studies have revealed that informal justice systems have continued to play a significant role in regulating the day-to-day lives of the members of various communities in Ethiopia (Dejene 2002, Pankhurst and Getachew 2008, Gebre *et al.* 2012) as they are 'more influential and affect the lives of more Ethiopians than the formal system, which is remote from the lives of many ordinary people' (Macfarlane 2007:488). The people favour these justice systems, which are more easily accessible, flexible, participatory and relevant to their lives (Pankhurst and Getachew 2008, Tsegaye *et al.* 2008).

The formal criminal justice system

Court structure and judicial process

Although Ethiopia is a multi-ethnic and multicultural society with various indigenous systems, successive rulers have pursued a policy of establishing a uniform, centralized and monist justice system. In the 1950s and 60s, Emperor Haile Selassie I launched a sweeping codification venture, introducing codes that were meant to be applied across the whole country and designed to supplant the various indigenous justice systems (Fisher 1971). With the adoption of the 1957 Penal Code, the Ethiopian State consolidated its monopoly over all criminal matters.

The 1995 FDRE Constitution has given some room to customary justice systems: through Articles 34(5) and 78(5) of the Constitution, disputes relating to personal and family matters can be adjudicated by customary courts based on customary laws. However, when it comes to criminal matters, Ethiopia continues to pursue its earlier centralist policy, in which the state assumed exclusive control over the prosecution and punishment of criminal cases. The 1995 Constitution declared Ethiopia a multicultural federal state with powers constitutionally shared between the federal government and the nine regional states that are members of the federation.

The nine regional states are further sub-divided into sub-regional structures, such as *woredas* (districts) and *kebeles* (the smallest administrative unit). The judiciary maintains a dual system of federal and regional courts. There are three hierarchical tiers of federal court: the Federal Supreme Court, Federal High Court and Federal First Instance Court. Likewise, the regional courts are structured into Regional Supreme Courts, Regional High Courts (also known in the regions as zonal court) and Regional First Instance Courts (*woreda* courts) (Art.78 of the 1995 Constitution). The structure of the regular courts does not extend to the *kebele* level, which is the lowest administrative unit. This means that criminal matters have to be sent to *woreda* courts, which makes the formal criminal justice system inaccessible to the rural population of Ethiopia who reside in remote *kebeles.*[2]

In terms of the criminal justice process, since crime is considered an offence against the state, the parties to a criminal dispute are limited to the public prosecutor and the defendant. Hence, on receiving information from any source about a crime, the police will conduct a criminal investigation (Arts. 22 & 23 of the 1961 Criminal Procedure Code). Based on Article 13 of the Criminal Procedure Code, only offences punishable upon complaint are left to the discretion of the injured party. Article 42 of the Code outlines certain cases where criminal proceedings will not be instituted.[3] The Article does not mention cases where the victim and the offender settle the matter through reconciliation as one of the grounds for not instituting proceedings or withdrawing a case at any point of the proceedings.

In the sentencing process following conviction, the judge takes the maximum and the minimum penalty fixed by the law for the crime as a framework, and then takes aggravating and extenuating circumstances into account. But here again, reconciliation agreements between the victim and the offender made out of court under indigenous justice systems are not mentioned as part of the extenuating circumstances outlined under Article 82 of the Federal Criminal Code.[4] In short,

---

2 Although social courts are found in urban centers, according to my informants, they are ineffective (interview with Borbor Bule, 2012).

3 According to Article 42 of the Ethiopian Criminal Procedure Code, no proceedings shall be instituted where: (a) the public prosecutor is of opinion that there is not sufficient evidence to justify a conviction: or (b) there is no possibility of finding the accused and the case is one which may not be tried in his absence: or (c) the prosecution is barred by limitation or the offence is made the subject of a pardon or amnesty; or (d) the public prosecutor is instructed not to institute proceedings in the public interest by the Minister or by order under his hand. 2) On no other grounds may the public prosecutor refuse to institute proceedings. 3) The public prosecutor shall institute proceedings in cases affecting the Government when so instructed by the Minister.

4 The general extenuating circumstances under which the court shall reduce the penalty are enumerated under Article 82, Sub-Article 1 (a-e) of the Federal Criminal Code. But reconciliation made between an offender and victims is not included.

the diverse customary rules, institutions and procedures seen in Ethiopia have no officially recognized jurisdictional space in the handling of criminal matters.

Before proceeding to the next section, let us look at some of the criminal matters covered by Article 538 of the Ethiopian Federal Criminal Code, which states that whoever causes the death of a human either intentionally or through negligence, no matter what the weapon or means used, commits homicide. Any person, who commits homicide, whether intentionally or negligently, shall be punished by a lawful judicial process and in accordance with decisions rendered thereby. The punishment to be imposed on a person guilty of intentional or negligent homicide shall be determined depending on whether the homicide was aggravated (Art. 539) or simple (Art. 540).

Article 539 of the Federal Criminal Code deals with aggravated homicide, stating that whoever intentionally commits homicide with such premeditation, motive, weapon or means, in such conditions of commission, as to show that he is exceptionally cruel, abominable or dangerous, or as a member of a band organized to carry out homicide or armed robbery, or to further another crime or to conceal a crime already committed, will be punished with rigorous life imprisonment or death. According to Article 540, the sentence for someone who intentionally commits homicide neither in aggravating circumstances nor extenuating circumstances as in Article 541[5] is rigorous imprisonment for between five and twenty years. The Ethiopian Federal Criminal Code also has a provision dealing with homicide by negligence.[6]

The Code also includes specific provisions that are relevant to the cases in this study dealing with bodily injuries. The Criminal Code categorizes bodily injuries into 'grave wilful injury' (Art. 555)[7] and 'common wilful injury' (Art. 556),[8] and anyone who intentionally or by negligence causes bodily injury to another or impairs his health, by whatever means or in any manner, is punishable.

5 Whoever intentionally commits homicide: a) by exceeding the limits of necessity (Art. 75), or of legitimate defence (Art. 78); or b) after gross provocation, under the shock of surprise or under the influence of violent emotion or intense passion made understandable and, in some degree, excusable by the circumstances, is punishable with simple imprisonment not exceeding five years.

6 Whoever negligently causes the death of another is punishable with simple imprisonment from six months to three years or with a fine of between two thousand and four thousand Birr.

7 Whoever commits grave wilful injury as provided under this Article is punishable, according to the circumstances of the case and the gravity of the injury, with rigorous imprisonment not exceeding fifteen years, or with simple imprisonment for not less than one year.

8 According to this article, anyone who commits wilful injury is punishable, according to the circumstances of the case and the gravity of the injury, with rigorous imprisonment not exceeding fifteen years, or with simple imprisonment for not less than one year.

The Borana indigenous justice system
Institutions, norms and dispute processes

The land of the Borana Oromo is an extensive territory straddling the Kenya–Ethiopia border (Leus 1995). In Ethiopia, the Borana Oromo belong to the larger groups of Oromo people with whom they share a common language and basic cultural values. Borana Zone is one of twenty-one administrative zones of the National Regional State of Oromia. While the Borana and Guji Oromo constitute the two major groups in the zone, smaller groups include the Gabra, the Burji and the Garri. The population of Borana Zone is approximately 1 million (CSA 2008). Most of the Borana are followers of the indigenous Oromo religion known as *Waqeffannaa* (Lasange *et al.* 2010).

The Borana land is covered with light vegetation/grass that favours pastoralism more than farming. Water and pasture are the two most important natural resources among the pastoral Borana. The study was undertaken in the semi-arid parts of Borana Zone where the informal justice system is functioning relatively well.

At the highest division in the Borana social system are the two exogamous halves of the society known as Sabo and Gona. These moieties are further subdivided or segmented into *gosa*, often translated as 'clan' (Asmarom 1973:39). The Borana constitute a corporate group, sharing many collective rights and obligations. Among the Borana, a clan is an enduring group that has considerable influence over the lives of individual members. Much of the social privileges, rights, duties, seniority position, and social identity of a person are based on clan membership. The clan is also the most important descent structure for 'disposing of a regular general assembly whose members recognize a common elder, *hayyu*' (Bassi 1994:19). While a person's clan comes to his assistance in times of difficulty, every member is also obliged to fulfil their obligations to the clan, which may include the digging and maintenance of water wells and providing contributions to the needy (Asmarom 1973:38).

The *gadaa* system

The Oromo are distinguished from many other Ethiopian people by their age- and generation system known as *gadaa*. As an indigenous governance system, *gadaa* has its own leaders who conduct political, economic, social, legislative, judicial, military and ritual responsibilities. Many authors have written about the complex *gadaa* system, emphasizing its role in recruiting warriors (Asmarom 2000), keeping the *nagaa boorana* – the ideal of keeping peace among all Borana groups (Dahl 1996:174, Aguilar 1996:191, Bassi 1996:157) – which is believed to be linked to the supernatural.

Other writers have praised the *gadaa* system as an example of egalitarian African democracy (Asmarom 2000).

The Borana *gadaa* system organizes and governs 'the life of every individual in the society from birth to death' (Asmarom 1973:8). At birth, every male becomes a member of a generation class (or set) called *luba*, which is determined by the generation class of his father. Every eight years, these classes climb up the 'gerontocratic ladder' and, as they reach the different age-grades, 'succeed each other every eight years in assuming military, economic, political and ritual responsibilities' (Asmarom 1973:8). The politically most powerful grade is the *gadaa* grade, which every generation set reaches after forty years and retains for eight years. The generation in power elects the *abbaa gadaa*[9] who, with his councillors, comprises the legitimate leadership of the Borana. Members of this leadership group are 'nurtured starting from the third *gadaa* grade to become leaders during the sixth *gadaa* grade when they reach the age of forty' (Ibrahim 2005:18). Women are not elected to participate in the *gadaa* governance system (PCDP 2005:26). Some authors seeking change have criticized the exclusion of women from the forums and processes of the customary justice system (Pankhurst and Getachew 2008:8).

Among the Borana, governing power is vested in the assemblies at various levels, at the apex of which is the *gumii gaayoo* (assembly of the *gaayoo*-public meeting place).[10] As an assembly formed from representatives of the major Borana clans, the *gumii gaayoo* is a pan-Borana assembly, which takes place every eight years at the mid-point of an *abbaa gadaa* period (Shongolo 1994:30). The *gumii gaayoo* has supreme authority over law-making and enforcement. During its sessions, the assembly proclaims new laws, amends old ones, and evaluates the *abbaa gadaa*. As a supreme judicial body, the *gumii* also resolves all disputes that could not be resolved at lower levels. No other Borana authority can reverse decisions made by the *gumii gaayoo* (Asmarom 1973, Bassi 2005, Shongolo 1994).

In addition to the *gumii*, several clan assemblies (*kora gosaa*) operate at clan levels. The clan assemblies meet annually and have the power to make decisions on all matters concerning the clan. They also resolve both criminal and civil disputes concerning clan members. Both *gumii gaayoo* and the clan assemblies have similar procedural rules. Every Borana assembly opens and closes with blessings (Bassi 2005:176).

Since the *gumii* meets only every eight years, the duty of enforcing laws and handling conflicts are left to the executive and the council of elders at each level. Executive power is in the hands of the *adulaa* council, which is composed of six elders – three from each moiety. The *abbaa gadaa* – who is in power for only eight

9 *Abbaa gadaa* (lit.: 'father of *gadaa*') is the head/leader of the *gadaa* governance system.

10 The term *gumii* refers to the assembly while *gaayoo* refers to the place where the assembly meets.

years – presides over the council. The *abbaa gadaa* and his councillors have attendants called *maakkala* (messengers) to enforce decisions. Each clan also elects *jaallabs* (representatives of clan assemblies) to enforce the decisions of the *gadaa* leaders (Homann *et al.* 2004:89).

The Borana clan-based social structure integrates cultural and territorial administrative arrangements that differ from the formal territorial administrative structures of the state. The localities are built into wider territorial units starting with the *olla* (village), the smallest family-based administrative unit comprising of about ten households. Next is the *jaarsa dheeda*, responsible for regulating seasonal access to grazing and water, and the *jaarsa madda*, responsible for grazing and water management at the local level. Finally, comes the *rabba gadda*, which has overall, customary jurisdiction over land, social and cultural issues, including conflict resolution (Muir 2007: n.p).

Aadaa seeraa: The Borana normative system

According to Borbor Bule, a well-known Borana oral historian (*argaa dhageetii*), the embodiment of Borana codes of conduct for social relations, natural resource management, food and dress are referred to as *aadaa seeraa*. The body of customary norms and laws are recognized by every Borana as binding, and they believe that the laws have maintained their well-being.[11] Depending on the context, *aadaa* (custom) has different meanings. In its broader sense, *aadaa* refers to a way of life that can be comprehended and reflected through and by one's daily practices (Bassi 2005:100). The term *seeraa* specifically refers to authoritative rules that serve as the basis for judgments given by the *hayyuu* (elders) in disputes. As Borana laws were made by the *gumii gaayoo* at some time in the past and are regularly restated, the elders can easily recall the laws applicable to a given case.[12] The Borana have specific laws dealing with physical injuries, personal property, theft, fines and punishment, among other things (Asmarom 2000:201).[13]

In general, among the Borana, the totality of the unwritten laws embedded in the *gada* system serves as a tool to determine rightful and wrongful acts and prescribe the measures to be taken when the laws are violated. As the Borana elder Jaatani Dida stated, the Borana consider their laws as the strongest instrument for the safeguarding and maintenance of the *nagaya borana* (peace of the Borana).[14] According to Asmarom (2000:27), 'how deep the sense of order is among the Borana can be gleaned from the fact that homicide – within their society – is virtually

11 Summary of an interview, August 2013.

12 As every single law gets discussed and repeated at *gumii gaayoo*, Borana elders know which laws are still operating and applicable (Asmarom 1973).

13 Interviews made with Borbor Bule and Waaqo Guyyo, two Borana elders, August 2013.

14 Interview, August 2013.

unknown'. Nowadays, although homicide is still rare among the remote pastoral Borana communities, it is on the increase around the towns and among the settled farming communities.

Borana indigenous dispute processes and outcome

The Borana believe in a cosmic order in which human beings live in harmony with one another, all beings, earth, nature and heaven (Gufu 1996). In Borana society, every day greetings constitute a form of preaching peace, and 'a sustained feud between groups or individuals is unacceptable' (Mamo 2008:48). As attested by Bassi, 'revenge, internal war and reciprocal fear do not have an institutional place' in the Borana social system (1994:27). In order to prevent the disruption of social harmony, the Borana resolve their disputes without any delay (Bassi 2005, Dejene 2002, Tena 2007).

The institution of *jaarsummaa* handles all kinds of disputes ranging from simple quarrels to the most serious criminal cases, such as homicide. The term *jaarsa* means 'elders', and *jaarsummaa* refers to the 'process of settling disputes by elders by way of reconciliation or negotiated settlement' (Arebba and Berhanu 2008:169). During *jaarsummaa*, the elders mainly aim to reconcile (*araara*) the parties and repair their severed relationship (Tarekegn and Hannah 2008:12). Since Borana laws do not distinguish between criminal and civil law, the judicial authority of the elders embraces all matters (Leus and Salvadori 2006). As Borbor Bule explained, disputes are resolved by the clan elders at the lowest possible level and only moved to a higher level if things cannot be settled.[15]

The formal dispute settlement process starts with the complainant submitting his case to the local elders. Every Borana believes that the *gaaddisa* ('shade where the elders sit') is a dwelling place of *Waaqa* (God), where only truth is spoken. As Jaatani Dida, a Borana elder, told me, for the Borana, the most detested act is lying (*soba*).[16] Having heard from the complainant, the elders ask the defendant to respond. The elders make sure that both parties have exhausted their submissions by asking them whether there are still things they want to add. Having obtained the required evidence, the elders discuss the facts and finally give their verdict based on the rule relevant to the case. If the defendant initially claims innocence and the evidence produced does not prove his guilt, the elders will declare his innocence. If the evidence proves the guilt of the suspect, the elders will hand out the appropriate sentence. Depending on the level at which the case was first heard, any party

15 Interview, August 2013.

16 Interview, August 2012.

dissatisfied with the decision may appeal to the next appropriate level, for example, the *kora gosaa* (clan assembly).[17]

Among the Borana, the worst sin against *Waaqa* and human beings is the intentional spilling of human blood. If a person kills or spills Borana blood, he makes himself impure (*xuraa'a*), and he will be expelled from the community to which he belongs unless cleansed through a reconciliation ritual (Bassi 1994:27). According to Waaqo Guyyo, a Borana elder, this embedded belief makes intentional killing rare among the Borana.[18] Borbor Bule explained that, if a homicide is committed, the common practice is that the killer will immediately report to his near relatives what has happened and go to a temporary sanctuary within his own clan, often with the clan leader. He will remain at the sanctuary until the victim's relatives are approached and the reconciliation process begins. No Borana clan will shelter anyone who has killed a fellow Borana with a view to hiding them from justice. Every Borana and every clan collaborates in discovering a killer. With the help of elders, the relatives of the offender approach the relatives of the victim asking for reconciliation, after which the elders may proceed to handling the case through Borana customary law.[19]

As I was told during a focus group discussions in Borana (July 2013), killers in Borana rarely deny that they have committed a crime. They usually admit their crime and ask for pardon and purification, so there is little dispute about the facts of the case. In most cases, the elders decide that the killer should pay a fixed number of heads of cattle as compensation (*gumaa*) to the victim's family. *Gumaa* is an indigenous institution that is part of the *gadaa* system used for settling blood feuds between persons, families, groups, clans and communities (Dejene 2007:59). The process of *gumaa* has ritual and material aspects. Paying compensation in the form of a fixed number of heads of cattle takes care of the material aspect of the reconciliation. Ritually, the offender provides a sheep for slaughter (*ijibbaata*), which symbolically washes away the blood of the deceased shed by the offenders' actions, and with this any feud between the parties is removed or avoided. According to my informants, the Borana have less interest in the material aspect of reconciliation and do not insist on receiving the whole amount of compensation since there is a belief that accepting the entire amount may lead to misfortune. According to Borana customary law, when a member of a clan commits a crime, his clan will pay the required compensation collectively. When the killer and the deceased belong to the same clan, there is a tradition of paying less compensation than is normally paid when the deceased and the killer belong to different clans. The Borana give

17 Summary of an FGD with Borana elders, July 2013.

18 Interview with Waaqo Guyyo, July 2013.

19 Interview, August 2013.

more weight to the ritual aspect of reconciliation, seeking a genuine apology from the offender with a view to pardoning him and restoring the disrupted harmony.[20]

In the rare cases where an accused refuses to admit guilt but is proved to have committed a crime, 'he is left in a state of suspension with a terrible sentence hanging over him and even if it is not executed by force, it can have very unpleasant social repercussions' (Bassi 2005:210). The formal way of excluding the recalcitrant from *nagaya borana* is through cursing (*abaarsa*) by the *gumii gaayoo*. The *abaarsa* excludes the recalcitrant offender from receiving blessing and prayers and any social and ritual support from all Borana, and even from exchanging greetings with them. In a pastoral life where everything, including water, is collectively used and administered through the clan system, a person cannot survive alone (Bassi 2005:110).

Criminal responsibility is individualized in the formal criminal justice system but, among the Borana, the principle of collective responsibility operates. Based on this principle, when a wrong is committed, the wrongdoer's clan is collectively held liable and has the responsibility to discipline him. In such a setting, the material costs of repeated wrongdoing by a habitual offender will generally be 'too great a strain on the resource of the clan' (Driberg 1934:239). To avoid such costs, the clan will withdraw the privileges and protection that flow from clan membership if a member repeatedly commits crime.[21]

The impacts of parallel justice systems with no mutual recognition

As mentioned above, both state law and customary law coexist in Borana, and both are applied not only in civil and family cases, which are supported by the Constitution, but also in criminal cases. As a rule, the police take every criminal case except upon complaint crimes[22] to the regular court, regardless of the preferences of the victim, the offender and the concerned community. Disagreement arises when the victim, the offender and the concerned community want their dispute to be settled out of court through customary law and the police insist that it be settled in the regular courts. In cases when the victim wants the case to be settled in the formal court, the community usually does not insist on having it resolved locally. However, since there is always a need for reconciliation under customary law, the offender may still be required to carry out the necessary conciliatory rituals and pay some compensation (*gumaa*) to the victim or their family (Pankhurst and Getachew 2008:30, Bassi 2005:209).

20 Summary of an FGD with Borana elders, July 2013.

21 Summary of an FGD with Borana elders in Gaayoo, August 2012.

22 In an upon complaint crime, the public prosecutor institutes proceedings against the offender at the request of the injured party.

To understand the impacts of the parallel operation of the Borana indigenous justice system and the formal justice system, it is necessary to look at some actual criminal cases. The cases presented here range from serious bodily injury to homicide. They are categorized broadly into cases settled exclusively outside the regular court, which did not lead to incarceration of the wrongdoers, and cases settled by the regular court, which led to conviction and imprisonment.[23] Cases settled by the state court were also handled by local elders arranging reconciliation between the parties in accordance with Borana customary law.

Cases settled outside court

The criminal cases discussed in this section were resolved exclusively through customary law. They include two cases of accidental homicide and one of serious bodily injury. In the case involving serious bodily injury, both the victim and the offender were interviewed. In the accidental homicide cases, one offender and two relatives of the victims were interviewed.

Case 1a: Serious bodily injury
The incident took place in Yabello town in the year 2012 as a result of a fight that broke out between two families. In that fight, Areero Dida was beaten and seriously injured by Kebede's[24] sons. Kebede's family members had originally came from Wollo and are Gurage and Amhara mixed ethnically (interview with Areero and W/o Yeshihune, Kebede's wife, May 2014).
According to Areero, after the beating, the police arrived at the scene and arrested Kebede. Areero's family took the case to court but, immediately after the incident, Kebede's family sent elders to Areero's family with a view to settling the case outside court through *araara* (reconciliation). In the beginning, Areero's family refused to accept the proposal, since the elders had failed to bring certain items needed when asking for forgiveness: *daraara* (tobacco used to signify a flower used for ritual purposes) and a sheep. Negotiations resumed once the elders returned with what was necessary under Borana *aadaa-seeraa*.
According to the victim, Areero, the elders from both sides wanted to know the scale of the injury he had suffered before a fair judgment and reconciliation could be made. Kebede's family took Areero to Hawassa for treatment and took respon-

23 The cases were gathered through interviews and focus group discussions with Borana elders, convicted offenders found in Yabello Zonal Correction Centre and victims of crime or their relatives.

24 Pseudonyms.

sibility for covering all the hospital and transport expenses.[25] After Areero had received medical treatment at Hawassa Hospital, Kebede's family gave his family a sheep (*hoolaa buula*) to slaughter for his recuperation. After the reconciliation, the elders who had participated signed a written confirmation of the reconciliation agreement and sent it to the court (interview with Areero, May 2014).

When asked about the reconciliation and its outcome, Kebede's wife[26] expressed her satisfaction. She stated that the court procedure could have taken a very long time and its outcome could have been much more severe. In her view, by resolving the case through *araara*, her husband not only avoided imprisonment, but a friendship with the victim's family was also established (interview with Yeshihune, May 2014). Although the offenders were ethnically, culturally and religiously different from the victim's family, they clearly emphasized the merits of Borana ways of resolving disputes. The victim was also pleased with the outcome of the reconciliation process. (Interview with Areero, May 2014)

In this case, although the parties to the dispute belonged to different cultural and ethnic groups, they both appreciated the process and outcome of settling their case out of court. Regardless of their ethnic background, the reconciliation process and the restorative outcome worked in favour of both parties: the harmony disrupted by the act of the offender was restored through the reconciliation; and the family of the offender covered all medical and other expenses thus avoiding his imprisonment.

Case 1b: Accidental homicide

This case took place in Areero Woreda of Borana in 2004. The perpetrator was a man called Galmo, who killed a fellow Borana, called Bona, from the Dambitu clan. The families of the two men were very close, so one day Galmo and Bona went out together in search of the wild animal that had killed and devoured three of their cows and escaped into the nearby bush. While in the bush, they spotted the animal and took cover to shoot it. Galmo thought he saw it behind a bush, and took aim and fired. Thereby, he accidentally killed Bona.

Immediately after the incident, the elders from Galmo's clan were sent to Bona's relatives. Bona's family accepted their request for *araara*, and the necessary rituals were performed. Although the offender's side was prepared to pay compensation, Bona's family declined it, as they viewed their son's death as an act of *Waaqa* (God). As such, making the offender responsible would be unjustifiable. In the meantime, the zone's police had heard about what happened and they arrested

25 The distance between Yabello and Hawassa is 298 km. Transport costs for an emergency patient are based on the agreement of the parties involved and the time taken, but are roughly between 750 and 1000 ETB (about 30–40 US Dollars at the time of the research).

26 Kebede's wife, Yeshihune (the mother of the young boys), was interviewed because Kebede was not around.

Galmo. They took him to Nagelle town and kept him under detention for more than sixty days. When the police came to the area to investigate, both families stated that, since God took the life of the deceased, there was no need for further investigation. They asked that Galmo be released, stating that the families had already reconciled. Since the police saw no point in continuing the investigation in the absence of witnesses, they set the offender free.[27] In the offender's view, the outcome of the *araara* process was the restoration of harmony between the two families, which was pleasing to both sides. (Summary of an interview with Galmo, May 2014)

In this particular case, the facts that the killing was purely accidental and the two families are closely related were important elements. The killing of Bona was viewed by his family as an act of God that was not intended by Galmo. With regard to unintentional killing, the Borana believe that making a person responsible for such accidental acts would anger God and result in some kind of disaster. Conversely, the Borana consider the intentional killing or spilling of human blood the most deplorable act, and believe intentional wrongdoing against another human being is a wrong committed against God. In intentionally disrupting harmony between human beings, the wrongdoer disrupts human relations with God (Summary of interview with Jaatani, August 2013).

Case 1c: Accidental homicide

One late evening in 2011, Teklu (who is a Borana), was driving his car at high speed towards Yabello town. Just before reaching the town, Teklu's car hit and killed Dawit (who is a Burji), who was walking back to Yabello. Immediately after the incident, elders from Teklu's side came to the deceased's family to ask for reconciliation (*araara*). Since it is against customary law to refuse *araara*, the elders' request was accepted. The two sides selected elders and formed a council to handle the matter outside the formal court. The offender took responsibility for covering all the expenses of the funeral and installing a gravestone at the burial site, and to cover the costs related to the visitors who arrived during the period of mourning.

When asked about their view of the reconciliation, Dawit's (the victim's) two sons said that *araara* mainly aimed to heal the wound caused by the act of the offender and to restore the harmony that has been disrupted by the offender's act. Because of the reconciliation, Teklu (the offender) was able to continue living with his family and avoid incarceration. Had the case been taken to court, Teklu himself and his family could have faced difficulties. The brothers stated that the reconciliation removed the feeling of insecurity and animosity between the two

27 Interview with a police officer, July 2013.

families. (Summary of an interview with Yonas and Yoseph,[28] sons of Dawit, May 2014)

In this case, the compensation paid by the family of the offender was limited to those expenses required to cover the expenses required for the mourning period and the building of monument on the burial site. The family did not give heads of cattle as *gumaa* as is normally the case.

All three cases discussed here were resolved through reconciliation (*araara*) between the parties involved and relatives from both sides. Where demanded, offenders genuinely apologized and paid compensation to the relatives of the deceased or to the victims for the harm they had caused. In return, they were pardoned, avoided incarceration and were reintegrated into their communities, which allowed them to live in harmony with the victim's relatives. The interviewed victims and/or their relatives acknowledged the importance of reconciliation in avoiding possible revenge and thus future conflict.

Once reconciled, the Borana are usually reluctant to appear and act as witnesses for the police. This is because appearing as a witness before a court of law and testifying against an offender is seen as disrespectful towards the elders who facilitated the reconciliation and as contrary to Borana customary law. Such a person would lose the support of their clan. Therefore, the Borana rarely act as witnesses in court after reconciliation, leaving the police unable to prove the guilt of a suspect and forced to release them.

Cases settled inside and outside the court of law

While the above-mentioned cases dealt with bodily injury and accidental homicide and could be settled exclusively outside the law courts, the following three cases deal with homicides brought before and resolved in the law courts. All the offenders were convicted and imprisoned. In addition, reconciliation rituals were performed and compensation paid in accordance with Borana customary law.

Case 2a: Murder

In the year 1993, a man was killed in a fight between two men. Raji,[29] the brother of the victim, told me that the offender, Malicha, was charged for murder, convicted and sentenced to six years imprisonment by the court. Raji claimed that the killing of his brother, Kutu, had been intentional and therefore Malicha deserved life imprisonment. But, in the eyes of the law, the crime committed by the offender was an ordinary homicide under Article 540 of the Federal Criminal Code.

28 Pseudonyms.

29 Pseudonym.

> The two families also went through reconciliation, with a view to avoiding animosity and revenge. The family of the offender accordingly paid twenty-seven heads of cattle as *gumaa*. (Summary of an interview with Raji, May 2014)

Both the formal justice system and Borana customary justice system were involved in handling this case, and this led to the offender being incarcerated and his family paying compensation. The offender and his family were dissatisfied with this, as among the Borana, the total number of head of cattle to be paid as compensation for a serious crime (*qakee*) such as killing a fellow Borana is thirty (Bassi 2005:109); in accepting twenty-seven heads, the victim's family had not been particularly generous.[30]

> Case 2b: Ordinary homicide
> Xadacha was 56 in 2014 when I interviewed him at Yabello Correction Center. He was from Yabello Woreda Carri *kebele*. He was accused of killing a woman whose name was Lokko B., for which he was convicted and sentenced to eighteen years imprisonment. During the interview, he claimed that he did not know anything about what happened at the time of the incident. There was contention over whether he was mentally well, and he was taken to a mental hospital in Addis Ababa, where he was given some kind of medicine and declared normal. From my own observation, Xadacha had some kind of disorder affecting his speech and acts. Nevertheless, he was found guilty and incarcerated. A letter[31] was written from the offender's *kebele* to Borana Zone High Court stating that reconciliation had been made according to Borana customary law. The letter indicated that approximately Birr 113,000[32] worth of Xadacha's assets, including cattle and goats, had been paid to the deceased's family. The letter was written to the Court with a view to securing the release of the offender, who had eighteen family members to take care of. Xadacha submitted the letter from his *kebele* to the court but the release request was rejected. (Summary of an interview with Xadacha, May 2014)[33]

Although within the range given for ordinary homicide, the eighteen years of imprisonment – just two years short of the maximum sentence – given to Xadacha

30 Although thirty heads of cattle is the normal amount of compensation to which the family of the deceased is entitled in murder cases, they usually receive less than the fixed amount.

31 This official letter Ref/No. W/B/G/C 013/06 dated *Miyaziaya* 16, 2006 Ethiopian Calendar was written by the chairman of Carri Kebele, Yabello Woreda.

32 This will be approximately between 4,500 and 5,000 in USD.

33 Out of the more than twenty prisoners I interviewed, six claimed that reconciliation agreements were made between the families in writing, but when presented to the court to seek release, the requests were rejected (summary of interviews made with prisoners on 29 July 2013 and 12 May 2014).

show that he did not have credible extenuating circumstance to lessen the punishment. Besides, the fact that the letter from the *kebele* did not mention anything about his mental state and records that he was able to pay a large sum of compensation suggests that the community considered Xadacha to be a person of sound mind, able to take full responsibility for his criminal act.

In this case, the offender's claim that he was of an unsound mind was disregarded by both systems. Similarly, the punishments imposed on the offender indicate that both systems considered his crime to be serious. This means that with regard to intentionally committed crime, both systems impose similar sanctions.

> Case 2c: Ordinary homicide
> In 2003 in Dirre Woreda of Borana Zone, two Borana men got into a fight that ended in homicide. Huqa and Galagalo went to a deep well (*eela*) – among the pastoral Borana, water drawn from such deep wells is used for watering animals and drinking and domestic purposes. According to Kashane, Galagalo's wife, there was a disagreement during which Huqa warned Galagalo that he would kill him. On their way home from the well, Huqa waited in a roadside bush and killed Galagalo. Huqa was soon arrested, charged, found guilty of homicide and sentenced to eight years imprisonment because he had admitted his guilt (summary of an interview with Kashane, May 2014).
> While Huqa was in prison, his family sent elders to the family of the deceased to make the necessary reconciliation. Huqa's family paid eighteen[34] heads of cattle to Galagalo's family as *gumaa*. Kashane's view regarding the punishment imposed on the offender by the court was that, since Huqa had killed Galagalo with full intention, he should have been sentenced to life imprisonment (summary of an interview with Kashane, May 2014).
> In this case, the offender was convicted by a court of law for the crime he had committed. But all the same, since restoring the harmony disrupted by the criminal act was necessary, reconciliation between the two families was made and *gumaa* was paid to the family of the deceased. (Summary of an FGD with Borana elders, July 2013)

While the family of the deceased agreed to have the case dealt with in the formal court, they were dissatisfied with the length of imprisonment imposed on the offender. Arguing that that the crime was committed intentionally, they wanted the court to impose a harsher punishment on the offender. On the other hand, the compensation (*gumaa*) Huqa had to pay locally was relatively low, as he and his victim

34 Among the Borana, the number of cattle to be paid as compensation is determined by elders who take into account the nature of crime, for example, the degree of cruelty. When it comes to the number actually received by the family of the deceased, depending on how they view the crime, the number may increase or decrease.

belonged to the same clan. Since the Borana believe the whole clan is responsible for a crime committed by its member, if a killer and the deceased belong to the same clan, the compensation is paid by their clan to the family of the deceased. If the crime was unintentional, compensation may not be received at all, or will be less.[35]

When one looks at the cases in both categories, the impacts of the cases settled outside the courts and those settled both inside and outside the courts are different. In the cases settled exclusively outside the court, the offenders paid only the customarily imposed sanctions and escaped incarceration. In the cases settled both inside and outside the court, the offenders were subject not only to incarceration but also to the compensation payment.

The study participants – prisoners, *gadaa* elders and justice officers – had divergent views on the parallel functioning of the two systems and their outcomes. The prisoners shared a feeling that they were victims of two competing legal systems. They maintained that the payment of *gumaa* in addition to imprisonment was an unjustifiable punishment. As mere addressees of the two normative orders, with no liberty to choose their preferred justice system, they felt powerless. They also expressed that being kept in isolation from their family caused them moral and material damage. Moreover, since compensation was paid by their families and clans, it could be seen as a kind of collective punishment and, in the prisoners' view, the cattle given as *gumaa* could instead have sustained their families while they were imprisoned and unable to take care of them.[36]

Borana elders blamed both the Oromia Regional State and the Federal State for failing to give some degree of recognition to their justice system. They maintained that reconciliation is user-friendlier in its process and outcome, and that, since the offender, the families from both sides and the community take part in resolving disputes, their justice system is participatory. In addition, they claimed that the material aspects of the injury are taken care of by compensation payment and the spiritual aspects needed to restore the harmony disrupted by the offender's wrongful are addressed through the reconciliation ritual. As the ritual of reconciliation requires a genuine apology, the offender is pardoned and continues to live in his community with no need for incarceration. They see their way of sanctioning as more constructive than incarceration, which has immense personal and social costs. The removal and distancing of the offender from his community for a long period of time is viewed as a vindictive measure with little socially constructive value.[37]

35 See case 1b above.

36 Summary of a FGD with offenders, August 2013.

37 Summary of an FGD with elders, August 2012.

When I asked whether the Borana justice system was effective in sanctioning criminals, the elders assertively stated that their system was highly functional, as it has its own mechanisms for punishing or excluding habitual offenders from the usual protection given to law-abiding clan members. They emphasized that all Borana share and value the *nagaya borana*. Since an unruly person disrupts *nagaya borana*, no clan wants to harbour a disruptive person. Therefore, generally every clan sees to it that all its members remain law-abiding in order to avoid compensation payment. To enduringly enjoy all the privileges and support offered by the clan, every member usually respects Borana laws. If a clan member becomes a habitual offender and disruptive, the clan simply withdraws all the privileges and support of clan membership. Nowadays, elders refer cases involving such people to the formal justice system.[38]

Representing the perspective of the justice officers, the President of the Borana Zone Justice Bureau remarked that the relationship between the two systems was not defined and regulated properly. Owing to this, he said, both the formal criminal justice system and Borana customary justice system were settling criminal disputes, including homicide and physical bodily injury, separately on the basis of their respective laws, procedures and institutions. As I was informed by a Justice Bureau officer, some converts to new religions and some individuals living in towns are now going to court when they think that the prosecutor or the police do not have the evidence to prove their guilt.[39] If the prosecutor fails to prove the guilt of the offender, she/he will be acquitted.[40] Such individuals, one justice officer from Borana Zone High Court, said, often try to make use of both systems opportunistically.

When asked when and why, in their opinion, the Borana preferred their own customary justice system, the justice officers stated that reconciliation based on customary law was preferred in all cases of accidentally committed homicide or physical injury. This is mainly because the people are more familiar with the rules, institutions and process, and because the outcome usually satisfies both parties.[41] Mangasha, Taaju and Tosha, three justice officers from Borana Zone High Court, reported that the families of offenders and victims often submit written requests

38 Summary of an FGD with elders, August 2012.

39 Individuals prefer the formal justice system not just because it is perceived as better but simply because the prosecutor may not have sufficient evidence to prove their guilt or the accused can produce false witnesses.

40 As Borbor Bule confirmed in an interview in August 2012. The prisoners also stated that there were some rich individuals who had escaped imprisonment by bribing judges or simply paying compensation (FGD with prisoners, July 2013).

41 Although some of the officers came to Borana from elsewhere, they are familiar with the Borana customary justice system (summary of interview made with justice officers, July 2013).

to the courts, asking that they accept the reconciliation made out of court, discontinue proceedings and release the offenders. In the justice officers' view, where the state law has not given the customary justice system the authority to handle criminal matters, there are no legal grounds for recognizing criminal dispute settlements made under customary laws.[42] The police and the public prosecutors gave the same reason for not accepting the written requests submitted to them with a view to seeking the withdrawal of cases. In short, based on the criminal law of Ethiopia, the officers stated that they had no legal authority to entertain such requests.[43] According to Ethiopian criminal law, a criminal case can only be dropped when there is a lack of evidence.[44] Thus, the only possible escape (if fortunate) from going to court, and the practice usually adopted by the Borana, is to encourage witnesses to refuse to appear or, if they are forced to appear, to withhold the necessary evidence. In such cases, the court will wait for some time before eventually closing the case file.[45] Although, as lawyers, the justice officers contended that their duties were to strictly adhere to the provisions of the law, some acknowledged the user-friendliness of the process and outcomes of Borana customary dispute settlement system, albeit while voicing some concern about its viability.[46]

In some cases the two systems overlap.For example, statements from both the families of victims and Borana elders show that, in cases of intentional homicide, they prefer the offenders to be incarcerated.[47] According to the elders, if those who intentionally kill others are allowed to avoid incarceration by paying *gumaa*, wealthy individuals might be encouraged to commit homicide. Because of this belief, criminals who intentionally commit homicide rarely evade court and escape incarceration, and – as seen above – victims' relatives may even express dissatisfaction with the term of imprisonment imposed by the law.[48]

In general, the cases presented above have shown that the Borana customary justice system recognizes the jurisdiction of the formal criminal justice system over cases of intentional homicide. In such cases, reconciliation between the families based on Borana customary law may help to create harmony. With regard to accidental or unintentional homicide, however, the lack of mutual recognition between

42 Summary of an interview with Taaju, February 2012.

43 Summary of interviews with Tariku, a police officer in July 2013 and with Abdub, a prosecutor in May 2013).

44 Article 42 of the Ethiopian Criminal Procedure Code.

45 Summary of interviews with police officers, Tariku in 2013, Tosha in July 2013 and Taaru, July 2013.

46 Lack of resources and strong enforcement mechanisms were some of the challenges mentioned by the officers.

47 Summary of interview with elders, August 2012.

48 See cases 2a and 2c above.

the two systems is viewed as a problem, particularly where the families of the offenders and the victims settle their cases out of court and the court disregards these settlements. With regard to unintentional homicide and physical injury, the benefits and costs of totally dismissing settlements made out of court have to be properly evaluated.

Summary and conclusion

Since Ethiopia is a society with pluralist normative orders, the Ethiopian justice system should be reflective of this reality. Yet, successive Ethiopian rulers have been reluctant to officially recognize the diverse customary justice systems, and the formal justice system continues to have exclusive control over the handling of criminal matters. However, even more than half a century after the sweeping codification that was meant to do away with normative diversity, the formal justice system still has not displaced Ethiopia's diverse customary justice systems.

The Borana community is one of many communities in Ethiopia whose customary justice system has survived, and the Borana continue to use it alongside the formal justice system, even in criminal matters. Due to its effectiveness in resolving disputes and maintaining peace and harmony, the Borana want their customary justice system to be given some degree of formal recognition and be supported by the Oromia National Regional State. They consider their justice system socially and culturally most appropriate for their distinct social setting and ask that the people's right to choose between the two systems should be extended to criminal cases, such as manslaughter (accidental homicide) and bodily injury.[49]

By giving limited space to the Borana customary justice system, the negative effects that result from the current lack of mutual recognition would be minimized. In addition, a reduction in the number of cases going to the courts and in the number of prisoners would ease the case backlog in the courts of law and reduce pressure on the prisons. What is more, giving some degree of recognition to the Borana customary justice system in cases of unintentional homicide and bodily injury would mean gaining the trust and support of those who want to settle such cases out of court.

Criminal justice reform would allow the Borana to resolve specified criminal disputes with Borana customary law. In order to do that, the leadership from both systems would need to work in partnership to determine the circumstances

49 In the negotiation, they can provide for the possibility of appeal to the regular court, determine the when and how of appeal of the appeal. Even in such cases the parties' freedom to opt for justice system of their own choice has to be respected.

in which the Borana customary justice system handles cases involving accidental homicide or bodily injuries. A defined partnership between both systems could help regulate their relationship and help establish certainty around when decisions made under Borana customary law in cases of unintentional homicide or bodily injuries can be rejected or accepted by the court of law.

Through negotiation, the leadership of both systems could specify how cases can be referred from one system to the other, and determine the nature of the relationship with the police and courts. They could also determine and agree upon the circumstances under which cases in the courts of law might be diverted to the customary justice system. When there is a defined and effectively regulated relationship between the two systems, the courts of law should have no difficulty in determining the particular criminal disputes over which Borana customary law has jurisdiction.

References

AGUILAR, Mario, 1996 “Keeping the peace of the Waso Boorana. Becoming Oromo through religious diversification”, in: Paul T. W. Baxter, Jan Hultin, Alessandro Triulzi (eds.): *Being and becoming Oromo: Historical and anthropological* inquiries, 162–177. Uppsala: Nordiska Afrikainstitutet

AREBBA Abdella and BERHANU Amenew, 2008 “Customary dispute resolution institutions in Oromia Region: The case of *Jaarsa biyyaa*”, in: Alula Pankhurst and Getachew Assefa (eds.): *Grass roots justice in Ethiopia: The contribution of customary dispute resolution*, 169–184. Addis Ababa: French Centre of Ethiopia Studies

ASMAROM Legesse, 1973 *Gada: Three approaches to the study of African society*. London: Free Press

2000 *Oromo democracy: An indigenous African political system*. Asmara: The Red Sea Press

BASSI, Marco, 1994 “Gada as an integrative factor of political organization”, in: David Brokensha (ed.): *A river of blessings: Essays in honour of Paul Baxter*, 15–30. Syracuse: Maxwell School of Citizenship and Public Affairs, Syracuse University

2005 *Decisions in the shade, political and judicial processes among the Oromo-Borana*. Asmara: The Red Sea Press

CENTRAL STATISTICAL AUTHORITY (CSA), 2008 *The 2007 population census of Ethiopia*. Addis Ababa: Central Statistical Authority

DAHL, Gudrun, 1996 “Sources of life”, in: Paul T W. Baxter, Jan Hultin, Alessandro Triulzi (eds.): *Being and becoming Oromo: Historical and anthropological inquiries*, 162–177. Uppsala: Nordiska Afrikainstitutet

DEJENE Gemechu, 2002 Some *aspects of conflict and conflict resolution among the Woliso Oromo of eastern Macha with particular emphasis on Guma.* Addis Ababa: Addis Ababa University (MA Thesis)

2007 *Conflict and conflict resolution among the Woliso Oromo of Eastern Macha: The case of the Guma.* (Social Anthropology Dissertation Series No.15). Addis Ababa: Addis Ababa University

DONOVAN, Dolores A. and GETACHEW Assefa, 2003 "Homicide in Ethiopia: Human rights, federalism, and legal pluralism", *American Journal of Comparative Law* 51 (3):505–552

DRIBERG, Herbert, J., 1934 "The African conception of law", *Journal of Comparative Legislation and International Law*, Third Series 16 (4):230–245

EMPIRE OF ETHIOPIA, 1961 *Criminal Procedure Code of the Empire of Ethiopia,* Proclamation No 185 of 1961. Addis Ababa: Negarit Gazeta

1957 *Penal Code of the Empire of Ethiopia*, Proclamation No 158 of 1957, Addis Ababa: Minister of the Pen (accessible online at https://www.refworld.org/pdfid/49216a0a2.pdf)

FEDERAL DEMOCRATIC REPUBLIC OF ETHIOPIA (FDRE), 2004 *Criminal Code of the Federal Democratic Republic of Ethiopia 2005*, Proclamation No. 414/2004. Addis Ababa: Berhanena Selam (accessible online at https://www.wipo.int/edocs/lexdocs/laws/en/et/et011en.pdf)

1995 Constitution, Proclamation No 1/1995. *Federal Negarit Gazeta* Year 1, No. 1, 21st August 1995. Addis Ababa: Addis Ababa: Federal Negarit Gazeta

FISHER, Stanley, 1971 "Traditional criminal procedure in Ethiopia", *The American Journal of Comparative Law* 19 (4):710–746

FORSYTH, Miranda, 2007 "A typology of relationships between state and non-state justice systems", *Journal of Legal Pluralism and Unofficial Law* 56:67–112

GEBRE Yntiso, FEKADE Azeze and ASSEFA Fiseha (eds.), 2012 *Customary dispute resolution mechanisms in Ethiopia* Vol 2. Addis Ababa: Ethiopian Arbitration and Conciliation Center

GUFU Oba, 1996 "Shifting identities along resource borders: Becoming and continuing to be Boorana Oromo", in: Paul T. W. Baxter, Jan Hultin and Alessandro Triulzi (eds.): *Being and becoming Oromo: Historical and anthropological enquiries*, 117–132. Asmara: Red Sea Press

HARPER, Erica, 2011 *Customary justice: From program design to impact evaluation.* Rome: International Development Law Organization

HOMANN, Sabine, Gemedo DALLE and Barbara RISCHKOWSKY, 2004 *Potentials and constraints of indigenous knowledge for sustainable range and water development in pastoral land use systems of Africa: A case study in the Borana lowlands of Southern Ethiopia*. Eschborn: Gesellschaft für Technische Zusammenarbeit (GTZ)

IBRAHIM Amae, 2005 *HIV/AIDS, gender and reproductive health promotion: The role of traditional Institutions among the Borana Oromo, Southern Ethiopia.* Addis Ababa: Artistic Enterprise

JENKINS, Morris, 2004 "Afro-centric theory and the restorative justice process: A productive response to crime and delinquency in the African American community", *Journal of Social and Social Policy* 3 (2):17–32

LASANGE, R., SEIFU A., M. HOOGLAND, A. DE VRIES, 2010 *Report on general characteristics of the Borana zone, Ethiopia.* Amsterdam: IVM Institute for Environmental Studies

LEUS, Ton, 1995 *Borana Dictionary: A Borana book for the study of language and culture.* Schijindel: Graf. Centrum

LEUS, Ton and Cynthia SALVADORI, 2006 *Aadaa Boorana: A dictionary of Borana culture.* Addis Ababa: Shama Books

MACFARLANE, Julie, 2007 "Working towards restorative justice in Ethiopia: Integrating traditional conflict resolution system with the formal legal system", *Cardozo Journal of Conflict Resolution* 8:487–509

MALAN, Jannie, 1997 *Conflict resolution wisdom from Africa.* Durban: ACCORD

MAMO Hebo, 2008 "The role of elders in conflict resolution: The case of Arsi Oromo with special reference to Dodolla district and its environments", in: Tarekegn Adebo and Hannah Tsadik (eds.) *Making peace in Ethiopia: Five cases of traditional mechanisms for conflict resolution,* 48–77. Addis Ababa: Peace and Development Committee

MARSHALL, Tony, 1999 *Restorative justice: An overview.* London: Home Office Research Development

MELTON, Ada, 2004 'Indigenous justice systems and tribal society' (accessible online at http://aidainc.net/Publications/ij_systems.htm, last accessed 29 April 2011)

MUIR, Ann, 2007 *Customary pastoral institutions today: SOS Sahel and Save the Children,* US Pastoral Livelihood Initiative (accessible online at http://www.fao.org/fileadmin/user_upload/drought/docs/43%20%20Customary%20Pastoral%20Institutions%20Study%20Ann%20Muir.pdf last accessed 3 August 2018

PANKHURST, Alula and GETACHEW Assefa (eds.), 2008 *Grass roots justice in Ethiopia: The contribution of customary dispute resolution. Addis Ababa*: French Centre of Ethiopia Studies

PASTORAL COMMUNITY PROJECT (PCDP), 2005 *Social analysis and indigenous livelihood strategy in Oromia pastoral communities.* Addis Ababa: WIBD Consult

PENAL REFORM INTERNATIONAL, 2000 *Access to justice in sub Saharan Africa: The role of traditional and informal justice systems.* London: Astron Printers (accessible online at www.penalreform.org, last accessed on 28 August 2012)

SHONGOLO, Abdullahi, 1994 "The Gumi Gaayyo assembly of the Boran: A traditional legislative organ and its relationship to the Ethiopian State and a modernizing world", *Zeitschrift für Ethnologie* 119:27–58

TAREKEGN Adebo and HANNAH Tsadik (eds.), 2008 *Making peace in Ethiopia: Five cases of traditional mechanisms for conflict resolution*. Addis Ababa: Peace and Development Committee

TENA Dawo, 2007 "Traditional moral values of the Oromo of Ethiopia: A philosophical appraisal of Gada System", *Ethiopian Journal of the Social Sciences and Humanities* 5 (2):71–80

TSEGAYE Regassa, URGESSA Genemo and TENA Yigezu 2008 *Restorative justice in Oromia: Baseline study*. Addis Ababa: Justice for All & Pf-Ethiopia

TWINNING, William, 2010 "Normative and legal pluralism: A global perspective", *Duke Journal of Comparative and International Law* 20:473–517

WOJKOWSKA, Ewa, 2006 *Doing justice: How informal justice systems can contribute*. Oslo: UNDP Oslo Governance Centre

ZEHR, Howard, 1990 *Changing lenses: A new focus for crime and justice*. Scottsdale: Herald Press

15. Combatting infanticide in Bashada and Hamar
The complexities behind a 'harmful traditional practice' in southern Ethiopia

Susanne Epple

Introduction

The Bashada and Hamar people are agro-pastoralists who live in a rather isolated part of southwestern Ethiopia where, until recently, the intrusion of the state was rather limited. Infanticide of allegedly impure children has been common and continues to exist today, despite the efforts by the government and NGOs to eliminate the practice. Abandoning the practice, as this paper argues, is so difficult because infanticide is linked to complex cultural explanations and beliefs that must be addressed in order to enable the people to lose their fears that change will affect their lives in an uncontrollable way.

Infanticide or infant homicide has existed in many societies on all continents, and continues to be practised in many of them. It is banned in most constitutions and has been the subject of debate at national and international levels as it contradicts universal human rights.[1] Legal prosecution, however, has not helped to lessen the occurrence of infanticide: while certain forms of infanticide that are deeply rooted in local culture have been driven underground, others, such as female foeticide, have been transformed into selective abortion and are, due to the availability of pre-birth sex-determination technologies, on the rise.

From the perspective of human rights, a child is a human being as soon as it is born. However, this is not a universally accepted understanding. Different societies or cultural contexts have differing ideas about the beginning of human life: its could be at the moment of conception, after certain months of pregnancy, after birth, or even several months after birth. Also, what makes a human being a social person and accepted member of a society varies, as humans are not merely

1 See the UN Convention on the Rights of the Child of 1989, especially article 6, which grants 'life, survival and development of every child', as well as Article 24(3), demanding that State Parties 'take all effective and appropriate measures with a view to abolishing traditional practices prejudicial to the health of children' (UN Committee on the Rights of the Child 2013).

biological, but also social bodies who are culturally constructed throughout their lives (La Fontaine 1985, Carrithers *et al.* 1985). In many societies, it is name-giving that marks the recognition of a baby as a social person (Lancy 2014), and this can be days, months or even years after birth. Once a child has been given a name, it is an acknowledged member of society, and infanticide – where it exists – is usually no longer a possibility (Feitosa *et al.* 2010:860).

Worldwide, the known reasons for infanticide (and/or abortion) also vary. They include a child's illegitimacy (concealing the pregnancy to avoid shame for the mother), poverty, preferences for a particular sex (usually for males), physical deformity of the child, unusual circumstances during the birth (breech births, foot-first births, vertex births, twin births), lack of time between two births (less than 2 years), and accusations of witchcraft. The decision to eliminate a child may lie with the community (if the child is believed to be abnormal or dangerous), or the mother (who might feel she cannot care for a baby born shortly after the birth of a sibling, for a handicapped child or for more than one child born at a time). Children are either actively killed by the parents or by members of the community, or indirectly killed through abandonment, neglect or harsh treatment. Often, infanticide is the result of a failed abortion (Encyclopedia of Population 2018:np).

Infanticide was common in Ancient Greece and Rome. Today, it is rather uncommonly done for cultural reasons in European and other Western countries.[2] Instead, factors such as poverty and parental mental illness play a greater role (Friedman and Resnick 2007). In many societies, such as in India and China and certain countries in Eastern Europe and the South Caucasus, the preference for the male sex is a reason for infanticide (also called 'femicide' or 'gendercide') (Warren 1985, http://www.gendercide.org/case_infanticide.html). The increased availability of prenatal sex-determination techniques has reduced the occurrence of infanticide in the last decades (Bashir 2011:48), but sex selective abortion (mostly female foeticide) seems to be on the increase (Working Group on the Girl-Child 2007:7, UN News 2003). Recently, 'reproductive tourism', e.g. when parents travel to countries such as Thailand where sex selective abortion is legal, seems to contribute to worsening ratios of female to male children, especially in China, India and Eastern Europe (ACHR 2016:5, 34–36). [3]

2 Infanticide was forbidden in Judaism and Christianity and strictly prohibited and severely punished in the Middle Ages. Possibilities to anonymously abandon an unwanted child and the legalization of abortion have greatly contributed to diminishing infanticide (Moseley 1985–86)

3 Liechtenstein has the highest differential between boys and girls with 126 boys to 100 girls. In Asia, the highest rate of male births is in China, with 115 boys to 100 girls. In Africa, the ratio between male and female births is relatively even, with Tunisia having highest differential: 107 boys to100 girls (ACHR 2016:3).

Infanticide is also still common in some indigenous communities, and poses major political and legal challenges to the governments concerned. In Brazil, for example, infanticide is practiced among certain groups in Amazonia. Their case has given rise to academic as well as political and legal debate on how to handle the issue. Some scholars, acknowledging cultural difference, argue that 'there is no moral difference between abortion, broadly legalized in most of the world, and the death of new-borns' (Singer 1993 in Scotti 2017:394, see also Feitosa *et al.*2010). Others emphasize that universal human rights should be given priority, stating that 'culture is not the greater good to be preserved, but the human being is' (Barreto 2006 in Scotti 2017:394). Feitosa *et al.* (2010) propose a middle way, suggesting that external agents (individual or institutional) should only intervene in indigenous societies in a way that allows and persuades the people to deliberate on certain cultural practices. External agents should stay out of the issue except to offer information and raise awareness, thereby providing the conditions for discussion.[4] Legal prosecution and the criminalization of indigenous people practicing infanticide, it is argued, would eventually worsen their social marginalization and might lead to the transformation of practices like infanticide into 'symbols of cultural identity' by the most conservative members of minority groups, and thus to their reinforcement (Scotti 2017:403).

In Africa, illegitimacy and the belief in witchcraft and curses appear to be important factors contributing to infanticide, while sex preference and poverty play a lesser role. Churches, especially those belonging to the Pentecostal and prophetic movements (charismatic, revivalist, etc.), are also contributing to the 'diffusion and legitimization of fears related to witchcraft, and in particular, child witches' in Africa (Cimpric 2010:15). Very little has been written on cultural explanations for infanticide in Ethiopia. Milner (2000:464) briefly mentions that twin births among the Amhara people are seen as abnormal. Without going into detail, Asmarom (1973) stated that among the Borana-Oromo, children who did not fit the rules of the *gada* generation system experienced various forms of infanticide or were put up for adoption. In the last decade, however, several groups living in South Omo Zone have become 'infamously famous' for the infanticide of children considered as 'impure' or 'cursed' (http://www.refworld.org/docid/559bd56b3b.html). National and international media have reported on such cases and the Ethiopian government and NGOs have been trying to address the issue.[5]

---

4 For more details on the legal debate on infanticide among Amazonian groups see Schramm (2010) and Scotti (2017).

5 http://omochildethiopia.org, https://ethiopia.savethechildren.net/news/hamer-community-says-we-no-longer-tolerate-violence-against-children, https://www.telegraph.co.uk/news/worldnews/africaandindianocean/ethiopia/9189136/Saving-the-condemned-children-of-Ethiopia.html, https://www.thereporterethiopia.com/article/peculiar-case-mingi, https://www christianitytoday.com/ct/2011/august/ethiopiariverdeath.html

'Impure children' in Bashada and Hamar

Among the Hamar, Bashada, Banna and Kara people,[6] certain pregnancies and children are perceived as ritually impure and dangerous to their families and/or the whole community. Among the children perceived as such are those conceived by unmarried girls, by betrothed girls who have not moved in with their husbands, and by married women who have not performed the necessary preconception rites. Once born, they are said to afflict their families, causing drought, disease, failed harvests, bird and pest plagues and the like.[7] People believe that aborting the foetus or eliminating the child after birth, followed by the performance of certain purification rituals, can avert such calamities.

When I began my research in Bashada in 1994/95,[8] I had already heard and read about the prohibition on girls conceiving or giving birth before moving in with their husbands. I had also heard about the '*mingi* children', allegedly impure children who were identified by the growth of their upper incisors before the lower ones. I knew girls and women who underwent abortions and sometimes heard rumours about infanticide, though mostly people talked about it as if it was history.

While most of the time the topic was avoided, the case of a girl who had grown her second teeth on the upper jaw first proved impossible to conceal, even though the mother tried to protect her daughter by hiding her. Initially, the community seemed to have tolerated her presence. However, whenever a harvest failed or rain shortage occurred, rumours surfaced that it was due to the *mingi* girl. The rumours were further reinforced, and allegedly confirmed, whenever the diviner consulted

6 The Bashada people speak the same language as the Hamar and Banna people and have an almost identical culture. Together with the Kara, these three groups form a cultural unit (Lydall 1976:393), within which intermarriage is allowed and common, and warfare prohibited. Officially labelled as a subgroup of the Hamar ethnic group, the Bashada people have their own history and origin, their own territory and their own ritual leader (*bitta*). In the past, they claim to have had cultural proximity to the Kara, with whom they reportedly share a common origin (see Epple 2010). In recent times, innovations and cultural change seem to occur first in Banna, which is geographically closer to Jinka, the zonal capital. Conversely, the southern parts of Hamar and Bashada, which are located far from urban influence, appear to be more conservative and resistant to interventions from outside.

7 The concept of human impurity exists also among other groups in South Omo, though with different implications. In the past, the concept of *mingi*, as well as the practice of infanticide, existed also among the Aari and Arbore people, though in a slightly different form from that of the above-mentioned groups.

8 I began research in Bashada in 1994 for my MA thesis and continued in 1998 for my PhD. Since my first stay I have visited Bashada regularly. The research for this chapter was done in the context of a project on legal pluralism in Ethiopia financed by the German Research Foundation (DFG) between 2016 and 2019 while I was hosted at the Frobenius Institute at Frankfurt University and an associate researcher at the South Omo Research Center (SORC) in Jinka, Ethiopia.

the sandal oracle about the reasons for the disasters.[9] This went on for several seasons until, in 1998, the community decided that the girl had to die or leave the area. While the mother had considered taking her child to the *bitta* Adeno (the ritual leader of the neighbouring Banna people who was said to be able to ritually cleanse *mingi* children), there was no guarantee that the community in Bashada would acknowledge the ritual cleansing. The family's second option was to convert to Christianity and move to town. In the end, the mother settled for a third option and gave her daughter to the Catholic Mission in nearby Dimeka town.[10] From there, the girl was later adopted by a foreign family living in Addis Ababa. Though many people in Bashada were convinced that she had caused the repeated calamities, all seemed relieved to see her leave the village alive.[11]

While the lives of this girl and others could be saved, efforts by the government, NGOs and individuals to convince the local population of the harmlessness of children labelled as *mingi* have been only partially successful. In Kara, for example, infanticide is said to have been widely given up, and some *mingi* children are now being raised in their villages. The same is true in a few settlement areas in Banna, Hamar and Bashada, but in most other places, premarital pregnancies are still ended through aborted, and *mingi* children are either given away for adoption outside the community, or secretly eliminated.

This paper aims to understand the local practice of infanticide, its underlying ideas and beliefs, and the reasons why these beliefs have been abandoned in some areas and not in others. Specifically it will focus on:

1) the local views, values, meanings and explanations pertaining to the practices of abortion and ritual infanticide within the context of harmful traditional practices (HTPs);
2) the strategies employed by government officials, NGOs and local private citizens to combat these practices;
3) the local reactions, forms of open and hidden resistance and consequent setbacks experienced;
4) the creativity, flexibility and patience of various actors that have led to partial changes and success stories.

9 Diviners (*moara*) in Bashada and Hamar claim to have the ability to find out the causes of disease and other individual or community level misfortunes by tossing a pair of ritual leather sandals (locally called *dunguri*) and interpreting the way they land on the ground.

10 A nearby small market town and seat of the district administration.

11 Anthropologist Nicole Poissonnier was doing research at that time in the same village. She was a close friend to the family and not only followed the case closely, but also helped to save the girl by communicating with the mission and finding an adoptive family.

Though the research focuses mainly on Bashada and Hamar, connections will be drawn with Kara and Banna, where local dynamics have led to a different handling of infanticide and abortion.

Human rights and local values: The contradictions

The relationship and contradictions between universal human rights standards and customary laws and values, as well as the problems arising during their implementation in local contexts, have stimulated scholarly debate in anthropology for a while.[12] The implementation of women's and children's rights into local contexts appears especially problematic, as the idea of gender equality and the emphasis on the rights of the individual often contradict and collide with local norms and values (Merry 2006, Hodgson 2011). Thus, while many officers argue for the strict employment of international standards worldwide at the international level,[13] at the grassroots level, local officials are struggling with the obvious contradictions, ethical dilemmas and local resistance, and finding that legal enforcement and the criminalization of culture do not necessarily lead to sustainable success, but often lead instead to conflict and resistance.

Local practices inconsistent with human rights have been labelled as 'harmful traditional/cultural practices'. While activists seem to have no doubts that certain practices deserve to be eradicated, some scholars have raised doubts about whether the labelling of certain practices as harmful is a viable or useful way of categorizing discriminatory practices across cultural contexts (Longman and Bradley 2015b).[14] Some went so far as arguing that emphasizing the harmfulness of certain cultural

12 See for example An-Na'im 1992, F. von Benda-Beckmann 2009, Eriksen 2001, Preis 1996. For case studies see Cowan *et al.* 2001, Foblet and Yassari 2013, Langfield *et al.* 2010.

13 For example, the 'Convention on the Elimination of all Forms of Discrimination against Women' (CEDAW), adopted by the UN General Assembly in 1979 aims to eliminate all practices that discriminate against women, even if it means changing cultural values, and even if women belonging to the culture concerned do not perceive them as harmful (www.un.org/womenwatch/daw/cedaw).

14 The term 'harmful cultural practices' was first coined in the 1950s in UN circles when calls were made to abolish 'customs, ancient laws and practices related to marriage and the family inconsistent with the Universal Declaration of Human Rights' (Longman and Bradley 2015b:11). See also Longman and Bradley (2015b) for the emergence of the term. Critiques of the term have said that the voices of the people concerned are often over-heard, thus labelling certain practices as harmful is yet another expression of Western dominance, as the definition of what is actually harmful, lies in the hands of the powerful. Besides, similar practices in the West are ignored in such debates and never labelled as culturally based and harmful (Grünbaum 2015, see Jeffreys 2005 on 'Harmful cultural practices in the West'.

practices is a way of distracting public attention from more severe problems affecting women and children, such as poverty.

Harmful traditional practices (HTPs) in Africa and Ethiopia: The policy contexts

The fight against 'harmful traditional practices' (HTPs) is mentioned as part of the 'Millennium Goals' and 'Sustainable Development Goals' of the African Union, which places a strong focus on women's and children's rights, and particularly on addressing sexual and gender-based violence (SGBV), removal of choice in marriage, sexual initiation, female genital cutting (FGC), opportunity marginalization (social and economic), and land and inheritance exclusion (African Union Commission 2012).

The African Union Commission (2012:2) has defined harmful traditional practices as 'forms of physical or psychological violence that prejudice the bodily integrity or mental well-being of women or girls on the basis of their inferior position in the social grouping that are considered to be long-established and community accepted practices deserving tolerance and respect.' Due to the continent's cultural diversity, there is no standardized list of harmful traditional practices in Africa. However, female genital cutting, sex and gender-based violence, violence related to bride price, forced and child marriage, wife inheritance and nutritional taboos, among others, exist in many African societies.

Ethiopia adopted the Universal Declaration of Human Rights (UDHR) and related conventions and treaties, and included laws protecting human rights of the individual into its 1995 Constitution and into numerous government and NGO programmes. The combatting of HTPs and the empowerment of women and children is among the country's top priorities as it endeavours to develop and modernize. In 2013, the Ministry of Women, Children and Youth Affairs prepared the 'National Strategy on Harmful Traditional Practices (HTPs) against Women and Children in Ethiopia' in collaboration with development partners. The document defined HTPs as 'traditional practices, which violate and negatively affect the physical, sexual, psychological well-being, human rights and socio-economic participation of women and children' (UNICEF 2015). According to UNICEF (2015:vi), there are about 140 HTPs that affect mothers and children in Ethiopia, and at least some of them exist in almost all ethnic groups. As they are part of local customs, they are defined as 'resistant to change', and UNICEF recommends the design of appropriate strategies for affecting change. However, as in other parts of the world, efforts to raise awareness and legal intervention have led to only partial successes and a variety of responses.

According to Jones *et al.* (2018b), over the last couple of decades legislation and policy concerning girls' and women's well-being and empowerment in Ethiopia has improved significantly, and a strong commitment to eradicating HTPs can be observed. Nevertheless, practical progress has been slow, and gender norms are proving particularly difficult to overcome. As Jones *et al.* (2018a) showed in a recent study in Amhara regional state, despite efforts by the government and NGOs to support girls' education and gender equality, many adolescent girls continue to face gendered discrimination. The authors also mention a kind of cultural backlash arising from the intensity of the government's discourse on women and children's rights. This backlash is reportedly evidenced by attempts to cover up weddings of underaged girls and boys by pretending that they are baptisms or other religious events (Jones *et al.* 2018:58). Other studies on southern Ethiopia have also reported on local resistance and clashes between government authorities and local population.[15]

Infanticide, abortion, and physical injury in Ethiopia: The legal contexts

The Ethiopian law deals with harmful traditional practices in various legal codes. Under the socialist Derg regime (1974–1991), efforts were made to unify all Ethiopian societies under a modernized umbrella, and many local practices were condemned. Since the EPRDF took over government, cultural difference has been celebrated and supported, albeit with limitations (see Epple/Thubauville 2012).

Any practices that contradict international human rights standards are labelled as HTPs and legally sanctioned. Articles 561 to 570 of the Criminal Code deal with 'Crimes committed against life, person and health through harmful traditional practices', especially those 'endangering the lives of and causing bodily injury to pregnant women and children' (Articles 561 and 562).[16] Such practices are punishable with 'fines or simple imprisonment from three months to one year'. Article 563 (Discretion of the Court) grants some flexibility in the application of the law, stating that the court may take a perpetrator's age, education, experience or social status into account and choose to give only a warning.

Article 544 specifically deals with 'infanticide', stating that it is punishable with simple imprisonment if committed by the mother while in labour (544(1)), and treated as homicide if the child is killed intentionally or by negligence (544(2)). The same laws apply to any instigators or accomplices to infanticide.

15 See for example LaTosky (2012, 2014) on the lip plates of Mursi women, Thubauville (2012) on bridal seclusion among the Maale, Epple (2012a) on girls' education in Bashada and Yohannes (this volume) on a major conflict between the Hamar and government authorities related to clashing values.

16 These include abortion, excision of the uvula of a child, removal of milk teeth, and preventing a child from being vaccinated as well as other practices considered as harmful by the medical profession.

Abortion is only allowed for medical reasons, for example, if either the health of the child or the mother is affected, or if the pregnancy is the result of rape or incest (Art 551).[17]

HTPs in South Omo Zone and Hamar Woreda

The South Omo Zone in SNNPR is home to sixteen officially recognized ethnic groups and known for its cultural diversity. The level of education among the mostly agro-pastoral or agrarian population is generally still low and, due to the relatively late penetration of the state in the area, knowledge about the national law is rather limited and scattered. The handling of HTPs in South Omo is particularly challenging because its cultures are quite diverse, and the people react differently to interventions from the outside.[18]

The zone and districts cooperate to identify HTPs. The Women and Children's Affairs offices in the various districts regularly visit the villages and, together with the local population, identify practices that could be considered as harmful. They then prepare and update the list of HTPs for their own district and submit it to the zonal authorities, where the lists are compiled and progress and setbacks evaluated. As the Head of the zonal Women and Children's Affairs Office, explained, these lists are updated annually to show which practices have been abandoned, continue to exist, or have been revived. The lists are then sent to the regional office in Hawassa. From there, further instructions on how to continue the work are sent back to the zone and from there to the districts. In addressing HTPs, the government gives the highest priority to those that threaten human life or cause physical injury.

At the zonal level, seventy-seven HTPs were listed as existing in six pastoral districts of South Omo in 2016 (South Omo Zone Women, Children and Youth's Affairs Department 2016). While some of them are unique to one or two of the respective ethnic groups (such as female circumcision in Arbore and Dassanetch,

17 Otherwise, abortion is punishable (Article 545,1) and leads to the imprisonment of the woman (and possible assistants) (Article 546). If the abortion was done against the will of the pregnant woman, it leads to rigorous imprisonment from three years to ten years of the 'aborter' (Article 547). If the abortion is done for financial gain, the 'aborter' also has to pay a fine, and if it was done by a professional – such as a doctor or nurse – he or she can be prohibited from practicing medicine for a limited period or even for life if they have undertaken numerous abortions (Article 548, 1, 2, 3).

18 See for example the baseline study on Hamar, Dassanech and Nyangatom districts by Save the Children Norway-Ethiopia (2011). See also LaTosky (2012, 2013, 2015) on Mursi women's lip-plates, Thubauville (2012) on bridal seclusion in Maale, and Epple (2012b) on whipping and physical punishment.

infanticide in Hamar, Banna-Tsamay and Maale, or the wearing of lip-plates in Mursi), there are practices that exist almost everywhere (for example, bride wealth, polygamy, reluctance to send girls to school).

HTPs in Hamar Woreda

Hamar Woreda has twelve listed HTPs. As the Head of the Women and Children's Affairs Office at the district level told me,[19] after years of awareness raising and information campaigns, certain practices have been abandoned, some are being practised less severely, and others have continued as before. The fight against HTPs related to the modification of the body for aesthetic reasons has been most successful, since these practices are voluntary and bear few ritual and social implications, serving rather as signs of strength, courage and social recognition.[20] HTPs related to marriage, including early marriage (below the age of 18), arranged marriage, abduction, polygamy, bride wealth, ghost marriage (marriage to a deceased person) and wife inheritance have proved to be more difficult to suppress, probably because giving them up has further implications for age and gender relations.[21]

The ritual whipping of girls and women during male initiations and the whipping of wrongdoers by their age-mates are likewise considered as cultural assets and have not been abandoned, although the severity of them has been reduced. The top priority, and the most difficult HTP to address, has been abortion and ritual infanticide.[22] While infanticide has reportedly been abandoned in Kara, it continues – along with abortion – in Hamar and Bashada for various reasons that will be explored in this paper.

19 Interview 24 March 2017 in Jinka.

20 In Bashada and Hamar these practices include the wearing of heavy iron rings around the arms and legs (*zau*) and the neck (*isante*), the breaking out of the lower incisors, and the cutting of decorative scars (*paala*). Decorative scars are commonly applied to the shoulders and chests of men who have killed an enemy. As homicide is prosecuted, such scarring of the chest is now only done is secret. The skin is sometimes still cut for medical purposes – such as to cure rheumatic pain – mostly by women.

21 In the 2016 report by the South Omo Women, Children and Youth Affairs Office (2016) ghost marriage (that is 'marriage to a dead man') and 'marriage through abduction' are said to have been eradicated. However, in conversations with the Women and Children's Affairs Office, it was said that abduction is still a problem, though on the decrease. During my stays in Bashada in 2016 and 2017 it was also clear that forced marriage and abduction is still prevalent, which shows how difficult it is not only to change certain practices, but also to follow up on practices that are illegal.

22 Another major priority is female circumcision in Arbore. The Arbore speak a different language and are also culturally quite different from the Hamar, Bashada and Kara, yet they share the same district. Over the last few years, female circumcision has been reduced in severity, although there is also resistance to change among the communities.

Abortion and infanticide

Abortion and infanticide based on the belief that a child is ritually impure is common in Hamar, Bashada, Banna and Kara.[23] The origin of the belief and exact beginning of the practice of infanticide is not known. When asked, people mostly explained that it has always been part of their culture.[24] Local explanations for the tradition emphasize the 'non-human' status and ritual pollution of such children. *Mingi* children – e.g. children born without the proper performance of preconception rites or whose teeth grow first on the upper jaw – are believed to harm their family. It is said that such children bring disease and misfortune, causing the deaths of their father, mother, and all their siblings, until they remain the sole survivor in the family and keep the family property to themselves. They are also believed to cause disasters that affect the whole community. When there is a severe drought or an invasion of pests in the fields, usually an oracle is consulted to identify the cause. If there is a child who has been suspected of being *mingi*, diviners may read in the oracle that they are responsible. In this way, the child becomes the scapegoat for a calamity (Lydall 2005).[25]

When members of the community come to forcefully take a *mingi* child away from their family, the parents usually try to protect their child vehemently. Families with many male members can resist more vigorously, so that those who came for the child may have to stay several days, trying to convince the family to voluntarily give up the child. The child is then taken to the bush and abandoned.

The alleged impurity of *mingi* children is strongly connected to the performance of the bridal and the preconception rituals that a woman has to undergo with her mother-in-law every time she wants to get pregnant. As Brüderlin (2012:100) has

---

23 Variations of the concept exist also in Maale and Ari. As one elderly Ari woman explained during a workshop at the South Omo Research Center (Epple/Brüderlin 2002:97–98), a child may only be conceived once the so-called 'feeding ritual' of its elder sibling has been performed (five months after birth), otherwise it will be *mingi*. The women from Ari, Hamar, Bashada and Banna who participated in the workshop all agreed that pregnancies conceived before the mother has had her first period after giving birth are especially dangerous or, as they expressed it, 'very, very *mingi*!' One of them called the concept of *mingi* a unifying cultural element of their cultures, which are also historically connected (Epple/Brüderlin 2002:99).

24 According to Lale Labuko the Kara speak of a child born several hundreds of years ago whose top teeth came first. The community suspected it might be a curse and when there was a drought some years later, the elders of the village related this to the child. The ritual leaders of Kara, Hamar and Banna then came together and decided that such children were impure and needed to be killed in order to prevent future calamities (https://www.thereporterethiopia.com/article/peculiar-case-mingi). The documentary film *The River and the bush* (http://omochildmovie.com) highlights the impressive effort and success of Lale Labuko in combatting infanticide in Kara.

25 In a way, the elimination of the child provides the community with a feeling of control over natural disasters and is, as such, comparable to witch-hunts.

explained, the prohibition on premarital pregnancies and the belief in the impurity of children conceived without the performance of the preconception rites serve as an indirect means of social control over married couples and their procreation, and gives a lot of power to mothers-in-law (see also Lydall 2005:163).

As local contraceptives do not exist and people have limited knowledge of fertile and non-fertile days, the only really effective method of avoiding an unwanted pregnancy is celibacy.[26] However, as virginity is not a precondition for marriage, premarital pregnancies occur from time to time. Sometimes, a betrothed girl may be impregnated by her prospective husband, who abducts her after getting tired waiting for his wife's father's consent to let her move in with him. During such abductions sexual intercourse is common, so that even girls who do not have a secret boyfriend may get pregnant and have to undergo an abortion.[27] A child conceived by a girl who has not moved in with her husband is referred to as *anzamo-nas* (lit.: 'girlhood child'). No matter who their biological father is, the parenthood of an *anzamo-nas* is neither socially nor ritually acknowledged, so the child is illegitimate and not considered as a fully human being (*edi*).

Within wedlock, the ideal time between pregnancies is considered to be two to three years. Once a child is strong enough to be weaned, its mother will perform the *gungulo* ritual with her mother-in-law, after which she is allowed to get pregnant again. If she gets pregnant before that, her child will be *mingi*. Husbands are advised to avoid sexual intercourse before the *gungulo* ritual has been performed, but as wives cannot easily reject a pushy husband, unwanted pregnancies within wedlock do occur. While still in the mother's womb, such children are called *wuta* ('unclean pregnancy'). If abortion fails and such a child is born, it will be *mingi* ('ritually impure').[28]

---

26 The performance of this ritual can be considered as a traditional kind of birth control that lies in the hands of the mother-in-law. It guarantees that the age gap between two siblings is not too short.

27 I was told during a conversation with two young Bashada women that if a girl refuses to have intercourse during abduction by her husband, he would suspect that she has a secret boyfriend (31 January 2017).

28 The concept of *mingi* appears also in other contexts of Hamar/Bashada culture, in the classification of animals, nature, and the temporal status of humans. Humans can be irreversibly *mingi* by birth (if the necessary rites were not performed before conception), by accident (if the genitalia or breasts of a man or woman are injured), or by impure behaviour (having sexual intercourse with a cow). Members of some ethnic groups or status groups are also called *mingi*, for example, the Tsamay (Tsamako), who have a reputation for being magicians, and blacksmiths, who are considered ritually impure. The ritual or magical abilities of these people is nevertheless venerated and used. The *bajje* people, a marginalized subgroup with great ritual responsibilities, are also sometimes called *mingi*, mainly because they do not kill children whose teeth grow on the upper jaw first, which means that in theory all of them could

The abortion or infanticide of a child of a premarital pregnancy is handled secretly to ensure that the prospective husband does not hear about it – unless he caused the pregnancy.[29] In cases where a married woman is known to have repeatedly carried and aborted a *wuta* ('unclean pregnancy'), her husband will be made responsible and accused of impregnating her with 'non-humans'. His agemates will warn him to avoid sexual intercourse until his wife has performed the necessary rites, so that she can bear an *edi* ('real human being').[30] If after this, the woman gets pregnant with a *wuta* again, the husband will be sanctioned and severely whipped by his agemates.

Both, *anzamo-nas* and *mingi* children are believed to bring misfortune such as drought, disease and plagues of pests or birds that eat the harvest. The only remedy is to remove them from the community. In Hamar and Bashada, the first choice is usually to terminate such pregnancies in the fifth or sixth month of pregnancy.[31] When abortion fails, the pregnant girl is kept hidden, perhaps in the fields, until the birth, and then the child is abandoned in the bush.[32] If the child of a married woman grows its first teeth in the upper jaw rather than the lower jaw,[33] this is interpreted as an indication that the mother has laid with the father before being ritually prepared, and the child therefore became *mingi*. In rare cases, children grow their adult teeth, rather than their milk teeth, in the upper gums first. This means they are identified as *mingi* only at the age of 7 or 8, but their fate is the same as that of younger children. The belief that if a *mingi* child is left alive all of its younger siblings will also become *mingi* puts extra pressure on the parents.

---

be children of *mingi* parents. See Brüderlin (2012:95ff) for a detailed summary of the existing literature.

29 According to Dal'o, a young married Bashada man, husbands are scared that their wife might die during an abortion, which is another reason why they get angry and threaten their wives' lovers. See also Brüderlin (2012) on different cases of premarital pregnancy in Hamar.

30 Girls and women who mourn the death of their children are comforted with the words: 'Don't cry, this was not a human. You will give birth to a human in the future!'

31 Premarital pregnancies and abortions are kept secret from the girl's father, elder brothers and prospective husband, as these would try to get hold of her secret boyfriend and beat or even kill him. For the same reason, girls try to hide the name of their lovers. To end a pregnancy, a local female expert will exert pressure on the girl's abdomen, though there is a belief that if a girl does not disclose her boyfriend's name, the abortion will fail.

32 During my research, I heard of several unwanted pregnancies. My impression was that the girls had internalized the idea that premarital pregnancies should be ended and therefore usually consented to an abortion. It is common for their secret boyfriends to contribute to the cost of the abortion, and young men assist each other in finding the necessary resources. Such pregnancies are usually an open secret among the youth and the female relatives of the pregnant girl.

33 See Brüderlin (2012) for a detailed description of marriage and bridal rituals, as well as the concepts of *wuta*, *mingi* and *dakka* used to refer to unclean conceptions and ritually impure children.

A woman carrying a *wuta* and mothers of *mingi* children are likewise considered unclean, and their pollution extends to their families and fields. Such women cannot fetch water, as this would allegedly pollute and dry out the waterholes. Their fields and crops are also considered *mulimidi* (polluted),[34] so that they can only be eaten but not be used as seeds or in exchange for goats or cattle. Their husbands cannot go hunting, as it would put them at risk to die, and none of the woman's close family members can go to initiations, as the cattle over which an initiate is supposed to leap would go wild. While a mingi child must be killed, its mother and her family and homestead can be ritually cleansed and reintegrated into community life. The procedure involves the slaughtering of a goat on a central path (*zarsi goiti*) by a ritual expert who then blesses and cleanses her homestead by spilling some of the goat's stomach contents in every corner. The slaughtering and cleasning is done in public so that everyone knows that after an unclean conception has been removed or a *mingi* child eliminated the appropriate cleansing rituals have been performed. The same rituals are done when a woman had a spontaneous miscarriage.[35]

Meeting the challenges in combatting abortion and infanticide

The settlement areas in Hamar and Bashada are relatively remote and scattered, making it difficult for the government to reach out and employ control mechanisms over their inhabitants. Besides which, abortion and infanticide take place in secret, so enforcing the law in this context is almost impossible unless people report such incidents to the police. Therefore, the government's emphasis has been on raising awareness in the region in the hope that this will slowly change the minds and beliefs of the people. Although, it has also taken action to exert legal pressure as well.

In the past two decades, the infrastructure in Hamar and Bashada has been improved, and all-weather roads have been built to most settlement areas. Health centres, schools, agricultural extension offices have been built in all *kebeles*, and local committees have been formed to address major issues in collaboration with the *likamamber* (lit. Amharic: 'chairperson'), who acts as an intermediary between the local community and the government.

However, the strong belief that children conceived and born without the proper ritual preparation bring disease and misfortune to the whole community is puting

34 The term *mulimidi* is, unlike the term *mingi*, also used in ordinary contexts to mean 'dirty', especially for water that has become muddy.

35 The cleansing is done by the *bajje*-man (ritual expert from a special subgroup living among the Hamar and Banne).

a lot of pressure on individual community members. Most government officials are well aware of the force of these beliefs, as they are native to the area themselves. Therefore, their work lies in both raising awareness raising and supporting individuals, while warning the community of the legal consequences of anyone caught committing infanticide. Delegations from the Women and Children's Affairs Offices, the Cultural Office, the Educational Office, the Justice Office and the Health Office regularly visit the villages to educate them about the harmfulness and illegality of certain practices, and to follow up on the changes people have promised to make.

In an effort to gain more control over childbirths and with the hope that this will help prevent abortion and infanticide, pregnancies are nowadays documented and followed up. In cooperation with the district Women and Children's Affairs Office, NGOs, the local health centres, and local health committees, pregnant women are identified and visited regularly and encouraged to go to the health centres in Dimeka or Turmi (small towns in Hamar district) when near to delivery. There, every pregnant woman is given free accommodation and health care until her baby is born and both are strong enough to return home. Through vaccination campaigns, the names of children are registered and their growth monitored. In the near future, the zonal administration is planning to issue birth certificates for all children, even those born in remote lowland areas. In collaboration with international NGOs, such as Save the Children, and with funds from UNICEF and the African Medical and Research Foundation (AMREF), financial support is being provided to individuals willing to raise *anzamo-nas* or *mingi* children. Omo Child – a local NGO – is helping raise awareness and providing shelter for such children in their orphanage in Jinka. The police and court are also involved through prosecutions and by raising awareness of the laws around infanticide. However, as mentioned above it is extremely difficult for them to locate cases of abortion or infanticide, and there have been very few convictions so far.[36]

In the following, some of the measures taken to reduce infanticide and abortion, as well as the local reactions towards them, are discussed in more detail.

---

36 Any major criminal issues and all cases of homicide are sent to the zone, so that cases of abortion and infanticide are sent to and handled at the Jinka court, e.g. the zonal capital. The former head of the prosecutors' office in Jinka, explained why the court has to show flexibility in handling cases of HTPs, "(...) The law says that one should keep law and order by prevention, e.g. teaching the people, and if after that the law is broken we have to prosecute them. But one cannot arrest all who violate the law here. If we do that, one would have to arrest almost all people. So, if for example someone's lower incisors are broken out by force here in Jinka, we have to act. But if it is done it Hamar (e.g. in the lowland villages), we leave it." (24 March 2017)

Saving lives through adoption

Encouraged by the government, some parents decide to give their children away for adoption, as *mingi* children raised outside the community by non-Hamar are no longer considered dangerous. The former representative of the Hamar people in the national parliament recalled how adoption was introduced under pressure from the socialist Derg regime (1974–1991),

> Already under the Derg it was said that people should not kill the *mingi* children. They said, 'It is a crime, it will be prosecuted. If you really believe that these children are impure, give them to the town's people, let them grow up there!' (...) People say that the rain would stop falling and there would be disease. But since the Derg, there have been many *mingi* children growing up in town, and today there still are. People have seen that there is disease in town and in the villages; rain is falling equally in towns and villages, there is no difference. It is a question of *barjo* (here: 'good fortune'), not of *mingi* children. (1 June 2017)

Many of these children grew up in Dimeka and Turmi, small towns in Hamar, or in Jinka, the zonal capital. Their relatives could see them – though not visit them – when they went to the weekly markets. Some of the children adopted during the Derg regime are among the first educated Hamar and have achieved high positions as officials in the local administration or as legal experts. As adults, they do not pose any risk when they visit the villages and eat and drink with the people and are treated like any guest from outside Hamar.[37]

While in the past only non-Hamar were willing to adopt and raise *mingi* children, today there is an increasing number of educated Hamar people living in the towns who believe that there is no danger in bringing up *mingi* children.[38] The NGO Omo Child has saved the lives of around fifty children who were given to them by parents or found abadonded in the bush.[39] However, while the orphanage s open to all children labelled as *mingi* or *anzamo-nas*, people in Bashada have said that

---

37 One of them, for example, became a lawyer and worked as head judge of the Zonal Court in Jinka. Another one was chief administrator in Hamar Woreda for some years. He underwent a purifying ritual as a young adult, was allowed to undergo initiation and married a local wife. As far as I could observe, the local reactions to this diverged: while some say that he was 're-born' and is a full Hamar now, others say that he is not fully *charangi* ('ritually pure'). Both have become active also in attempting to fight infanticide with the help of international NGOs and churches (see http://gtliconnect.blogspot.de/2011/11/creating-mingi-friendly-communities.html, and http://galataministries.org).

38 The mother of the current Women and Children's Affairs Officer of Hamar Woreda, for example, is bringing up two *mingi* children in Dimeka. She found one of them abandoned in the bush, while the other one was brought to her by its father.

39 The NGO recently changed its name to Omo Hope (see https://www.omohope.org). Besides the orphanage, the organization is very active in raising awareness and has significantly con-

parents who do not know any of the NGO's staff personally are still hesitant to approach the organization.

Enforced and supported upbringing of impure children

Nowadays, the government is making increased efforts to convince families and communities to keep their *mingi* children. In the 1990s and early 2000s, there were no *mingi* children growing up in the villages, but during my research in 2016 and 2017, I heard of several cases.

During meetings organized in Turmi and Dimeka, government officials had discussed the issue with the *likamambers* from the various *kebeles*, asking them to convince their communities. An elder from Bashada remembered these meetings as follows:

> The government said to us (about *mingi* children), 'You are giving them to the *gal* (non-Hamar). And then, when they study, grow up and come back, they eat and drink in your houses. Why are you eating with them? You used to kill them! You used to throw them down crevices! You said the sun would get hot, and the rain would stop falling. But now that is not the case. Now (as they were saved and grew up in town), the rain never stopped falling. You were wrong!'
> (After they talked like that we said), 'Eeeh, we have accepted that.'
> Now, the government is saying that we should raise them in the villages. Over there in Dalmi (settlement area in Bashada), there are two children. There is also one in Argude (settlement area in Bashada), it is raised here. (Interview, 19 November 2016)

While this elder gives the impression that many people are now convinced that *mingi* children are harmless, others said that acceptance is limited to a few places in Hamar. Both, local people as well as government workers told me that they knew that infanticide had not been given up. Many local people also expressed their doubts that *mingi* children were really equal to other children. Although leaving them alive was seen as generally good, it was suggested that they should go to school and live a town life rather than be locally initiated and married.

The former Women and Children's Affairs Officer of Hamar Woreda recounted the case of an *anzamo* child who, at the time of the interview in 2016, was 4 or 5 years old and living around Turmi town. She had become involved in the case when she took the child to the hospital after birth and fed it until she could convince the mother to keep it. To protect both child and mother from the enraged husband, she had also had to involve the police. Later, she convinced the community elders

---

tributed to the abandonment of infanticide in Kara, the birthplace of Omo Child's founder, Lale Labuko.

to let the mother and child return. Finally, the husband accepted the child and, after some years, the wife gave birth to more children with him.[40]

While there are more and more individual cases of surviving *mingi* children and *anzamo* children, there seems to be a growing and more outspoken resistance to the acceptance of *anzamo-nas* in the communities. During my fieldstay in 2016, the case of two Hamar girls who had refused to abort their premarital pregnancies was discussed widely in Bashada. The girls were taken to the clinic in Turmi, where they were given health care, protection from their families and support during delivery. The Head of the Women and Children's Affairs Office in Hamar district explained the strategy behind giving them shelter and financial support in town for a couple of years:

> The mothers should start loving their children. Once they got used to their children, we will send them back to the village. That is the psychology (she used the English word here) we want to use. The girls' husbands, hopefully, will later also accept the children as theirs. (Interview, 27 March 2017)[41]

After returning to the villages, I was assured, the mothers and their children will to be regularly visited by government officials and receive financial support to ensure their wellbeing. In addition, the families will have to sign a document saying that they would do no harm to them, in the knowledge that they will be sent to prison if anything did happen to the children.[42]

The case of these two girls stirred discussions in Bashada, and some people openly opposed bringing up an *anzamo-nas*. A Bashada elder summarized people's feelings:

> The people here say, 'Why should we accept such a child? The family of the man who impregnated her has to raise the child! (...) We do not agree with the government!' When we said so the government people responded, 'So, advise your

40 Summary of an interview held on 25 January 2017.

41 She added that people in Kara were now raising *mingi* children in the villages without problem, and that such families received some financial support. According to her, in 2017 there were fifteen *mingi* children being raised in Dus village (the biggest settlement area in Kara).

42 The former Women and Children's Affairs Officer of Hamar Woreda recounted the case of an *anzamo-nas*, then aged around 4 or 5, living around Turmi town with the support of Save the Children and the Women and Children's Affairs Office. The husband has accepted it and the couple subsequently had more children together. She explained: 'For that case, the elders had called me (to take the child to town). After the child was born, I took it to the hospital for 18 days. I fed the baby and finally convinced the mother, and later the community elders, to keep it, so that eventually the mother and child could return. In the beginning, I worked on this alone. But then I had to also involve the police, because the husband of the girl was bad at first and threatened to kill the baby, so the police had to stop him.' (Interview, 25 January 2017).

> daughters (not to get pregnant)!' (Then we said), 'Eh, so we will better hand over our daughters to their husbands at early age, before they grow up and start playing around with boys!' We have accepted the *mingi* talk, but we did not accept the talk about the *wuta* and *anzamo* children. (Interview, 19 November 2016)

As is indicated here, the unclear social status of an *anzamo* child creates a problem, as by local definition social descent is only determined once a wife has moved in with her husband and performed all necessary rituals, no matter who the biological father of a child is. Therefore, children born before that cannot become members of the husband's lineage. On the other hand, any child born after the necessary rites have been performed will be fully accepted and considered as the child of their social father, even when it is known that someone else fathered the child.[43]

In the above account, the elder suggested that to prevent premarital pregnancies girls could be given to their husbands at an early age, knowing that underage marriage is another target of the government. In the past, Hamar girls moved over to their husbands' homes at a young age, and grew up under the supervision of their in-laws until they were physical maturity enough to be given to their husbands. While Hamar girls often still get married (i.e. the marriage is sealed) at an early age, they now grow up in their parents' house until the age of 18 and older. This has made it difficult to prevent premarital relationships, and the risk of premarital pregnancy has increased immensely. With his remark, the government's demand to let girls get betrothed and married at adult age was indirectly challenged: it was shown that from a local perspective it is contradictory to control the girls and avoid premarital pregnancies, and at the same time forbid abortions and infanticide.[44] Without saying it directly, it was indicated that abortion and infanticide of *anzamo* children would continue if the problem of premarital pregnancies is not be addressed otherwise.

---

43 There are cases in which a husband was absent for several years (in prison) and later thanked the man who slept with his wife while he was away, thereby enabling him to return to a fully-grown family. In other cases, where husbands are not happy that their wives have given birth to children from a secret lover, their anger should only be addressed towards the lover, and not toward the children.

44 Efforts to inform the youth about contraception, as well as awareness raising on HIV, free distribution of hormone injections or condoms seem not to reach everywhere and are not always effective. During a conversation with a young Bashada women, I learned that many fear that they would not be able to get pregnant for some time after receiving a hormone injection or that condoms might get lost inside the body of a woman. Therefore, they claimed, many females did not use them.

Expanding control mechanisms, awareness raising and legal prosecution

As indicated earlier, both abortion and infanticide are done secretly and hardly ever reported to the police and the court. Consequently, government institutions depend on the cooperation of the community to prosecute such cases. Efforts to register pregnant women and newborn children have given some control over newly born children.

According to a prosecutor at Hamar Woreda Court, very few parents have sought legal support after their child was labelled *mingi* and killed. He suspected that social pressure played a major role in preventing parents from coming forward. As many people continue to be convinced that these children are dangerous, parents fear being ostracized by the community if they refuse to hand over their child. Therefore, even individuals who do not believe in *mingi* tend to give their child away for adoption.

Equally rare are reported cases of abortion. The majority of girls who get pregnant before marriage comply with an abortion, as they have internalized that it is a cultural prerequisite to live with their husband and bear socially accepted children. Besides, as shown above, bringing up an *anzamo-nas* means having to withstand the whole community, live in town for a while – if not forever if the government officials' negotiations are not successful – and risk the marriage. A judge at the Hamar Woreda Court remembered only one case of a reported abortion. Here, an elderly woman had forced her daughter-in-law to interrupt her pregnancy:

> When her daughter-in-law moved in with her son, she was already pregnant [by someone else]. The mother-in-law said, 'This child is not my son's child. We have not finished the (bridal preconception) rituals!' and aborted the child by force. Later, she was accused of murder here in town. Her daughter-in-law had submitted a letter [to the police]. 'My child was killed! This old woman killed my child! I am not going to live in that place anymore! I will go to school now!' she said, and then the police arrested the mother-in-law. The young woman is in school now. (Interview, 29 March 2017)

This case of forced abortion was especially delicate. Though I did not have the chance to talk to her in person, reporting her mother-in-law to the police must have been a drastic step for the young woman. As custom dictates that cases should first be discussed with the elders and reported to the police only through the militia or the *likamamber*, circumventing the elders is strongly disapproved. Anyone doing so is locally perceived as *d'abbi* (wrongdoer) and has to pay a fine to the elders or is otherwise sanctioned. In this case, the woman had to sever relations with all her-in-laws and move to town.

Government collaboration with ritual leaders

Despite years of awareness raising and legal pressure, abortions and infanticide have still not been abandoned. Therefore, the government recently decided to involve the ritual leaders (*bitta*) to ban these practices through local custom.

The ritual leaders in Hamar, Bashada and Banna [45] are said to be descendants of brothers who once left Aari and migrated south and there is a strong connection between the ritual leaders of the three groups. Until today, the *bittas* are venerated for their ritual power, though some of the former prohibitions surrounding their hereditary office have been weakened: while in the past the *bittas* were not allowed to leave their own territory and meet other *bittas* face-to-face, today, they often meet during meetings organized by the government in Dimeka and Turmi, in Jinka (the zonal capital) and even in Hawassa (the regional capital).

One of the Banna *bittas*, Adeno Garsho, was already known in the 1990s to have developed a ritual that could cleanse *mingi* children: through a kind of symbolic rebirth he could turn them into 'real human beings'.[46] However, when during my fieldstay in 1998–99 people in Bashada mentioned him to me, many also expressed their doubts on the effectiveness of his ritual. Those who believed he coud really turn a *mingi* child into a 'real human' feared that the transformation would not be accepted in Bashada and their children remain outcasts.

When harmful traditional practices began to be addressed under the EPRDF regime, *bitta* Adeno offered to be of help. During a Banna-Tsamay Woreda council meeting in 2005, his son, Kotsa Adeno, declared that they would do all they could to stop certain HTPs. During the course of numerous field visits and talks, seventy-two practices were identified as HTPs, of which forty-eight were considered as being most critically affecting human life. The highest priority was given to the practice of killing *mingi* children. A young educated man[47] from Banna recounted:

> *Bitta* Adeno Garsho called the representatives from the Women and Children's Affairs Office, and also the *kogos* and *parkos*[48] from their respective areas in Bannaland. He also invited the Banna representatives in the national parliament, the zonal administrators and regional government bodies to his own home. Here, he slaughtered a pure female sheep that had never given birth before (*yati sebani*)

45 There are two *bittas* in Banna, two in Hamar and one in Bashada.

46 *Bitta* Adeno's grandmother originally came up with the idea of abandoning the killing of *mingi* children (Gele Bani, 30 May 2018).

47 He is the son of a *kogo* (ritual expert and fire-maker), has a university degree and has been working for the local government in Banna and Jinka.

48 *Kogo* and *parko* are ritual experts. While the *kogo* is a ritual fire maker who performs protective rites for the cattle, the *parko* is the counterpart to the *bitta* and performs rituals for the cattle and the bees. The *parko* is also said to be able to move the stars when they have left their usual paths, and thereby prevent drought and disaster.

> at his ritual gateway (*kerri*) and addressed his ancestors [asking them to allow him to abandon infanticide]. Next, he took parts of the sheep's heart, tongue and stomach and put them onto the gateway [for the ancestors]. He ate some of it himself and then shared it among the elders and the people, saying: 'From this day on I have abandoned this practice! Let my children grow up in peace and freely!' About one year later, around forty-eight HTPs, including *mingi*, were registered as being abandoned in Banna land. [49] (Interview, 30 May 2018)

Other *bittas* followed Adeno's example and began denouncing the killing of *mingi* children. The former Hamar representative in the national parliament recounted:

> First *bitta* Adeno stopped it, maybe 5 or 6 years back. He also stopped the killing of the first-born child [of the Gatta clan].[50] (...) Then *bitta* Muga [the other Banna *bitta*] followed. In Lala, the Hamar *bitta* Bankimaro said during a public meeting, 'These are children of humans! If their teeth grow first on the upper jaw, to call them *mingi* is the talk of the past. Let it be gone!' (...). There is also, Elto [the other Hamar *bitta*]. But his talk is moving back and forth. He accepts some things and rejects and resists to others. (Interview, 1 June 2017)

However, despite the *bittas*' efforts, infanticide has not been easily given up and continues in many places.

Local reactions to external interventions

Generally, there appears to be no linear progression in combatting HTPs in Hamar and Bashada: the changes are scattered and not sustainable everywhere. This be-

49 According to him, today most of the Banna people go to Adeno's house if one of their children appears to be *mingi* (i.e. their first teeth in the upper jaw), especially since 2006. Nowadays, there are many children in Banna who have been ritually cleansed and have grown up with their families. Some live in Jinka, in the Omo Child orphanage. Most of these former *mingi* children are still underage and have not yet married. He expects that the *mingi* children who were cleansed can participate in any ritual and marry anyone from Banna. To understand whether such children have been totally accepted locally one would have to observe the marriage choices of individual families.

50 The different clans have their own prohibitions, abilities and rules. In the past, the Gatta clan used to kill all women's first-born children. In Bashada, I was told that it was their *parko* (ritual expert) Nakwa, my host father, who first abolished the killing of first-born girls and later also of first-born boys. Being Gatta himself, when his wife she finally gave birth – after 8 years of trying – he decided that the child should not be killed. Later, when his own son's wife gave birth to a boy, he also decided that the child should not be killed as his daughter-in-law had lost twins before. Though he abandoned the practice for Gatta children, this abandonment did not automatically oblige others to follow and I heard of a subsequent case of Gatta infanticide in a different family.

came sadly obvious in 2014 and 2015 when, in an act of resistance against the government, infanticide was revived in an area in Hamar where some parents had been raising their *mingi* children in the village.

Revitalization of infanticide as resistance

According to informants from the area, in the past they had been pressurized to send the *mingi* children to school. Some of those who received an education in Dimeka and Jinka made a career and came back as government officials. They were locally accepted, though again not without some pressure from the government side. The fact that they were able to support their families and communities financially also gave them some local leverage. [51] More recently, children were also educated in the newly built schools in the villages.

In 2014 a violent conflict erupted between some *kebeles* in Hamar and the government. Though the causes of the conflict and its triggers are complex, the main underlying reasons were related to continuous pressure from the government to send more children (especially girls) to school, to stop hunting in the national parks, and to end certain cultural practices (see Yohannes, this volume, for details). When the situation escalated at the end of 2014, the Hamar physically attacked the district administrator, police and other government representatives, destroyed government institutions, such as schools and health posts, and decided to return to their own ways. As part of their resistance, they revived certain practices in order to strengthen their own identity and as a sign that they rejected the new culture imposed on them. Among those practices was infanticide.

The former chief administrator of South Omo Zone and by then representative of the Hamar in the national parliament was called to help resolve the conflict. He recounted how the elders of the area emphasized their autonomy when they revitalized the practice of infanticide:

> With this conflict they have started it again. They said, 'In the past, this was our custom. This government told us to stop, but now we will do it again! We will turn back to our old practices!' (...).
> It was mainly the *zarsi* [community of males]. 'We are the ones who make the *bitta* a *bitta*, we are the ones who select the *ayo* (spokesman)! When we, the *zarsi*, say so, it will be given up! But if we say that there exist *mingi* children, there will be!'
> So, now they are killing them again. By then, there were four or five children killed, even big children who were attending school. (...). (Interview, 1 June 2017)

51 Oral information from Yohannes Yitbarek, who has been doing research in the conflict areas since 2016.

During the time of the conflict, some parents moved to town or gave their children to friends in town in order to save their lives. The discord between government and local popluation only really calmed down in 2017, partly because some of the government officials who had contributed to the escalation were taken to prison. The killing of *mingi* children who had been living in the community can be seen as a drastic way of restastance against the government when the pressure got too high.

Faking rituals

When the conflict became less severe, the government organized more meetings in an attempt to pick up its own efforts and reinforce the *bittas'* efforts to end the most prioritized HTPs.

In June 2016, for example, representatives from the local and regional government, with support from Save the Children, organized a meeting in Turmi involving men and women from Hamar and Bashada. The three ritual leaders (two from Hamar and one from Bashada) were invited to ritually abandon several harmful traditional practices, including the ritual infanticide of *mingi* children, early marriage, the exclusion of girls from education and the ritual whipping of girls and women during male initiation.[52]

The abandonment ritual was held again in Bashada, with only the Bashada *bitta*. However, it later came out that the rituals had not been done properly, neither in Hamar nor in Bashada. In both cases, certain ritual elements – invisible to outsiders – were changed, which rendered the whole event ineffective and non-binding. As a young Bashada man, who had participated in the ritual in Bashada, explained, no one felt obliged to abide by the ritual until it was repeated in the proper way:

> The first time the branches they used were from the wrong tree, a kind we don't use for rituals. 'These are *gal* [highland Ethiopians] coming to the ritual. What is the problem [with using the wrong tree]?' people had said [*laughs*]. 'They are like small children, they don't know!' The people tricked the government simply to appease them.
>
> But the administrator of Hamar Woreda was also there. He is Hamar and he had understood what the elders had done. So, he called them back! 'These were wrong trees that you used! Erect *baraza* [tree used for rituals]! Slaughter a sheep,

52 Save the Children has been involved in raising awareness on harmful traditional practices in Hamar, Dassanech and Nyangatom since 2010. It cooperates with the Women and Children's Affairs Offices and some other relevant stakeholders. As part of a revised strategy, and with funding from Save the Children Italy, in collaboration with the regional government, it organized the above-mentioned ritual (https://ethiopia.savethechildren.net/news/hamer-community-says-we-no-longer-tolerate-violence-against-children).

> go down to the river! I know all about it!' And then they did it all again, this time in the right way. (Interview, 27 March 2017)

The involvement of the *bittas* was not without pressure from the government side. As the *bittas* need the support of their communities to change cultural practices, they could not force their people to abandon the belief that *mingi* children were dangerous and give up infanticide. Instead, they pretended to cooperate with the officials, but actually altered the ritual.[53] Currently, new efforts are being made by the government to discuss with the communities, especially in those *kebeles* where resistance has been strong and violence has erupted.

Summary and conclusion

The practice of infanticide and abortion in Bashada and Hamar (as well as in Banna and Kara) is closely linked to the idea of personhood. Children conceived before marriage (*anzamo*-children) are considered as illegitimate and can never achieve the status of an accepted social person (*edi*). Such pregnancies, therefore, are usually ended through abortion. If the abortion fails, the children are eliminated after their birth. Accepting these children as persons seems most difficult in Bashada and Hamar, where people have resisted accepting them despite pressure from the government and many attempts to raise awareness of its undesirability. The status of children considered as ritually impure (*mingi* children) is only visible several months after birth: when their first teeth grow on the upper instead of the lower jaw, this indicates that preconception rites were not performed properly. Their status allegedly makes them – similar to child-witches in other countries – dangerous for their families and the whole community. They are believed to be equipped with supernatural powers who can afflict and kill their parents and siblings and bring disease and drought to all. Explanations for the status of such children differ: while an *anzamo* child cannot be a social person because it lacks a social father and therefore identity, a *mingi* child has been born outside the ritual order, which is believed to make them hazardous and a carrier of imbalance and disaster. The elimination of *mingi* children provides the local population with a feeling of control over uncontrollable events (like any other ritual or magic), and restores the social and ritual order. Defining births as legitimate only after marriage (until recently common also in the western world) and the performance of bridal rituals grants

53 Also, in Kara, where the practice of infanticide is said to have been abandoned completely, there are still few individuals who are not following the decision of the majority and ritual performance of their ritual leader, so that the awareness raising efforts of NGOs and government are continuing there, too (oral information by the managing director of the NGO OMO child).

a clear social status to all legitimately conceived children, even if their biological father is different from the social one.

The belief in *mingi* children also serves as an identity marker, especially in opposition or confrontation with the cultural other. During an intercultural workshop in which many women from different ethnic groups in South Omo participated, several women from Banna, Bashada, Kara and Ari explicitly drew a boundary between their groups and others from Arbore and Dassanech, emphasizing that they had certain rites necessary for a child to become human and that they practised infanticide on impure children (see Epple/Brüderlin 2004:chapter 7.14). Although I do not know how common the view is that infanticide creates a feeling of unity, the revitalization of the killing of *mingi* children that emerged from the armed conflict between the Hamar and the government in 2014 showed that infanticide can easily be evoked as an identity marker. As several informants from those rebellious *kebeles* confirmed, the reinvigoration of infanticide was not only a return to past traditions that were only reluctantly given up under government pressure, it was also an act of revenge, demonstrating distance and resistance to the pressure to change. It emphasized the Hamar people's otherness and independence, as Scotti (2017:403) predicted.

Efforts to combat abortion and infanticide must take all these cultural meanings and beliefs into account, and acknowledge that too much pressure and the criminalization of culture can have adverse effects. At the official level, it appears that this has been accepted, and is reflected in the emphasis on awareness raising over strict law enforcement. Practically, however, it seems that too many meetings and one-sided discussions have led to fatigue and frustration among the local population, who – feeling pressurized – pretend to agree and fake rituals to please the government.

So, what can be done? The results of the combination of efforts (awareness raising, support for individual families, offers to adopt children, pressure from the government) made in Kara, where infanticide of *mingi* and *anzamo* children has almost stopped, is encouraging, and interventions should continue, with a focus on providing information on issues related to infanticide. To avoid frustration in the communities, which might lead to more resistance, rather than placing too much stress on values and laws, continued education on the real causes of natural disasters and disease would help reduce the fear of *mingi* children. Better explanations about birth control and provision of contraceptives could help avoid unwanted pregnancies from the beginning. Debates on values, and possibly on the outside image of the groups, might help them question their identity markers and lead to changes in attitude. As one Kara man said after years of awareness raising and discussions with the government, NGOs and educated Kara men: 'We do not want to be known for killing our children anymore!'[54] Yet, as Feitosa *et al.* (2010) have suggested, such discussions should probably be done in a more participatory way, and not provide all the answers from the beginning.

Despite the many drawbacks and problems, as the Head of the Women and Children's Affairs Office in Hamar Woreda (herself from Hamar) positively and realistically remarked:

> What is called *dambi* (tradition, custom) will not disappear in one day! It is something that needs a lot of time! (Interview, 27 March 2017)

References

AFRICAN UNION COMMISSION, DEPARTMENT OF SOCIAL AFFAIRS, 2012 *Harmful traditional practices towards women and girls in Africa*. Addis Ababa: African Union

AN-NA'IM, ABDULLAHI (ed.), 1992 *Human rights in cross-cultural perspectives: A quest for consensus.* Philadelphia: University of Philadelphia Press

ASIAN CENTRE FOR HUMAN RIGHTS (ACHR), 2016 *Female infanticide worldwide: The case for action by the UN Human Rights Council.* New Delhi: ACHR (accessible online at http://www.indiaenvironmentportal.org.in/files/file/Femalefoeticideworldwide.pdf, last accessed 31 October 2018)

ASMAROM Legesse, 1973 *Gada: Three approaches to the study of African society.* New York: Free Press, London: Collier–Macmillan

BASHIR, Samina, 2011 "Infanticide and diminished responsibility: In conflict with International Human Rights Law and Islamic legal norms", *Pakistan Journal of Islamic Research* 8:45–60

BENDA-BECKMANN, Franz von, 2009 "Human rights, cultural relativism and legal pluralism: Towards a two-dimensional debate", in: Franz von Benda-Beckmann, Keebet von Benda-Beckmann and Anne Griffiths (eds.) *The power of law in a transnational world*, 115–134. Oxford and New York: Berghahn

BRÜDERLIN, Tina, 2012 "The incorporation of children into the society: Pre- and postnatal rituals among the Hamar of southern Ethiopia", *Working papers of the department of Anthropology and African Studies 135*, Institut für Ethnologie und Afrikastudien, Johannes Gutenberg-Universität Mainz (accessible online at https://www.ifeas.uni-mainz.de/Dateien/AP135.pdf, last accessed 1 August 2018)

54 This statement was made by a Kara man during the time when strong efforts were being made in Kara to overcome infanticide. He can be seen in John Rowe's documentary film *The River and the Bush* (Rowe 2015).

CARRITHERS, Michael, Steven COLLINS and Stephen LUKES (eds.), 1985 *The category of the person: Anthropology, philosophy, history*. Cambridge: Cambridge University Press

CIMPRIC, Aleksandra, 2010 *Children accused of witchcraft: An anthropological study of contemporary practices in Africa*. Dakar: UNICEF WCARO (accessible online at https://www.unicef.org/wcaro/wcaro_children-accused-of-witchcraft-in-Africa.pdf, last accessed 1 November 2018)

COWAN, Jane K., Marie-Bénédicte DEMBOUR, Richard A. WILSON (eds.), 2001 *Culture and rights: Anthropological perspectives*. Cambridge: CUP

ENCYCLOPEDIA OF POPULATION, 2018 "Infanticide" (accessible online at http://www.encyclopedia.com/social-sciences/encyclopedias-almanacs-transcripts-and-maps/infanticide-1, last accessed, 20 October 2018)

EPPLE, Susanne and Tina BRÜDERLIN, 2004 *The pride and social worthiness of women in South Omo*, Working papers of the department of Anthropology and African Studies 78, Institut für Ethnologie und Afrikastudien, Johannes Gutenberg-Universität Mainz (accessible online athttp://www.ifeas.uni-mainz.de/Dateien/AP78.pdf, last accessed 1 August 2018)

EPPLE, Susanne and Sophia THUBAUVILLE (eds.), 2012 "Cultural diversity in Ethiopia: Between appreciation and suppression" (Special focus issue), *Paideuma* 58

EPPLE, Susanne 2012a "Selective resilience: Local responses to externally induced cultural change in southern Ethiopia", *Paideuma* 58:197–212

2012b "Harmful practice or ritualized guidance? Reflections on physical punishment as part of the socialization among the Bashada of southern Ethiopia", *Rassegna di Studi Etiopici* 3:69–102

2010 *The Bashada of southern Ethiopia: A study of age, gender and social discourse*. Köln: Köppe

ERIKSEN, Thomas Hylland 2001 "Between universalism and relativism: A critique of the UNESCO concept of culture", in: Jane K. Cowan, Marie-Bénédicte Dembour, Richard A. Wilson (eds.) *Culture and rights: Anthropological perspectives*, 127–148. Cambridge: CUP

FEDERAL DEMOCRATIC REPUBLIC OF ETHIOPIA (FDRE), 2013 *The Federal Democratic Republic of Ethiopia National Human Rights Action Plan 2013–2015* (acc. online at http://www.ehrc.org.et/PublicationsandReports/Publications)

FEITOSA, Saulo Ferreira *et al.*, 2010 "Bioethics, culture and infanticide in Brazilian indigenous communities: the Zuruahá case", *Cad. Saúde Pública, Rio de Janeiro* 26 (5):853–878

FOBLETS, Marie-Claire and Nadjma YASSARI (eds.), 2013 *Legal approaches to cultural diversity*. Leiden/Boston: Martinus Nijhoff

FRIEDMAN, Susan Hatters and Philip J. RESNICK, 2007 "Child murder by mothers: patterns and prevention", *World Psychiatry* 6 (3):137–141

GRÜNBAUM, Ellen, 2015 "Epilogue: Harm and well-being: Cultural practices and harmful global practices", in Chia Longman and Tamsin Bradley (eds.) *Interrogating harmful cultural practices: Gender, culture and coercion*, 193–20. Farnham: Ashgate

HODGSON, Dorothy L. (ed.), 2011 *Gender and culture at the limits of rights*. Philadelphia: University of Pennsylvania Press

JEFFREYS, Sheila 2011 *Beauty and misogyny. Harmful cultural practices in the West.* London and New York: Routledge

JONES, Nicola *et al.*, 2018a "'Sticky' gendered norms. Change and stasis in the patterning of child marriage in Amhara, Ethiopia", in Caroline Harper *et al.* (eds.) *Empowering adolescent girls in developing countries: Gender justice and norm change*, 43–62. London and New York: Routledge

2018b "The politics of policy and programme implementation to advance adolescent girls' well-being in Ethiopia", in Caroline Harper *et al.* (eds.): *Empowering adolescent girls in developing countries: Gender justice and norm change*, 62–80. London and New York: Routledge

LA FONTAINE, Jean S., 1985 "Person and individual: Some anthropological reflections", in: Michael Carrithers, Steven Collins and Steven Lukes (eds.): *The category of the person: Anthropology, philosophy, history*, 123–140. Cambridge *et al.*: Cambridge University Press

LANCY, David F., 2014 "Babies aren't persons": A survey of delayed personhood", in: Hiltrud Otto and Heidi Keller (eds.) *Different faces of attachment: Cultural variations on a universal human need*, 66–112. Cambridge: Cambridge University Press

LANGFIELD, Michele, William LOGAN and Máiréad Nic CRAITH, 2010 *Cultural diversity, heritage and human rights: Intersections in theory and practice*. London and New York: Routledge

LATOSKY, Shauna, 2012 "A form of self-harm? Opening the dialogue on 'harmful cultural practices' in southern Ethiopia", *Paideuma* 58:229–244

2013 *Predicaments of Mursi (Mun) Women in Ethiopia's Changing World*. Köln: Köppe

2015 "Lip plates, 'harm' debates, and the cultural rights of the Mursi (Mun) women", in: Chia Longman and Tamsin Bradley (eds.) *Interrogating harmful cultural practices: Gender, culture and coercion*, 169–192. Farnham: Ashgate

LONGMAN, Chia and Tasmin BRADLEY (eds.), 2015a *Interrogating harmful cultural practices: Gender, culture and coercion*. Farnham: Ashgate

2015b "Interrogating the concept of 'harmful cultural practices", in: Chia Longman and Tasmin Bradley (eds.) *Interrogating harmful cultural practices. Gender, culture and coercion*, 11–30. Farnham: Ashgate

LYDALL, Jean, 1976 "Hamer", in: M. Lionel Bender (ed.) *The Non-Semitic Languages of Ethiopia*, 393–438. East Lansing, Michigan: Michigan State University, African Studies Center

2005 "The power of women in an ostensibly male-dominated agro-pastoral society", in: Thomas Widlok and Tadesse Wolde (eds.) *Property and equality 2: Encapsulation, commercialization, discrimination*, 152–172. Oxford, New York: Berghahn

MERRY, Sally Engle, 2006 *Human rights and gender violence: Translating international law into local justice.* Chicago and London: The University of Chicago Press

MILNER, Larry Stephen, 2000 *Hardness of heart/hardness of life: The stain of human infanticide*. Lanham, New York, Oxford: University Press of America

MOSELEY, Kathryn L., 1986 "The history of infanticide in western society", Issues Law Med. 1 (5):345–361

PREIS, Ann-Belinda S., 1996 "Human rights as cultural practice: An anthropological critique", *Human Rights Quarterly* 18 (2):286–315

ROWE, JOHN, 2015 *Omo child: The river and the bush* (film). Little Pass Films

SAVE THE CHILDREN NORWAY–ETHIOPIA, 2011 *Baseline survey on the most prevalent HTP and sanitation practices among the community of the Hamer, Dassenech, and Nyangatom Woredas of the South Omo Zone in the SNNPRS.* Addis Ababa (accessible online at https://www.norad.no/globalassets/import-2162015-80434-am/www.norad.no-ny/filarkiv/ngo-evaluations/baseline-survey-on-the-most-prevalent-harmful-traditional-practices-htps-and-sanitation-practices-in-hamer-dassenech-and-nyangtom-woredas-of-south-omo-zone-of-snnpr-ethiopia.pdf, last accessed 19 April 2018)

SCHRAMM, Fermin Roland, 2010 "The morality of infanticide at the crossroads between moral pluralism and human rights culture", Cad. Saúde Pública, Rio de Janeiro, 26(5):853–878 (acc. online at https://pdfs.semanticscholar.org/ba47/4bc988514c73d193576e304c91e3ba1cc270.pdf, last accessed 2 November 2018)

SCOTTI, Guilherme, 2017 "Human rights and multiculturalism: The debate on indigenous infanticide in Brazil", *Bio Law Journal – Rivista di Bio Diritto* 3:387–403

SOUTH OMO WOMEN AND CHILDREN'S AFFAIRS DEPARTMENT, 2016 *Report sent to the Women, Children and Youth's Affairs Bureau on HTPs in the six pastoral and agro-pastoral woredas* 2009 (2016) (unpublished manuscript)

THUBAUVILLE, Sophia, 2012 "Brides behind bars: Maale women as captives between tradition and development", *Paideuma* 58: 213–228

UN COMMITTEE ON THE RIGHTS OF THE CHILD (CRC), 2013 *General comment No. 15 (2013) on the right of the child to the enjoyment of the highest attainable standard of health* (Art. 24), 17 April 2013, CRC/C/GC/15, accessible online at http://www.refworld.org/docid/51ef9e134.html, last accessed 1 November 2018

UNITED STATES DEPARTMENT OF STATE 2015, 2014 *Country Reports on Human Rights Practices – Ethiopia, 25 June 2015* (accessible online at http://www.refworld.org/docid/559bd56b3b.html, last accessed on 1 November 2018)

UNICEF ETHIOPIA, CHILD PROTECTION SECTION AND MEDIA & EXTERNAL RELATIONS SECTION, 2015 *Harmful traditional practices: Briefing note* (accessible online at https://www.unicef.org/ethiopia/Child_Marriage_and_FGM_2015.pdf; last accessed, 1 April 2019)

UNITED NATIONS, 1989 *UN Convention on the Rights of the Child* (accessible online at https://downloads.unicef.org.uk/wp-content/uploads/2010/05/UNCRC_united_nations_convention_on_the_rights_of_the_child.pdf?_ga=2.2298224.1797821837.1541070582-1811260057.1541070582, last accessed 1 November 2018)

UN NEWS, 2003 *UN agency deplores infanticide of girls in India; praises government for study* (accessible online at https://news.un.org/en/story/2003/10/83772-un-agency-deplores-infanticide-girls-india-praises-government-study, last accessed 3 October 2018)

WARREN, Mary Anne, 1985 *Gendercide: The implications of sex selection*. Totowa, N.J.: Rowman & Allanheld

WORKING GROUP ON THE GIRL-CHILD, 2007 *A girl's right to live: Female foeticide and girl infanticide: Report published on the occasion of the United Nations Commission on the Status of Women 51st Session, 26 February to 9 March 2007* (accessible online at https://wilpf.org/wp-content/uploads/2014/07/2007_A_Girls_Right_to_Live.pdf, last accessed 31 October 2018)

Webpages

http://www.gendercide.org/case_infanticide.html

http://www.refworld.org/docid/559bd56b3b.html

https://www.omohope.org

http://omochildmovie.com

https://ethiopia.savethechildren.net/news/hamer-community-says-we-no-longer-tolerate-violence-against-children

https://www.telegraph.co.uk/news/worldnews/africaandindianocean/ethiopia/9189136/Saving-the-condemned-children-of-Ethiopia.html

https://www.thereporterethiopia.com/article/peculiar-case-mingi

https://www.christianitytoday.com/ct/2011/august/ethiopiariverdeath.html

www.un.org/womenwatch/daw/cedaw

http://gtliconnect.blogspot.de/2011/11/creating-mingi-friendly-communities.html, and http://galataministries.org)

16. Clashing values

The 2015 conflict in Hamar district of South Omo Zone, southern Ethiopia

Yohannes Yitbarek

Introduction

Hamar Woreda is a district in southern Ethiopia that has, until recently, been rather detached from the centre. Like most of their ethnic neighbours in South Omo Zone, the Hamar people are agro-pastoralists who have lived somewhat autonomously for a long time in the district. Despite their incorporation into the Ethiopian nation state in the late-nineteenth century, the Hamar were able to continue an independent lifestyle, with limited contact with the subsequent central governments. Since the mid-1990s, the government's attempts to actively include all ethnic groups and develop remote areas have changed many things, and interactions between local communities and government have become frequent. These encounters between different people and their value systems have led to innovations, but also tensions and conflict. In 2014/5, growing tension between the local authorities and the Hamar community over their clashing values escalated into a serious armed conflict. The resolution of the conflict could only be achieved with much effort, concessions on both side, and a better understanding of and respect for some of the key values of Hamar society. This chapter looks at the causes of the tension, the reasons for the escalation of the conflict and the efforts made by both sides to resolve it. In doing so, I explore the differing value positions, perspectives and strategies employed by local government agents and the Hamar people to achieve their goals.[1]

1 The fieldwork for this research has been done as part of my PhD project at the Max Planck Institute (MPI) for Social Anthropology, Halle/Saale, Germany. All fieldwork expenses were covered by the department of Integration and Conflict of MPI. I have conducted fieldwork between September 2016 to September 2017. The data for this research was gathered through structured and semi structured interviews with local people and local government authorities in Hamar.

The Hamar and their relation with the Ethiopian state

The Hamar are one of the largest groups in South Omo Zone of the Southern Nations, Nationalities and People's Regional State (SNNPRS). According to the Central Statistical Agency, the Hamar population was estimated to be 59,160 in 2007 (CSA 2008). The Hamar speak their own South Omotic language. Their economy combines the rearing of animals (goats, sheep, cattle), farming (sorghum, maize, varieties of beans), apiculture, and hunting and gathering (Strecker 2010:87). They live in mountainous and lowland areas, in settlement areas consisting of several homesteads. Close relatives are usually clustered together within one homestead.

The Hamar social and political organization is rather egalitarian and could be called acephalous or, as Amborn (2018), puts it 'polycephalous', which means that they have no central leader or chief; rather they live a kind of 'regulated anarchy', where seniority and the rhetorical skills of individuals play a role in daily affairs and conflict resolution. The Hamar have two ritual leaders, locally called *bitta*,[2] one from the Gatta clan and the other from the Worla clan, who are responsible for the spiritual well-being of the country, but do not have any political power. They have twenty-four exogamous clans under two moieties (Strecker 2006b:87).

Like the other groups in South Omo, the Hamar were incorporated into the Ethiopian state by Emperor Menelik II at the end of the nineteenth century (Donham and James 2002, Lydall 2010, Strecker 2013, Tsega-Ab 2005). Under the succeeding governments of Ethiopia, they were governed by rulers whose staff consisted mainly of central and northern Ethiopians. As Jean Lydall (2010:322) noted, in the immediate period after Menelik's conquest and also later during Emperor Haile Selassie's rule (1931–1974), the governors made no effort to condemn the culture and tradition of the conquered groups; instead they emphasized cultural difference to justify their dominance. Their relations with the local community were confined to issues concerning the 'adjudication of inter-group conflicts' and the 'collection of taxes' (Lydall (2010:322). With the coming to power of the socialist Derg regime (1974–1991), a few development projects (schools, road, market schemes and relief aid programmes) loaded with 'a civilizational bias' (Abbink 1997:2) were introduced to the Hamar, as well as to other groups in Southern Ethiopia.

After the downfall of the Derg in 1991, the change of government significantly transformed the relationship between the central state and most of the local groups in Ethiopia, including the Hamar. The ruling party, the Ethiopian People's Revolutionary Front (EPRDF), adopted the language of democracy, peace and development, and abandoned a highly centralized, unitary state in favour of what is

2 The term '*bitta*' literally means 'the first' and refers to the first ancestor of the Hamar to settle in the area. It also means 'the first' in authority and 'the first' in transcendental and ritual power (see Strecker 1976:30).

commonly known as 'ethnic-based federalism', giving constitutionally based equal power to all ethnic groups and individuals (Belete 2008:447). Since then, the Hamar, like other groups in Ethiopia, have been exercising the right to govern their own affairs. They are also entitled to the 'right to development', to education, health services, markets and infrastructure.

Although introduced with the objective of improving living standards (FDRE 2015), these development packages contravene Hamar values and have triggered conflicts between the local population and the district administration. Over the past few years, the relationship between the local population and the administration of Hamar Woreda has been increasingly tense. Numerous small and large disputes led to an open and armed confrontation that reached a climax in 2015 when open war broke out between the Hamar and the district police. In its aftermath, the conflict continued to engage local, regional and national officials as well as the Hamar people, and to this day it has not been fully settled.

The issues that led to the outbreak of the conflict have been topics of intense debate among the Hamar community, the local authorities, residents of Dimeka, and others who were directly or indirectly involved or affected by the conflict. The Hamar mention two major issues as the causes of the conflict: the denial of access to the Mago National Park; and problems related to the schooling of girls. On the other hand, the local authorities blame the Hamar for being resistant to modernity, characterizing the communities involved in the conflict as rather 'closed', locked in their own traditions and stubbornly opposed to any change, citing the Hamar people's rejection of education and their insistence on hunting game and grazing in the Mago National Park as evidence.

Having looked deeper into the topic and talked to many individuals on both sides, I will argue here that the main cause of the conflict is the clash between two different value systems: the rather mobile agro-pastoral production of the Hamar and the top-down development approach of the government.

Universal human rights, particular cultures and national interests

Over the past decades, social and economic development programmes aimed at changing the lifestyles of pastoral and agro-pastoral communities have been widely introduced by the Ethiopian government. Education provision and the need to reduce gender disparity in the schooling system and other social service projects are among the key priorities of the government's social development programme. These programmes are usually framed in the context of universal human right discourses, such as the 'education for all' programme established at the Dakar UN Forum in 2000, and the Convention on the Elimination of All Forms of Discrimination against Women (CEDAW) adopted in 1979. The implementation of these social development programmes has generated different responses among local communities, local administrations, national governments and international organizations. To understand these dynamics, it is necessary to contextualize the discussion within the broader debate and negotiation about and legal uses of 'human rights' and their conjunction with 'particular cultures' (Cowan *et al.* 2001:1, Johansson 2017:611). The pervasive use of 'universal rights' and the way these rights are implemented in local contexts, and resisted by and negotiated in particular cultures and societies offers a more meaningful insight to comprehend the applicability of universal rights in local settings.

According to Johansson (2017:613), the debate between 'universal rights' and 'particular cultures' has existed since the adoption of Universal Declaration of Human Rights (UDHR) in 1948. The preamble of the UDHR affirms that 'Peoples of the United Nations (...) faith in fundamental human rights, in the dignity and worth of the human person, in the equal rights of men and women and of nations large and small' (UN 1948:1). The assembly also proclaims the UDHR as 'a common standard of achievement for all peoples and all nations' (ibid). Following the adoption of the UDHR, countries around the world, including Ethiopia, have ratified several human right conventions. Many have even gone further, enacting legislation, creating mechanisms and putting into place a range of measures to ensure the protection and realization of rights within their jurisdictions. Anthropologists and other social scientists have nevertheless criticized this universalistic approach to the implementation of human rights on the basis of cultural relativism.

Cultural relativism, which has been advocated since the early twentieth century by the American anthropologist Franz Boas and his students, has become the core of the human rights discourse. The main argument of cultural relativism is that all cultures and value systems, despite their diversity, are equally valid (Dahre 2017:616), and that culture is a complex whole with parts so intertwined that none of them can be understood or evaluated without reference to the other parts and the cultural whole (Lawson cited in Hossain 2015:3). Hence, according to the cultural relativist view, human rights cannot be universal but are culturally relative. Moreover, advocates of universalism have been criticized for their failure to detail the circumstances of implementation of rights in particular cultures and societies. Hossain (2015:1) for example, argues that 'in states where arranged marriages are common, one would expect clause 2 of Art 16 of the UDHR ("marriage shall be entered in to only with the free and full consent of the intending spouse") to be routinely disregarded'. Thus, some authors argue, as universal rights are unresponsive to cultural differences, they are instruments of oppression (Forst 1999:35). Certain rights – such as women's, marriage, social and economic rights and the right to education – have even been criticized as attempts to universalize western values and impost them on non-western societies (Hossain 2015).

The discussion on universalism and cultural relativism seems to be animated by a contest between the desire to establish universal rights on the one hand, and the awareness of cultural differences on the other (Cowan *et al.* 2001:4). At times, arguments promoting or opposing either universalism or relativism are instrumentalized to advance the political and economic interests of certain groups. In the context of the conflict between the Hamar and the government, for example, one can see the inconsistent position of the government in its advocacy of certain rights over others. For example, the right to education for girls is among the cardinal issues in the rights discourses of the government. As such, it was among the main reasons for the 2015 open confrontation between the police and the Hamar communities. The Hamar refused to send their girls to school due to certain cultural norms, and their resistance was aggravated by serious problems, such as sexual harassment, at the schools in town. The other trigger for the Hamar–government conflict was the government's restriction of the Hamar people's right to hunt and graze their animals in the Mago Park and its surroundings. The government considered such behaviour to be damaging to wildlife and biodiversity and did not view it as part of the social and economic rights of the indigenous people, as stipulated in Art. 5 of the United Nations Declaration on the Rights of Indigenous Peoples (UNDRIP).

The lack of uniform positions towards universal rights and particular cultures makes the debate between universalism and relativism more compelling, and shows how both concepts are essentialized by different actors to promote their interests. Hence, as Cowan *et al.* (2001:6) argue, rather than seeing universalism and cultural relativism as two opposing forces, one should see the tension between the positions as part of an on-going social process in which universal and local values are negotiated and evaluated in relation to each other. Furthermore, posing the choices in such a dichotomous way ignores the extent to which the different actors – local people, governments and international organizations – have negotiated these contradictions and redefined both the meanings of rights and culture (Merry 2001:32).

Recent national development priorities in Ethiopia

According to government reports, Ethiopia is working towards achieving broad-based, accelerated and sustained economic growth in order to outpace the predicaments posed by poverty. In the public discourse, poverty is considered as an existential threat to the country and its people (FDRE 2015:4). The only viable option considered by the government to tackle these challenges of poverty was to design a comprehensive national development plan aimed at bringing fast and sustained economic growth. Hence, since 2002, the Ministry of Finance and Economic Development (MoFED) has implemented four successive national development plans guided by an overall development policy agenda of eradicating poverty. These include the Sustainable Development and Poverty Reduction Programme (SDPRP), the Plan for Accelerated and Sustained Development to End Poverty (PASDEP), the First Growth and Transformation Plan (GTP I), and the Second Growth and Transformation Plan (GTP II).

The first, the SDPRP (2002/03–2004/05), emphasized the transformation of the rural economy in general and the agricultural sector in particular. The plan's overriding focus was on agriculture as the engine of growth with a huge potential to fuel the growth of other sectors of the economy by facilitating surplus production, market creation and provision of raw material and foreign exchange (FDRE 2002:iii).

The second, PASDEP (2005/06–2009/10), built on the goals pursued under the SDPRP. The plan was designed to bring accelerated growth to the economy through a particular focus on private sector development and commercialization of agriculture, industry and urban development (MoFED 2007:1).

The third, the GTP I (2010/11–2014/15), was designed with the objective of achieving the Millennium Development Goals (MDGs). It focused on improving the quantity and quality of social services, especially education, health and other infrastructural developments, thereby hoping to achieve macroeconomic stability and enhance productivity in agriculture and manufacturing sectors (FDRE 2010:7). During the GTP I period, several massive development projects were implemented, such as the construction of dams for hydroelectric power, sugar factories and cotton plantations as well as the creation of mechanized agricultural estates, especially along the major river valleys of the Awash, the Gibe-Omo, the Wabe Shebelli, the Beles, and the Abay (Blue Nile). Many of these development projects are situated in the pastoral and agro-pastoral inhabited lowland peripheries of the country, which are considered by the government as 'less inhabited' and endowed with 'abundant' and 'virgin' land.

According to government reports, the main aim of these development projects is to improve the living standards of the pastoral and agro-pastoral population, mainly by integrating them into the mainstream national economy and by facilitating social development though improving pastoral livelihoods and asset bases, basic social services, and institutional setup (FDRE 2008:8). In doing so, various government and non-government organizations (NGOs) are working towards changing the lifestyle of these communities.

Generally, since the introduction of GTP I, and even more so since the fourth national development plan, the GTP II (2014/15–2019/20), emphasis has been given to boosting the national economy and improving the standard of living of all citizens, in order to maintain the vision of Ethiopia becoming a 'middle income country by 2025 through sustaining the rapid, broad based and inclusive economic growth, which accelerates economic transformation and the journey towards the country's renaissance' (FDRE 2015:2).

The four national development programmes mentioned above share a focus on modernizing agriculture as the main driver for rapid economic growth and development. Additionally, the programmes presume the move toward the middle-income country can be achieved through centrally planned and installed development plans.

The type of development approach promoted by the EPRDF basically emanated from and is guided by the developmental state[3] ideology of the government. The developmental state ideology – often associated with the economic polices followed by East Asian governments (e.g. South Korea and Taiwan) – underscores the importance of state intervention, shared vision orientation, central planning, coordination of development projects, and commitment to building human capital (Planel 2014:421). It has been Ethiopia's overarching development approach since 2001 (Fana 2014:67). Under the developmental state ideology, the government has promoted state intervention in economy and society, or 'a revolution from above' (Aaron 2017:48), to transform the economy. This kind of development approach usually disregards local realities, values and complexities and is geared towards securing fast national economic growth.

Development and related conflicts in South Omo

As mentioned earlier, the government considers the lowland peripheries as important outlets for its ambition to foster fast and sustained economic growth (Markakis 2011:291). In South Omo, recent projects include the Kuraz Sugar Development Project (KSDP) along the banks of the Omo River, and the villagization programme in the *woredas* of Bodi, Mursi, Gnangatom,[4] Dassanech and Hamar. Several other state-backed but privately owned large-scale agricultural investments have also been put in place in the last few years.

Presently, the KSDP is the largest irrigation-based agricultural development scheme in the country, with 175.000 hectares of land and a plan to build five sugar factory units. The KSDP project area encompasses Salamago and Gnangatom Woredas from South Omo, the Surma and Meinit-Shasha districts of Bench-Maji and Diecha district of Kefa Zone. Most of the people living in and around the

3 Even scholars continue to debate the conceptual understanding of developmental state, following Mkandawire (2001:3), I define 'developmental state' as a state 'whose ideological underpinnings are developmental and one that seriously attempts to deploy its administrative and political resources to the task of economic development'.

4 Also: 'Nyangatom'.

project area are agro-pastoralists who rely on animal husbandry and flood-retreat cultivation from the Omo River. With regard to the transformational impact of the KSDP project, Kamski (2016:6) has noted two main impacts: 'the alteration of the natural landscape' and the abrupt transformation of the socio-cultural sphere caused by migrant labour workers and the state-directed villagization of local people.

Although the project has so far not been implemented across all 175,000 hectares of land, the land-clearing process and the construction of waterworks and roads have brought new challenges to the local people and their environs. Buffavand (2018:298), for example, has noted with regard to the Mela:[5]

> When the bulldozers had just started to raze the bush belt to the ground, large animals in particular were in disarray, having lost their shelter. (...) Mela certainly deplored the loss of their resources: game meat but also diverse edible plants, medicinal plants, trees for house and bee-hive construction, dry-season grazing plants for cattle, etc., were disappearing with the bush belt.

The conversion of riverbank land for estates and the construction of the Gibe III dam have also greatly affected the practice of flood recession agriculture (Turton 2011:166, Kamski 2015:6).

As the construction of the Kuraz sugar factories in Salamago and Gnangatom Woredas is still on-going, everyday resistance in its different forms is arising from the local groups near the project areas. One source of conflict in Bodi and Mursi areas, for example, is the issue of accidents and injuries to people and their cattle caused by the sugar plantation's vehicles on the areas bumpy and damaged roads. On 4 December 2017, for example, twelve truck drivers were killed by the Bodi after a Bodi man was killed in a car accident. Public and private trucks frequently run between Jinka, headquarters of the South Omo Zone, and Hana, the small town near the sugar factory, and factory workers are often the targets for retaliation for accidents on the road.

Privately owned large-scale agricultural investments are another cause of contention, as illustrated by the case of the conflict that arose between a cotton plantation investment near the Woito River, the Birale Agricultural Development Private Limited Company and the Tsamakko community in South Omo. The Tsamakko were dispossessed of their land by the cotton farm and, in the confrontations that resulted, workers from the farm and members of the Tsamakko community were killed (Gabbert 2014:29, Melese 2009:280). Such conflicts between private investors and local communities are also very common in other regions of Ethiopia (for example Gambella).

5 The Mela people also called under the ethnonym Bodi.

South Omo has also attracted the attention of the government in the area of eco-tourism development, as is evidenced in the strict enforcement of wildlife protected areas (WPAs). These include the Omo National Park, Mago National Park, Tama and Chelbi Wildlife Reserves, Murle and Welishet Sala Controlled Hunting Areas. In order to protect the animal population, the local population are prohibited from entering such areas to hunt or to graze their animals, while tourists are allowed in to both see the animals and sometimes to hunt. The prohibitions have been enforced more strictly in the last decade, which has led to repeated conflicts between WPA scouts[6] and the local communities.

The Hamar, Banna, Bashada, Ari and the Mursi are among the groups who live in the adjoining area of one of the recently contested protected areas – the Mago National Park. They enter the park to hunt wild animals and graze their cattle and the recent stricter enforcement of the law become a source of conflict, causing the loss of human life among the local hunters and the scouts been hired by the government to protect the area. When four scouts in the Mago Park were killed during a clash with poachers in 2015, the relationship between the local communities and the park authorities became very tense and full of ambivalence.

Another area of development intervention in South Omo is the provision of schooling and other social service projects[7] aimed at improving the standard of living of the agro-pastoralists. Numerous primary schools have been built in different *woredas* (districts) of South Omo, and special awareness programmes have been organized to convince parents to send their children to school. Recently, more and more pressure has been exerted on parents who have resisted. This and the issue of the protection given to girls who have run away from home to join school have become another major source of conflict between the administration and some groups in the region (Epple 2012, Maurus 2016). In particular, the campaign to send girls to the boarding schools in town is being more and more resisted, as there have been many cases of undesired marriage with town people (and abandonment of previously arranged marriages), unwanted pregnancies and abortion, and a general abandonment of local values.

Conflicts between the Hamar and the government

The conflict that arose between the Hamar and the *woreda* administration in 2015 can be considered as the third in a line of wars fought since the incorporation of the

6 Most of the scouts working in the Mago Park are from the neighbouring groups: Banna, Ari and Hamar.

7 The social service projects being implemented in the region include: primary and secondary schools, public health services, veterinary services, market and rural road construction programmes.

Hamar into the Ethiopian state. The first war was fought with the soldiers of Emperor Menelik's army when they invaded and incorporated the Hamar and neighbouring groups into the Ethiopian state. In an account given by Baldambe, a Hamar elder, of his father's experiences during that time, he recounted how the Hamar had first fought and resisted and were later devastated by Menelik's army (Strecker 2013). Their catastrophic defeat by Emperor Menelik's army cost the Hamar an entire generation, and they were forced to live in exile in the lands of the Dassanech for many years.

The second violent encounter took place in a place called Assile in southern Hamar in 1948. This conflict with Emperor Haile Selassie's soldiers is still fresh in the memory of the Hamar and is remembered as the 'Assile war'. The Hamar's frequent cattle raiding of the Borana and the intervention of Haile Selassie's administration to secure the return of the looted cattle are considered as the causes of the Assile war. The war was devastating and took numerous human lives on both sides. Cattle died and Hamar houses were burnt down. For almost fifty years after the Assile debacle there was not any open conflict between the Hamar and government soldiers. The third and most recent conflict between eight Hamar kebeles[8] and the Hamar Woreda administration erupted in January 2015.

According to informants from both sides, the animosity between the administration and the community started in 2012, when the Woreda administration introduced a rifle registration programme with the objective of controlling illicit arm possession among the community. The Hamar were unhappy with the programme, insinuating that the local administration was helping the government to abuse the gun registration and licensing system so that they could later confiscate the guns from the people who had registered. They traced an analogy from Haile Selassie's time when, after much debate, the Hamar had handed over their arms to the governors for registration, only to find the weapons were never returned but sent instead to the central administration in Addis Ababa. They feared the same thing would happen during the 2012 registration programme.

The government considered the resistance of the Hamar to the rifle registration programme as a violation of the rule of law and a sign of disobedience to the government. As higher officials in the Woreda administration told me, because of Hamar resistance, the administration failed to meet its obligations with regard to the registration and licensing programme.

The already unpleasant relationship between the Hamar and the authorities became worse in the context of the open confrontations with poachers in the Mago

8 The Hamar *kebeles* most vigorously involved in the conflict with the government were Worro, Shanqo Qelema, Shanqo Wolfo, Lala, Achi Mussa, Achi Algone, Kufur and Gedback. The government and the town people alike refer to these kebeles as the 'security cluster *kebeles*'.

National Park and repeated cases of Hamar girls running away to the towns for education. In 2015, the Woreda administration's attempt to bring poachers to court and to try to stop any future encroachment in to the park turned into an open confrontation between the Hamar youngsters and the police in a place called Worro. The clash resulted in the deaths of six policemen and one elementary school teacher, and in the destruction of public service centres, including schools and health centres. From January 2015 to November 2017, government activities in these villages were curtailed by the security problem and no public servant dared to work in those villages. In the following, a detailed account of the main conflict will be given, followed by an analysis of the events and circumstances that led to it.

The armed conflict

The open confrontation between the police and the Hamar took place in a village called Worro on 15 January 2015. On that day, a team from the Hamar Woreda administration that included the police, the vice administrator and the head of security, as well as representatives of local elders from the nearby villages,[9] went to Worro to bring poachers, accused of poaching in the Mago Park, to the court. [10]

Before that day, the Hamar Woreda administration and the Mago Park Office had held a series of consultative meetings with the community of Worro, Shanqo Qelema, Shanqo Wolfo and Lala *kebeles* on how individual and group-hunting activities in Mago Park were damaging its fauna and flora. In those meetings, representatives of the local administration had asked that the Hamar hand over poachers to the police. In Worro *kebele* alone, the local administration had listed seventeen suspected poachers sought by the police. After a long discussion, the elders of the village through their *bitta* (ritual leader) requested the government to let the poachers pay fines instead of going to court. However, the government rejected the appeal and instead to send the police into the villages.

The team went to Worro with the aim of peacefully negotiating the issue of poachers and girls' education with the community. However, the police officer I interviewed from the team explained to me that, since the Hamar in Shanqo Qellema village had severely beaten the Chief Administrator and other officials at a previous

9 Community elders included in the team were from Bashada, Errä Qaisa, Errä Umbule, Shanqo Qelema and Lala *kebeles*. The elders were selected on the basis of their closeness to the *kebele* administration and their perceived community influence.

10 According to my informants from the Mago National Park Office, in the years from 2012/13 to 2014/15, of the 65 registered poaching cases, 43 were from Hamar *kebeles*, mostly Dimeka *Zuria*, Worro, Shanqo, and Lala.

meeting,[11] the security office found it necessary that the team go with an armed police force, carrying Kalashnikovs and machine guns.

Two days before the team went to Worro, the police fired machine guns in the outskirts of Dimeka town. The sound of the gunshots was heard all over Hamar. According to the police, the machine guns were fired for two reasons: to see if they worked, as they were remnants from the Derg's regime and had not been used for the last two decades; and to intimidate the people in Worro and neighbouring *kebeles*, who were known to be resistant, and convince them to hand over the poachers to justice. Having tested the machine guns, the team entered Worro *kebele* in the evening of 14 January 2015. One of the policemen who was part of the group remembered the situation as follows:

> We arrived in Worro at 4:00 pm in the afternoon. We wanted to spend the night in some of the rooms at Worro Elementary School. Soon, our members (the police members) went to fetch water in the nearby river to cook food for dinner. At that time, we were in peace. Later when it got darker, we sent those elders who were with us to the village to inform the community about the arrival of the team and a plan to hold a meeting the next day. But the elders who carried our message were chased away by the Worro community who told them that they were *gal* (literally: enemy), not Hamar. Shortly after, a woman from the village came and told us that we were surrounded by armed Hamar men from the village. She said, 'You have to go...you have to escape...go...go...!' But the higher officials from the *woreda* administration refused the woman's advice. We spent a very tense night. Outside, we heard shouting, war songs and the firing of rifles by the young Hamar.
>
> The next morning, we woke up early. Again we sent the elders to the village to appease and persuade the people to come talk with us. When some members of the police went to the river to fetch water and prepare breakfast, the Worro youngsters started firing at them. The elders were also chased and even beaten up by the 'resistant fighters'. Everything went out of control. Our police members flew into the bush and escaped to Dimeka town. The elders also ran to other villages. A few policemen, including me, and the *woreda* authorities remained in the school. There followed a time of shooting with the Hamar during which two policemen were killed and four highly wounded. We were encircled from all sides. Of course, we did not have the basic knowledge of the terrain. The 'resistant fighters' came and said 'put down your rifles!' When we put down our rifles, they

11 The beating of the Chief Administrator and other officials happened shortly before the Worro conflict. According to some Hamar and government official informants, the beating was attributed to the grievances that the Hamar have in relation to the pressure of girls' education and the problems in the park. Some informants also told me that the beating was started by some drunk Hamar youngsters in the village.

> took our Kalashnikovs and our machine guns and then we remained alone. To be frank, the police did not shoot at the people, we were actually firing into the sky. The authorities who were with us ran to one elder's house, near the school.
> Around 12:00 am, a special police force came from Jinka, the headquarters of the South Omo Zone administration. First, they took the wounded policemen to hospital. The bodies of those who had been killed were down at the river area. When the special police force asked the community to give them the bodies, the Hamar refused. Then, the Special Police Force and the Hamar fought in the afternoon and four more members of the police and one female teacher from the village were killed. The day passed without any achievement on the side of the police. At night, it was decided that all of us should retreat to town. We dispersed in different directions, left the dead ones in the village and returned to Dimeka (to the town) during the night. (Interview, 4 December 2016, in Dimeka)

Soon after, the Hamar began to destroy all public centres in Worro, including schools, health centres and veterinary service centres. Properties were taken. The news quickly spread all over Hamar, and people in other places, such as Shanqo (both Shanqo Qellema and Shanqo Wolfo), Lala, Achi Mussa, Achi Algone, Kufur, also started destroying public service centres. All the government workers fled to the towns and the eight villages remained inaccessible to the government until Feb 2017.

The roots of the conflict

'Territorialisation of conservation space' versus local economy and social identity

As mentioned above, one of the contested arenas for the Hamar and the local government is the 'territorialisation of conservation space' (Robbins 2004) in the Mago National Park. The Park, with 2,162 km^2, was established in 1978 with the assumption that the area was 'uninhabited' and 'free from human activity' and therefore required protection from human and animal encroachment (Turton 2011:166). In reality, there are six groups – the Banna, Hamar, Kara, Muguji, Mursi and Ari – living in and around the Mago Park (Nishizaki 2005:32, Turton 2011:150). Others, such as the Tsamakko, Konso, Arbore and Dassanech, come from further away to hunt animals for trophies and meat, place beehives, and extract timber (Strecker 2006b:135).

As part of the current government's commitment to promoting eco-tourism development and building a climate-resilient green economy, laws prohibiting entry to and hunting in the park are being enforced more strictly than at any time in the past, and sanctions range from the financial to imprisonment. The strict enforcement of the law collides with the interests of the pastoralists, who feel that not only their livelihood but also the key values of their culture are under threat. One Hamar elder explained:

> We have a long tradition of going to the bush to hunt game. In the past, when our sons herd cattle, they used to go with spears, nowadays they have guns [...]. They need them for two reasons: first, to protect the cattle from raiders and from dangerous animals such as hyenas; and second, to prove their manhood by killing trophy animals so that the community knows they are ready for marriage.
> We were told that our boys are killing animals and that these animals are sources of income for the government. So, the government is very concerned about them. They (the government) told us that tourists from far away are visiting to take photos of these animals and that they are paying money for that [...]. We have no problem with that. Our problem is the grazing land. We worry about where to graze our cattle and goats. That is why our boys travel such a long way to Mago. (Interview, 2 December 2016, in Lojera)

As the account shows, hunting plays an important role in the socialization of Hamar men, who want to prove their manhood by killing game – a venture a male should go through in order to become a *donza*, a married and 'competent adult man' (Lydall and Strecker 1979b:77). Though not a compulsory precondition for marriage, hunting is considered important in the eyes of the community. Successful hunters of big game are given special recognition and celebrated for a whole season, during which they adorn themselves and paint their foreheads with clay.[12] While men traditionally go on special hunting trips, herders also kill wild animals to protect their herds and their own lives from dangerous animals, as I was told by Hamar herders I spent some days with in their cattle camps near the Mago Park and the adjoining area of Omo river.

The Mago Park is used to graze cattle especially in times of drought. According to the Hamar Woreda Pastoral Affairs Office, the dramatic increase in the encroachment of herders into the park seen over the past 10–15 years. This has been caused by a shortage of grazing land resulting from an increasing cattle population, drought and the allocation of land to investors. In the past, when they had fewer cattle, the Hamar used to graze their animals near their homesteads, and only seasonally took their animals to places further away. Over the past two decades they have started to travel with their herds to Kizo, an area near the Omo River, close to the Karo community settlement area. As the Kizo area has been under the control

12 For example, when someone kills a hyena he shaves off all his hair. He takes some pure white paint and smears it on his head. When a person kills an elephant, lion, leopard or buffalo, he smears red ochre on his forehead (see Lydall and Strecker 1979b:78).

of the Ethiopian Rift Valley Safari (also called the Murle Controlled Hunting Station) since 1984, the Hamar face difficulties grazing and watering their cattle in the area. The scouts and manager of the hunting station told me that when the herders encroach on the controlled hunting territory, they sometimes shoot game indiscriminately, which causes disputes between the scouts and the herders. Moreover, the size of the Kizo area was reduced in 2012 by the allocation of 10,000 hectares of land to foreign investors, who established the Omo Valley Cotton Farm.[13] Since then, the Hamar have had little access to the grazing land in the area and to the Omo River to water their animals. Even worse, many goats, sheep and cattle have fallen into the large ditches dug by the investors to fence their farmland. This all led to disputes with the investors[14] that eventually forced the Hamar to move their animals further, to the Mago Park, and led them again into conflict.

In the Park, as I observed, the Hamar have recently begun to build cattle camps and live there more permanently. Repeated attempts to remove herders and hunters from the Park territory has resulted in conflict and the deaths of some scouts.

The *woreda* administration and the Mago Park authorities organized several meetings with community elders and herders during which they suggested the destocking of cattle and promoted other income-generating economic activities. In an interview, a local expert of pastoral affairs told me:

> The Hamar give high value to the size of their herds. They do not worry about the quality of their cattle. What they worry about is to maximize the herd size and thereby increase their social status. We told them to decrease their herd, to sell some and diversify their income strategies outside the pastoral economy. Recently, we have been observing a change in climate, and there is a lack of grazing land and water […]. Some people have accepted our advice and started to live a 'modern life'. You can see, for example, Hamar guys transporting people from their village to the town by motorbike. But these are only few. Most still continue to keep their cattle […]. Because of the lack of pasture, they recently moved their herds to Mago National Park. It is this encroachment to the park, which later caused the Worro conflict. (Interview, 16 May 2017, in Dimeka)

13 The plantation was established in June 2013 by Turkish investors, mainly to supply cotton to a sister company called ELSE Addis Industrial Development PLC, located in Adama town. When I arrived in Hamar for fieldwork in September 2016, the investors had been expelled by the government for issues pertaining to their failure to repay a loan they had received from the Ethiopian Development Bank.

14 Government officials from Hamar Woreda told me about a case from 2014. Hamar herders were grazing their cattle near the farm when some of the animals entered the farm territory. The cattle were detained for a day and this caused an open clash between the farm's guards and the herders. The dispute was only settled by the intervention of the *woreda* administration.

This account shows that authorities accuse the Hamar pastoralists of having 'irrational' cultural norms related to their cattle that drive them to own large herds as a symbol of wealth, status and prestige. This is a common misconception held by many policy makers in the Horn of Africa and elsewhere in the world. The government, on the other hand, argues in terms of market economy and financial benefit, encouraging the Hamar to reduce the size of their herds, start ranching, fatten their animals and supply them to the market. This, it is argued, is the best way to diversify their means of income, which would improve their standard of living. In addition, it would reduce the damage done to the Park and the surrounding environment by the cattle. During meetings, I heard government officials addressing notable cattle owners among the Hamar, asking them why they did not sell some of their cattle, build dorms for rent in the town, buy motorbikes, and wear clothes like the town people. However, the Hamar, particularly the older generation with whom I held focused group discussions, are reluctant to take such advice from the authorities.[15]

One of the reasons for this reluctance is the wide-ranging social, economic, and ritual importance livestock has among the Hamar. For example, besides being used for food in the household (for milk and meat), cattle serve an important function in social bonds and networks. A typical kind of social relationship in South Omo is the institution of bondfriendship (Girke 2010), in Hamar called *beltamo*. Among males, bondfriendship exists over territorial and even ethnic boundaries. Bondfriends exchange and herd each other's cattle, and support each other in difficult times.[16]

For the Hamar and other neighbouring groups, sharing animals has a number of advantages over the cash economy. Hence, the institution of bondfriendship plays a significant role in maintaining social and economic cooperation and solidarity among the community and beyond. For cattle owners, it is an opportunity to establish a widespread social network on which they can fall back in times of need. It is also a mechanism for spreading one's cattle over a wide territory and thereby making it less vulnerable to epidemics affecting only one area. For poorer or young men, it provides a means of establishing their own herd, or overcoming

15 There are a very few Hamar who have built houses, bought motorbikes, and wear clothes like the town people. Most of them are close to the administration and are mentioned as positive exemplars during such meetings.

16 The cattle exchanged are called *bannewak*. Often, such an exchange begins with someone asking a cattle owner to give him a cow so his children can drink milk. The person making the request may give a gift such as honey in return. If the owner agrees to give a cow, the receiver has an obligation to look after the cow well. He is not allowed to slaughter or sell the cow or its offspring, but he may use the milk. Some of the calves will go to the owner, others are kept by the receiver.

difficult times, for example, when someone who owns no cattle needs to feed small children.

The economic system of the Hamar is thus very different from the government's market-oriented system. It is not, as Jean Lydall (2010:315) noted, primarily intended for commercial exchange, but rather has an equalizing effect: poor families receive cattle from the rich, and 'any produce in excess of domestic needs is used for special events (e.g. initiation or marriage), celebrations (e.g. harvest festival), exchange (e.g. goats for grain in time of hunger) or marriage (e.g. bride wealth)'.

'National educational' imperatives versus the place of girls in Hamar

Modern education in Hamar and in most of southern Ethiopia was introduced during the reign of Emperor Haile Selassie (1931–1974). The Emperor placed a strong emphasis on the expansion of education to strengthen the national unification project and to bring about the country's development. In southern Ethiopia, the establishment of schools was mainly targeted towards educating the children of administrators, police and settlers from the north. Sending children from local communities to school was not common except and only a few children of local dignitaries (such as ritual leaders) went to a boarding school in Addis Ababa (Epple 2012:198, Lydall 2010:7).

During the Derg regime (1974–1991), there was an emphasis on the expansion of education in rural areas. As Lydall (2010:15) pointed out, 'one of the first things the Derg did after taking power was to establish schools in rural towns where previously there were none. In Hamar, for example, schools were set up in Turmi and Dimeka'.

The EPRDF government has labelled education as one of the fundamental human rights of school age children in Ethiopia. Education is considered a key to development, democracy and peace-building within and among the Nations, Nationalities and People of Ethiopia. The emphasis on the expansion of education is evidenced in the construction of numerous schools even in remote areas. In Hamar, there are twenty-three primary schools in five clusters (Dimeka, Turmi, Shanqo, Kara, and Arbore), and two secondary schools in Dimeka and Turmi towns. The current Hamar local administration is committed to the expansion of education and other social services in the *woreda*. One of my informants from the local Education Office explained the office's recent efforts in Hamar Woreda as follows,

> For a long time the Hamar were among the less privileged and disadvantaged groups in South Omo. Most of them are still illiterate and only look after the cattle. They do not have educated boys and girls; they do not really know the world outside their own […].
>
> With our developmental government, a new hope and vision is in the making.

> The government is committed to expanding different infrastructures in the whole country especially to benefit groups that were disadvantaged under the previous regimes [...].
> In Hamar, we are working hard to implement the 'education for all' programme of the government. Education is a key to the development of a community and it broadens the horizon of people's life. We are building schools, health centres, and veterinary posts with the aim to improve the way of life of our community. (Interview, 10 November 2016, in Dimeka town)

The five-year education plan[17] (2014/15–2019/20) of Hamar Woreda shows that the administration is striving to expand the coverage of primary school education to all the *woreda's kebeles*, and to reduce gender disparity in the enrolment children to schools. To attain its vision, the office has been undertaking a series of awareness raising activities, including meetings with the community and campaigning about the importance of education for the future of the country, the pastoral and agro-pastoral community and their children.

From these campaigns, it is obvious that education has become loaded with expectations of a good life and well-paid job in town. When I asked my host brother, a Hamar schoolboy, to explain what modern life means to him, he told me it meant 'to be able to wear *gal*[18] clothes, to ride a motorbike, to have a mobile, to eat *injera*,[19] to live in Dimeka town and to get a government salary'. At the same time, among those who are educated and close to towns life allegiance to the Hamar way of life has become stigmatized as 'traditional', 'backward' and 'resistant to development and modernity'. My informant from the Education Office stated:

> The Hamar are conservative and stick to their traditional way of life [...]. One manifestation of this is their lack of interest in sending their children to school, especially the girls. They don't know the value of education. For example, they don't send boys (especially first born sons) to school because they believe an educated boy will not bury his father, inherit his father's property and continue the Hamar way of life. With the girls, the problem is even worse. The Hamar believe that if a Hamar girl moves to a town, she will never come back. They also use their girls as a means to accumulate wealth through bride wealth, which often enables them to get many cattle and goats [...].

---

17 The five-year education plan was prepared by the Hamar Woreda Education office to attain the vision of the National Growth and Transformation Plan on Education.

18 The term *gal* literary means 'enemy' (see Lydall 2010). It is also used to refer to non-Hamar, mainly highland Ethiopians.

19 *Injera* is a fermented sourdough flatbread traditionally made from teff flour. It is the main staple food in highland and Central Ethiopia, and has recently also become popular in other parts of the country.

> Nevertheless, over the past years, the *woreda* administration has been working hard to tackle these 'traditional' attitudes despite resistance and conflict. (Interview, 21 December 2016, in Turmi)

In the discourse of the *woreda's* Women, Children and Youth Office, girls are commonly depicted as 'slaves of their husbands', 'exploited creatures', 'sold for cows' and 'forced by their parents into marriage', sometimes with old men. This representation is presented in opposition to women's rights and the public discourse on gender equality, as prescribed by international human rights advocacy groups and the Ethiopian government.

As part of their efforts to get more Hamar girls into school, annual educational campaigns, led by Hamar Woreda's Education Office, Women Children and Youth Office, and administration, are being organized in all *kebeles*. The main agenda of these campaigns pertains to the right of girls to education. The denial of this right, it is propagated, will result in bad consequences for the parents, such as fines and even imprisonment. Concomitantly, girls are told about their right to go to schools and that they should report any denial of this right to their respective *kebele* administration and/or to the police or the Woreda Court.

This high-level campaign is highly controversial in Hamar and generates much resistance for various reasons. First, girls in Hamar are seen as indispensable to continue Hamar culture and economy. A good/respected Hamar girl is one who is skilful and knowledgeable of all agro-pastoral and household tasks: she collects firewood, fetches water, grinds flour and prepares food and coffee, cleans the compound and, most importantly, cultivates fields of sorghum, beans and other produce. People fear, and experience has shown, that if girls go to school they do not learn to become competent Hamar women capable of coordinating and running an agro-pastoralist household (Lydall 2010:323).

Second, the Hamar are worried about voluntarily and involuntarily pre-marital sexual affairs and pregnancy, which occur in the context of school education, especially among those who live in the hostels at town. While virginity is not a condition for marriage in Hamar, premarital pregnancies are traditionally considered as impure and need to be aborted or the children killed after birth. As abortion and infanticide are prohibited by the law, schoolgirl pregnancies create a lot of problems for the girls and their families. Therefore, parents find it hard to send their daughters to hostels, where they are not properly supervised.

Third, educated girls usually insist on choosing their own partner, which means that Hamar parents are unable to arrange marriages for them and that they will not receive any bride wealth. Such marriages, made outside the agro-pastoral economy, do not bring any livestock to the family, and are less likely to expand the social and kinship network of the household. Moreover, as descent is patrilineal, if a girl marries a non-Hamar her own children will not be considered as Hamar and are thus lost to the community. One Hamar elder told me:

> I have a daughter, she is my second daughter. Now, she is grown up. I raised her like the other small girls in Hamar. She used to fetch water for her mother, clean the enclosure of goats and the homestead. Later, when she became a matured girl she was engaged to a Hamar boy from Assile area [...]. Shortly after her engagement, she joined the school at Dimeka.
> I had a difficult time with her future husband and his family, as they were disappointed with her education. Even worse, she is not living in Dimeka anymore. What would you do when your daughter disappear in the bush, in the town? I have lost my daughter. She is now in Jinka, I heard that she is a cleaner of a hotel in Arkesha (part of Jinka). She is neither attending school nor coming back to Hamar. Her family begged her to come back to us, but she is not listening anymore (Interview, 20 February 2016, Lojera).

The above case shows that it is difficult for her parents to stay in control of a girl's life once she has gone to school. Many such girls are regarded as lost to their Hamar families and the community; no longer fully integrated into Hamar society, they are seen as destined to live in the towns. As a counter reaction, some Hamar have become active 'traditionalists', who strongly oppose girls' education.

As became clear during interviews and many informal conversations, it has become common for girls in several villages in Hamar to be sent to school and their resistant parents sanctioned. The pressure put on the families played an important role in causing the 2015 conflict in Hamar. One case in particular aggravated the hostility between the Hamar and the *woreda* administration. Muga, one of the two Hamar *bittas*, told me about the sudden disappearance of seven girls and the shock it caused in Hamar.

> In Hamar, we have a special place for girls. You see, the girls are the future mothers. They take care of their children; they are responsible for the continuation of Hamar as a community. We need our young girls to learn about Hamar culture. Recently, the government has been forcing the Hamar to send their children to school. But, it should not be forces. It is our own sons, the educated Hamar men who are now administering the country, who are lobbying and persuading our girls to go to town for schooling against our will.
> Within one week, seven girls from my country ran away to Dimeka: three from Buska, three from Lala, and one from Shanqo Wolfo. First, we did not know that they were in Dimeka. We, the Hamar, were worried and started to search for them in different villages. Six of the girls except the one from Buska village had already been engaged and their parents had received bride wealth, from their future husbands (Interview, 8 March 2017, Buska).

When the Hamar requested the return of the girls, they were told that it was the right of the girls to go to school and that they would stay in town to do that. The family's feelings and interests, as well as their wish that their daughters become 'competent Hamar wives and mothers' (Lydall 2010:12) and fit into the local forms of life and obligations to kin were discounted.

Albeit with difficulty, I had the chance to meet and talk to one of these seven girls, who was at the time in the fourth grade at the Dimeka Boarding School. She told me the reasons why she ran away from her family. These included her interest in attending school and becoming a civil servant like Goiti, Head of the Women and Children's Affairs Office and the only Hamar woman in the *woreda* cabinet. She explained that her father had died when she was small, so she grew up with her mother and brothers. When her older brother chose a husband for her, she disagreed and went to Dimeka. Right now, she is the only one of the seven girls attending school in Dimeka. The other girls, as the Head of Women and Children's Affairs Office told me, are in Jinka; some are selling coffee on the streets and others are, according to rumours, working in the hotels as bar ladies. Her office, together with the *woreda* administration, was planning to convince the girls to return to school in Hamar or reunite with their parents.

During the Worro conflict, when the *woreda* police and the security team marched to Worro to bring poachers to the court, the Hamar were already resentful because of the situations of these and other girls, and this fuelled the open confrontation.

Efforts to resolve the conflict

A few days after the Worro conflict, the Southern Nations Nationalities and People Government took the initiative to start a peace dialogue with notable elders of the Hamar. The proposed strategy was to persuade the Hamar to attend a peace meeting, and to find a 'trustable' mediator who could serve as a peace broker between the community and the government. The man identified was Awoke Aike.[20] Awoke is among the first educated generation of the Hamar and was Chief Administrator of South Omo Zone from 2000 to 2006 and served as a representative of the Hamar in the Ethiopian Parliament from 2007 to 2016.

In the days after Awoke's arrival in Hamar, he and other government officials started to deliberate on possible ways to convince the Hamar to enter the peace dialogue. They first approached Elto Gino, one of the *bittas*, to help them. After a few

---

20 He is the son of Aike Berinas (also called Baldambe), a former spokesman of the Hamar and friend and key informant of the anthropologists Ivo Strecker and Jean Lydall (see Lydall and Strecker 1979b).

days of negotiation, the *bitta* agreed to hold meetings with the government people, who guaranteed him that neither police nor security would make him accountable for the mess in Worro.

The first peace meeting was held between the Hamar *bitta*, some Hamar elders who accompanied him, and government representatives at the Kaeske River, near Dimeka town. The two main issues discussed were firstly, the government's desire that the elders persuade the young Hamar men to stop the war and refrain from destroying further public service centres; and secondly, that the rifles taken from the police and the property stolen from schools and health centres (such as chairs, tables, refrigerators) be returned.

Before entering the discussion, the elders requested that the authorities first talk about who was responsible for causing the war. The *bitta* and his spokespersons argued that the government soldiers who came with machine guns to attack the peaceful community were liable for the trouble. They added that the community, and particularly the Hamar youngsters, did nothing wrong except defend themselves from the bullets of the soldiers. The elders made clear that the government and its police force were at fault. The elders also mentioned that making peace in any way would only be attainable if the government was willing to allow the elders to solve problems in their own way and not insist on 'rigid rules', sending the police to the community and bringing the so-called 'criminals' in to court. As *bitta* Elto recounted:

> I said to Berki, then chief administrator of Hamar, and to Burka, head of security, to give us time to talk with our sons, with those they call poachers. I also said to them 'Do not insist on deadlines!', for they gave us a two week time frame to handover the poachers to the police.
> We Hamar said to them: 'Bringing peace is not like buying coffee from the market! It requires time and will only be achieved gradually.'
> The elders from the far away areas like Assile, Wungabaino, Bashada, Errä Umbule and Errä Qaisa also told them: 'Do not send police to the peaceful settlement areas.' We also told them that the poachers would pay fines in cash but not go to jail. But they (the government officials) did not agree and sent police (Interview, 20 May 2017, in Worro).

The way the Hamar manage conflicts and ensure order is completely different from what the government officials aspired to do. Among the Hamar, any cases of wrongdoing are presented to the *zarsi*, the community of adult men sharing a common residence area. Depending on the issue at stake, after careful deliberation, the wrongdoer might be told to apologize and to give a cow or goat as compensation to the person he has harmed. In some cases, he will be asked to slaughter a cow to the *zarsi* and feed them. The main aim is to restore social peace between conflicting parties and to reintegrate the wrongdoer into the community. As such, the Hamar practise what is called 'restorative justice' (Damren 2002:83). State law, based on the principle of retributive justice is meant to punish wrongdoers, so that 'the issue of bringing the poachers and others who resisted girls education to the court was a matter of enforcing "rule of law"', as one of my informants from the *woreda* administration put it. It was with this orientation that the police and the security team went to Worro, and this was strongly criticised by the Hamar elders during the peace talks.

Informants from both sides recounted that Awoke and a few government officials accepted the view of the elders and confessed that the administration's decision to send police had been completely wrong. But other officials opposed it and did not show any sense of guilt. Instead, they insisted on identifying those Hamar who had killed policemen and destroyed public property. Therefore, the first peace meeting ended without any meaningful consensus or detailed discussion of the agendas set by the authorities. The officials who felt that their previous decisions had been right later put *bitta* Elto in jail for four months, claiming that he had instigated the Worro conflict. The imprisonment of the *bitta* in Dimeka caused a second violent clash between the Hamar and government soldiers in May 2015, a situation that was only ended when he was freed.

A second peace meeting was then held in November 2015, in the presence of the president of SNNPR. This time, *bitta* Elto refused to attend out of fear and distrust of the government officials. In the meeting, the president openly offered an apology for what had happened in Worro because of the administration's decision to send the police force. He also announced that the government had pardoned all Hamar involved, including those who had killed police officers in Worro and those who had destroyed public service centres. It was also promised that those officials who had given the command to the police would be held accountable for their decisions and removed from their positions. The regional government's vigorous response to the situation laid the foundation for a new administration in Hamar and facilitated a real peace dialogue between the authorities and the community.

Following this meeting, the new administration in Hamar soon organized meetings in the different *kebeles*. The new administrator, Walle Alma, wanted to speak to *bitta* Elto in person, but only managed to do so with the intervention of the *ayo* (spokesman) of Worro.[21] Finally, Walle was allowed to come to Worro on the condition that he comes alone, without any police (security guards) or car. Walle agreed and went the next day, bringing coffee as a gift to the *bitta* to ask him for forgiveness. The *bitta* accepted the apology wholeheartedly and blessed the new

21 He travelled twice to the village but was not able to meet the *bitta*. Instead, the *ayo* told him to leave a message for the *bitta*. When Walle insisted on meeting the *bitta* personally, with the intention of admitting the mistakes of the government and asking for the bitta's blessings, finally the *ayo* agreed to help him.

administrator. This was the beginning of a new phase in relations marked by real peace dialogues.

I attended several meetings in Turmi and Dimeka during which the Hamar and the new administration agreed to set up a joint peace committee, which included elders, herders, women and local government representatives. Once it had been established, the peace committee agreed to communicate community concerns to the government and to consult one another. Some of the rifles that had been taken during the war were also returned to the administration, and the residents of Worro agreed to restore the public service centres.

However, the main causes of the conflict – hunting and grazing in the Mago Park and the issue of girls' education – remain unresolved. Park authorities continue to blame the Hamar for hunting in Mago Park, even though the Hamar usually express their willingness to stop hunting and tend to condemn poachers in meetings. The Hamar are more concerned about herding and grazing in the Park and are asking the government about the future of their local economy. And, I have observed that the government allowed the Hamar and other neighbouring groups to graze inside the park, and also supplied fodder from far away areas – from Maze Park, near Gofa, and from the Kuraz Sugar Factory – during the 2017 drought in the region.

Summary and conclusion

To fully understand what led to the 2015 conflict between the Hamar and the local government it has been necessary to study the relationship between both parties, taking their respective values, intentions and motivations into account. These included the wider social, cultural and economic base of the Hamar and the developmental priorities of the Ethiopian government.

From the Hamar side, three factors can be seen as the underlying causes of their conflict-laden relationship with the local administration: their strong attachment to hunting as a mechanism for proving manhood and elevating one's social status; their subsistence economy, which is partly based on cattle herding and demands the constant search for grazing land and watering points; and the value given to girls as agents for the continuation of the Hamar as a group and as a source of bride wealth.

From the local administration's side, centrally designed development projects – such as the conservation schemes to foster eco-tourism development, the strict enforcement of law, and the 'education for all' programme – along with the view that these programmes are inviolable prerequisites for the eradication of poverty and fostering of economic development are responsible for the contention with the local community.

The case presented here is that the escalation of the conflict when the Hamar Woreda administration decided to send armed police to Worro resulted in unwanted consequences for both sides and – in hindsight – could have been avoided. As the accounts from Hamar elders reveal, the contested issues – hunting and grazing in the Mago Park and female education – could have been addressed and at least partly resolved through an open dialogue between the elders and the *woreda* officials.

Given the high social value attached to hunting game among the Hamar, their suggestion that illegal hunters pay fines to the government instead of going to jail was in fact an offer to compromise with the park authorities. Yet, it was interpreted as resistance to government authority. As the president of the SNNPR and the new administration admitted during the post-conflict peace meetings, the order given to the police was a serious mistake that caused the loss of human life on both sides and the destruction of public property. The overgrazing and entry of herders into the Mago Park was, at least partly, the result of the allocation of grazing land to investors, which restricted the herders' access to grass and watering points. As the Hamar economy is to a large extent derived from animal husbandry, the development programmes implemented in the area should have considered this reality and ensured the availability of livestock routes and access to riverbanks. Hamar resistance to sending their girls to school was only partly based on the important role played by girls in the Hamar household economy and their central place in the continuation of Hamar as a group. These cultural aspects may not change fast, but Hamar concerns about their daughters' security in the boarding schools in towns could be more easily addressed. Instead of exerting pressure on parents to send their daughters to school, more attention should be given to awareness raising and ensuring the overall protection and wellbeing of girls in the towns.

To conclude, the Worro conflict and its resolution can teach us a lesson about how and why things can go wrong when two different values systems come together. While in such situations the more powerful partner – usually the government – often 'wins' and subjugates the weaker one, the Hamar case was different as their land is still rather inaccessible and they are heavily armed. Besides, nowadays many local government officials are native Hamar, which means that they have a good knowledge of the local culture and values, even if they no longer share it. The way the issue was finally resolved shows that not only mutual understanding, but also tolerance, flexibility and patience are needed to live peacefully together in a culturally and legally plural country.

References

ABBINK, JON, 1997 "The shrinking cultural and political space of East African pastoral societies", *Nordic Journal of African Studies* 6 (1): 1–15

AMBORN, Herrmann, 2018 *Law as refuge of anarchy: Societies without hegemony or state.* Cambridge: IT Press

AARON Tesfaye, 2017 *State and economic development in Africa: The case of Ethiopia.* Cham: Springer International

BELETE Bizuneh, 2008 *An agrarian polity and its pastoral periphery: State and pastoralism in the Borana borderlands (Southern Ethiopia), 1897–1991*. Boston: University of Boston (PhD Thesis)

BUFFAVAND, Lucie, 2018 *Vanishing stones and the hovering giraffe: Identity, land and the divine in Mela, South-West Ethiopia*. Halle: Martin-Luther University Halle-Wittenberg (PhD Thesis)

CENTRAL STATISTICAL AUTHORITY (CSA), 2008 *The 2007 population census of Ethiopia*. Addis Ababa: Central Statistical Authority

COWAN, Jane K., Marie-Bénédicte DEMBOUR and Richard A. WILSON (eds.), 2001 *Culture and rights: Anthropological perspectives*. Cambridge: Cambridge University Press

DAMREN, Samuel, 2002 "Restorative justice: Prison and the native sense of justice", *Journal of Legal Pluralism* 47:83–111

DEMBOUR, Marie-Bénédicte, 2001 "Following the movement of a pendulum: Between universalism and relativism", in: Jane K. Cowan, Marie-Bénédicte Dembour and Richard A. Wilson (eds.) *Culture and rights: Anthropological perspectives*, 56–79. Cambridge: Cambridge University Press.

DONHAM, Donald and Wendy JAMES, 2002 *The southern marches of Imperial Ethiopia*. Oxford: Currey

EPPLE, Susanne, 2012 "Local responses to externally induced cultural change. The introduction of formal education in Bashada (Southern Ethiopia)", *Paideuma* 58:197–211

FANA Gebresenbet, 2014 "Securitisation of development in Ethiopia: The discourse and politics developmentalism", *Review of African Political Economy* 41:64–74

FEDERAL DEMOCRATIC REPUBLIC OF ETHIOPIA (FDRE), 2002 *Ethiopia: Sustainable development and poverty reduction program*. Addis Ababa: Ministry of Finance and Economic Development

2007 *Ethiopia: Building on progress: A plan for accelerated and sustained development to end poverty* (PASDP). Addis Ababa: Ministry of Finance and Economic Development

2008 *Draft policy statement for the sustainable development of pastoral and agro-pastoral areas of Ethiopia*. Addis Ababa: Ministry of Finance and Economic Development

2010 *Growth and transformation plan (GTP) 2010/11–2014/15*. Addis Ababa: Ministry of Finance and Economic Development

2015 *The second growth and transformation plan (GTP II) (1015/16 – 2019/20) (draft)*. Addis Ababa: Ministry of Finance and Economic Development

FORST, Rainer, 1999 "The basic rights to justification: Toward a constructivist conception of human rights", *Constellation* 6 (1):36–60

GABBERT, Christina, 2013 "The global neighbourhood concept: A chance for cooperative development or festina lente". Paper presented at the conference on *Large Scale Agricultural Investments in Pastoral Lowlands of the Horn of Africa: Implications for Minority Rights and Pastoral Conflicts*. IPSS (Institute for Peace and Security Studies), Addis Ababa University, 26–27 April 2013

GIRKE, Felix, 2010 "Bondfriendship in the cultural neighbourhood: Dyadic ties and their public appreciation in South Omo", in: Christina Gabbert and Sophia Thubauville (eds.) *To live with others: Essays on cultural neighbourhood in southern Ethiopia*, 68–98. Köln: Köppe

HOSSAIN, Shanawez, 2015 "Development and human security in Asia: An analysis from human rights and cultural relativism point of view". Brac Institute of Governance and Development (BIGD), BRAC University, Working Paper No 28:1–15

JOHANSSON, Dahre, 2017 "Searching for a middle ground: Anthropologists and the debate on the universalism and the cultural relativism of human rights", *The International Journal of Human Rights* 21 (5):611–628

KAMSKI, Benedikt, 2015 "Agricultural investments in Ethiopia's South Omo Zone: Widening the perspective on regional externalities". Paper presented at the *Annual World Bank Conference on Land and Poverty*. Washington DC, 23–27 March 2015

LYDALL, Jean, 2010 "The paternalistic neighbour: A tale of the demise of cherished traditions", in: Christina Gabbert and Sophia Thubauville (eds.) *To live with others: Essays on cultural neighbourhood in Southern* Ethiopia, 314–334.Köln: Köppe.

LYDALL, Jean and Ivo STRECKER, 1979a *Work Journal: The Hamar of Southern Ethiopia Vol. I.* Hohenschäftlarn: Renner

1979b *Baldambe explains: The Hamar of Southern Ethiopia Vol. II.* Hohenschäftlarn: Renner

MARKAKIS, John, 2011 *Ethiopia: The last two frontiers*. Oxford: Currey

MAURUS, Sabrina, 2016 "Times of continuity and development: Visions of the future among agro-pastoral children and young people in southern Ethiopia", *Anthropochildren* 6:1–24

MELESSE Getu, 2009 "The effects of investment on the livelihoods of the Tsamako in the Wayto Valley", in: Alula Pankhurst and François Piguet (eds.) *Moving people in Ethiopia: Development, displacement and the state*, 264–284. Oxford: Currey

MKANDAWIRE, Thandika, 2001 "Thinking about developmental states in Africa", *Cambridge Journal of Economics* 25 (3):289–313

NISHIZAKI, Nobuko, 2005 "Differing local attitudes toward conservation policy: A case study of Mago National Park, Ethiopia", *African Study Monographs* Suppl. 29:31–40

PLANEL, Sabine, 2014 "A view of a bureaucratic developmental state: local governance and agricultural extension in rural Ethiopia", *Journal of Eastern African Studies* 8 (3):420–437

RICHMON, Malcolm, 2005 *The value impress: Toward a normative account of educational administration*. Toronto: University of Toronto (PhD Thesis)

ROBBINS, Paul, 2004 *Political Ecology: A Critical Introduction*. Oxford: Blackwell

STRECKER, Ivo, 2006 "Cultural variation in the concept of face", in: Ivo Strecker and Jean Lydall (eds.) *The perils of face. Essays on cultural contact, respect and self-esteem in southern Ethiopia*, 83–104. Berlin: Lit

2010 *Ethnographic chiasmus: Essays on culture, conflict and rhetoric*. Berlin: Lit

2013 *Berimba's resistance. The life and times of a great Hamar spokesman as told by his son Aike Berinas*. Vienna: Lit

TSEGA-AB Kassa, 2005 *Administrative history of Gäläb and Hamär Bakko Awraja, south-western Ethiopia*. Addis Ababa: Addis Ababa University (MA Thesis)

TURTON, David, 2011 "Wilderness, wasteland, or home? Three ways of imagining the Lower Omo Valley", *Journal of East African Studies* 5 (1):158–176

UNITED NATIONS 1948 *Universal declaration of human rights*, adopted 10 December 1948. GA. Res. 217 AIII. United Nations Document a/810. N

17. Glossary

A

aadaa custom, tradition, culture (Oromo)

aadaa seeraa Borana normative system

Aariaf (also: Aaraf) language of the Aari

abaarsa curse (Borana)

abbaa bokkuu lit: 'father of the sceptre', senior position in Oromo lineage system and in *gadaa*, responsible for decision-making

abbaa gadaa lit.: 'father of *gadaa*', leader of the *gadaa* governance system (Oromo)

abbaa seeraa legal expert (Oromo)

abegar conflict resolution mechanism practised by elders who claim to have hereditary divine power (Amhara of Wollo)

abunzi mediation system in Rwanda

ad'a culture (Siltie)

adulaa council composed of elders from each moiety holding executive power (Borana), senior councilor within the *gadaa*-system (Oromo)

afaan OromoOromo language

afi evil eye (Aari)

aish person with the evil eye (Aari)

akonatari lit.: transferor of land in traditional land transactions (Sidama)

alem world (Amharic), self-designation of non-Protestants in Aari, where it could be translated as 'traditionalist'

anje blessings (Aari)

ansewa Siltie highlanders

anzamo-nas lit.: girlhood child, refers to children conceived before marriage (Bashada, Hamar, Banna)

araara reconciliation (Borana)

araqé local liquor

argaa dhageetii oral historian/oral history/anecdote (Borana)

atbia dagnia local judge (Amharic), established by the government

awliyā saint, guardian (pl.) (Arabic)

awneya marginalized craft workers (blacksmiths, tanners, and potters) among Siltie people
awraja third administrative tier below the province/region during the Imperial (1931–1974) and the Socialist Derg regime (1974–1991)
awraja qadis judges assigned to a specific area (see *awraja*)
'Ay berimka' 'Do not judge!' (Aari expression)
Ayidama customary mechanism to resolve conflicts between different Gamo communities
ayle slave descendants (Gamo)
ayo spokesman and intermediary between the local communities and the government (Bashada, Hamar, Banna, see also: *likamamber*)
aysafte woni heathen work (Aari)

B

babi hereditary ritual king (Aari)
bajje marginalized subgroup with ritual responsibilities (Bashada, Hamar, Banna)
balabat landlord during the Imperial regime (1931–1974)
baliqe elder (Siltie)
bannewak cattle exchanged among bondfriends in Hamar
barjo good fortune (Bashada, Hamar)
bashi displaying fear (Aari)
berche notions of the right to justice in Siltie, see also *tur* and *fero*
bida'a unwanted innovation (Siltie)
birr Ethiopian currency
bitta lit.: 'the first' (Hamar), refers also to 'the first' in authority and transcendental and ritual power, title for ritual leader among Hamar
bul lit.: untied, also: absolved (Aari)
buts to acknowledge/confess wrong-doing (Aari)

C

caffee places of law-proclamations, law-giving assembly (Oromo)
caffee taa'icha lit.: '[he] who was at [the place of] the law gathering', (also: *jaarsa caffee*), expert in customary law (Oromo)
chako oath (Gamo)
charangi ritually pure (Bashada, Hamar, Banna)

D

d'abbi wrongdoer (Bashada, Hamar, Banna)
dakerka imprison (imperative, Aari)

dakri lit.: tying, term is used for imprisonment in the *kebele* prison, and for banning a wrongdoer from active religious participation for a specified number of months (Aari)
dannawa form of land tenure in Sidama, (communal land)
danya judge (Amharic)
daraara tobacco used ritual purposes (Borana)
dax'ilsi offence (Aari)
dem adreq shimgilinna conciliation aimed at stopping a lengthy conflict between families that involved a cycle of retaliatory killings (Amhara)
deme keleb lit.: 'impure blood' (Amharic)
demutha religious experts (Gamo)
dere (plural: *dereta*), self-administered community in Gamo
dere cima council of elders in Gamo
dere dulata public assembly in Gamo
detsmi lit.: heaviness, also greatness of a person (Aari)
digela (also *tsoma* or *manna*), craftworkers (Gamo)
dofen norti girank lit.: truly from the stomach, full heartedly (Aari)
dosi potsh opening a dossier (Aari)
dubusha public assembly place in Gamo

E

edi human being (Bashada, Hamar, Banna)
eela deep well (Borana)
ensete false banana
ercho certain grass used to purify the wrongdoers and their relatives from *gome* (ritual pollution in Gamo)
erq conciliation between disputants whose relationship had already broken down in an earlier conflict (Amhara)

F

fenter special feast in Sidama to mark the conclusion of a *kontract* (hybrid form of land law)
fero notions of the right to justice in Siltie, see also *tur* and *berche*
ferezagegne local cassation court judges (in Siltie)
Fetha Nagast 'law of the kings' (Amharic)
foollee one of the stages in the *gadaa* grade system (Tulama Oromo)

G

gaaddisa shade where the elders sit, dwelling place of god (Borana)
gabinti economic growth (Aari)
gacaca Rwandan customary courts
gadaa (also: *gada*) age and generation system of Oromo people
gadho traditional palace in Gamo, residence of the *kawo*
gal enemy (Bashada, Hamar, Banna), term also used for highland Ethiopians
galta elders (Aari)
gemet assessment (Amharic)
gasaa maga (also: *ogade*), mediator between two or more communities (Gamo)
gerad clan leader (Siltie)
geta elders from related lineages serving as ritual helpers (Aari)
gichit aswegaj lit. 'conflict prevention/resolution' (Amharic), quasi-formal, state-initiated conflict resolution institution consisting of elders and representatives of government offices
gika beat (Aari)
godmi hereditary ritual specialists (Aari)
gome transgression of a social norm or sin that causes pollution of the wrongdoer and misfortune, disease and natural calamities for the whole society (Gamo)
gosa clan (Sidama, Oromo)
gote smallest state administrative level below *kebele*, consists of less than 500 people (in Siltie)
gumaa blood price/compensation to victims of crime (Tulama-Oromo, Borana)
gumii gaayoo pan-Borana assembly, taking place every eight years at the mid-point of an *abbaa gadaa* period, has supreme authority over law-making and enforcement
gumma blood money/compensation in case of homicide (Siltie)
gurri afak lit.: done just with the mouth, not full-heartedly (Aari)

H

halaqa initiate in small sized *dere* in Gamo
hadiya gifts (Islamic law, Siltie)
hayyuu senior position in Oromo lineage system and in *gadaa*; lineage senior acting as judge (Oromo)
hiba gift (Sharia law)
hisbint dassken helping people up, refers to duty of offender to provide food and drink for all cell members who participated in conflict resolution (Aari)
hoolaa buula sheep slaughtered for recuperation of sick person (Borana)
huduga initiate in medium sized *dere* in Gamo

I

iddir informal burial insurance and bereavement association common in many parts of Ethiopia
ijibbaata sheep for ritual slaughter (Borana)
'indapsi antam ay kashishka!' lit.: 'Do not make your brother pay!' (Aari expression implying that being a Christian one should forgive)
injera fermented sourdough flatbread traditionally made from t'eff flour
irki mother's brother (Aari),
isante iron rings worn by girls and women around their necks (Bashada, Hamar, Banna)
isgoota pleading ceremony, during which a killer's side plead for reconciliation (Tulama-Oromo)

J

jaallaba representative of clan assembly enforcing decisions of the *abbaa gadaa* (Borana)
jaarsa elder (Tulama-Oromo)
'jaarsaaf jeedhi!' lit.: 'For the sake of elders!' (part of blessing, Tulama-Oromo)
jaarsa dheeda administrative unit responsible for regulating seasonal access to grazing and water (Borana)
jaarsa madda administrative unit responsible for grazing and water management at the local level (Borana)
jaarsa Waaqaa lit.: 'elder of God', member of a court run by spirit mediums (Oromo)
jaarsummaa conflict resolution through elders (Oromo)
jahil ignorant of Islamic knowledge (Siltie)

K

karta tradition (Aari)
kashi beday 'There is not a lot of fines!' (Aari expression)
kashka fine (imperative, Aari)
kawo title for hereditary ruler in Gamo
kebele lowest administrative level
kerri ritual gateway (Bashada, Hamar, Banna)
k'esh customary mode of dispute resolution, reconciliation (Aari)
kilil region (Amharic)
k'itat punishment (Amharic)
kisi lawsuit (Amharic), term used in Dell/Aari for the process of dealing with disputes through state institutions
kogo ritual fire maker (Bashada, Hamar, Banna)
kontract new hybrid form of land law in Sidama

koota sharecropping arrangement used to match land with labour and/or other inputs in Sidama
kora gosaa clan assembly (Borana)
kotsa share-cropping arrangement (Aari)

L

lafa abba torbbaatama lit.: 'land of seventy people'; referring to a specific piece of land over which 70 people are claiming ownership in Tulama-Oromo land
lafa etege land of Empress Menen, wife of Emperor Haile Selassie (Tulama-Oromo)
'*Lafaaf jedhi!*' 'For the sake of earth!' (part of blessing, Tulama-Oromo)
likamamber (from Amharic: 'likamenber'), spokesman and intermediary between the local communities and the government (Bashada, Hamar, Banna, see also: *ayo*)
liqa form of dispute settlements based on local holy men (*waliye*) among the Siltie (see also *mawlid* and *warrie*)
luba generation class (or set) among the Borana

M

mad'a customary courts of the Afar people
maga kind of mediator within the same *dere* (self-administered community in Gamo)
mahberawi firdebet Social Court for property and monetary claims in Dell/Aari (Amharic)
makkala messengers enforcing decisions of *abbaa gadaa* and council of elders (Borana)
malla farmers (Gamo)
majlis institution administering Muslim affairs
mana craft workers (Gamo, Aari)
mashayik religious figure, dead or alive, popularly recognized as honourable Islamic symbols by the majority of Muslims (see also *waliye*)
mawlid form of dispute settlements based on local holy men (*waliye*) among the Siltie (see also *liqa*, and *warrie*)
mawlid-un-nabi Prophet Mohammed's birthday celebration
mawlid al-mashayik local religious leader/figure's celebration day where by a dispute settlement is conducted (Siltie)
mele'ata guba'e assembly delegates; platform for reconciliations by Church elders (Amharic)
mengist government (Amharic)
mengiste higi law of the government (Amharic), expression used in Aari

meret komitee committee for legal issues at the *kebele* level dealing with land disputes in Dell/Aari (Amharic)
mesaki family head (Siltie)
miks begging (Aari)
militia auxiliary policeman
mingi ritually impure (Bashada, Hamar, Banna, Kara)
mikitil woreda lit.: 'subdistrict', administrative unit below the *woreda* (district) in the past
moara diviner (Bashada, Hamar, Banna)
moro head of sub clan (Siltie)
mulimidi polluted (Bashada, Hamar, Banna)
mushro disease affecting anyone breaking an oath (Amhara)

N

nagaa boorana peace among all Borana groups
negane forgiveness (Aari)
nisah teykate to take confession (Aari expression referring to the Christian duty to confess wrongdoings).
norti stomach, locus of feelings (Aari)
nikah Islamic marriage contract (Siltie)

O

Odaa Nabee tree serving as regional assembly place for the Tuulama-Oromo
ogade (also: *gasaa maga*), mediator between two or more *dere* (self administered communities in Gamo)
ollaa lit.: 'neighbour', also: village, neighbourhood (Borana)
oogliya spirit (Oromo)
ooshsha conflict (Gamo)

P

paala decorative scars (Bashada, Hamar, Banna)
parko ritual expert (Bashada, Hamar, Banna)

Q

qaalluu ritual leader, also spirit medium (Oromo)
qadi judge in Sharia court
qalla lowlanders (Siltie)
qakee serious crime and sanction (Borana)

R

raga local legal expert (Siltie)

raaba gadda administrative unit having customary jurisdiction over land, social and cultural issues, and conflict resolution (Borana)

S

'Sabi an negane!' 'May God forgive you!' (Aari)

sabite gami divine punishment (Aari)

sabite higi God's law (Aari)

sabite woni service to God (Aari)

seeraa Oromo law

Shafie Islamic school of thought

sharafic upper class people tracing their origin to the Hashemite and the Prophet Mohammed's family among the Siltie people

shimma coolness, harmony (Aari),

shimagillé lit.: 'old' (Amharic); refers to elder assigned for conflict resolution (Amhara)

shimgilinna lit.: 'aging' (Amharic), conflict resolution through elders (Amhara)

soba lie (Borana)

songo highest clan council (Sidama)

susaa qantso compensation (Gamo)

T

talak unilateral divorce or release of wife from marriage (Sharia law)

tekonatari transferee of land in traditional land transaction (Sidama)

toidi lineage head (Aari)

toksi belittling someone (Aari)

tsha'x'a testify under oath (Aari)

tsoma (also: *manna* or *digela*), craftworkers (Gamo)

tur notions of the right to justice in Siltie, see also *fero* and *berche*

U

utuwa form of land tenure in Sidama (private land)

W

waliigaltee agreement (Tulama-Oromo)

waliye religious figure, dead or alive, popularly recognized as honourable Islamic symbols by the majority of Muslims (see also *mashayik*)

wakf inalienable charitable endowment in Sharia law
Waaqa higher spiritual being, sky, God (Oromo, Borana)
'Waaqaf jeedhi!' 'For the sake of God!', (part of blessing, Tulama-Oromo)
wana firdebet Main Court (Amharic)
Waaqeffannaa indigenous Oromo religion, (also neo-traditional)
warrie form of dispute settlements based on local holy men (*waliye*) among the Siltie (see also *mawlid* and *liqa*)
wesiya last will (Islamic law, Siltie)
wofa legesse spirit medium used by people seeking remedies to resolve conflict (Amhara people of North Shewa)
woleba dominant majority of farmers and traders (Siltie)
woreda district (Amharic)
wule contract (Amharic)
wuta unclean conception or pregnancy (Bashada, Hamar, Banna)

Y

yati sebani female sheep that never gave birth, used for ritual slaughtering (Bashada, Hamar, Banna)
xuraa'a impure (Borana)
ye-akkababi bahil lit.: according to the local culture (Amharic), refers to customary law
ye-abatader hig lit.: the laws of the fathers (Amharic), refers to long-established system of beliefs, values, and norms used for promoting peace and resolving conflicts (Amhara)
ye-afer seb low class people believed to be native to the Siltie area
ye-bad baliqe
shengo/chale local chiefs' assembly (in Siltie)
ye-bahil meberez lit.: dilution of culture (Amharic), expression used by elders referring to loss of conflict resolution culture among the youth and general community (Amhara of Ankober)
ye-betezemed guba'e lit.: family council (Amharic), settles disputes that arise between husbands and wives (Amhara)
ye-burda baliqe shengo hamlet elders assembly (Siltie)
ye-giligil shimgilinna conciliation between parties in an on-going disagreement (Amhara)
ye-hager shimgilinna lit.: country level conciliation (Amharic), larger and complex conflicts resolved by influential elders selected from the wider community (Amhara)
ye-mewta baliqe supra-village assembly (Siltie)
ye-sebeka guba'e

shimagillée lit.: council of parish elders (Amharic), council of respected community and Church members operating between church members (Amhara of Ankober)
ye-sefer shimgilinna lit.: village conciliation (Amharic), small or relatively uncomplicated conflict in a neighbourhood or village handled by the village elders (Amhara)
ye-siltie serra local mode of governance among the Siltie people

Z

zarsi community of adult men of a given residence area (Bashada, Hamar, Banna)
zarsi goiti central path where many people pass (Bashada, Hamar, Banna)
zera fine (Amharic)
zia local representative of the ritual king (Aari)
zau iron rings worn by women around arms and legs (Bashada, Hamar)

18. Contributors

ABERRA DEGEFA is Assistant Professor at the School of Law at Addis Ababa University. He has LLB and LLM degrees in Law, a post-graduate diploma from ISS, The Hague and a PhD degree in Social Work and Social Development from Addis Ababa University. He did extensive field research among the Borana people of southern Ethiopia. His areas of research interest include constitutional law, legal pluralism and indigenous knowledge and justice systems.

DESALEGN AMSALU has a BA degree in English Language and Literature, LL.B in Law, MA in Ethiopian Studies, and PhD in Social Anthropology from Addis Ababa University. He has been a researcher at the Institute of Ethiopian Studies since 2008, and lectures at the Department of Social Anthropology at Addis Ababa University. He has done extensive fieldwork in north western and central Ethiopia since 2008, and has published on topics related to social marginalization, legal pluralism, ethnic identity, inter-ethnic relations and the lived experience of ethnic groups under the federal regime. Currently, he heads the research unit at the Institute of Ethiopian Studies at Addis Ababa University.

SUSANNE EPPLE has MA and PhD degrees in Social Anthropology from Mainz University. She has been employed as scientific assistant in Social Anthropology at the University of Mainz, and as Assistant Professor at Addis Ababa University and associate researcher at Hamburg University. Since 1994, she has undertaken extensive fieldwork in southern Ethiopia on issues related to gender and age in pastoral societies, social discourse and identity, cultural contact and change, hereditary status groups, legal pluralism and human rights. She is the author of numerous articles, one monograph: *The Bashada of southern Ethiopia: A study of age, gender and social discourse* (2010), and two edited volumes: *The state of status groups in Ethiopia: Minorities between marginalization and integration* (2018) and *Creating and crossing boundaries in Ethiopia: Dynamics of social categorization and differentiation* (2014). Currently, she is a researcher at the Frobenius Institute in Frankfurt, Germany, and research affiliate at the South Omo Research Center in Jinka, Ethiopia.

GEBRE YNTISO is a Professor of Social Anthropology at Jinka University, Ethiopia. He earned his BA degree in Sociology and Social Administration and his MA degree in Social Anthropology from Addis Ababa University, Ethiopia, and obtained his PhD degree in Anthropology from the University of Florida, USA. Besides teaching, he has served as Chairman of the Department Sociology and Social Anthropology and Dean of the College of Social Sciences at Addis Ababa University, and is currently President of Jinka University. He has undertaken extensive studies on population displacement, resettlement, interethnic relations, environment and livelihoods, civil society organizations, violent extremism, conflict handling, culture and development, and disadvantaged groups. As well as publishing many book chapters and articles in major journals in Africa, Asia, Europe and USA, he has co-edited the following books: *African virtues and the pursuit of conviviality: Exploring local solutions in light of global prescriptions* (2017); *Customary dispute resolution mechanisms in Ethiopia*, Volume I and II (2011, 2012); and *Displacement risks in Africa: Refugees, resettlers, and their host population* (2005). He is widely recognized for initiating and supporting community-based development projects.

GETACHEW ASSEFA is Associate Professor of Law at Addis Ababa University. He received his education in Ethiopia, the USA, Finland and Australia, and obtained his PhD Degree in Comparative Constitutional Law from the University of Melbourne, Australia. He has over 20 years of experience in academia, research and private practice as attorney at law, and has served as consultant to various governmental and non-governmental organizations. He is the author of numerous articles that have appeared in various national and foreign-refereed journals, including the *American Journal of Comparative Law* and the *International Journal on Minority and Group Rights*, and has edited three books: *Economic, social and cultural rights in* Ethiopia (2016, with Muradu Abdo and Yonas Birmeta), *Ethiopian Constitutional Law with comparative notes and materials: A textbook* (2012), and *Grass-roots justice in Ethiopia: The contribution of customary dispute resolution* (2008 with Alula Pankhurst). He served as interim Dean of the College of Law and Governance Studies of Addis Ababa University from 2014 to 2015. His areas of interest include Ethiopian and comparative constitutional law and federalism, human rights law, African Constitutionalism, alternative dispute settlement and traditional (informal) justice systems, law and religion, children's and women's rights, administrative law, local governance, and Ethiopian and comparative judicial systems.

JULIAN SOMMERSCHUH is a lecturer in Social Anthropology and Practical Philosophy at the University of Cologne. He holds a PhD in Social Anthropology from Cambridge (2019), and has carried out long-term fieldwork with the Aari people of southwestern Ethiopia. Julian's ethnographic work examines religious conversion and economic transformations in a rural community. He has broader interests in values, moral economy, and normative change.

KAIREDIN TEZERA has an MA in Social Anthropology from Addis Ababa University and received his PhD in Social Anthropology in 2018 from the International Graduate School of African Studies (BIGSAS) at Bayreuth University, Germany. He has done extensive fieldwork in Siltie and Gurage Zones in southern Ethiopia on issues related to ethnicity, legal pluralism, local governance systems, the protection of women's rights in plural legal settings and social mobility. He has authored an article on the role of religious institutions for peace building (2017) and three books: *Siltie history and culture* (2012, in Amharic), *The local government system of the Siltie* (2013) and *Dynamics of identity formation and legal pluralism: The case of customary, state and religious dispute resolutions* (2018). Currently, he is employed as Assistant Professor of Social Anthropology at the Department of Social Anthropology, Addis Ababa University.

KARL-HEINZ KOHL is Professor Emeritus of Cultural Anthropology at the Goethe University in Frankfurt, where he also headed the Frobenius Institute from 1996 to 2016. From 1988 to 1996 he was Professor at the University of Mainz, and from 2001 to 2002 Theodor-Heuss Professor at the New School for Social Research in New York. Since 2005 he has been a member of the Berlin-Brandenburg Academy of Sciences. From 2007 to 2011 he served as President of the German Anthropological Association. He has published extensively on the history of anthropology, on anthropological methods and epistemology, and on the image of indigenous peoples in the West; another main focus of his research is the study of kinship, myth and ritual based on his own ethnographic fieldwork in Eastern Indonesia. Among his recent books are: *Ethnologie – die Wissenschaft vom kulturell Fremden* (3rd ed. 2012) and, as co-editor, *The end of anthropology?* (2011).

MELAKU ABERA is an Assistant Professor of Social Anthropology at Jimma University, Ethiopia. He obtained a diploma in History from Bahir Dar University, and earned his BA degree in History, his MA in Ethiopian Studies and his PhD in Social Anthropology from Addis Ababa University. Since 2003, he has been teaching and advising students at Jimma University and actively participated in Community Based Education. For his MA and PhD degrees, Melaku has done ethnographic fieldwork among the Tulama Oromo of central Ethiopia on topics related to land, conflict and legal pluralism. His research interests include contemporary Ethiopian history and politics, ethnicity, conflict, legal pluralism and internal displacement.

MOHAMMED ABDO has a PhD from Ghent University, Belgium (2015). He has been a full-time Assistant Professor at School of Law and Federalism, Ethiopian Civil Service University since 1998, and also teaches at the School of Law, Addis Ababa University. He has authored a number of articles and book chapters related to issues such as national human rights institutions, legal pluralism and the issues related to the Nile River, and has published two monographs (*Civil procedure* and *Law and religion in Ethiopia*) and one textbook (*Ethiopian administrative law*). He has also managed research projects, acted as a consultant, and written numerous research reports and policy briefings.

MURADU ABDO holds a PhD in Law from the University of Warwick. He received his undergraduate degree in Law from Addis Ababa University and his LL.M degree from the University of San Francisco. He has published journal articles, book chapters, book reviews, comments and textbooks in the areas of land law, property law, customary law, human rights and legal history in Ethiopia. He has also edited books on law and development, human rights and legal pluralism, and has served on a number of editorial committees for law journals and research papers. His research interests include law and development, land policy and law, customary legal systems and human rights. Muradu Abdo is an Associate Professor at Addis Ababa University, School of Law.

ANDREA NICOLAS is a social anthropologist and postdoctoral researcher. She received her PhD from Free University in Berlin. She has worked at the Max Planck Institute for Social Anthropology in Halle and, in the realm of the International MaxNetAging Programme, for the Max Planck Institute for Demographic Research in Rostock. She has also been affiliated to the Graduate School of Cultural Contacts and Scientific Discourse at the University of Rostock. Currently, she is working at the African Studies Information Centre at Johann Wolfgang Goethe University, Frankfurt/Main. In recent years, she has carried out extensive fieldwork in Northeast Africa, among the Oromo and Amhara groups of Ethiopia. Her research interests include age, generation, mediation, conflict resolution, law and legal pluralism, along with issues of comparative research and research methodology. She is the author of *From process to procedure: Elders' mediation and formality in Central Ethiopia* (Wiesbaden 2011), and co-editor of the volumes *Growing up, growing old: Trajectories of time and lives* (Oxford 2013, with Ian Flaherty) and *Travel, agency, and the circulation of knowledge* (Münster 2017, with Gesa Mackenthun and Stephanie Wodianka).

TEMECHEGN GUTU received a BA degree in History from Jimma University and an MA degree in Social Anthropology from Addis Ababa University. Since 2010 he has been employed as a lecturer in Social Anthropology at Arba Minch University and was head of the department from May 2016 to October 2017. From October 2017 to September 2018 he was Director of the South Omo Research Center (SORC) in Jinka. Currently, he is pursuing an Advanced Masters degree in Cultural Anthropology and Development Studies at KU Leuven, Belgium. As part of the program, he is doing research on development intervention and the feeling of insecurity among the Nyangatom. He has done extensive fieldwork among the Alle and Gamo people of southern Ethiopia on issues related to polygamy, parenting practices, traditional administration, legal pluralism, weaving and ethno-medicine. His research interests are related to political and legal anthropology, development anthropology, social relations, indigenous knowledge and livelihood.

YOHANNES YITBAREK received his BA in History and MA in Social Anthropology from Arba Minch University in 2008 and Addis Ababa University in 2011 respectively. From 2012 to 2016, he was a lecturer of Social Anthropology, and head of the department of Sociology and Social Anthropology at Arba Minch University. From 2015 to 2016, he was also the Director of the South Omo Research Center (SORC) in Jinka. He has done research on issues related to intra-regional resettlement and inter-ethnic relations among the Kulsi and Amhara resettlers in Jawi district, northwestern Ethiopia, and resettlement and settler–host relations between the Konso and the Bodi pastoralists in southern Ethiopia. As a PhD candidate at the Max Planck Institute for Social Anthropology in Halle/Saale, Germany, he is currently looking at Hamar–government relations in the context of the local community encounter with state-sponsored development projects.